China's Road
to DISASTER

Contemporary China Papers

Australian National University

Series Editor: Jonathan Unger
Australian National University

Titles in this series published by M. E. Sharpe are:

No. 20: THE PRO-DEMOCRACY PROTESTS IN CHINA
Reports from the Provinces
Edited by Jonathan Unger

No. 21: USING THE PAST TO SERVE THE PRESENT
Historiography and Politics in Contemporary China
Edited by Jonathan Unger

No. 22: DIRECTORY OF OFFICIALS AND
ORGANIZATIONS IN CHINA
A Quarter-Century Guide
Malcolm Lamb

No. 23: CHINESE NATIONALISM
Edited by Jonathan Unger

No. 24: CHINA'S ROAD TO DISASTER
Mao, Central Politicians, and Provincial Leaders in the Unfolding of
the Great Leap Forward, 1955-1959
Frederick C. Teiwes
with Warren Sun

China's Road to DISASTER

Mao, Central Politicians, and
Provincial Leaders in the
Unfolding of
the Great Leap Forward
1955-1959

Frederick C. Teiwes with Warren Sun

An East Gate Book

M.E. Sharpe
Armonk, New York
London, England

An East Gate Book

Copyright © 1999 by M. E. Sharpe, Inc.

Library of Congress Cataloging-in-Publication Data

Teiwes, Frederick C.
China's road to disaster : Mao, central politicians, and
provincial leaders in the unfolding of the great leap forward,
1955–1959 / Frederick C. Teiwes with Warren Sun.
p. cm. — (Contemporary China papers)
"An East gate book."
Includes bibliographical references and index.
ISBN 0-7656-0201-6 (hardcover : alk. paper).
ISBN 0-7656-0202-4 (pbk. : alk. paper)
1. China—Politics and government—1949–1976. I. Sun, Warren.
II. Title. III. Series.
DS777.75.T43 1998
951.05′5—dc21   98-15299
CIP

Printed in the United States of America

The paper used in this publication meets the minimum requirements of
American National Standard for Information Sciences—
Permanence of Paper for Printed Library Materials,
ANSI Z 39.48-1984.

⊗

BM (c) 10 9 8 7 6 5 4 3 2 1
BM (p) 10 9 8 7 6 5 4 3 2 1

To Our Respective Teachers

Fred Teiwes Honors Doak Barnett

Warren Sun Honors Wang Gungwu

CONTENTS

TABLES AND PHOTOGRAPHS

Tables

Photographs

ABBREVIATIONS

Organizations and Policies

CCP	Chinese Communist Party
FFYP	First Five-Year Plan
ICBM	Intercontinental Ballistic Missile
NDU	National Defense University
NPC	National People's Congress
PLA	People's Liberation Army
PRC	People's Republic of China
SEC	State Economic Commission
SFYP	Second Five-Year Plan
SPC	State Planning Commission

Publications and Publishing Agencies

AJCA	*The Australian Journal of Chinese Affairs*
CB	*Current Background*
CQ	*The China Quarterly*
NCNA	New China News Agency
PDA	*Communist China 1955-1959: Policy Documents with Analysis*
SCMP	*Survey of China Mainland Press*
SS	*The Secret Speeches of Chairman Mao*
SW	*Selected Works of Mao Tsetung*

WM	*The Writings of Mao Zedong*
XHBYK	*Xinhua banyuekan* [New China Semi-Monthly]
ZGDSRWZ	*Zhonggong dangshi renwu zhuan* [Biographies of Personalities in CCP History]
ZGDSYJ	*Zhonggong dangshi yanjiu* [Research on CCP History]

PREFACE

More than with most studies, this book began as a result of a number of different intellectual and practical considerations, and took on more as the research progressed. The initial practical impetus came from the need for a paper to be delivered to a conference on Chinese Communist history during the pre-Cultural Revolution period. This led fairly directly to an examination of the moderate economic policies of 1956-57 — the program of "opposing rash advance." The intellectual impetus for this was first in the recognition that this issue had only been dealt with in passing in our previous work, and that on the surface the events of this period as depicted in the existing literature were at considerable variance with our understanding of a completely dominant Mao Zedong as the pivot of Chinese elite politics. This, in turn, was linked to a certain frustration with the residual influence of the "two line struggle" model which we had hoped to demolish in various earlier works. Simply put, would a detailed examination of economic policy in this period confirm our overall assessment of Chinese politics, and would it provide sufficient evidence to convince the sceptics?

As the research developed, particularly as a result of extensive interviews with a significant participant in the economic policy-making process in both 1956-57 and 1958-59, our attention was increasingly drawn to the momentous drama of the Great Leap Forward which followed upon and was intimately linked to opposing rash advance. Not least, we became transfixed by the question of how such an enormous tragedy as the Great Leap famine which claimed millions of lives came about and who was responsible. In some senses the answers have long been apparent, but a deeper political understanding has been missing. Indeed, for such a watershed event it is remarkable how little sustained and detailed attention has been given to the politics of the Great Leap Forward. The conventional wisdom adopted by most accounts did little more than adapt with limited research the Cultural Revolution perspective of, crudely put, anti-Maoist elements attacking the Chairman and implementing the moderate policies of 1956-57, Mao defeating his opponents by the end of 1957 and launching the radical leap and enforcing his views until 1960, and then being again shunted to the sidelines by a dominant group of moderates as the disasters of the leap became undeniable. Needless to say, we believed this wide of the mark, and in the event our detailed examination provides a multi-faceted analysis of just how far such interpretations stray from the reality.

While the general dearth of serious work on the politics of opposing rash advance and the Great Leap was one reason for undertaking this study, our assessment of the major studies of national-level politics during this period by Roderick MacFarquhar and David Bachman also contributed to our determination to proceed. (Also demanding recognition is Jean-Luc Domenach's fine local study, *The Origins of the Great Leap Forward: The Case of One Chinese Province*.) The first two volumes of MacFarquhar's classic trilogy, *The Origins of the Cultural Revolution*, cover the period of our study from a leadership conflict perspective, and the second volume on 1958-60, easily the best existing study of the leap, provides much with which we agree. The deeper our research, however, the more we have been impressed with the important matters where we differ; moreover, the vast amount of new material available in the decade and a half since MacFarquhar wrote, we believe, allows a considerably more complete and accurate account than was possible then. Bachman's more recent institutional interpretation, *Bureaucracy, Economy, and Leadership in China: The Institutional Origins of the Great Leap Forward*, was a major stimulus. While we believed from the outset his analysis was as wrong-headed as it was thought-provoking, it was clearly something to be taken seriously. As a result our interpretation in turn deals seriously with bureaucratic politics, but not only places it in a far different relationship to leadership politics than does Bachman but also differs on the nature of the dominant institutional conflict. Another benefit to our study deriving from Bachman's work is that it encouraged us to assess systematically the roles and responsibility of a variety of actors in the system, including not only the economic bureaucracies he emphasizes and the top leadership which is the focus of MacFarquhar's work, but also Mao's personal staff and especially provincial leaders who provided such a crucial dynamic in the emergence and evolution of the Great Leap.

If the ultimate result of this study has been to reinforce our conception of a Mao-dominated politics, and beyond that to enrich our understanding of the nuances of how this was manifested, we have also again learned the salutary lesson of how difficult it is to get to the "truth" of Chinese Communist elite interaction. Of specific note in this regard is that we have had to revise considerably our understanding of the role of Chen Yun during the utopian stage of the Great Leap in 1958. Whereas previously both documentary evidence and the accounts of Party historians in interviews had led us to believe that this most cool-headed leader had basically been inactive during the phase of wild dreams and reckless behavior, we are now convinced that he played a much more active role in carrying out the wishes of his leader — acting according to, as Mao put it, his strong sense of discipline. While it is clear that Chen did, as previously understood, play a critical role in curbing the excesses of the Great Leap when the opportunity arose, we now know that he was deeply involved in such key leap hallmarks as the 40 articles on agriculture and especially the backyard steel furnaces. Chen remains for us one of the most fascinating of Chinese leaders, and we await with interest future surprises concerning his role as research continues on other topics. Since, we believe, we were not being systematically misled in this instance but rather that Chinese scholars themselves came to flawed conclusions based on inadequate information, albeit an inadequacy arguably the result of conscious distortion by higher authority, we can only rededicate ourselves to the diligent pursuit of evidence married to a scepticism of sources in order to avoid future misconceptions.

Many people contributed to this study but one must be singled out. While Chris Buckley joined the project late in the day in a research capacity, his tireless work has greatly enhanced the end product. Even before coming "on board," Chris read the manuscript and made the perspicacious suggestion that an examination of the post-leap retreat as seen in the saga of the Anhui responsibility system would extend the theme of the study to a totally different situation which paradoxically demonstrated the same underlying political dynamic — and this has been done in Epilogue 2. In his research role Chris has uncovered various new materials and suggested numerous improvements to the manuscript, as well as preparing the two Appendices to the book. All in all, his contribution has been considerable.

A number of individuals commented upon various stages of the manuscript and/or assisted with valuable research material: David Chambers, Dave Denny, Keith Forster, David Goodman, Nancy Hearst, Lin Yousu, Tony Saich, Odd Arne Westad, Xu Bing, and especially Peter Kuhfus all receive our gratitude. Thanks also go to Timothy Cheek and Tony Saich, and institutionally to The Colorado College and the National Endowment for the Humanities, for organizing the 1993 conference where the analysis of opposing rash advance first saw the light of day, and to Tim and Tony for their permission to use an updated version of the chapter which appeared in their edited volume, *New Perspectives on State Socialism in China.*

The research upon which this study is based would not have been possible without the financial support of the University of Sydney's research grants scheme and Research Institute for Asia and the Pacific, the Pacific Cultural Foundation, the Ian Potter Foundation, and especially the Australian Research Council. The ARC's very generous support over a considerable period of time has been the bedrock upon which this and other recent studies have been built. Institutional support was also provided in various ways by our home institutions, the University of Sydney's Department of Government and Monash University's Department of Asian Languages and Studies, while the Contemporary China Institute of the School of Oriental and African Studies, the International Institute for Asian Studies at Leiden University, the Nordic Institute of Asian Studies in Copenhagen, and the Sinological Seminar of the University of Heidelberg helped sustain a year of writing in Europe. The efforts of David Shambaugh, Rick Edmonds, Kitty Yang, Stefan Landsburger, Börge Bakken, and Susanne Weigelin-Schwiedrzik in facilitating this European sojourn are particularly appreciated.

In converting our manuscript into the form you see here particular thanks is owed the Australian National University's Contemporary China Centre, its head Jonathan Unger who graciously arranged for the study's inclusion in the Centre's Contemporary China Papers and its preparation for publication, and to Heli Petryk who skillfully produced the camera-ready pages. Back in

Sydney Lyn Fisher meticulously prepared the index, while Nancy Hearst at Harvard proofread the manuscript. And at M. E. Sharpe, as on so many previous occasions, Doug Merwin gave the essential support for the project, while Angela Piliouras and Patricia Loo provided technical and editorial advice and coordination.

In our recent studies it has become *de rigueur* to offer special thanks to the many Chinese scholars and some former officials whom we have interviewed. The thanks is no less real for being repeated yet again. In the case of this study our lengthy interviews with an important figure in the events of the period were of exceptional value, while the interviews as a whole provided both important new information and perceptive insights. While within any group there is considerable variation in terms of grasp of information, subtlety of thought, and simple personal reliability, we again come away impressed with the intellectual seriousness and basic honesty of our interviewees as a whole.

Finally, longer-standing support must be acknowledged. Our families again sustained us throughout the arduous efforts that have gone into this book. But on this occasion we would like to recognize another type of support provided by the teachers who so stimulated our interest in and shaped our understanding of Chinese politics and history. Fred Teiwes expresses his gratitude to the man who drew him to the study of modern China and provided a model of careful, empirical scholarship that he has tried to emulate in his own work — A. Doak Barnett. Warren Sun wishes to acknowledge great indebtedness to his mentor — Wang Gungwu — whose balanced mind, caring heart, and elegant historical scholarship has inspired him to pursue the career of a humble scholar. It is to these respected *laoshi* that we individually dedicate this book.

Sydney and Melbourne
April 1998

CHRONOLOGY OF IMPORTANT EVENTS, 1955-62

July 5-6, 1955   Li Fuchun presents FFYP (1953-57) on lines of Soviet model. Investment rate in heavy industry even higher than first Soviet plan; projected growth set at 14.7 percent p.a. in industry, 4.3 percent p.a. in agriculture.

July 31, 1955   Mao addresses conference of provincial secretaries on agricultural cooperativization. Sharply critical of Central Rural Work Department and Deng Zihui for slow pace of development. Speech launches intense mass mobilization outstripping Mao's own goals.

October 4-11, 1955   6th Plenum of 7th Central Committee endorses even higher cooperativization targets and attacks Deng Zihui's policies as "right opportunism." Deng makes self-criticism.

November 1955-
January 1956   Mao consults provincial leaders on agricultural development, leading to ambitious 12-year program (the 40 articles).

December 5, 1955   Liu Shaoqi conveys Mao's views criticizing "rightist conservatism" in economic thinking and calling for faster development. Initially broad leadership enthusiasm, including from Zhou Enlai. Slogan of "more, faster, better, more economical" formulated.

December 1955-
April 1956   "Small (or first) leap forward" under influence of anti-conservatism line. Ambitious targets pursued by central ministries and provinces, resulting in economic dislocations.

January 1956   Mao declares basic victory of socialism over capitalism on basis of ownership transformation in agriculture and similar processes underway in industry, commerce, and handicrafts. New emphasis on construction as main task leads to effort to enlist support of intellectuals at conference addressed by Mao and Zhou Enlai.

January 10- February 7, 1956	Planning and financial conference under Zhou Enlai, Li Fuchun, and Li Xiannian winds back demands of ministries and provinces for additional investment funds, but overall investment level reflects anti-conservative orientation.
February 14-25, 1956	20th Congress of Soviet Communist Party produces strain in Sino-Soviet relations as a result of Khrushchev's denunciation of Stalin without warning and other matters. Overall relations remain close, although CCP publishes its own "balanced" view of Stalin on April 5th.
April 25-28, 1956	Enlarged Politburo meeting hears Mao's "Ten Great Relationships" report, based on his briefings by 34 economic ministries over the preceding months, indicating the need for adjustments to the Soviet model of development. Proposals leave basic approach and methods of the model unchanged. At the same meeting Mao proposed a ¥2 billion increase in investment against the views of Zhou Enlai and virtually all present. Mao's demand adopted, but Zhou persuades him to relent during a private meeting shortly after the conference. At the conference Mao also takes further steps to win over intellectuals by proposing "Let a Hundred Flowers Bloom, Let a Hundred Schools of Thought Contend" slogan.
May-early June 1956	Zhou Enlai pushes attack on left excesses at State Council meetings. Undertakes discussions on a new budget with Li Xiannian, Li Fuchun, and Bo Yibo, resulting in a "crew cut" reduction of 5-6 percent in capital construction funding.
May 12, 1956	SEC established under Bo Yibo with responsibility for annual economic plans.
June 15-30, 1956	Systematic program of "opposing rash advance" takes shape and is pushed by Zhou *et al.* at NPC session in various reports, most notably Li Xiannian's report on financial work. At a more political level, the program is articulated in a June 20 *People's Daily* editorial criticizing rash advance as well as conservatism.

July-August 1956	Preparation of revised SFYP under Zhou Enlai's personal leadership, reducing targets formulated by the SPC in May. Chen Yun involved in final reductions.
summer 1956	SEC under Bo Yibo sharply cuts spending proposals of ministries and provinces for 1957 from ¥24.3 to ¥15 billion over strong objections.
September 15-27, 1956	Eighth Party Congress approves SFYP (1958-62), again based on Soviet model and projecting growth rates of 20 percent p.a. in industry and 7 percent p.a. in agriculture. Congress also endorses economic construction as focus of all work and relegates class struggle to a secondary and fading position.
October-November 1956	East European crises in Poland and Hungary result in tightening of political atmosphere, until Mao revives Hundred Flowers policy in early 1957.
October-November 9, 1956	Zhou Enlai reviews 1957 plan and launches new attacks on left excesses. Gains support for general effort with the backing of Chen Yun, Li Xiannian, and Bo Yibo.
November 10-15, 1956	2nd Plenum of 8th Central Committee. Later declared by Mao to be the "peak" of opposing rash advance. Zhou makes systematic critique of the left, calling for slower pace of development and changes to unrealistic goals of the 40 articles. Mao, although warning against "pouring cold water on the masses," offers general and specific support.
November 1956-March 1957	Further consideration of 1957 targets by economic leaders, including Zhou, Chen Yun, Bo Yibo, and Jia Tuofu. Figure of ¥11.1 billion finally endorsed at February-March national planning conference.
January 10, 1957	Central economics work small group established under Chen Yun's leadership. Li Fuchun, Bo Yibo, Li Xiannian, and Huang Kecheng named members.
January 18-27, 1957	Conference of provincial secretaries. Policy approach emphasizing Chen Yun's "three balances" adopted. Mao endorses approach and praises Chen, but also makes first critical reference to opposing rash

advance, in this case concerning agricultural cooperativization.

February 27, 1957   Mao's speech on "Contradictions among the People" relaunches the Hundred Flowers, now with the new radical edge of encouraging non-Party people to criticize the CCP. After several months of official efforts to encourage speaking out, this results in a torrent of criticism by May.

June 8, 1957   Anti-Rightist Campaign launched in response to intellectuals' spring criticisms. The campaign affected most urban sectors by the fall and was extended to the countryside from late summer, with the movement in both areas lasting well into 1958. Effect is to raise doubts about reliability of intellectuals as a force for socialist construction, although there is no immediate impact on economic policy.

June 26-
July 15, 1957   NPC session focuses on refutation of "bourgeois rightists." Zhou Enlai declares national economy in 1956 a "leap forward" rather than a "rash advance." Overall policy continues according to Chen Yun's emphasis on balance, however, and Zhou reaffirms 20 percent cut in capital construction.

September 20-
October 9, 1957   3rd Plenum of 8th Central Committee. First signs of new economic approach emerge late in the plenum, particularly with Mao's concluding speech on October 9 when he criticized opposing rash advance and the "blowing away" of the 40 articles and the policy of "more, faster, better, more economical." Mao's changing thinking also reflected in his redefinition of the main contradiction from one with economic backwardness to the class contradiction between the proletariat and the bourgeoisie.

November
2-21, 1957   Mao visits Soviet Union. Encouraged by the Soviet sputnik and ICBM, he declares "the east wind is now prevailing over the west wind." Close relations with Moscow reflected in October 15 Soviet agreement to supply China with a sample nuclear bomb. Domestic implications in Mao's enthusiasm over Soviet steel advances he wished to see emulated at home, and in his response to Khrushchev's goal of overtaking the U.S. in

economic production in 15 years with a pledge to overtake Britain in the same period.

November 13, 1957   *People's Daily* editorial unveils first use of "Great Leap Forward" slogan.

winter 1957-58   Mass water conservancy campaign. Following November-December provincial meetings emphasizing anti-conservatism and ambitious agricultural development, the campaign is launched with some places promising to meet the 40 articles' 12-year water conservancy targets in 2 years. The movement not only created a heated mass mobilization atmosphere, it also produced the need for larger-scale rural collective organization that led to the people's commune by mid-1958.

December 1958   Mao highlights growing importance of provincial leaders by praising reports of Zhejiang's Jiang Hua and Shanghai's Ke Qingshi which emphasized the proletariat-bourgeoisie contradiction, ordering Zhou Enlai to read Jiang's report, and his secretaries to revise it for publication in the *People's Daily*.

January 2-4, 1958   Hangzhou conference. Mao raises methods for leading economic construction, especially the relations of politics and administration and the technological revolution, criticizes Zhou Enlai, and expresses discontent with Bo Yibo.

January 11-22, 1958   Nanning conference. Mao continues to emphasize work methods, sharply rejecting Soviet approaches and instead stressing political leadership, mass mobilization, and local initiative, themes written into his 60 articles on work methods issued on February 19, with important input by provincial leaders. Articles include expanded version of Bo Yibo's Nanning proposal for "two sets of books" involving required and "strive for" targets that would produce rampant escalation of targets. Most significantly, Mao raised the issue of opposing rash advance to the level of a political mistake and criticized by name Zhou Enlai, Chen Yun, Li Xiannian, and Bo Yibo, thus creating a situation where "no one could say anything different."

March 8-26, 1958   Chengdu conference. Mao continues to press emphasis on technical revolution, criticism of opposing rash advance, and smashing superstitious belief in experts and Soviet practice around overall theme of speeding up economic construction. "Strive for" 1958 targets of 33 and 16.2 percent increases over 1957 in industry and agriculture respectively approved. Top leaders, including Liu Shaoqi, Zhou Enlai, and Chen Yun, forced to make self-criticisms at "rectification seminars," while Mao's "personality cult" was strongly pushed.

March-June 1958   Establishment of economic coordination regions. Raised by Mao at Chengdu, these bodies played a key role in the escalation of Great Leap targets. Formally approved on June 1st.

May 5-23, 1958   2nd Session of 8th Party Congress. General line of "going all out, aiming high, and achieving more, faster, better, and more economical results in economic construction" adopted. Mao reduces time to overtake Britain to 7 years and projects reaching U.S. levels in 15 years. Political pressure continues with provincial leaders prominent; Zhou Enlai, Chen Yun, Li Xiannian, and Bo Yibo required to make written self-examinations. Provincial leaders also prominent in new appointees to Central Committee, including Shanghai's Ke Qingshi and Sichuan's Li Jingquan who are raised to Politburo level, along with agricultural czar Tan Zhenlin.

May 27-   Military affairs conference focuses on criticism of
July 22, 1958   Soviet style "dogmatism." Mao emphasizes similarity to erroneous Soviet economic methods.

late May-   Escalation of 1958 steel targets from 8-8.5 million to
June 19, 1958   10.7 million tons, doubling the 1957 figure. Key factors include input of economic coordination regions competing to catch up with Ke Qingshi's East China region, and various central economic officials, including Li Fuchun, Bo Yibo, and Wang Heshou, responding to Mao's desire for higher targets in personal meetings with the Chairman.

June 1, 1958

New Central Committee theoretical journal *Red Flag* begins publication. Under editorship of Chen Boda becomes an important voice for Great Leap radicalism.

June 9, 1958

Politburo considers Zhou Enlai's resignation as Premier but decides no change necessary. This followed Mao's declaration at the Party Congress that Zhou *et al.* were good comrades and the issue of opposing rash advance had been settled.

June 10, 1958

Decision to establish new central small groups, including financial and economics small group replacing economics work group set up in January 1957. Chen Yun retained the leading position, with a membership of Li Fuchun, Bo Yibo, Li Xiannian, Tan Zhenlin, Wang Heshou, and Zhao Erlu, but the group's role is reduced to completely advisory functions subordinate to Party Secretariat.

July 1958

Ministry of Agriculture estimates 1958 grain output at 1,000 billion catties, 2.7 times the actual 1957 output.

July 31-
August 3, 1958

Khrushchev visits Beijing. Differences on international and Sino-Soviet issues, including Soviet proposals for joint military facilities and the impending late August-early October Taiwan Straits crisis, lead to major strains in the relationship.

August 17-31, 1958

Beidaihe conference. Height of leap forward utopianism, with decision on setting up people's communes, formal endorsement of steel and other wild targets, and projections of rapid transition to communism. Chen Yun given responsibility for achieving steel target using Mao's "backyard furnaces" method, as well as key role in providing coordination of China's rapid construction program. SPC regains control of annual planning, SEC made responsible for "grasping production," and Deng Xiaoping exercises key role in enforcing high targets.

mid-late
October 1958

Mao inspection tour of North China produces awareness of significant problems with the Great Leap. Consults provincial leaders and (somewhat later) various top leaders and central economic officials, and assigns particularly important role to his own secretaries in uncovering problems.

November 2-10, 1958	First Zhengzhou conference. Mao launches effort to "cool down" the leap by criticizing excessive targets, chaotic conditions in the communes, and efforts to achieve an immediate transition to communism, and by advocating the need to obey "objective [economic] laws." Nevertheless, Mao's message is profoundly ambivalent as he warns against "pouring cold water on the masses," still endorses wildly ambitious targets, and orders the establishment of urban communes.
November 21-December 10, 1958	Wuchang conference (November 21-27) and 6th Plenum of 8th Central Committee (November 28-December 10). "Cooling down" process continues although various participants resistant to the trend, especially provincial leaders. Mao continues with ambivalent mix of warnings against the left and enthusiasm for continuing leap activism. Major 6th Plenum policy decisions to relegate the transition to communism to the more distant future, authorize commune readjustment, reduce various industrial targets, and postpone setting up urban communes. The plenum also accepted Mao's proposal that he not serve another term as PRC Chairman, with the position subsequently assumed by Liu Shaoqi in April 1959.
December 1958-February 1959	Inspections by Mao and other leaders produce even greater awareness of seriousness of the situation. Zhou Enlai, Deng Xiaoping, Chen Yun, and others attempt to moderate policy further, but with little effect. Mao encourages Chen but then responds harshly to his suggestions in early January. Mao's own rural investigations in January and February result in gradual moderation in his thinking.
January 26-February 2, 1959	Beijing conference of provincial secretaries. Despite some moderate sentiments on Mao's part, 6th Plenum targets unchanged. Chen Yun, unnerved by Mao's early January attitude, offers self-criticism. Mao's concluding speech stresses again pushing forward, that defects were but one finger out of ten, and there would be a leap forward every year.
February 27-March 5, 1959	Second Zhengzhou conference. Focusing on commune problems, Mao adopts a *comparatively* consistent anti-left posture criticizing egalitarian practices and over-

centralization, excessive corvee labor, and the collectivization of household items, while advocating a more relaxed pace and the policy of 3-level ownership and accounting, with the brigade as the basic unit. Nevertheless, Mao still warns of "right opportunism" and fails to bring significant pressure to bear on leftist provincial leaders.

March 25- April 5, 1959	Shanghai conference (March 25-April 1) and 7th Plenum of the 8th Central Committee (April 2-5). Further moderating measures for the communes and somewhat reduced steel and other targets adopted. Divisions appear among provincial leaders over feasibility of leap targets. Mao proposes 9 points on work methods that stress listening to different opinions and encourages the "Hai Rui spirit" of criticizing the emperor, yet he expressed sharp dissatisfaction with his economic officials, reaffirmed his rejection of opposing rash advance, and launched a wide-ranging attack on a large number of senior leaders. Although the plenum formally endorsed Mao's retirement as head of state, he emphasized concentrating power under his supreme command.
April-June 1959	Readjustment of 1959 steel target. Chen Yun, bolstered by Mao's approving remarks at Shanghai that his cautious views the previous winter had been correct, placed in overall charge of the readjustment. "Reliable" target reduced from 16.5 million tons at Shanghai to 13 million tons and approved by Mao and Politburo on June 13. At June 12-13 meeting Mao, Zhou Enlai, and Li Fuchun also emphasize comprehensive balance in the economy, but Mao still endorses carrying out "more, faster, better, more economical" guideline. Meeting also notable for Mao's self-criticism regarding his inadequacies in economic construction.
April 29, 1959	Mao's circular letter to Party cadres on rural production denounces "mere bragging" and demands production targets be based on reality.
June 22, 1959	Mao meets Henan leader Wu Zhipu. Despite his call for realism in April 29 letter, Mao is highly encouraged by Wu's excessive claims for grain production and asks

him to prepare materials on Henan's experience with communal mess halls for the forthcoming Lushan conference.

June 1959-
July 1960

Serious deterioration of Sino-Soviet relations over series of international issues, plus Soviet criticism of Great Leap. Key steps include Soviet June 1959 cancellation of nuclear weapons assistance, April 1960 CCP systematic criticism of "modern revisionism" which began open polemics, and July 1960 withdrawal of Soviet advisers from China.

July 2-
August 16, 1959

Lushan conference (July 2-August 1) and 8th Plenum of 8th Central Committee (August 2-16). Following early stage of conference where efforts to correct leftist errors gingerly undertaken at Mao's urging, Mao reacts furiously to Peng Dehuai's private letter of July 14 which called for bolder rectification of errors. With conference thrown into disarray, fierce criticism of Peng, Zhang Wentian, and others launched. At the subsequent plenum, Peng, Zhang, Huang Kecheng, and Zhou Xiaozhou were removed from their positions, but further reductions in several key targets were approved.

late August 1959-
mid-1960

Anti-right opportunist campaign launched against those with views similar to those of Peng Dehuai. Harsh movement undermines efforts to curb left errors, underpins new leap forward surge, and thus greatly worsens already serious famine conditions.

January 7-17, 1960

Shanghai expanded Politburo meeting. Adopts 1960 economic plan setting excessive targets and calls for transition from team to commune-level ownership in 8 years.

late May 1960

Party Center issues directives on economic situation. May 28 directive addresses severe food shortages by allocating emergency grain to Beijing, Tianjin, Shanghai, and Liaoning, while other measures reduce food and cloth rations. But May 30 directive approves much higher targets, such as 21-22 million tons of steel compared to 18.4 million tons set in January.

| June 14-18, 1960 | Shanghai expanded Politburo meeting. Main focus on international situation, but Mao warns of blindness in construction and calls for study of economic laws. |

July 5-
August 10, 1960   Beidaihe conference. Conference curtails capital construction, ends practice of 2nd set of "strive for" targets, and delays transition to commune-level ownership, but Great Leap and communal mess halls are affirmed. Li Fuchun and Zhou Enlai propose 8-character principle of "adjustment, consolidation, filling out, and improvement" to guide economics work.

November 3, 1960   Urgent directive on people's communes (the 12 articles). Calls for 3-level ownership system with the team as the basic unit, private plots to occupy 5 percent of cultivated land, and rectification of egalitarianism and erroneous cadre work styles.

December 24, 1960-
January 18, 1961   Beijing conference (December 24-January 13) and 9th Plenum of 8th Central Committee (January 14-18). Further retreat authorized, including cuts to capital construction, increasing private plots to 7 percent of cultivated land, compensation for property seized during the leap, and increases in agricultural procurement prices. Decision taken to import food. Mao warns against haste in construction and declares 1961 a year of investigation and research, thus laying the basis for experimentation and additional policy adjustments.

March 15-23, 1961   Guangzhou conference. Under Mao's leadership 60 articles on people's communes are formulated, which further liberalize rural policy by reducing the size of communes and brigades and decentralizing authority within the commune. Extensive debate on contracting production to individual households, notably Anhui's responsibility fields which had developed since the 12 articles, with Mao initially indicating support but quickly adopting a more restrictive attitude.

April-
December 1961   Major extension of household responsibility systems at grass roots despite official restrictive policy. In Anhui, responsibility fields extend from implementation in nearly 40 percent of production teams at the end of the Guangzhou conference to over 90 percent by the end of the year. Much of expansion due to peasant and low-

level cadre initiative, but additional boost from Mao's relatively positive attitude in July conversation with Anhui leader Zeng Xisheng.

May 21- June 12, 1961

Beijing conference. Major changes to 60 articles allowing disbanding of mess halls with Mao's backing. Steel target cut from 18 to 11 million tons, and decision taken to rehabilitate cadres wrongly punished during the anti-right opportunist campaign. Mao makes self-criticism but Liu Shaoqi prudently decides not to circulate it.

August 23- September 16, 1961

Lushan conference. Criticism of failure to carry out seriously the 8-character principle, especially in not implementing cuts in industrial production quotas. 70 articles on industry approved to strengthen management rules and regulations within enterprises. Mao maintains that the economic situation had hit bottom and could only improve.

2nd half of 1961

Considerable criticism directed at household contracting, as in Hu Yaobang's report after investigations in Anhui which declared responsibility fields dangerous and threatening to collective organization. November Party Center directive holds household contracting not in accord with the collective economy. By end of year Mao apparently determines decentralization to the team level, as in his September 29 proposal to make the team the basic rural accounting unit, was as far as he was prepared to go.

January 11- February 7, 1962

7,000 cadres conference. Conference reviews recent experience and engages in broad debate. Liu Shaoqi reports for the Central Committee; with Mao's approval Liu's report gives extensive analysis of shortcomings since 1958 but formally upholds the general line. Mao gives speech on inner-Party democracy, including a self-criticism, but Lin Biao and Deng Xiaoping praise the Chairman. Meeting also sees attacks on Anhui's responsibility fields, leading to the removal of Zeng Xisheng and the reorganization of the Anhui provincial Party committee.

February
21-23, 1962

Xilou conference. Presided over by Liu Shaoqi, the meeting takes bleaker view of the economy than that at the 7,000 cadres conference. Liu and others conclude that the economy was "on verge of collapse." Chen Yun plays prominent role and, at Liu's suggestion and with Mao's assent, becomes overall economic czar with his appointment as head of the central financial and economics small group formally made on April 19. Under Chen new sharp cuts in construction and investment adopted.

March-July 1962

Individual farming and household contracting continue to spread despite official policy. Various officials conduct rural investigations, leading a diverse set of actors, including Liu Shaoqi, Deng Xiaoping, Chen Yun, Li Fuchun, Deng Zihui, and Mao's secretary Tian Jiaying, to adopt relatively positive attidudes toward household contracting by May-June. Although showing some tolerance of household contracting, Mao reacted badly to strong advocacy by Chen Yun and Tian Jiaying in early July, causing Liu and Deng Xiaoping to alter course.

May 7-11, 1962

Beijing conference. Presided over by Liu Shaoqi, the meeting reviews the economic situation, emphasizes achieving comprehensive balance in priority order of agriculture, light industry, and heavy industry, further curtails construction, closes down enterprises, and reduces numbers of workers and staff.

July 25-September
27, 1962

Beidaihe conference, preparatory and formal sessions of 10th Plenum of 8th Central Committee. Despite initial expectations of a moderate outcome, as the conference proceeded Mao increasingly voiced discontent on a broad range of issues, including overestimating the seriousness of the situation, overall economic policy, concessions to individual peasant production, and the rehabilitation of "right opportunists," and criticized Liu Shaoqi, Zhou Enlai, Chen Yun, Deng Zihui, and Jia Tuofu among others. At this time Chen Yun and Deng Zihui were removed from positions of influence, with Deng's Rural Work Department abolished on November 9th. Although economic and rural policies remained cautious, significant change in ideological direction emerged under Mao's slogan "never forget class struggle."

China's Road
to DISASTER

Since [the August 1958] Beidaihe conference the Party's leading cadres have truly grasped economic work and construction. Formerly this did not extend beyond Chen Yun, Li Fuchun, [and] Bo Yibo, [but] now everyone does it.... In the past everyone carried out revolution, [while] economic and construction [work] was entrusted to some of [our] comrades. The Secretariat [and] Politburo didn't discuss it much, [we] just went through the motions.... [But] starting from last year, although some disorder emerged, everyone grasped industry.

> — Mao Zedong commenting on changes in economic policy making during the Great Leap Forward, Lushan, July 10, 1959, cited in "unpublished Chinese document no. 6," p. 163.

When Mao did not personally intervene, the system functioned more or less by standard procedures. The government dealt with issues, there were local discussions and feedback to the Center. But whenever Mao intervened this could no longer be sustained, the waters were muddied, and in 1958 there was no planning.

> — Post-Mao observations of a leading ministerial official during 1955-59, interview, March 1993.

Mao cannot be entirely blamed because he was deceived by false reports sent by ambitious officials. As always in China, the Emperor is never wrong, only misled by his ministers who flatter him and who in turn are deceived by dishonest lower-ranking officials. On the other hand, they cannot be blamed either, because they have no choice but to follow orders from above. So in the end no one is responsible.

> — Peasant reflections concerning responsibility for the Great Leap famine 30 years later, as paraphrased by Jasper Becker, *Hungry Ghosts: China's Secret Famine*, p. 285.

INTRODUCTION

In 1956 and for most of 1957 the economic policies of the People's Republic of China (PRC) were modest and realistic. Moreover, the processes by which these policies were decided were comparatively orderly and largely in the hands of officials with some specialized knowledge of economic issues. Yet by the start of 1958 these policies were rejected and their main architects were under severe political attack. Out of this maelstrom emerged the Great Leap Forward, an unprecedented program for economic development and social transformation that was utopian in substance and chaotic in implementation. And out of that came one of the great tragedies of the twentieth century, the Great Leap famine of 1958-62 that took anywhere from 15 to 46 million lives, if not more.[1]

How does one account for the dramatic shifts in Chinese economic policy during the mid and late 1950s which marked the road from realism to disaster? By the end of 1955 the euphoria surrounding that year's "high tide" of agricultural cooperativization spread to economic policy and produced the first leap forward. Yet by late January 1956, moves were afoot to wind back overambitious expectations, moves which by the middle of the year had developed into a comprehensive program of "opposing rash advance" (*fanmaojin*). Changing political circumstances notwithstanding, this basic approach remained in place until the fall 1957 Third Plenum where Chairman Mao Zedong criticized *fanmaojin* and set in motion a process which, by May 1958 at the latest, resulted in the Great Leap Forward. It was, to use official imagery, a pattern of U-shaped development, with upsurges of mass mobilization in 1955 and 1958-59 contrasting to the sober emphasis on balance in 1956-57. It was also a contrast between the obviously forceful role of Mao in the former and latter periods and the Chairman's much lower profile, at least as far as economic policy was concerned, in the middle period which might be considered the most "bureaucratic" phase of the Maoist era.[2]

---

[1] For reviews of various estimates of the toll of the famine, see Jasper Becker, *Hungry Ghosts: China's Secret Famine* (London: John Murray, 1996), ch. 18; and Dali L. Yang, *Calamity and Reform in China: State, Rural Society, and Institutional Change Since the Great Leap Famine* (Stanford: Stanford University Press, 1996), pp. 37-38. See also Thomas Bernstein's careful assessment completed a decade earlier, "Stalinism, Famine, and Chinese Peasants: Grain Procurements during the Great Leap Forward," *Theory and Society*, May 1984. For a recent PRC assessment placing the likely toll in the lower end of this range, see the article by Li Chengrui of the State Statistical Bureau in *Zhonggong dangshi yanjiu* [*Research on CCP History*, hereafter *ZGDSYJ*], no. 2 (1997), pp. 1-14.

[2] See Frederick C. Teiwes, "'Rules of the Game' in Chinese Politics," *Problems of Communism*, September-December 1979.

Yet by fall 1958 Mao himself began to sense that something was amiss and, over the next eight months, made repeated calls for greater caution. But notwithstanding various policy adjustments, by mid-1959, on the eve of the watershed Lushan conference, China had reached a stage of grave peril, a peril which even then had begun to be manifested in mass starvation.

Surprisingly, given the unprecedented nature of the Great Leap Forward and the magnitude of the resulting human tragedy, not to mention the well-recognized links between these developments and the Cultural Revolution, relatively little in-depth scholarly attention has been devoted to the *politics* surrounding the emergence and development of the Great Leap. Although much has long been known about the nature of PRC economic policies over the 1955-59 period and even concerning some key political features — e.g., the relative leeway given to the regime's economic specialists before the leap, and Mao's unwillingness to question the basic *line* of the leap even after he became aware of serious problems, few studies have provided comprehensive interpretations of the political process involved on the basis of detailed research, while even these, in our judgment, are incomplete or unpersuasive. This book, through a close examination of specific events and the utilization of new sources, seeks to fill the gap with its own explanation of this critical period, in the process confronting both general misconceptions in the literature and the few existing analyses based on penetrating research.

The book also addresses an additional issue: the question of responsibility. In seeking an overall interpretation of events, the study looks systematically at a range of concerned actors, both individual and institutional, thus providing a perspective generally absent in the existing literature.[3] Analytically, this approach allows the elucidation of the interests and behavior of such actors, and thus of their policy influence and general clout in the developments of the period. But more than analysis is involved; the extent of the disaster resulting from individual and collective actions calls out for some assessment of blame and complicity. Thus in telling our story we seek both to conceptualize the political roles of the participants, and at the same time try to come to grips with the disturbing question of how such a tragedy was allowed to occur.

Existing Interpretations and New Analysis

The literature on Chinese politics to date offers two major approaches to the emergence and development of the Great Leap Forward, approaches which form the backdrop against which the analyses of the following chapters are written. The long-dominant approach focuses on the politics of the top

---

3   David Bachman's study (see n. 5, below) is the exception, although its coverage is limited to the pre-Great Leap period and does not, in our view, make several critical distinctions — *viz.* spending ministries *versus* economic coordinating agencies, and provincial Party leaders as separate from a more amorphous "Party as agent of social transformation."

leadership, on the power and policy interests of a small number of leaders at or slightly below the Politburo level. The main variant of the leadership politics interpretation postulates conflict between a "radical" tendency, always depicted as led by Mao, and a more variable "conservative" grouping of the Chairman's alleged opponents, with major policy shifts reflecting the changing fortunes of the competing coalitions.[4] The major alternative interpretation, advanced in the early 1990s by David Bachman,[5] focuses on institutions — particularly central bureaucracies — as the true makers of economic policy, and explains the key decision to launch the Great Leap in terms of bureaucratic politics. In this view Politburo leaders are either coopted by their organizations or, as in the case of Mao, reduced to choosing among competing bureaucratic options. There are still competing coalitions within the Politburo, but they are fundamentally seen as expressions of institutional interests.

The leadership politics interpretation can be traced to the Cultural Revolution and its polemical interpretation of pre-1966 Chinese Communist Party (CCP) politics as a "two line struggle" along the lines indicated above, an interpretation used by the authorities to justify the contemporaneous purge of Mao's alleged "opponents." Much of the Western scholarship which appeared in the immediate wake of the Cultural Revolution in the late 1960s and 1970s slavishly adopted this official designation of political fault lines, even if the "two lines" were normally translated into either personal ("Maoists" *versus* "Liuists") or social science ("revolutionary modernizers" *versus* "managerial modernizers") terminology. Apart from adopting official interpretations, scholarship of this type generally suffered from superficial research; rather than relentless attention to detail the tendency was to skim the surface, find evidence seemingly fitting the "two line" model, and present the result as mature analysis. A further consequence was that much of the resultant writing was descriptive rather than truly analytic. Having uncritically accepted the fundamental notion of an ongoing conflict between Mao and

---

4   The most significant example is Parris H. Chang, *Power and Policy in China* (University Park: The Pennsylvania State University Press, 1975). While suffering from some of the shortcomings discussed below, Chang's book is notable for both the clarity (and some subtlety) of its propositions and its focus on several key issues of economic policy — e.g., the Draft 12-Year Agricultural Program (the 40 articles).

5   *Bureaucracy, Economy, and Leadership in China: The Institutional Origins of the Great Leap Forward* (New York: Cambridge University Press, 1991). For a critical review of Bachman's book (together with Bachman's response), see Frederick C. Teiwes, "Leaders, Institutions, and the Origins of the Great Leap Forward," *Pacific Affairs*, vol. 66, no. 2 (Summer 1993). The present study, while broadly consistent with that review, greatly extends the analysis and modifies several points. For another critique of Bachman, see Alfred L. Chan, "Leaders, Coalition Politics, and Policy-Formulation in China: The Great Leap Forward Revisited," *The Journal of Contemporary China*, Winter-Spring 1995, and Bachman's reply in the Summer 1995 issue of the same journal, "Chinese Bureaucratic Politics and the Origins of the Great Leap Forward."

other leaders, analysis was often reduced to describing the apparent ups and downs of the "struggle" — largely on the basis of skewed information released during the Cultural Revolution.[6]

Far superior to nearly all other leadership politics analyses of the period are the first two volumes of Roderick MacFarquhar's study of the origins of the Cultural Revolution.[7] In contrast to the thinness of much "two line" analysis, MacFarquhar's work is based on exhaustive research into all available sources at the time of writing. In substance, moreover, his analysis of leadership conflict is much more fluid and complex than that of most other writers. Eschewing "two line" interpretations, MacFarquhar does not force Mao into a "radical" box and he assesses the positions of other leaders on the basis of detailed empirical evidence rather than according to the broad brush of Cultural Revolution attacks. Nevertheless, there is a fundamental point of agreement between MacFarquhar and less sophisticated "two line struggle" analysts: Mao's power is far from absolute, he is subject to various challenges, and even when riding high Mao's position is sustained by political calculations on the part of other actors rather than by their instinctive obedience.

In the leadership politics interpretation Mao's power is decidedly variable. In the initial period under study up to the fall 1957 Third Plenum, a time when policy ostensibly followed impulses alien to Mao (at least from a Cultural Revolution perspective), the Chairman allegedly suffered a relative loss of clout *vis-à-vis* other top leaders. Assertedly shifting coalitions within the leadership overruled or delayed the Chairman's preferences, such as those concerning the speed of economic development; Mao is depicted as someone *unable* to carry the day, or at least unable to carry it without great difficulty. When he did prevail, as in launching the first leap forward in winter 1955-56, he was often forced to draw on "outside" forces, specifically provincial Party leaders, to overcome central opponents, while in the case of opposing rash advance he is "compelled" to accept the new program while suffering a political "setback" or even "eclipse."[8]

---

[6] For an early critique of the "two line struggle" model first published in 1974, see Frederick C. Teiwes, *Leadership, Legitimacy, and Conflict in China: From A Charismatic Mao to the Politics of Succession* (Armonk: M. E. Sharpe, 1984), ch. I. For a detailed rebuttal of the model's claims originally published in 1979, see idem, *Politics and Purges in China: Rectification and the Decline of Party Norms 1950-1965*, 2nd ed. (Armonk: M. E. Sharpe, 1993).

[7] Roderick MacFarquhar, *The Origins of the Cultural Revolution 1: Contradictions among the People 1956-1957* (New York: Columbia University Press, 1974), and *The Origins of the Cultural Revolution 2: The Great Leap Forward 1958-1960* (New York: Columbia University Press, 1983). The recently published final volume, *The Origins of the Cultural Revolution 3: The Coming of the Cataclysm 1961-1966* (New York: Columbia University Press, 1997), takes the story up to the onset of the Cultural Revolution itself.

[8] See Chang, *Power and Policy*, pp. 2, 19, 30-33; and MacFarquhar, *Origins 1*, pp. 57ff,

While, as we shall see, there are good reasons for rejecting the above interpretation, ironically the leadership conflict model is less developed for the subsequent period where its substantive view of a dominant Mao accords to the facts. Here the real difficulty for this interpretation lies in its inability to explain adequately how a weak Mao (whose weakness assertedly was due both to setbacks on economic policy and, even more so, to failures and disputes associated with the Hundred Flowers and Party rectification in spring and summer 1957[9]), was able to reverse his fortunes so decisively and quickly at and following the Third Plenum. Indeed, in MacFarquhar's explanation, "Mao desperately needed a new initiative to restore his tarnished credibility [in fall 1957],"[10] thus making the Chairman's personal political vulnerability the key to the emergence of the Great Leap Forward. Yet in MacFarquhar's and lesser accounts the question of the means by which Mao turned his situation around remains elusive.

Most analyses in the leadership politics mode, moreover, having posited Mao's victory over his opponents following the Third Plenum, treat the entire period up to the Lushan conference as a time of "radical" ascendancy albeit with a slow swing to the right from late 1958, but give little attention to how Mao maintained the upper hand.[11] MacFarquhar's subtle and gloriously detailed account of this period of the Chairman's unchallenged leadership goes furthest in grappling with this issue, describing other leaders as swept along by his vision and unwilling to argue for moderation without his lead, and the entire process (apart from some political calculation and tradeoffs) is attributed to Mao's "sheer personal dominance." While we do not dissent from these latter conclusions, as will become apparent we believe they do not go nearly far enough.[12]

86-91, 122ff.

[9]   The outstanding example of the view that Mao was under pressure as a result of the Hundred Flowers and Party rectification is MacFarquhar, *Origins 1*, parts 3 and 4. For the counterargument of a dominant Mao on these issues, see Teiwes, *Politics and Purges*, pp. xxii-xxvi and chs. 6-7.

[10]   Roderick MacFarquhar, "The Secret Speeches of Chairman Mao," in *The Secret Speeches of Chairman Mao: From the Hundred Flowers to the Great Leap Forward* (hereafter *SS*), edited by MacFarquhar, Timothy Cheek, and Eugene Wu (Cambridge: Harvard Council on East Asian Studies, 1989), p. 14.

[11]   E.g., Chang's discussion of the post-Third Plenum period is largely descriptive of policy developments with little attention to his "radicals" *v.* "conservatives" perspective; see *Power and Policy*, pp. 55ff, 69ff, 96ff. The main exceptions are to note attacks on alleged opponents of the Great Leap at the time of the May 1958 Party Congress (pp. 77-78), and to posit a slow decline in "the influence of the radical elements" starting with the Wuhan Plenum (pp. 102, 109-10).

[12]   See MacFarquhar, *Origins 2*, pp. 131, 333-35. MacFarquhar's picture of Mao's personal dominance stops well short of the reality. Thus he portrays Chen Yun and possibly even Zhou Enlai as prepared to say no to the Chairman albeit not to confront him, views Liu Shaoqi's support of the Great Leap as partly due to political calculation concerning the

If the leadership conflict interpretation ultimately derives from Cultural Revolution "revelations" and polemics, Bachman's alternative explanation is the child of American political science.[13] The framework of Bachman's study, as he notes, was heavily influenced by the "new institutionalism" literature which was making its influence felt in American academic circles in the 1980s. In applying the insights of this school to Chinese politics in his extensively researched and closely argued analysis, the aim was to demonstrate the "full impact of institutions — how they structure, channel, and constrain political action in China."[14] While such a perspective had already become influential in analyses of the post-Mao reform period,[15] Bachman's claim that his study fundamentally revises conventional views about the nature of the leap, and by extension the politics of the Maoist period generally, is fully justified. The focus on institutions, and especially the claim that they ultimately shaped policy at least in the economic realm, stands in sharp relief from the previously dominant emphasis on power struggles among the top leaders and Mao's bold individual initiatives.

While Bachman's institutional approach is truly innovative, it involves similarities as well as contrasts to the leadership politics interpretation. With regard to Mao's role and influence, it shares a sense of the Chairman's limitations, with special attention to the constraints allegedly operating on him. Bachman agrees that Mao's power was variable, with the Chairman assertedly significantly weakened by the failure of the Hundred Flowers experiment.[16] Although in some respects Bachman grants Mao more clout in 1956-57 than the leadership conflict analysts, and he certainly demonstrates a more subtle grasp of Mao's shifting economic thinking than most, fundamentally the treatment of the Chairman and his key colleagues is even more dismissive of their roles. Mao and other top political generalists are seen as largely ignorant of economic matters and unable to formulate innovative proposals; they could choose among alternatives but those alternatives were the products of the concerned bureaucracies. While the high-ranking leaders in

---

Party's and his personal power, particularly his assumption of the chairmanship of the PRC in 1959, identifies Politburo members with allegedly greater allegiance to other top leaders than to Mao, and argues that even some provincial-level leaders were seemingly willing to criticize Mao indirectly. *Ibid.*, pp. 56-57, 58, 61, 158-59, 334; and *Origins 1*, pp. 311-15. *Origins 3*, with the benefit of 15 years of new material, goes further in the direction of a dominant Mao, picturing him as "a suspicious Olympian Jove, ready to strike down with lightning bolts" (pp.vii-viii).

13   For a succinct statement pointing to the dangers of following both CCP interpretations and American academic fashions, see Frederick C. Teiwes, "A Critique of Western Studies of CCP Elite Politics," *IIAS Newsletter*, Summer 1996, p. 37.

14   Bachman, *Bureaucracy*, pp. xi, 7, 29.

15   Most significantly Kenneth Lieberthal and Michel Oksenberg, *Policy Making in China: Leaders, Structures, and Processes* (Princeton: Princeton University Press, 1988).

16   Bachman, *Bureaucracy*, pp. 5, 27. Bachman, however, inconsistently rates Mao's power highly elsewhere; see pp. 42-43, 157, 216.

charge of the relevant organizations might have considerable economic expertise, they are treated as representatives of their institutions. Exactly how bureaucratic specialists, their responsible leaders, and the political generalists interact is unclear in Bachman's schema, but the basic assertion is that political action is shaped decisively by institutional interests. For Mao and other generalists it was a matter of coopting the policies of the "winning coalition" and then adding their own concerns. In this interpretation Mao's contribution to the Great Leap was more a matter of style than substance.[17]

The crucial "coalitions" for Bachman are bureaucratic. The origins of the Great Leap, and by extension the course of the conflict over rash advance, are found in a struggle between two institutional groupings, a "financial coalition" led by Chen Yun representing the Ministry of Commerce[18] and Minister of Finance Li Xiannian concerned with achieving a balance between revenue and expenditure, and a "planning and heavy industry coalition" led by State Planning Commission (SPC) chief Li Fuchun and State Economic Commission (SEC) head Bo Yibo[19] which sought to maximize resources for investment in heavy industry and thus increase the pace of development, positions that are rooted in the organizational missions of the respective groupings. While an ill-defined Party organization concerned with social transformation is given a role in determining the final victory of the "planning and heavy industry coalition," in this analysis Mao had no fixed position on economic policy, but instead shifted his support from one bureaucratic coalition to another, eventually hitching his star to the ascendant bureaucratic force.[20]

One of the clearest differences between the leadership politics interpretation and Bachman is that he rejects the dominant view of a dramatic shift in policy at and following the Third Plenum in fall 1957. He challenges

[17] See Bachman, *Bureaucracy*, especially pp. x, 6-8, 158-59, 205.

[18] There is an empirical difficulty in this characterization in that Chen became Minister of Commerce in November 1956, well after not only the beginning of the *fanmaojin* story, but also after the basic start of Bachman's analysis with the Eighth Party Congress. Earlier Chen had played a major role in drafting the initial five-year plan, and subsequently in January 1957 he became head of the five-person small group with overall responsibility for economics work, with Li Fuchun, Bo Yibo, Li Xiannian, and Huang Kecheng as his deputies.

[19] Bo became head of the new SEC which was responsible for annual plans in May 1956, but he could be considered in the "planning and heavy industry coalition" earlier by virtue of his responsibility for industry and communications since 1953. Before that, however, he had been Minister of Finance.

[20] See Bachman, *Bureaucracy,* pp. 8, 59ff, 96ff, 237-40, and *passim*. Bachman neither deals with the developments in opposing rash advance in the first half of 1956 nor makes more than passing mention of the issue thereafter, but his analysis of the programs of the two "coalitions" makes it clear that he believes the financial group was seeking to moderate growth, in opposition to the planners' desire to push construction forward; see *ibid.*, pp. 59, 61-62, 76-77, 107.

conventional interpretations which picture the Great Leap program as the product of "a fever from Mao's brain" with little connection to the preceding period,[21] taking to task, as we do, the failure of the leadership conflict model to explain why the policy reversal came about with relatively little intra-elite opposition. Bachman's answer is that the turnaround was not sudden, but rather that there had been a gradual buildup of pressure for a new direction from about March 1957, with the "planning and heavy industry coalition" relentlessly subduing its bureaucratic opposition and its program of balanced (slower) growth, increased reliance on markets, and greater investment in agriculture and light industry at the expense of the heavy industry sector. In this interpretation Great Leap policies such as decentralization, the development of small and medium-scale industry, and providing inputs for agriculture through investment in industry did not emerge suddenly in late 1957, but had been gaining the upper hand under the auspices of the planners over the previous six months, with the result that all essential ingredients of the leap, except for the people's communes, were on the agenda by mid-1957 — well before being formally ratified, and endorsed by Mao, at the Third Plenum. Continuity, rather than sudden change, is seen as the essence of the policy process.

Yet if Bachman's institutional interpretation is dramatically different on this score, it ironically suffers from the same fate as leadership conflict explanations in failing to provide a convincing explanation of developments once the leap began. In fact, he makes the misleading claim that if he has succeeded in demonstrating the power of institutional analysis for the frenetic Great Leap, it serves to enhance the general explanatory model as applied to PRC politics more broadly. But Bachman's analysis does *not* deal with the Great Leap years; instead the detailed research is confined to the September 1956-October 1957 period which, as already noted, was the most bureaucratic of the Maoist era. As a result there is no empirical testing of the model against developments once the movement is launched; indeed, Bachman's brief comments on the leap itself, while arguing that once launched it served the interests of the "planning coalition" particularly by increasing investment in heavy industry, nevertheless acknowledge that the planners were vulnerable to the increasing role of the Party and "its extreme flight from reality" during the leap, a characterization which, we believe, still understates the threat to planning interests.[22] In short, the presumptive winners of the bureaucratic

---

21   The exception, in the leadership conflict model, concerns the political situation created by disputes over the Hundred Flowers (see above, n. 9) and the heightened tension created by the subsequent Anti-Rightist Campaign in summer 1957.

22   Bachman, *Bureaucracy*, pp. 210-11. Bachman's brief account of the post-Third Plenum period (pp. 206-13) is basically incompatible with his general argument since the "coalitions" do not drive or shape policy but instead are at the mercy of forces originating in the leadership and Party.

Bachman, "Chinese Bureaucratic Politics," p. 40, also calls attention to the work of

conflict wound up faced with profoundly antithetical policies which are largely ignored by Bachman's analysis.

While seeing the major shifts of policy as fundamentally a product of high-level elite politics, the new analysis offered here differs from previous studies of both the leadership conflict and bureaucratic models by, first and foremost, arguing the unchallenged political dominance of Mao throughout the entire 1955-59 period. That such a situation existed even during the "bureaucratic" phase of 1956-57 has been supported by the virtually unanimous testimony of substantial numbers of Party historians who have been interviewed over the past decade. For such historians Mao's unchallenged leadership in the mid-1950s is axiomatic. Scholars from a variety of institutions made such observations as: "Mao had absolute power over the Center"; "at that time it was impossible to oppose Mao, to oppose the emperor"; and "due to Mao's great prestige since Yan'an it was impossible to find comrades with very different opinions from his." Indeed, the senior historian making the latter observation went on to say that when leaders found themselves with different opinions from the Chairman they tended to ask where they had gone wrong, why they couldn't keep up with Mao. As these statements indicate, Mao had an unusual — indeed absolute — authority among his leadership colleagues and the Party more generally, an authority derived fundamentally from the revolutionary success of 1949. His perceived exceptional ability to solve the mysteries of revolutionary struggle in the face of overwhelming odds created a deep faith that he could chart a course others could not see. At another level, leaders whose whole lives had been devoted to the revolution could not separate their life work from loyalty and ultimately obedience to the man who seemingly had produced the improbable victory — even when events suggested he was no longer infallible.[23]

Mao's dominance had been demonstrated on the eve of the events examined here by the almost passive acceptance of his decision to overturn the consensus position (a position he had forcefully endorsed a few months

---

other scholars such as David M. Lampton on the politics of medicine (see "Health Policy During the Great Leap Forward," *The China Quarterly* (hereafter *CQ*), no. 60 [1974]) which indicates an ability on the part of some institutions to protect some of their organizational interests during the Great Leap. This causes us no difficulty since the efforts of officials to seek organizational advantage in a policy calling for advance on *all* fronts, modern as well as traditional, could only be expected. The point is that largely noninstitutional forces shaped the developing leap forward program, often to the detriment of some of the notionally most powerful organizations of the regime.

23 The statements quoted were by Party historians from the Museum of the Chinese Revolution, the Party History Department of the People's University of China, and the CCP Central Party School in 1992, 1991, and 1990 respectively. For an overview of the benefits and limitations of interviewing on Party history, see Frederick C. Teiwes, "Interviews on Party History," in Timothy Cheek and Tony Saich, eds, *New Perspectives on State Socialism in China* (Armonk: M. E. Sharpe, 1997). On the sources of Mao's unquestioned legitimacy within the leadership, see Teiwes, *Leadership*, ch. II.

earlier) on the speed of agricultural cooperativization in mid-1955.[24] This, of course, was an area — social revolution — where Mao's special credentials were widely acknowledged within the elite. His overwhelming power was even more dramatically revealed slightly earlier in a case of high-level power conflict, the 1953-54 purge of Gao Gang and Rao Shushi, which provided extensive evidence of a court politics where other key leaders accepted absolutely the Chairman's authority, sought to promote their own policy interests by convincing him of their preferences, and attempted to advance or retain their political positions by interpreting his often ambiguous cues.[25]

But if court politics was the dominant mode of leadership politics, how was it manifested in the economic policy area where, as of late 1955, Mao made no special claims and where policy outcomes in 1956-57 were ostensibly "un-Maoist"? Moreover, how and why was the political process transformed from one where Mao's ultimate authority was unchallenged to one where, by the January 1958 Nanning conference, all actors were transfixed by his will? There is a final puzzle: if Mao was, as we claim, so extraordinarily dominant from the Nanning conference on that whenever he forcefully expressed a preference the overwhelming majority of the leadership fell in behind his views with a surprising degree of enthusiasm, and no actor ever contemplated differing with the Chairman in such circumstances, then why were his oft-repeated calls for greater moderation from fall 1958 of such limited effect? These are the central questions our Mao-centered analysis must address.

Dealing with these questions will require an examination of not only Mao's own thinking and motivations and the roles of his key colleagues in the immediate "inner court" of the Politburo, but also of the more institutional actors of what can be loosely characterized as an "outer court" which clearly did play significant roles in both influencing and implementing policy, notwithstanding Bachman's overestimation of their importance. Thus the aim of this analysis is not simply to explain the major decisions which led to the *fanmaojin* program and the Great Leap. It also seeks to examine the mode of policy making in the distinctive periods concerned, with attention to the roles of a number of key actors. These are the Chairman himself, other key leaders at the apex of the system, the relevant central bureaucracies including both coordinating bodies and spending ministries, the provincial Party leadership, and, more intermittently, the Chairman's personal staff and the central Party apparatus.[26] While Mao-centered, the study examines the interests and clout of

---

24   See Frederick C. Teiwes and Warren Sun, eds, *The Politics of Agricultural Cooperativization in China: Mao, Deng Zihui, and the "High Tide" of 1955* (Armonk: M. E. Sharpe, 1993).

25   See Frederick C. Teiwes, *Politics at Mao's Court: Gao Gang and Party Factionalism in the Early 1950s* (Armonk: M. E. Sharpe, 1990).

26   Missing from this list is China's military establishment simply because we find no evidence of it playing a significant role concerning economic policy in the late 1955 to

the various players operating around the Chairman, and analyzes how bureaucratic as well as leadership politics were altered by the dramatic shifts in both policy and modes of policy making. Finally, as already indicated, we delve into responsibility for the great tragedy which was unfolding by 1959.

A Methodological Note

We have relied on a wide range of sources drawn from different periods in conducting our research. These include the contemporary documentary record from the 1950s, obviously an essential source for the verification of events. We have also made significant use of materials from the Cultural Revolution era, particularly versions of Mao's speeches made available by Red Guard sources. But our most important sources date from the reform era: we have relied heavily on both post-Mao Party history sources and interviews with Chinese Party historians and a small number of participants in the events themselves.

Each of these broad categories of sources have their strengths and weaknesses and have been relied on to different degrees by various authors. Returning to the contemporary sources is not only *de rigueur* for checking the claims of memoirs, interviews, and other after-the-fact accounts, it also provides a rich vein of information concerning actors not normally in the public eye. This, however, is variable, with some periods such as the mid-1950s providing a much more detailed record of policy advocacy than later periods when the public media was much more concerned with propaganda and considerably more sparing with useful information. In this light it is not surprising that Bachman's study, which focuses on 1956-57, differs from ours not only in interpretation but in reliance on sources. In contrast to our extensive use of post-Mao sources, Bachman's analysis is fundamentally based on the open documents of the mid-1950s although it is supplemented by a wide range of reform era documentary sources, some Cultural Revolution materials, and seemingly a very limited number of interviews. Placing primary emphasis on contemporary documents, however, is subject to all the limitations of traditional Pekinology: we only see what someone has deemed fit for public consumption, while the politics behind open statements must be inferred on the basis of (often very) incomplete evidence. Indeed, the fundamental methodological assumption that what appears under an individual's name represents that person's views is clearly flawed; post-Mao sources demonstrate that views often associated with Mao's "opponents" in fact appeared only after his careful review and vigorous editing.[27] As a result,

---

mid-1959 period. For further discussion, see the Conclusion to this study, below, pp. 198-99.

[27]   See the discussion in Frederick C. Teiwes, "Mao Texts and the Mao of the 1950s," *The Australian Journal of Chinese Affairs* (hereafter *AJCA*), no. 33 (1995), especially pp. 135, 138-39.

many interpretations which seem reasonable on the basis of contemporary texts turn out to be seriously mistaken when more information becomes available.

As already suggested, Cultural Revolution sources have been profoundly influential in shaping the leadership conflict interpretation, although in MacFarquhar's case in conjunction with an exhaustive reading of contemporary sources and some post-Mao materials.[28] The distortions of polemic denunciations of disgraced leaders cannot be overestimated, yet at the same time much useful information concerning behind the scenes activities emerged from both official and Red Guard sources during these years, information which has also been harnessed in post-Mao Party history studies.[29] Generally speaking, while any specific claim from these sources must be treated with caution, on the whole the problem is not false information but instead biased interpretation, something which could always be mitigated by a careful reading of contemporary sources[30] and can now be tested by the richer vein of post-Mao materials. But of all the Cultural Revolution materials the most valuable are transcripts of Mao's previously unpublished speeches released by Red Guard organizations. While clearly selective, these speeches were treated as sacred texts by the young revolutionaries, and their verbatim, unpolished nature provide an invaluable insight into not only the confused nature of Mao's thinking but the real situation faced by those who had to contend with an all powerful Chairman.[31]

Post-Mao sources too are not without problems including selectivity and political constraints concerning sensitive issues. Yet in comparison to any previous period the materials available are far more extensive and objective. Rich documentary collections, detailed chronologies, revealing memoirs, and serious academic history all contribute to a depth of understanding impossible during earlier periods.[32] The nature, coverage, and limitations of the most

---

28   The latter, of course, were the post-Mao materials available when *Origins 2* was published in 1983. For MacFarquhar's assessment of early post-Mao sources, see *ibid.*, pp. 434-35.

29   For example, the authoritative Hu Sheng, ed., *Zhongguo Gongchandang qishinian* [The CCP's Seventy Years] (Beijing: Zhonggong dangshi chubanshe, 1991), makes substantial use of such materials.

30   See especially MacFarquhar's admirable evaluation of attacks on Liu Shaoqi's political report to the 1956 Party Congress in *Origins 1*, pp. 160-64.

31   Of particular value for this analysis are the Red Guard texts translated in *SS*. For an insightful overview of Red Guard Mao texts, see Timothy Cheek, "Textually Speaking: An Assessment of Newly Available Mao Texts," in *ibid.*

32   In addition to Party history journals, books by Party historians, chronologies, documentary collections, and participant memoirs, we have also used six unpublished Chinese documents which cover the events of this period in great detail, They are identified as "unpublished Chinese documents nos. 1-6," and deposit copies are available at the Menzies Library, the Australian National University, and the Fairbank Center Library, Harvard University. They are discussed in detail in our Annotated Bibliography.

important post-Mao materials used in our research are discussed in some detail
in the Annotated Bibliography at the end of this volume; here we only mention
briefly two of the most outstanding. First, the 13 volumes (including four on
the years primarily in question) of *Mao Zedong's Manuscripts since the
Founding of the State* provide not only an extraordinary detailed account of
Mao's changing views and concerns, but also an exceptional window into the
interaction among the leader, his leading colleagues, and a wide range of
official bodies. And second, Bo Yibo's magnificent memoirs encompass not
only a detailed reconstruction of many of the crucial events of the period
under study,[33] but also offer a palpable sense of how one of the central actors
in our story actually felt when confronted by an aroused Mao.

Finally, separate mention must be made of the interview sources that have
opened up during the reform era. For this particular study we have interviewed
over two dozen Party historians specializing in the 1955-59 period or other
relevant topics, as well as a small number of participants, consisting of a
central bureaucrat from the heavy industrial sector throughout the entire
period, a key provincial Party leader over these same years, a provincial Party
committee staff member in 1958-59, four officials who attended major Party
conferences in 1958-59 including both the central bureaucrat and key
provincial leader, and two individuals who worked for Mao.

Perhaps the overriding lesson to be derived from extended contact with
professional Party historians in particular, but not excluding most of the
participants interviewed, is that these are on the whole modest and serious
individuals with high standards of historical evidence. Notwithstanding the
various restrictions which have affected their writings, scholars of Party
history are thoroughly empiricist in the best traditions of Chinese
historiography. Although working in an area where there are inevitable gaps in
information, they are not happy without a solid factual basis for their
conclusions. Party historians are sceptical of their sources noting, for example,
that memoir material is of variable quality and often unreliable. They are also
candid about the limitations of their knowledge, willingly admitting where
they have not seen materials and carefully distinguishing where they are
offering their own analysis in the absence of specific evidence. Such
meticulous behavior creates considerable confidence for those instances where
scholars report the contents of a particular document they have read or offer
conclusions based on familiarity with extensive archival material or other
sources.

While the limitations on interviews and other post-Mao sources should
not be understated, and important blank spots in the story remain, when
combined with the contemporary record and key Cultural Revolution

---

33   This was based not simply on Bo's recollections of the period, but equally significantly
on his unmatched archival access as one of the most powerful post-Mao Party elders and
as a member of the most authoritative Party body overseeing Party history activities, the
three-person Party history leadership small group (*dangshi lingdao xiaozu*).

materials they allow a much more detailed and discriminating analysis than what was previously possible. The nuanced story which results both revises previous understandings about and provides new perspectives on the events of the mid to late 1950s that culminated in the great famine.

The study which follows is divided into four detailed chapters. In Chapter 1 we examine the emergence and continuation of the opposition to rash advance in 1956-57. Here we go into considerable detail concerning the events of this well-known but largely unexamined phase of PRC economic policy to analyze the complex interaction of leadership and bureaucratic interests. We find a vigorous bureaucratic politics, but one fundamentally different from that hypothesized by Bachman: instead of competing coalitions organized around financial and planning functions, the real source of institutional conflict was between those, budgeteers and planners alike, charged with the overall coordinating responsibilities, and actors in both the spending ministries and provinces seeking maximum resources for their specific tasks and areas. Furthermore, we elucidate a situation where the locus of power was not in institutions but in top Party leaders, with Mao in the paradoxical position of being all powerful but somewhat remote from economic decision making.

Chapter 2 addresses explicitly the question of the origins of the Great Leap Forward, analyzing the forces and circumstances giving rise to the new program, reviewing the issue of linkages to previous developments, and providing an analysis of the political dynamics of policy change in late 1957 and early 1958. Here the issue of continuity/discontinuity is examined, with the seeming policy continuities between 1956-57 and the leap analyzed in some detail, and found to be more superficial than fundamental. Moreover, our examination of political dynamics reveals an even more abrupt change of political direction, although not of concrete policy, at the Third Plenum than previously imagined. In addition, the discussion of events at the January 1958 Nanning conference which, it is now clear, must rank with the Lushan meetings 18 months later in significance, provides an astonishing picture of personal power and an elite that virtually unanimously followed Mao due to a combination of fear and belief. The analysis further elucidates the special role played by provincial Party leaders in the process. Finally, we offer a new explanation of why Mao lurched into uncharted waters with a program that not only overturned the policies of his trusted lieutenants, but in the process reversed his own positions of the previous period.

Chapter 3 takes up the story from the start of 1958 as enthusiastic acceptance of Mao's new program led to a series of utopian measures. It examines the process whereby a series of top-level Party meetings from January to August created unprecedented pressure for unattainable results, and also provides a detailed analysis of the dramatic escalation of steel targets during the May-June period. These investigations assess the personal timidity of top leaders seeking to avoid the "rightist" label, the special dynamics of competition among individuals, organizations, and areas, the continuing radical role of provincial leaders, and the peculiar bureaucratic inversion whereby the previously supreme coordinating agencies were now forced to dance to the tunes of key spending ministries.

Chapter 4 turns to the developments where awareness of the shortcomings of the leap became a central factor of political life. It examines the circumstances which saw Mao become the first leader to doubt openly the fantastic claims emerging from lower levels in fall 1958, asking how and why the Chairman himself of all CCP leaders became the spokesperson for greater realism. It then asks why it was so difficult for Mao's many calls for moderation in the November 1958-summer 1959 period to make a more significant impact. In pursuing this issue we examine the timid attempts of leaders such as Chen Yun to make use of Mao's "realistic" impulses and the emergence of different views within the various categories of actors including provincial Party leaders. But in seeking to explain the failure to achieve a more systematic rectification of the leap's flawed policies, we conclude the key element was Mao's own ambivalence and constantly changing signals. When the detailed study concludes on the eve of the July-August 1959 Lushan conference, Mao's continuing concern with the lack of realism was a factor for more forceful action, but his ongoing lack of constancy severely compromised the likelihood of such an outcome.

In the Conclusion we review our overall findings and systematically examine the interests, behavior, and calculations of each of the categories of actors considered throughout the study. We are left with the depressing summary observation that *no one* was willing to stand up to Mao despite the gathering signs of unprecedented disaster. This is followed by two epilogues, the first a review of developments at the Lushan conference which, despite a certain (limited) boldness on the part of Peng Dehuai and others in airing problems caused by the Great Leap, nevertheless illustrates the ongoing complicity of key leaders in Mao's mistakes, a complicity which resulted in a new lurch to the left that greatly accelerated the famine. The second epilogue on the 1960-62 period when reversals of policy did take place while millions starved also suggests a fundamental continuity with earlier developments — the system stood paralyzed while Mao hesitated, and key policies that helped reverse the situation were ultimately discarded once Mao turned against them. Finally, the Appendices list participants in the key Party conferences of 1958-59 and translate available texts of early 1958 self-criticisms by top Party leaders, and the Annotated Bibliography provides a critical discussion of the most important sources used in this study.

Chapter 1

OPPOSING RASH ADVANCE, 1956-57[1]

The period of opposing rash advance from early 1956 up to the fall 1957 Third Plenum[2] was indeed an "un-Maoist" interlude in terms of the Chairman's greatest passions, not to mention the demonology of the Cultural Revolution. How can this be squared with our view of a dominant Mao? If neither the leadership conflict interpretation of Mao's presumed relative loss of clout *vis-à-vis* other top leaders nor the bureaucratic explanation of policy being driven by institutions are adequate, why were the policy outcomes as they were and what was the nature of the political process? Long recognized factors such as Mao's confidence in Chen Yun and other specialist leaders in the economic sphere (and his own lack of expertise concerning these matters) and the

---

[1] An earlier version of this chapter appeared as Frederick C. Teiwes with Warren Sun, "The Politics of an 'Un-Maoist' Interlude: The Case of Opposing Rash Advance, 1956-57," in Timothy Cheek and Tony Saich, eds, *New Perspectives on State Socialism in China* (Armonk: M. E. Sharpe, 1997), pp. 151-71. The present version is basically unchanged, apart from a relatively small number of corrections and additions resulting from further research. The most significant new information is that concerning the elusive incident in April 1956 when Mao proposed a ¥2 billion increase in capital construction spending; see below, pp. 27-29. Also of particular note is a partial revision in our assessment of Zhou Enlai's performance (p. 48). Finally, we have also added a detailed table (pp. 36-39) of capital construction targets during and beyond the period analyzed.

[2] The precise dating of the *fanmaojin* interlude varies in different accounts with Bo Yibo, *Ruogan zhongda juece yu shijian de huigu* [Reflections on Certain Major Decisions and Events], vol. 1 (Beijing: Zhonggong zhongyang dangxiao chubanshe, 1991), p. 561, stating it lasted from early 1956 to early 1957, while Mao (see the Red Guard collection *Xuexi wenxuan* [Selected Study Materials], vol. 2 [October 1957-1958] [Beijing: 1967], p. 188, and Ma Qibin, Chen Wenbin, Lin Yunhui, Cong Jin, Wang Nianyi, Zhang Tianrong, and Bu Weihua, eds., *Zhongguo Gongchandang zhizheng sishinian (1949-1989)* [The CCP's Forty Years in Power, 1949-1989], rev. ed. [Beijing: Zhonggong dangshi chubanshe, 1991], p. 137) regarded it as originating in June 1956 and lasting until late summer 1957, i.e., roughly up to the September-October Third Plenum. The best dating is to consider the effort as spanning both periods, with a comprehensive program forming in mid-1956 after limited initial measures, and the basic approach continuing to the Third Plenum, although the major measures to slow the economy had been completed by early 1957.

relatively robust expression of bureaucratic interests in the mid-1950s provide important clues to the general picture, but until the outpouring of new sources beginning in the early 1980s both detail and fuller understanding remained elusive. The contributions of post-Mao Party history has changed this situation significantly.

Standard Party history accounts, as opposed to the full range of new documentation, are closer to the leadership conflict than the bureaucratic model, but without the implication of a major struggle between Mao and other top leaders. In these accounts two opposing lines of thinking concerning economic construction did exist from early 1956 to the Third Plenum, and they reflected the views of Mao on the one hand and Premier Zhou Enlai, Chen Yun, and others (including both top planning and financial officials) on the other. However, rather than causing major political conflict, the differences were managed by Mao obeying the wishes of the majority.[3] Yet when the full range of the new evidence available from the reform era is examined, a more subtle and complex picture emerges that is both at variance with each of the major existing Western interpretations and which goes well beyond the stylized official overview.

The Origins and Development of Opposition to Rash Advance

The problem of rash advance clearly originated in the exaggerated expectations produced by the rapid development of agricultural cooperatives in the summer and fall of 1955, as well as in the atmosphere created by the sharp attacks on rightist conservativism which so influenced the cooperativization drive.[4] In both aspects Mao was at the forefront of extending the rural transformation experience to the economic sphere. In October 1955 he began to sense conservativism in economic policy when he received a report from Li Fuchun's SPC which proposed targets for the entire period to 1967, targets which a dissatisfied Chairman considered too low.[5] About this time Mao also became disenchanted with the execution of the 1955 plan and was not fully mollified even when Zhou Enlai made a self-criticism and the SPC demanded more activism from ministries and provinces in drawing up 1956 economic plans. The key moment came on December 5 when Liu Shaoqi conveyed Mao's criticism of right conservative thought in the economy to a meeting of 122 Central Committee members and responsible officials of

---

3   E.g., see *Dang de wenxian* [The Party's Documents], no. 2 (1990), p. 9.

4   See Teiwes and Sun, *The Politics of Agricultural Cooperativization*, pp. 14, 107ff.

5   Tong Xiaopeng, *Fengyu sishinian (dierbu)* [Forty Years of Trials and Hardships (second part)] (Beijing: Zhongyang wenxian chubanshe, 1996), p. 350, reports Mao's dissatisfaction with SPC projections for the end of the Third Five-Year Plan in 1967: 60 billion catties for grain, 56 million piculs for cotton, 18 million tons for steel, and 280 million tons for coal. Overall, industry was to grow by 8.6 percent annually in the First, 9.9 percent in the Second, and 10.1 percent in the Third Five-Year Plans.

leading Party, government, and military organs. Liu quoted Mao as saying that it was necessary to use the opportunities created by the more relaxed international situation of 1955 to speed the pace of development and that the crucial thing was "to oppose rightist thought, to oppose conservatism." Liu further amplified the message with some comments of his own, which contrasted sharply with what would become the dominant theme of *fanmaojin,* when he observed that the development of real things was not balanced, and that attempting to manage affairs in a balanced manner would only lead to problems.[6]

In the same period, believing that, much as the continuing high tide of cooperativization had laid down a standard for socialist transformation generally, an increased pace of agricultural growth could set a precedent for speeding up overall economic construction, in mid-November Mao convened meetings in Hangzhou and Tianjin with Party secretaries from 15 provinces which produced 17 articles on agricultural development. In December the Chairman drafted a notice inviting opinions from provincial-level leaders on the 17 articles, and on the basis of consultations involving these local leaders and concerned central officials, the 17 articles were expanded into the ambitious 40 article 12-year Draft Program for Agricultural Development which was formally adopted by the Supreme State Conference in January 1956.[7] Thus on this key issue which was so important in setting the tone for the ambitious push for rapid development in early 1956, provincial leaders had a direct input in fueling Mao's enthusiasm for intensified agricultural growth. Moreover, as Mao toured the provinces at the turn of the year, provincial leaders took the opportunity to complain of overcentralization and inadequate central government funding of the economic development of their areas, as we shall see in somewhat more detail later.[8]

While Mao's personal role in creating the new atmosphere and pushing specific projects such as the Draft Agricultural Program was crucial, there is little evidence of any contrary voices within the leadership in late 1955. The top bodies of the Party and state adopted without argument the measures and symbols which characterized what became known as the first leap forward. In addition to the 40 articles, the Party Secretariat approved Mao's late December preface to *Socialist Upsurge in the Chinese Countryside* which urged criticism of rightist and conservative thinking "without stop" and called for speeding up not only the socialist transformation of handicrafts and capitalist industry and commerce, but also industrialization and the development of science, culture, education, and other fields of work. Also endorsed in this period were anti-rightist guidelines for the projected Eighth

---

6   Bo Yibo, *Huigu,* vol. 1, pp. 521-25; Lin Yunhui, Fan Shouxin, and Zhang Gong, *1949-1989 nian de Zhongguo: Kaige xingjin de shiqi* [China 1949-1989: The Period of Triumph and Advance] (Zhengzhou: Henan renmin chubanshe, 1989), pp. 614-15.

7   Bo Yibo, *Huigu,* vol. 1, pp. 523-24; and Ma Qibin, *Zhizheng sishinian,* pp. 105, 107.

8   See below, p. 58.

Party Congress. And enlarged Politburo meetings further approved the "committee to promote progress" (*cujin weiyuanhui*) to push forward agricultural development[9] and the slogan "more, faster, better, and more economical" (*duo, kuai, hao, sheng*),[10] initiatives which together with the 40 articles were the three things that, in fall 1957 at the Third Plenum, Mao complained had been "blown away" by *fanmaojin*.[11]

Although the kind of political pressure Mao had generated during cooperativization was clearly operative here, the evidence suggests that there was a genuine and broad support for more rapid growth. Both oral sources and Bo Yibo's memoir account claim strong enthusiasm within the leadership and "the whole Party" for boosting construction. In bureaucratic terms, *at this stage* the Ministry of Finance joined the spending departments and the localities in approving the new thrust. Given his preeminent role subsequently in pushing the *fanmaojin* program, the attitudes of Zhou Enlai are of particular interest. As Bo Yibo put it over 35 years later, at the end of 1955 the Premier like other leaders was "filled with exaltation" over a high tide of construction, a position seemingly also shared by Chen Yun who helped to formulate the crucial 40 articles. When Zhou addressed the conference of intellectuals in mid-January it was also in the spirit of opposing right conservatism, but by that point events were unfolding which would very soon force an initial reassessment. As Premier, Zhou had to contend with the consequences of significantly increased targets proposed by both central ministries and localities. As early as November-December, driven by the desire to avoid the rightist label, direct orders from both Zhou and the SPC, and the opportunity to expand spending on their organizational functions or local areas, such units began the frenzy of setting unrealistic targets which marked the first leap forward. Pushed also by a new national objective of fulfilling the First Five-

---

9   Although widely thought merely to refer to the spirit of exerting greater efforts for agricultural construction rather than to an actual body, this obscure organ was proposed by Mao and, ironically in view of later developments, Chen Yun was made responsible for it. Shi Zhongquan, *Zhou Enlai de zhuoyue fengxian* [Zhou Enlai's Distinguished Commitment] (Beijing: Zhonggong zhongyang dangxiao chubanshe, 1993), p. 329n.

10 There is some uncertainty as to the authorship of the slogan. According to the first volume of Bo Yibo's reflections, *Huigu*, p. 526, Zhou Enlai had begun to create the slogan even before Liu's December 5 conveying of Mao's comments. Together with Bo Yibo he proposed the guideline of "more, faster, better" which quickly won Mao's complete approval, and later Li Fuchun added the more restrained "more economical." Bo's second volume (Beijing: Zhonggong zhongyang dangxiao chubanshe, 1993), p. 661, and other Party history sources, however, credit Mao with raising the first three exhortations, but with Li Fuchun again contributing *sheng*.

11 Bo Yibo, *Huigu*, vol. 1, pp. 525-26; *Jianguo yilai Mao Zedong wengao* [Mao Zedong's Manuscripts since the Founding of the State], vol. 7 (January 1958-December 1958) (Beijing: Zhongyang wenxian chubanshe, 1992), pp. 204-205; *Selected Works of Mao Tsetung* (hereafter *SW*), vol. V (Peking: Foreign Languages Press, 1977), pp. 491-92; and oral sources.

Year Plan (FFYP) in four years, this "small leap" would last well into spring 1956.[12]

Zhou was now faced with excessive demands on state resources. Although the joint planning and financial conference (i.e., the third national planning conference) which met in Beijing from January 10 to February 7 was convened under the anti-rightist banner and the SPC presented ambitious targets including a 22 percent overall industrial growth rate for 1956, during this conference spending ministries and the provinces pushed for even higher targets and demanded large investments. While the SPC proposed a hefty increase in total capital construction investment to ¥14.85 billion, the demands put on the table reached ¥18 billion and then ¥20 billion plus, producing considerable concern on the part of Zhou and the CCP's economic architect, Chen Yun. At the symbolic level, Zhou sought to deal with the situation by balancing the need for opposing conservatism with an equal imperative to avoid blind rash advance. In speeches in late January and early February he emphasized the approach of seeking truth from facts, avoiding unrealistic goals, and guarding against too fast development. In some striking phrases he enjoined that "on no account [should we] raise the slogan, 'Realize industrialization at an early date,'" and while it was necessary to avoid pouring cold water on the masses, "cold water can be useful for leaders who get carried away, for it may sober them up."[13]

More concretely Zhou, working with Li Xiannian and Li Fuchun, began to press for a reduction of targets with the result that the capital construction investment target was pushed back down to ¥14.7 billion, a situation which led the Premier to joke that the joint conference, which actually continued to work for the next year, had become a committee for promoting retrogression (cutui weiyuanhui), i.e., the opposite of the committee for promoting progress. Several things stand out from this process. First, there was no division in principle between the SPC and the Ministry of Finance over the necessity of reining in unrealistic plans; moreover, the two organizations worked together in achieving the ¥14.7 billion figure. Some evidence of the influence of

---

12   Bo Yibo, *Huigu*, vol. 1, pp. 526-27, 530-31; *Dang de wenxian*, no. 2 (1988), p. 9, and no. 4 (1993), p. 64; and oral sources. Regarding Chen Yun, Mao commented in 1958 that he, Zhou, and Chen had all been "very active" about the 40 articles; Li Rui, *"Dayuejin" qinliji* [A Personal Record of the "Great Leap Forward"] (Shanghai: Shanghai yuandong chubanshe, 1996), p. 204. More specifically, Chen, who had been engaging in rural investigations, endorsed in January 1956 the 40 articles' ambitious output per *mu* goals for 1967; see *Chen Yun yu Xin Zhongguo jingji jianshe* [Chen Yun and New China's Economic Construction] (Beijing: Zhongyang wenxian chubanshe, 1991), pp. 161-62. The first leap is well described in the existing literature; see especially MacFarquhar, *Origins 1*, pp. 26-32.

13   Bo Yibo, *Huigu*, vol. 1, pp. 531-33; Liao Gailong, ed., *Xin Zhongguo biannianshi (1949-1989)* [Chronicle of New China, 1949-1989] (Beijing: Renmin chubanshe, 1989), pp. 97-98; *Selected Works of Zhou Enlai*, vol. II (Beijing: Foreign Languages Press, 1989), pp. 195-96; and oral sources.

organizational missions is available, however, in the sense that the Ministry of Finance reportedly was the most concerned, with Li Xiannian particularly active in dealing with the problem. Yet, according to oral sources, the key figure without question was Zhou Enlai whose work style of minute attention to detail led him to focus on the problem early and to carry out joint research with the Finance Ministry which had itself become aware of the problem almost simultaneously. Zhou's key contribution was both the vision and political will to deal with the question. Given the atmosphere of the time, the general desire for economic development, and the feeling of many leaders that given the relatively smooth economic performance of the previous three years high targets would not be a problem, Zhou's willingness to pour cold water was, in the view of one senior Party historian, quite extraordinary. But it must also be pointed out that the actual measures taken at this juncture were pale in comparison to what happened later. This *fanmaojin* appears to have been limited to the 1956 capital construction target, and the result was simply to pare things back to the already ambitious targets advanced by the SPC. Moreover, when the SPC presented its draft 1956 plan later in February it reflected the anti-rightist spirit and contained ambitious targets, and it was formally approved by Zhou's State Council on March 25.[14]

This leaves the question of Mao's role, and the relationship between the Chairman and Premier. While Party historians are adamant that the efforts of Zhou and associates were aimed at the lower levels and not at the Chairman, the position adopted was clearly at some variance with Mao's enthusiasm at the turn of the year. Yet in one sense, the very fact that Zhou's fairly modest results could be seen in retrospect as "courageously doing a little bit"[15] speaks volumes for Mao's authority. Zhou, moreover, drew on that authority when arguing for moderation, citing the Chairman's January injunctions not to attempt things which cannot be realized, that ministries should fix targets on a realistic basis, and to avoid "left" adventurism. Party history analyses today, however, while observing that Mao had considered the question of "leftist" errors and put forward many correct and reasonable opinions which Zhou then developed, conclude accurately (with the benefit of hindsight) that these efforts were not the Chairman's main emphasis — an emphasis suggested by his late February urging of heavy industry leaders Wang Heshou and Lü Dong to pursue faster growth than the Soviet Union's and his early March remark that "Our understanding of the real situation has advanced a step, but it has also brought about a rightist tendency."[16] Nevertheless, one of the most

---

14   Bo Yibo, *Huigu*, vol. 1, pp. 532-33; *Dang de wenxian*, no. 2 (1988), p. 11; Tong Xiaopeng, *Fengyu sishinian*, p. 352; Li Ping, *Kaiguo Zongli Zhou Enlai* [Founding Premier Zhou Enlai] (Beijing: Zhonggong zhongyang dangxiao chubanshe, 1994), p. 355; and oral sources.

15   *Dang de wenxian*, no. 2 (1988), p. 11.

16   See *ibid.*, no. 5 (1992), p. 43; and *Zhou Enlai jingji wenxuan* [Selected Works of Zhou Enlai on the Economy] (Beijing: Zhongyang wenxian chubanshe, 1993), p. 251. Mao's

authoritative writers on Zhou Enlai, Shi Zhongquan, concludes that Zhou and the vice premiers responsible for the economy believed their efforts to curb rashness did not oppose the Chairman's position but merely corrected shortcomings in work, and this lack of apprehension on their part meant courageous measures could be taken.[17] In any case, there is no evidence of any reaction on Mao's part to the specific activities of Zhou et al. While it is hard to believe that the Chairman was not briefed on the situation, Party historians know of no response on his part and conclude that he was basically silent on the unfolding situation. Given that the problem was conceived of as a question of practical work, as concerning the deficit rather than the Party's line, oral sources find this understandable.

The situation changed in early April when problems of serious shortages and waste caused by excessive growth became obvious. In these circumstances Zhou and Chen Yun determined that the 1956 plan was still reckless, they began measures to curb the excesses, and, in the view of one Party history account, Zhou Enlai truly began to push fanmaojin. Moreover, in addition to the 1956 plan, Zhou and Chen concluded that the rates of construction in the draft 1957 plan and Second (SFYP) and Third Five-Year Plans were also maojin. One of the important measures taken was to emphasize the importance of balance, especially materials balance, a theme particularly developed by Bo Yibo who was now placed in charge of "balancing work," a step which foreshadowed the creation of the SEC under Bo with responsibility for annual plan implementation the next month. Overall, Party history sources stress the cooperative efforts of Zhou, Chen, and Bo in combating rash advance at this juncture.[18]

---

remark is from Gu Longsheng, ed., Mao Zedong jingji nianpu [Chronicle of Mao Zedong on the Economy] (Beijing: Zhonggong zhongyang dangxiao chubanshe, 1993), p. 374. The memoir account of his meeting with Wang and Lü (Minister and Vice Minister of Heavy Industry respectively until May 1956 when the ministry was abolished and they took up similar positions in the new Ministry of Metallurgy) is from Mianhuai Mao Zedong [Cherish the Memory of Mao Zedong], vol. 1 (Beijing: Zhongyang wenxian chubanshe, 1993), pp. 68-69.

17   Shi Zhongquan, Zhou Enlai, p. 319. In this period, moreover, Zhou was clearly in tune with Mao when he claimed the 40 articles could be overfulfilled ahead of time through mass initiative; see Chang, Power and Policy, p. 19.

18   Dang de wenxian, no. 2 (1988), p. 11, and no. 2 (1990), p. 8; Lin Yunhui, Xingjin de shiqi, pp. 622-24, 626; Bo Yibo, Huigu, vol. 1, pp. 533-34; "unpublished Chinese document no. 1," pp. 8-10; and MacFarquhar, Origins 1, pp. 59-60. Tong Xiaopeng, Fengyu sishinian, p. 353, reports that SPC Vice Chairman Zhang Xi was also given responsibility for balancing work along with Bo Yibo.

In addition to the link between the SEC and balancing work, the concept of a "planning and heavy industry coalition" is weakened somewhat by the appointment of Minister of Light Industry Jia Tuofu as Bo's ranking deputy on the SEC; see Hu Hua, ed., Zhonggong dangshi renwu zhuan (hereafter ZGDSRWZ) [Biographies of Personalities in CCP History], vol. 46 (Xi'an: Shaanxi renmin chubanshe, 1991), p. 288.

The problem, however, was to a large extent political. It was not simply that many leading figures within the Party still harbored serious *maojin* tendencies and various ministries continued to demand increased capital construction funds, but even more to the point the issue became "an extremely large political question" because of the anti-right conservative atmosphere created by Mao. Thus something of an impasse developed in many localities where, under the influence of the anti-rightist criticism, lower levels demanded more construction while the upper levels didn't dare to put all their cards on the table.[19] In this context, a remarkable, if still obscure, encounter took place at a late April Politburo meeting.[20] While Zhou, backed by Chen Yun, apparently argued that the capital construction budget was still too high, Mao, who rarely attended Politburo meetings even in the mid-1950s, on this occasion came and instead proposed a ¥2 billion increase. In the ensuing discussion only Li Fuchun supported Mao,[21] with the majority arguing that there was no money for such an increase. Although this has been cited by Party historians as a case of a "democratic" Mao accepting the views of the majority, in fact the meeting ended with the Politburo approving the proposal when the Chairman insisted on his view.[22] Mao's acceptance of the "majority"

---

[19] Lin Yunhui, *Xingjin de shiqi*, pp. 626-27; Bo Yibo, *Huigu*, vol. 1, p. 533; *Dang de wenxian*, no. 2 (1988), p. 11; and "unpublished Chinese document no. 1," pp. 9-10.

[20] Only a handful of published sources, insofar as we can determine, make brief references to this event during the enlarged Politburo meeting of April 25-28: exceedingly terse mentions in Shi Zhongquan, *Mao Zedong de jianxin kaituo* [Mao Zedong's Arduous Pioneering] (Beijing: Zhonggong dangshi ziliao chubanshe, 1990), p. 212, Li Ping, "Zhou Enlai," in *ZGDSRWZ*, vol. 49 (Xi'an: Shaanxi renmin chubanshe, 1991), p. 108, and *Dang de wenxian*, no. 2 (1992), p. 53; and the somewhat more substantial descriptions in Li Ping, *Kaiguo Zongli*, p. 356, and Jin Chongji, ed., *Zhou Enlai zhuan* [Biography of Zhou Enlai] (Beijing: Zhongyang wenxian chubanshe, 1998), vol. 3, p. 1227. In addition, "unpublished Chinese document no. 1," pp. 10-11, and Xiong Huayuan, "Zai xiandaihua jianshezhong de fenqi" [Differences of Opinion concerning Modernizing Construction], in Lin Zhijian, *Xin Zhongguo yaoshi shuping* [Commentary on New China's Important Affairs] (Beijing: Zhonggong dangshi chubanshe, 1994), pp. 138-39, provide some further detail, while much of the sense of the meeting comes from oral sources specializing on the period or Zhou Enlai. Interestingly, the authoritative *Zhou Enlai nianpu 1949-1976* [Chronicle of Zhou Enlai, 1949-1976], 3 vols. (Beijing: Zhongyang wenxian chubanshe, 1997), makes no mention of this development in accord with the principle of not emphasizing conflict within the leadership.

[21] While "unpublished Chinese document no. 1," p. 10, refers to "one or two" (*gebieren*) persons who backed the Chairman, the oral sources consulted have consistently indicated a single individual. Recently, one such senior source confirmed our suspicion that the person was Li Fuchun. Li's support seemingly had both organizational and personality aspects. In organizational terms, Li's SPC had put forward the ambitious SFYP targets in February that were now under attack from Zhou Enlai and Chen Yun. More important in our view, Li was one of the leaders most prone to following Mao's lead without hesitation. Cf. below, p. 50.

[22] According to one of the most authoritative sources on Zhou Enlai in an interview,

position actually came shortly after the meeting, on May 2, when a worried Zhou pursued the matter with him privately, explained in great detail the shortages in funds, and (although it apparently was a tense encounter[23]) seemingly obtained his agreement that no money should be spent on additional investment.

What further can be said about this unusual development? First, according to some senior oral sources, Mao's proposal to the Politburo meeting was not his own but that of a lower-level unit, perhaps a province, which had appealed for his support; indeed, shortly before the Politburo meeting various ministries called for spending increases totaling ¥350,000.[24] In a situation where Zhou's push for reductions had cut deeply and on a broad front into what such units sought during the first leap, many complaints from below reached the Center. That Mao was sympathetic seems certain, although it is difficult to gauge the temperature of the meeting in the absence of a detailed record.[25] In any case, when Mao insisted his view was accepted, notwithstanding the fact that the Premier and Chen Yun argued the contrary position and no one, with the single exception of Li Fuchun, had backed the Chairman.

In the larger sense, however, Mao was still open to persuasion, as seen in his acceptance of Zhou's argument on May 2nd. It appears that in some respects the Mao-Zhou meeting did not go smoothly. When Zhou, increasingly concerned that the Politburo's action was unsustainable, told Mao that as Premier he "could not in good conscience agree with this decision," the Chairman reportedly became unusually angry. Yet it seems this sudden outburst of temper did not prevent Mao from conceding the specific points Zhou raised in his "patient persuasion" of his leader.[26] By his own testimony

---

Beijing, 1997. This person was deeply involved in the preparation of Zhou's biography which, quoting Hu Qiaomu, only says that Mao "maintained his own point of view to the end, and then announced the end of the meeting." Jin Chongji, *Zhou Enlai zhuan*, vol. 3, p. 1227. Cf. below, n. 26.

23   See the account below.

24   See *Dang de wenxian* bianjibu [*The Party's Documents* editorial department], ed., *Gongheguo zouguode lu* [The Road Travelled by the People's Republic] (Beijing: Zhongyang wenxian chubanshe, 1991), pp. 278, 280. The senior oral source cited in n. 22, above, however, regards the proposal for increased spending as largely Mao's own idea.

25   While one Party historian deduced that the Politburo exchange had been "heated," as with most others questioned he lacked access to records of the meeting. The fundamental problem is that no *detailed* record seemingly exists since Mao had from an early post-1949 stage ruled against notetaking that might inhibit discussion. Instead, only brief summaries of decisions taken apparently exist for Politburo meetings.

26   Li Ping, *Kaiguo Zongli*, p. 356, and Jin Chongji, *Zhou Enlai zhuan*, vol. 3, p. 1227, present the rather confrontational account of the Mao-Zhou meeting based on the recollection of Mao's secretary, Hu Qiaomu. Its general tone stands in contradiction with the brief accounts of the Mao-Zhou meeting in "unpublished Chinese document no. 1,"

this was a time when Mao had started to change his views in the direction of greater moderation; a year later he declared that "I, too, craved for greatness and success. Only as recently as March and April [1956] did [I] begin to change."[27] Moreover, at the same Politburo conference Mao delivered his famous address on the "Ten Great Relationships," a speech that while still seeking rapid growth, recognized that better balance in the short run was a necessary precondition to speedy development.[28] In any case, the conference ended without a formal resolution but with what Mao later termed a "gentleman's agreement" (*junzi xieding*). While the content of any such agreement is unclear, at least in Mao's recollections it included the symbols of the anti-rightist push — the 40 articles and *duo, kuai, hao, sheng*.[29] Mao undoubtedly still felt that reasonably rapid growth was on the cards as he left Beijing following the May Day celebrations on a provincial tour where he would continue to pursue economic issues,[30] but any understanding presumably allowed Zhou and the leading economic officials to get on with the task of coping with the problems of the upsurge.

The Premier and other leaders soon extended the *fanmaojin* approach. Zhou moved quickly, as in January-February, on both the symbolic and practical fronts. On May 11 he declared at a State Council meeting that opposition to conservatism and rightism had been going on for eight or nine months and it shouldn't go on any longer, thus in this internal setting ignoring the public approach of opposing both right and "left" deviations. Canvassing such problems as excessive capital investment, the explosion of costs resulting from wage reforms and the rapid growth of the urban work force, the overextension of credit, and deficit spending which resulted in printing currency, Zhou engaged in new budget discussions with Li Xiannian, Li Fuchun, and Bo Yibo during May. The Ministry of Finance produced a new

---

p. 11, and Xiong Huayuan, "Zai xiandaihua jianshezhong de fenqi," p. 139, which emphasize Zhou's "patient persuasion," and it is certainly incomplete in not addressing where the issue of the level of investment was left, simply stating that Mao left Beijing soon after his outburst. It should be noted that the available sources do not state explicitly that Mao accepted Zhou's arguments, but we surmise that he was "patiently persuaded" and that certainly Zhou would not have immediately begun to push opposition to rash advance without the Chairman's assent. Significantly, Mao did not raise this incident in his distorted *ex post facto* complaints about Zhou.

27   *SS*, p. 372. This cooling can be seen in Mao's April 1956 statement that "Without [national] balance, national industrialization can't be achieved" (*The Writings of Mao Zedong, 1949-1976, Volume II, January 1956-December 1957* [hereafter *WM*], edited by John K. Leung and Michael Y. M. Kau [Armonk: M. E. Sharpe, 1992], p. 70) — a view at sharp variance with that of Liu Shaoqi in December 1955 when conveying the Chairman's criticism of right conservatism.

28   See *SW*, V, 285-86.

29   See Mao's May 23, 1958, remarks in *Xuexi wenxuan*, vol. 2, p. 188.

30   *Mao wengao*, vol. 6 (January 1956-December 1957) (Beijing: Zhongyang wenxian chubanshe, 1992), pp. 116-19.

budget in early June and Zhou pressed home his views at State Council
Standing Committee meetings on the 1st and 5th. Arguing forcefully that even
after the efforts of the January-February joint conference, the capital
construction target was still *maojin*, the 1956 budget needed a crew cut and
the March ¥14.7 billion target should be cut down by at least a further 5 to 6
percent to ¥14 billion, and pressure would have to be applied to achieve the
reductions, Zhou together with both planning and financial leaders[31] faced
substantial opposition from the spending departments which not only had their
various bureaucratic interests, but some of which complained that the anti-
rightist struggle was being abandoned. It took all the Premier's persuasive
powers, as well as Party discipline, to bring these officials into line. While
various ministers dutifully echoed the *fanmaojin* line at the National People's
Congress (NPC) session later in the month, it is clear that many parts of the
economic bureaucracy were unhappy with the policies enforced by Zhou and
the leaders of both the top planning and financial bodies. All the top economic
officials were involved in the effort although, with good reason as we shall
see, oral sources regard Li Fuchun's support as less wholehearted than that of
his colleagues.[32]

At the same time as this concrete struggle with the economic
bureaucracies, the issue was being further developed at a more political level
and involved officials with noneconomic responsibilities. In May a conference
of the Center endorsed opposition to the "two isms" (*lianggezhuyi*),
conservatism and rash advance, as the theme for the upcoming NPC session.
At the conference Liu Shaoqi demanded that the Propaganda Department
write a *People's Daily* editorial on this question. The task was then overseen
by propaganda chief Lu Dingyi who echoed the Premier's bold remarks about
eight months of anti-conservatism being enough when he observed on June 1
that anti-right conservatism was being sung to the skies and the need was to
emphasize opposing blind rash advance. Once Lu revised his department's
draft, Mao's secretary, Hu Qiaomu, made further revisions, including the
presumptively sensitive example of the double-wheeled plow, an item from
Mao's beloved 40 articles, as an excessive target. Liu Shaoqi also made
revisions and finally submitted the editorial to Mao whose only response was

---

31   There is some contradiction in the sources concerning precisely who administered the
      crew cut, with Shi Wei in *Dang de wenxian*, no. 2 (1990), p. 8, and a speech by Zhou
      Enlai in *Zhou Enlai jingji wenxuan*, p. 261, claiming Bo Yibo and Li Fuchun proposed
      this measure, while Bo himself, *Huigu*, vol. 1, p. 535, maintains he and Li Xiannian were
      responsible, a version also found in Tong Xiaopeng, *Fengyu sishinian*, p. 353. Yet
      another version (Xiong Huayuan, "Zai xiandaihua jianshezhong de fenqi," p. 139)
      assigns responsibility to Li Fuchun and Li Xiannian. Finally, Jin Chongji, *Zhou Enlai
      zhuan*, vol. 3, pp. 1228-29, notes the involvement of all three economic officials.

32   Bo Yibo, *Huigu*, vol. 1, pp. 534-35; *Dangshi yanjiu* [Research on Party History], no. 6
      (1980), p. 38; *Dang de wenxian*, no. 2 (1988), pp. 12-14; Lin Yunhui, *Xingjin de shiqi*,
      pp. 627-28; Tong Xiaopeng, *Fengyu sishinian*, p. 353; *Zhou Enlai jingji wenxuan*, pp.
      253-62; oral sources; and below, pp. 34, 49-51.

the now famous notation, "[I do] not [want to] read [this]" (*bu kanle*).[33] Although retaining the anti-conservativism slogan, this decidedly cautious document went to press on June 20.[34]

Mao's enigmatic comment, according to oral sources, caused no concern at the time as other leaders felt they had the Chairman's broad approval for their approach.[35] Indeed, a senior Party historian claims that there is no doubt that Mao was aware of and endorsed all the key measures of June despite *bu kanle*. In early 1958, however, under the radically different circumstances of an emerging Great Leap Forward, Mao bitterly attacked the editorial as directed at him.[36] In the twisted Cultural Revolution version which has been widely accepted in the West, the episode is treated as a case where Mao was overruled on policy, or at least casually insulted, and *bu kanle* represented his barely suppressed fury. The reality, as already suggested, was quite different. First, as various Party historians emphasize, it is only *in retrospect* that we can conclude that Mao had reservations about both the editorial and *fanmaojin* more generally. To their knowledge nothing clear and direct was expressed by him at the time. Particularly striking is the involvement of Hu Qiaomu, who was not only Mao's secretary but also one of the most acute observers of the Chairman's many moods and who on various occasions warned other leaders to back off when they risked the leader's displeasure.[37] That Hu would dare to raise sensitive issues in his revisions of the editorial strongly suggests he at least *perceived* Mao's attitude as supportive of the general thrust of opposing rash advance.[38]

Nevertheless, the best reconstruction would be that Mao was at least

---

[33] While often taken as expressing Mao's objection to the editorial, the surface message is "There is no need for me to read this, I leave it to you."

[34] Bo Yibo, *Huigu*, vol. 1, pp. 534, 536-38; and oral sources.

[35] These sources further stated that the absence of a more detailed response was not unusual, particularly since Mao was outside of Beijing. According to Li Ping, *Kaiguo Zongli*, p. 358, however, Mao had already returned to the capital when he received the editorial. Either version is credible since the Chairman was in central China in early June but was receiving foreign representatives in Beijing by June 13 (He Ping, ed., *Mao Zedong dacidian* [Dictionary of Mao Zedong] [Beijing: Zhongguo guoji guangbo chubanshe, 1992] p. 168), while according to Bo Yibo, *Huigu*, vol. 1, pp. 537-38, the draft editorial was revised by Lu Dingyi, Liu Shaoqi, and Hu Qiaomu and passed on to Mao "around June 10."

[36] *Mao wengao*, vol. 7, p. 34.

[37] On Hu's sensitive handling of the Chairman and his top colleagues, see, e.g., the discussion of Hu's warning to Chen Yun in late 1958, below p. 140. Cf. Bo Yibo's belief at the time that he was acting in accord with Mao's wishes, *Huigu*, vol. 1, p. 536.

[38] In the case of the double-wheeled plow there is reason to believe Hu correctly perceived Mao's opinion. At the Third Plenum the Chairman declared he had insisted on its cancellation from beginning to end. See the Red Guard collection covering 1957-61, *Xuexi ziliao* [Study Materials], vol. 2 [1957-61] ([Beijing: 1967]), p. 97.

mildly upset,[39] although certainly well short of the ferocity he expressed in 1958. Speculatively, it arguably was the case that Mao's reservations had less to do with *policy* than with ideological *formulations*. Mao most likely was concerned with the unbalanced presentation of the editorial concerning the "two isms," and particularly with the misrepresentation of his own (sacred) words. Thus he subsequently claimed that his views had been deliberately distorted when the editorial quoted his statement from *Socialist Upsurge in the Chinese Countryside* that one shouldn't attempt to do what was impossible, but deleted his linked comment on opposing conservatism.[40] If this was the case, it represented an established pattern on Mao's part.[41]

While any reservations on Mao's part remained basically hidden, objections were expressed by others. According to the recollections of Chen Pixian, a leading Shanghai official at the time, the June 20 editorial caused dissatisfaction among comrades who always wanted to surpass what was allowed by objective conditions and obstinately attempted things that could not be achieved. What types of people were these? Chen only mentioned the main responsible person in Shanghai, i.e., Party First Secretary Ke Qingshi, who "used the opportunity to reveal his dissatisfied feelings."[42] To the extent Ke was representative, this again points to provincial-level leaders as a major source of opposition to *fanmaojin*, along with the central spending ministries. This suggests not that Mao was encouraging such leaders, something for which there is no evidence, but that in the absence of a strongly articulated pro-*fanmaojin* position on the part of the Chairman these figures felt they had leeway to express their discontent.[43]

With the *fanmaojin* program now clearly in place, work in summer 1956 covered a broad front, with Zhou Enlai taking charge of "the second stage of opposing rash advance work." In this he was assisted by most of the CCP's chief economic officials, Chen Yun, Li Xiannian, and Bo Yibo — but not by Li Fuchun who was busy in Moscow negotiating Soviet economic assistance.[44] While the problem with the 1956 plan was considered solved,

---

39   Some historians go further and picture a "very dissatisfied" Chairman, but even in these accounts he did not raise any objections at the time. See *Dang de wenxian*, no. 2 (1992), p. 53.

40   *Dangshi tongxun* [Party History Bulletin], no. 12 (1987), p. 32.

41   This tendency had already surfaced during the events surrounding the Gao Gang affair; see Teiwes, *Politics at Mao's Court*, pp. 42-43, 57-58, 62-71.

42   *Women de Zhou Zongli* [Our Premier Zhou] (Beijing: Zhongyang wenxian chubanshe, 1990), pp. 81-82.

43   This is a similar situation to that in early 1955 concerning the new policy to slow down the development of cooperatives. This met considerable local resistance until Mao personally endorsed the policy in a forceful manner. See Teiwes and Sun, *The Politics of Agricultural Cooperativization*, pp. 8-10, 15.

44   Li, however, made a contribution by reporting from Moscow in mid-August the Soviet government's view supporting moderate targets. Bo Yibo, *Huigu*, vol. 1, p. 544.

now the drafting of the 1957 annual plan by Bo's SEC demanded attention. Starting in July, this involved cutting back ministerial and local demands for ¥24.3 billion in capital construction to ¥15 billion. But the most important aspect of the "second stage" concerned preparing the SFYP for the upcoming Eighth Party Congress. In May the SPC had presented a second version of the plan, but this had involved only slight reductions from the first proposal, with the result that few departments prepared revised plans of their own for the Congress. In this context Zhou called a State Council meeting on July 3-5, declared the first draft *maojin* and the new one unreliable and dangerous, and with the support of all the other top economic leaders then in Beijing obtained unanimous agreement on the need to reduce further the plan's targets. Zhou then personally took charge of formulating the SFYP, and working closely with SPC personnel produced a third version by the end of July. The following month at the Beidaihe summer resort Zhou and Chen Yun made further revisions which then became the official proposal to the Congress.[45]

In the process of drafting the plan and other documents for the Party Congress, a couple of interesting developments occurred. First, again reflecting Zhou's seeming boldness throughout the entire *fanmaojin* story, the Premier deleted from the documents references to both *duo, kuai, hao, sheng* and the 40 article Draft Agricultural Program, two of the three things, along with the committee for promoting progress that Zhou had already jokingly dismissed, which Mao would subsequently complain had been blown away. In the former case, Zhou concluded that in fact lower levels focused on "more" and "faster" to the detriment of "better" and "more economically," thus making it preferable to delete the entire slogan,[46] while it had been clear since the spring that the 40 articles had been a major factor in producing wild targets. In another, more mysterious instance, an unknown person[47] increased the proposed wool and grain targets in the documents. Zhou responded by changing the targets back to the original figures, and added the comment that "these targets have been approved by Chen Yun." While Mao's reaction to these developments at the time remains less than completely clear, contrary to Cultural Revolution claims and some Western analysis, he controlled the drafting process for the Eighth Congress documents from beginning to end, and specifically endorsed Zhou's SFYP report, giving it a "very good." In the second instance, moreover, when the documents were again reviewed and Mao noticed the grain target had been raised even higher, the Chairman

---

[45]   *Dang de wenxian*, no. 2 (1988), p. 14, and no. 2 (1990), p. 8; Lin Yunhui, *Xingjin de shiqi*, pp. 630-32; "unpublished Chinese document no. 1," pp. 16-18, 22; and oral source.

[46]   According to Shi Zhongquan, *Zhou Enlai*, pp. 322-23, Zhou and other leaders thought this action was very natural and not in conflict with Mao's thinking.

[47]   The leading ministerial official from the period whom we interviewed extensively speculated that this person was Li Fuchun. Our own guess, however, is that it was more likely to be Tan Zhenlin, the leading radical responsible for agriculture during the Great Leap, given that agricultural targets were at issue.

declared the figure should be lowered in line with the proposal of the State Council. Finally, at the time of the Congress in September Mao highly praised Chen Yun who had been so important in shaping overall economic policy as well as vetting specific targets. Throughout the entire process leading to the Eighth Congress, whatever reservations he may have had, Mao gave no sign of anything other than support for the new economic policies.[48]

If Mao was largely benign toward *fanmaojin* at the time of the Party Congress, his attitude at the Second Plenum of the new Central Committee in November was seemingly more complex. In an *ex post facto* judgment Mao declared that while anti-rash advance began with the June 20 editorial, it reached its peak with the Second Plenum; he further stated that at the plenum he "compromised" (*tuoxie*) with the tendency, a situation which lasted to the Third Plenum nearly a year later when his position was "restored" (*fubi*).[49] Indeed, at the Second Plenum itself, although Mao proclaimed "*complete agreement*" with the meeting's results,[50] at the same time he seemingly began to express subtle criticisms of the *fanmaojin* approach. This ambiguous position on the Chairman's part must be seen against the background of events both leading to and at the plenum.

In the six weeks from the Eighth Party Congress to the Second Plenum Zhou Enlai began to review the 1957 annual plan which had been formulated during the summer by Bo Yibo's SEC. While this plan which sharply cut the spending proposals of various ministries and localities from ¥24.3 to ¥15 billion had met their considerable opposition, Zhou considered that the plan was still excessive. At a meeting of the State Council Standing Committee from October 20 to November 9, the Premier led an investigation of both the implementation of the 1956 plan and the control figures for the 1957 plan, and concluded that both the annual plan and the long-range plan were rash (*maole*). Zhou thus declared the need to criticize the "left," although to ease the anxieties of some participants he added that this was not a question of left or right tendencies in the political sense, and said the aim was to protect balance in economic construction. Joining his efforts with those of Chen Yun, Li Xiannian, and Bo Yibo (but seemingly not Li Fuchun[51]), Zhou reportedly

---

48   Bo Yibo, *Huigu*, vol. 1, p. 546; Shi Zhongquan, *Zhou Enlai*, p. 324; *ZGDSYJ*, no. 2 (1990), pp. 64-66; *Wenxian he yanjiu* [Documents and Research], no. 7 (1984), p. 25; "unpublished Chinese document no. 1," p. 18; Chang, *Power and Policy*, pp. 21-23; *Mao wengao*, vol. 6, pp. 167-69, 199; Teiwes, "Mao Texts," pp. 138-39; and oral sources.

49   *Dangshi wenhui* [Party History Collection], no. 2 (1989), pp. 7-8.

50   While Mao's "complete agreement" was indicated in a *People's Daily* report at the time, it is now clear this was written by the Chairman himself; *Mao wengao*, vol. 6, p. 247.

51   Although Li Fuchun had by this time returned to China (we do not know his whereabouts after early October to the end of 1956, however), all Party history accounts exclude him from the list of those pushing *fanmaojin* in this period. Li's speech to the Party Congress, nevertheless, was firmly in the oppose rash advance mode; see *Li Fuchun xuanji* [Selected Works of Li Fuchun] (Beijing: Zhongguo jihua chubanshe,

was able to clarify the thinking of leaders of government departments concerning the danger posed by rash advance, and gain their unanimous support for slowing the pace of construction, although no concrete target was apparently agreed upon.[52] During the discussions which also continued after the plenum, various planners supported widely differing figures, with some advocating that the ¥15 billion target remained suitable, Bo Yibo proposing ¥12.5 billion, and his chief deputy Jia Tuofu arguing for a figure in the ¥10-11 billion range. Interestingly, in this process the State Construction Commission, which had a direct bureaucratic responsibility for the heavy industry sector, proposed a moderate target of ¥12 billion. Zhou and Chen Yun inclined to Jia Tuofu's proposal, with a State Council Standing Committee meeting chaired by Chen approving a figure of ¥11.4 billion in December before a target of ¥11.1 was finally adopted by the February-March 1957 planning conference.[53] These targets, as well as earlier capital construction targets proposed since fall 1954 and those subsequently put forward for the remainder of 1957, during the Great Leap, and through to the collapse of projections in 1961 are summarized in Table 1 (pp.36-39).

When the plenum convened on November 10, Zhou addressed the main agenda item of the 1957 plan in his opening speech. While there is some question as to whether Zhou adequately briefed Mao concerning his report,[54] in several respects Zhou's address exhibited appropriate political sensitivity: the Chairman was frequently mentioned and his authority was invoked to support several of the Premier's points; the "unprecedented burst of enthusiasm for socialist construction" since the high tide of cooperativization and the "highly successful" FFYP were duly noted; and the basic proposal to reduce the scale of capital construction was couched in terms of promoting "continued advance." But the substantive message was a sober one. Zhou argued that the overall economy and especially heavy industry should grow at a slower pace,[55] that unrealistic targets such as that for steel threatened to unbalance other branches of the economy, and the targets recently laid down

---

1992), pp. 179-89. Cf. below, n. 60.

[52] *Dang de wenxian*, no. 2 (1988), pp. 15-16, and no. 4 (1993), pp. 64-65; Lin Yunhui, *Xingjin de shiqi*, pp. 632-33; and "unpublished Chinese document no. 1," pp. 23-24. According to Fang Weizhong, ed., *Zhonghuarenmingongheguo jingji dashiji (1949-1980 nian)* [Chronology of Economic Events in the PRC, 1949-1980] (Beijing: Zhongguo shehui kexue chubanshe, 1984), p. 181, Zhou proposed a target of ¥12.47 billion at the plenum, while Bo Yibo, *Huigu*, vol. 1, p. 558, reports that Zhou mentioned a proposal, presumably by the SEC, of ¥13.1 billion in his report.

[53] ZGDSRWZ, vol. 46, p. 289; Bo Yibo, *Huigu*, vol. 1, p. 555; Ma Qibin, *Zhizheng sishinian*, p. 121; Li Ping, *Kaiguo Zongli*, p. 358; and "unpublished Chinese document no. 1," pp. 26-27. In the exchange between Chan and Bachman (see above, p.7n5), both erroneously treat these developments as occurring in 1957 rather than 1956.

[54] See below, n. 88.

[55] On the specific point of heavy industry growth Zhou was in fact in accord with the position stated by Mao five days later at the close of the plenum; *WM*, II, 179-80.

Table 1: CAPITAL CONSTRUCTION TARGETS, SEPTEMBER 1954-DECEMBER 1961

Date/Occasion	Proposed by	1955	1956	1957	1958	1959	1960	1961	1962
September 20, 1954	SPC[a]	8.87							
February 8, 1955	SPC[b]	9.80							
July 5, 1955	Li Fuchun			42.74*					
July 6, 1955	Li Xiannian	9.59							
September 1955	SPC		11.27[c]						
October 4, 1955	Party Center		higher[d]						
soon after October 4	SPC	9.79[e]							
by November 1955	Ministries/provinces		14						
November 29, 1955	SPC	9.17							
December 31, 1955	**Actual total for 1955**	9.3[f]							
January 5, 1956	Ministries/provinces		15.3						
January 10-February 7, 1956/	SPC		14.85						
3rd nat'l planning conference	Ministries/provinces		18-20						
by February 10, 1956	Ministries/provinces		17						
February 10, 1956	Zhou Enlai[g]		14.7						
February 22, 1956	SPC		14.73[h]						
April 14, 1956	Ministries		+0.35						
late April, 1956[i]	Mao		+2						
June 5, 1956	Zhou Enlai[j]		14						
June 21, 1956/NPC	Bo Yibo		14						
July 1956/SEC conference	Ministries/provinces			24.3					
	SEC			15					c.85**
September 1956	Zhou Enlai/Liu Shaoqi[k]								
October 18, 1956	Ministries/provinces		15.24						
	SEC		14						
November 10-15, 1956/	SEC[l]			13.1					
2nd Plenum	Zhou Enlai			12.47					
around and after 2nd Plenum	"some people"			15					
	Bo Yibo			12.5					
	Jia Tuofu			10-11					
	State Construction Commission			12					

Date	Source/Actor			
late November 1956	Zhou Enlai/Chen Yun	10		
December 17, 1956	Chen Yun/State Council Standing Committee	11.4		
December 31, 1956	Actual total for 1956		14.8[m]	
January 3, 1957	SPC			140**
February 22-March 11, 1957	Bo Yibo	11.1[n]		
June 26, 1957/NPC	Zhou Enlai	11.1		
June 29, 1957/NPC	Li Xiannian	11/47.2*		
July 1, 1957/NPC	Bo Yibo	11.1		
July 25-August 22, 1957	SEC	11.6[o]		
December 4, 1957	Zhou Enlai/SEC	12.567		
December 7, 1957	Zhou Enlai	12.617		
November 28-Dec 12, 1957	6th national planning conference	13.05[p]		
December 28, 1957	Zhou Enlai/Finance Ministry	12.736		
December 31, 1957	Actual total for 1957	14.33[q]		
	Actual total for FFYP	55		
January 15, 1958/Nanning	SEC	13.4		
February 1, 1958	Li Xiannian	14.57		
February 3, 1958	Bo Yibo	14.58[s]		
May 6, 1958	SEC/Party Center	17.5		305**
June 16, 1958	Li Xiannian		45	
June 17, 1958	Bo Yibo	20[t]		
June 27, 1958	Party Center/Ministries	23		
around mid-June 1958 and after	Ministries/provinces			
August 28, 1958/Beidaihe	SEC		50	385**[u]
	SPC		36	
November 28-Dec 10, 1958[v]	Party Center/SEC	26.9[w]		
December 31, 1958	Actual total for 1958			
early April 1959/7th Plenum	Li Fuchun		26-28	
June 8, 1959	Zhou Enlai		24	
June 13, 1959	SPC		24	
September 4, 1959	State Capital Construction Commission/ SPC		28.1	

Date/Occasion	Proposed by	1955	1956	1957	1958	1959	1960	1961	1962
October 25–November 16, 1959/	SPC						34		
8th national planning conference	State Capital Construction Commission/SPC					31.1			
December 31, 1959	**Actual total for 1959**					35[x]			
April 1960	Li Fuchun						32.5		
September 30, 1960	SPC							27.5	
December 1960	Li Fuchun[y]							19.4	
December 31, 1960	**Actual total for 1960**						38.9[z]		
January 1961	SPC							16.7	
April 1961	SPC							12.9	
July 17–August 21, 1961	SPC**							7.83	
early December 1961	Zhou Enlai, Chen Yun, Deng Xiaoping, Li Fuchun								5
December 31, 1961	**Actual total for 1961**							12.7[ab]	

Unit: billion yuan   *FFYP total   ** SFYP total

Sources:
Bo Yibo, *Huigu*, vol. 1, pp. 524, 531-35, 541, 554-55, 558, 560; Ma Qibin, *Zhizheng sishinian*, pp. 102, 104, 106, 109, 121, 129, 135, 137, 139, 146, 156, 158, 166, 172-73; "unpublished Chinese document no. 1," pp. 10-11, 16-18, 22-24, 26-27; Lin Yunhui, *Xingjin de shiqi*, pp. 614-15, 620-21, 626, 628, 632; *Zhonghuarenmingongheguo guomin jingji he shehui fazhan jihua dashi jiyao 1949-1985* [Outline of Events in PRC National Economic and Social Development 1949-1985] (Beijing: Hongqi chubanshe, 1987), pp. 61, 69, 74, 78-79, 83, 87, 89, 90, 93, 95, 98, 105-106, 111, 114, 116-17, 121, 123, 127, 129, 133, 137, 140, 142-43, 149, 155, 157, 159, 163-64, 168, 173, 177-78; Liao Gailong, *Xin Zhongguo biannianshi*, pp. 97-98; *Dang de wenxian*, no. 2 (1988), pp. 11-16, no. 4 (1993), pp. 64-65; Li Ping, *Kaiguo Zongli*, pp. 355-56, 358-59; Fang Weizhong, *Jingji jingji zhuanti dashiji, 1949-1965* [Chronology of PRC Special Economic Topics, 1949-1965] (Henan: Henan renmin chubanshe, 1989), pp. 202, 206-207, 209-10, 214, 635, 639, 641, 643; *Zhou Enlai nianpu*, vol. 2, pp. 76, 104, 105, 112, 235; *ZGDSRWZ*, vol. 46, p. 289; Cong Jin, *1949-1989 nian de Zhongguo: Quzhe fazhan de suiye* [China 1949-1989: The Years of Circuitous Development] (Zhengzhou: Henan renmin chubanshe, 1989), pp. 33, 118, 120, 137; *Gongheguo zouguode lu*, pp. 204-205, 278, 280, 282, 284, 287, 291; Liu Guoxin, ed., *Zhonghuarenmingongheguo shilu* [True Record of the PRC], vol. 1, part 2, *Jueqi yu fendou—Gongheguo dansheng zhichu, 1953-1956* [The Rising (Nation) and Marching Forward—The Early years of the Republic] (Changchun: Jilin renmin chubanshe, 1994), pp. 1322, 1351, 1383.

Notes:

[a] At the 1st national planning conference.

[b] At the 2nd national planning conference; approved by the Party Center on April 25, 1955.

[c] Approved by the Party Center on October 4, 1955.

[d] At the start of the 6th Central Committee Plenum the Party Center issued a directive demanding "higher targets whenever possible." The SPC reacted accordingly by asking each ministry and province to set more positive targets.

[e] Our calculation is deduced from *Guomin jingji he shehui fazhan jihua dashi jiyao*, p. 78.

[f] As reported in *Guomin jingji he shehui fazhan jihua dashi jiyao*, p. 79; and Ma Qibin, p. 105. Alternative figures are 10.03 (Fang Weizhong, p. 161), 9.17 (Bo Yibo, vol. 1, p. 524), 8.63 (Zhao Dexing, p. 214), and 8.2 (Li Ping, p.358).

[g] With the assistance of Li Fuchun and Li Xiannian; often labeled "the February retreat."

[h] Representing a 70.6 percent increase over 1955; approved by the State Council on March 25, 1956.

[i] During enlarged Politburo meeting, April 25-28.

[j] With the assistance of Li Fuchun, Li Xiannian, and Bo Yibo; referred to as "the 5 percent crew cut."

[k] In reports to the 8th Party Congress

[l] Referred to by Zhou Enlai without identifying the issuing agency; we assume that this was the SEC given its responsibility for annual planning.

[m] This represents a 59 percent increase over 1955. As reported in Ma Qibin, p. 119; and *Guomin jingji he shehui fazhan jihua dashi jiyao*, p. 93. Alternative figures are 15.58 (Fang Weizhong, p. 183), 13.99 (Bo Yibo, vol. 1, p. 560), and 15.52 (*Gongheguo zouguode lu*, p. 205). The disparity between these last two figures fits well with Mao's later remark that 1.5 billion yuan were overdrawn for 1956 capital construction investment; see Li Rui, *"Dayuejin" qinliji*, p. 65.

[n] Presented at the 4th national planning conference. Represents a 20.6 percent decrease compared to 1956.

[o] Representing a small increase over the 1957 target, thus demonstrating unchanged policy in the pre-Third Plenum period. Presented at the 5th national planning conference; approved by Zhou Enlai on September 1.

[p] Thus the significant jump of nearly 2 billion yuan took place after the Third Plenum.

[q] Representing a 3 percent decrease compared to 1956.

[r] Of this figure, 13.83 billion yuan was to be funded from the central government's budget, while 0.74 billion was to be self-funded (*zichou zijin*), i.e. provided by the concerned ministries and provinces themselves.

[s] Approved by the February 1958 NPC meeting.

[t] This figure was reached by the Party Center and ministries asking for a 2.5 billion yuan increase on top of the SPC's May 6 figure.

[u] Representing a 680 percent increase over the FFYP.

[v] During the 6th Central Committee Plenum, Wuhan.

[w] Representing an 88 percent increase over 1957.

[x] Representing a 30 percent increase over 1958.

[y] At the 9th national planning conference.

[z] Representing an 11.1 percent increase over 1959.

[aa] At national planning conference.

[bb] Representing a 67.2 percent decrease compared to 1960.

by the Eighth Congress only six weeks earlier needed adjustment. He even called for changes to unrealistic goals in the 40 articles, commenting that some had already been crossed out, although in this case he cited Mao's statement when the program was first raised that changes could be made during implementation. All in all, Zhou made a forceful statement of the necessity for even more *fanmaojin*.[56]

A complete reading of the materials available concerning the Second Plenum suggests that Mao's subsequent rationalizations concerning the meeting were greatly exaggerated. Although claiming in 1958 that the plenum, like the April Politburo meeting, produced no "clear resolution" (*mingque jueyi*) but only another "gentleman's agreement," and that the tense international and domestic political situation following the disruptions in Poland and Hungary prevented his dealing with *fanmaojin*, in fact Mao did address economic questions and "completely agreed with" the session's "guiding principles" (*fangzhen*) and "measures" (*cuoshi*), including specific targets. Mao's known comments were broadly supportive of appropriate reductions in expenditures of money and materials. In a small group meeting he raised a number of opinions which all supported Zhou's policies, and in his closing speech on the 15th — at least in the Red Guard version — his discussion of economic issues allowed that doing less next year was nothing to worry about and the important thing was for "construction to remain consistent and steady." Given the difficulties created by Mao's anti-right conservative guideline throughout the opposition to rash advance, perhaps the Chairman's most crucial comment occurred toward the end of Zhou's speech when the question of left and right came up. Mao asked what sort of rightism was involved. Liu Shaoqi responded it was rightism over the speed of construction, to which Mao rejoined that this kind of rightism was acceptable.[57]

But Mao's views are best known from his closing speech on the 15th — i.e., the official 1977 *Selected Works* version of it. In this version Mao did not deal directly with the specific proposals raised by Zhou and approved by the plenum. Instead, he spoke in a more philosophical vein with the apparent aim of offsetting any excessive pessimism which might have grown out of Zhou's report; in historian Shi Zhongquan's view Zhou's words must have been distasteful and very grating to Mao's ears.[58] Mao began with the question of

---

56   *Selected Works of Zhou*, II, 233-44. Chen Yun took a similar line, calling for going a bit slower for one or two years; see "unpublished Chinese document no. 1," p. 25.

57   Bo Yibo, *Huigu*, vol. 1, pp. 556, 559, vol. 2, p. 641; *Mao wengao*, vol. 6, pp. 244-47, vol. 7, p. 205; and *WM*, II, 179-83. The only exception we have found to Mao's support for the *concrete policies* advocated by Zhou *et al.* is the assertion in *Dang de wenxian*, no. 2 (1992), p. 54, that at the plenum Mao advocated increasing the 1957 budget a bit, although even in this account he did not clearly oppose the meeting's policy orientation.

58   Shi Zhongquan, *Zhou Enlai*, p. 325. Shi further described Mao as "very dissatisfied," while other sources assessed varying degrees of discontent on his part.

whether one should advance or retreat, or (using terms that had been supercharged in 1955[59]) get on or off the horse. Characteristically, the answer was a dialectical one: life required both but, with special reference to the economy, balance was temporary and imbalance absolute.[60] The cadres and masses were to be advised that the economy was both advancing and retreating, but mainly advancing in a wave-like manner. Like Zhou, Mao noted that mistakes had been made in the FFYP, but he argued that these could become useful lessons. The important thing was to "protect the enthusiasm of the cadres and masses and not pour cold water on them." Mao did not comment directly on the new budget proposal in this version, but he hinted at some impatience with excessive caution by complaining that the use of "safely reliable" to describe the budget was tautological. Yet the Chairman did not express any hope for rapid advance even in this rendering of his speech; the masses might want to pursue the impossible in which case it would be necessary to explain the real situation to them while at the same time sustaining their enthusiasm. It was a subtly different message from that of Zhou Enlai, but given Mao's acceptance of Zhou's policies and, as Bo Yibo recalled, the fact that he made no criticisms at the time, it was a message whose significance could, as emphasized by a senior Party historian, only be seen in retrospect.[61]

In his closing speech Mao also took up the theme of combating waste and building the country through thrift, and in this regard he had already made a concrete proposal for a production increase and austerity campaign at the small group session. In making a self-criticism for his role in promoting *fanmaojin* 18 months later, Zhou Enlai claimed that soon after the plenum the Party Center, in accord with Mao's remarks to the small group meeting, adopted an active policy and launched such a nationwide production increase and austerity movement which began to change the situation created by opposing rash advance, although *fanmaojin's* unhealthy influence was still felt. Such austerity movements, however, were quite compatible with a cautious economic approach, and when Chen Yun launched the movement at

[59] As a result of Mao's criticism of the slowing down of cooperativization; see *SW*, V, 201-202.

[60] The view of balance as temporary or relative is often taken as an indication of a pro-growth position; cf. Bachman, *Bureaucracy,* p. 106, concerning Li Fuchun's use of the concept at the Eighth Congress. The same concept, however, was used in uncontrovertibly go-slow statements, as by Minister of Finance Li Xiannian at the 1957 NPC; see *Current Background* (hereafter *CB*), no. 464, p. 11. The point is that "relative balance and absolute imbalance" only become relevant when the philosophical principle drives economic policy, something it did not do for either Li Fuchun or Li Xiannian in 1956-57, but did, as Party history sources note, under Mao's direction during the Great Leap. See *Dang de wenxian*, no. 2 (1992), p. 56.

[61] *SW*, V, 332-37; and oral sources.

the start of 1957 it was explicitly to deal with difficulties *created by rash advance*.[62]

As had happened in 1953,[63] basic economic policy stayed the same, while some of Mao's political and rhetorical concerns were accommodated. Certainly the chief economic policy makers continued to see rash advance as the main concern. In early January 1957 Chen Yun, Li Xiannian, Bo Yibo, and Li Fuchun advocated continued measures against rash advance at a small meeting called by Mao to discuss economic work. The basic unity of both planning and financial officials was again demonstrated at the conference of provincial Party secretaries later in the month when Chen Yun praised Bo's Eighth Congress views on proportional development[64] and Li Fuchun complained of dizziness with rash advance in 1956 planning. A major feature of the conference as a whole was the emphasis on reducing the scale of capital construction. This overall approach was particularly prominent in early 1957, culminating in the February-March planning conference decision to reduce 1957 capital construction investment by 20 percent from the 1956 level to ¥11.1 billion, and it continued to guide economic policy up to the Third Plenum.[65]

For Mao's part, the evidence strongly suggests he went along with this approach. As Bachman has skillfully argued,[66] Mao's contradictory and ambiguous views on the economy generally came down on the side of moderation in late 1956-early 1957. In December 1956 he even went so far as to liken China's economic policy to the Soviet New Economic Policy of the 1920s, commenting that this policy had in fact been carried out for too short a time. And at the January conference of provincial secretaries Mao was greatly

---

[62]   *SW*, V, 336; Cong Jin, *Quzhe fazhan*, pp. 124-25; and *Dangshi yanjiu*, no. 6 (1980), p. 40.

[63]   During the Gao Gang affair Mao had directed severe ideological strictures against Bo Yibo's tax policies, but in the end the actual changes in policy were minor; see Teiwes, *Politics at Mao's Court*, pp. 62-71.

[64]   This, of course, did not mean complete agreement on every point. As Bachman, *Bureaucracy*, p. 78, has pointed out, Chen Yun did indicate some differences over the precise proportions advocated by Bo at the Congress, and he also raised some doubts about the SEC projections for 1958.

[65]   Bo Yibo, *Huigu*, vol. 1, p. 541; Cong Jin, *Quzhe fazhan*, p. 34; Ma Qibin, *Zhizheng sishinian*, p. 123; Fang Weizhong, *Jingji dashiji*, pp. 184-85; and "unpublished Chinese document no. 1," p. 27. According to a senior Party historian who read Li Fuchun's report to the conference, it was *exactly* in the spirit of Chen Yun's views. Apart from providing further evidence of the consensus of top economic officials, we see this as another indication of Li's propensity to follow Mao since in this period the Chairman highly praised Chen. Cf. above, p. 27; and below, p. 50.

[66]   Bachman, *Bureaucracy*, pp. 170-82, gives an admirably subtle account of Mao's shifting views over the entire 1955-57 period. His conclusion concerning late 1956-early 1957 (p. 174) is framed in terms of Mao siding with the "financial coalition," a position rejected by this analysis, but it is consistent in policy terms with what is argued here.

impressed by Chen Yun's analysis of the economy which, by articulating a comprehensive argument for the three balances (budgets, credit, and materials), provided the classic rationale of *fanmaojin*, and he held Chen up for high praise.[67] Yet while Mao warned against boasting during the meeting, at the same time he spoke out against underestimating achievements.[68] And in the middle of his supportive attitude toward Chen's economic thrust, Mao made a critical reference to "*fanmaojin*" on January 18:

> Minister of Agriculture Liao [Luyan] ... says in effect that he himself feels discouraged and so do the responsible cadres under him, and that the cooperatives won't work anyway and the [40 articles are] no longer valid. What do we do with a person who feels discouraged? ....
>
> The year before last there was a struggle against a rightist deviation, and last year a struggle against "rash advance," which resulted in another right deviation. By this I mean the right deviation on the question of socialist revolution, primarily that of socialist transformation in the rural areas.[69]

Reading this literally, Mao focuses on noneconomic issues, specifically problems concerning agricultural cooperatives, yet at the same time he broadens the matter by raising the 40 articles. Once again with the benefit of hindsight, some Party historians see his comments as a very subtle criticism of the general process.[70] Whether Mao actually had such an intention or was simply reflecting a still vague sense of unease remains unknowable, but in the view of a leading provincial official present on the occasion Mao's comments had nothing to do with the *fanmaojin* program for the overall economy but were clearly aimed to refute doubts about the cooperatives.[71] In any case, in

---

[67]   *Ibid.*, pp. 77, 176-77; and *Dang de wenxian*, no. 6 (1989), pp. 33, 35. In this period Mao was also especially solicitous of China's capitalists; see *Dang de wenxian*, no. 6 (1988), pp. 29-30.

[68]   "Unpublished Chinese document no. 1," p. 28.

[69]   *SW*, V, 351.

[70]   Interestingly, Bo Yibo makes no mention of this incident in his richly detailed reflections. Shi Zhongquan, *Zhou Enlai*, p. 325, however, concludes that the Chairman's remarks already carried a "sting." See also Xie Chuntao, *Dayuejin kuanglan* [Raging Waves of the Great Leap Forward] (Henan: Henan renmin chubanshe, 1990), p. 12.

[71]   Interview, Beijing, 1997. This former provincial leader observed that Mao was dealing with a trend of thought within the Party that cooperatives had not produced great results in 1956, that many peasants — especially rich peasants — were not enthusiastic and felt household production was better, and as a result some cadres were not keen to promote the cooperatives. Interestingly, given the absence of evidence concerning a significant military role in policy developments during the period of our study (see below, pp. 198-99), our source also noted that Mao was concerned that some military cadres had complained on behalf of the peasants.

the context of his other actions at the time it is not surprising that the Chairman's remarks caused no particular concern.

After early 1957 *fanmaojin* faded as a issue of policy debate until Mao forcefully raised it at the Third Plenum. This seemingly was due to the fact that, after a year's struggle, the cutting back of targets and expenditures had achieved an acceptable level. At the same time, however, although further reductions were not required, the watchword of economic policy remained balance up to the Third Plenum. Even the Anti-Rightist Campaign did not alter this basic orientation, and the budget and plan approved during the summer remained cautious.[72] That campaign, however, caused some political discomfit and the need for rhetorical readjustment. The advocates of *fanmaojin* found themselves in the uncomfortable position of having their policies echoed by non-Party "rightists" during the ill-fated Hundred Flowers, although in this they were not unique as Mao himself had been similarly caught out on more than one occasion.[73] Nevertheless, at the June-July 1957 NPC, while presenting essentially the same economic policy and reaffirming the 20 percent cut in capital construction, Zhou Enlai attacked the rightists for characterizing economic performance in 1956 as rash advance, and instead claimed the economy had actually undergone a "leap forward" (*yuejin*).[74] As will be argued subsequently, these political circumstances contributed greatly to the emergence of the Great Leap Forward by the end of the year.

The continuing dominance of the *fanmaojin* approach throughout summer 1957 can perhaps be seen most graphically in the activities of China's leading planners, Li Fuchun and Bo Yibo, over the May-August period. Initially in the context of Party rectification and the Hundred Flowers, Li and Bo toured Xi'an, Chengdu, and Chongqing to address economic problems. Subsequently, as the political situation began to change, they addressed a national design conference in Beijing, and with the Anti-Rightist Campaign firmly in place in July-August, Bo dealt with planning issues in speeches to the NPC, the fifth national planning conference (the second in 1957 following the February-March conference), and local cadres. In all these statements Li and Bo, similar to their colleagues from the "financial coalition,"[75] emphasized the sentiments of "better" and "more economically" to the virtual exclusion of "more" and "faster" from the *duo, kuai, hao, sheng* slogan which would soon reappear with the Great Leap Forward. Their emphasis throughout was on thrift, modest

---

[72]   See, for example, the reports of Li Xiannian and Bo Yibo to the NPC in *CB*, nos. 464 and 465.

[73]   For examples of "rightist" opinions similar to Mao's views, see Teiwes, *Politics and Purges*, pp. 195, 209-11.

[74]   *Communist China 1955-1959: Policy Documents with Analysis* (hereafter *PDA*), with a foreword by Robert R. Bowie and John K. Fairbank (Cambridge: Harvard University Press, 1965), p. 307.

[75]   See especially Li Xiannian's late June speech to the NPC in *CB*, no. 464, pp. 3-31.

investment, step-by-step industrialization, and comprehensive balance.[76] Gradual change was also the theme of the July-August national planning conference which concluded with a recommendation for a slight increase in capital construction investment in 1958.[77] Perhaps most remarkable, speaking at the Third Plenum on October 5, a mere four days before Mao's attack on *fanmaojin*, Li Fuchun was still articulating the cautious line, using the formula of the famous June 20, 1956, *People's Daily* editorial to warn of both rash advance and conservatism.[78] The end of *fanmaojin* came as a surprise to virtually all CCP leaders and bureaucrats and as a severe jolt to many of the most important, as we shall see in more detail in the following chapter's discussion of the origins of the Great Leap Forward.

The Politics of Opposing Rash Advance

In comparison to the subsequent Great Leap Forward, Mao's role in the *fanmaojin* process was clearly not only not as crucial, but in some important senses peripheral. Yet Mao was certainly not overruled in these developments. While the evidence suggests a somewhat different inclination on the Chairman's part and some subtle expressions of reservations, at no time were his specific proposals rejected.[79] Moreover, there is ample evidence that he not

---

[76] *Xinhua banyuekan* (hereafter *XHBYK*) [New China Semi-Monthly], no. 11 (1957), pp. 90-91, no. 12 (1957), pp. 104-105, no. 13 (1957), pp. 134-37, no. 17 (1957), pp. 206-208, no. 18 (1957), pp. 206-207; New China News Agency (hereafter NCNA), Beijing, July 1, 1957, in *CB*, no. 465, pp. 1-23; and *Jianshe yuekan* [Construction Monthly], no. 8 (1957), in *Union Research Service*, vol. 8, no. 25, pp. 433-55. This analysis runs directly counter to the interpretation of the same events using the same sources in Bachman, *Bureaucracy*, pp. 121-28, which claims that *duo, kuai, hao, sheng* was the explicit theme of a "blitz" organized by Li and Bo (see p. 122). Contrary to Bachman, in all their spring and summer statements Li and Bo nowhere used the "more, faster, better, and more economical" concept as an overarching theme, nor did they even *mention* the *duo, kuai, hao, sheng* slogan.

The analysis of the "blitz" in Teiwes, "Leaders, Institutions, and the Origins," pp. 249-50, was flawed as a result of taking at face value Bachman's assertion that such a "blitz" existed in rhetoric (if not policy) and questioning Chinese scholars as to the reasons for such a development. The scholars questioned, while clearly unaware of a "blitz," in turn took the question at face value and offered Mao-centered interpretations as to how it *could* have happened. Subsequent to the article, further interviews led a senior Party historian to check relevant sources, resulting in his conclusion that there was no evidence for a "blitz." For further detailed criticism of Bachman's "blitz," see Chan, "Leaders, Coalition Politics, and Policy-Formulation," pp. 68-70.

[77] *XHBYK*, no. 18 (1957), pp. 206-207; and NCNA, Beijing, 22 August 1957, in *Survey of China Mainland Press* (hereafter *SCMP*), no. 1602, p. 18, no. 1607, pp. 34-36.

[78] *Li Fuchun xuanji*, p. 212. Actually, Li reversed the June 20 formula by giving rash advance pride of place.

[79] A possible minor exception was Mao's reported call for a higher 1957 budget at the

only raised no objections to the anti-rash advance approach, but also that he approved it in both general and specific terms. Mao's restrained posture was clearly not a sign of disinterest in the economy. He not only wanted to extend the "high tide" of cooperativization to economic development, but he quickly picked up Liu Shaoqi's idea of briefings by the economic ministries, a process which resulted in the famous "Ten Great Relationships." In all this Mao was seeking faster economic growth; he specifically saw the ministerial briefings as leading to a more rapid pace of development than that achieved by the Soviet Union.[80] Yet in the process he apparently became attuned to the concerns of his economic specialists, and over the 1956-57 period tempered his underlying desire for fast growth with a respect for "objective economic laws." Clearly he had a high regard for the administrative and economic capabilities of Zhou Enlai and Chen Yun in particular and was prepared to grant them considerable leeway in running the economy, even though at the same time the influence of his anti-right conservative inclinations caused them repeated difficulties in accomplishing what they felt was necessary.

Further elaboration of Mao's relatively quiescent performance is required, however. Party historians in interviews raised a number of factors apart from his respect for the expertise of the economic specialists. A number of considerations of personal and Party style come into play. As a person with direct experience of the Chairman put it, when he might not agree with something Mao would sometimes say nothing and wait for an occasion to state his views. Mao's propensity to hold his tongue when unsure of an issue or only mildly annoyed dovetailed with other aspects of his personal work style and CCP norms in the mid-1950s. One aspect, frequently mentioned by Party historians, was the relatively "democratic" life within the leadership at this time, notwithstanding Mao's recently demonstrated capacity to act in one-man imperial style.[81] While this was reflected in the expectations of the top elite as a whole based on the practices of the previous decade and the belief that differences with Mao were not fatal, and was deepened in 1956 by attention to the democracy question resulting from the criticism of Stalin at the Soviet Twentieth Party Congress, it was more significantly a product of Mao's own *modus operandi*. As Party historians observed, at this juncture it was Mao's style to let colleagues air their views, accept majority views where he had no strong contrary opinions, and let responsible officials get on with the job of implementing agreed policies without his close involvement. This, of course, was not obeying the majority as standard Party histories claim, but a deliberate

---

Second Plenum (see above, n. 57), but information on this development is unusually meager. If Mao did indeed make such a suggestion, we surmise that, unlike his proposal for increased capital construction spending at the April Politburo meeting, he did not insist on his view.

80   See Bo Yibo, *Huigu*, vol. 1, p. 528.

81   The relevant cases being the criticism of Bo Yibo in 1953 and Deng Zihui in 1955. For an overview of Party democracy in this period, see Teiwes, *Politics and Purges*, pp. xlviii-l.

approach especially to areas where he felt less sure of himself. Also of relevance is that concrete economic work was not considered the type of major political question where the Chairman's close supervision was required, although this factor should not be exaggerated.[82] Finally, a great deal of the Chairman's time and energy in 1956-57 went into political issues like the Hundred Flowers and international problems, such as those facing the international communist movement after Poland and Hungary.

This, in turn, left considerable scope for other leaders. Of particular significance in the whole *fanmaojin* story was Zhou Enlai. Zhou's boldness and persistence in pushing the opposition to rash advance was remarkable and possibly suggests more political steel in the Premier's personality than is often acknowledged. What is striking is not simply Zhou's efforts to overcome bureaucratic resistance, but especially his willingness to touch politically sensitive matters as in deleting references to the 40 articles and *duo, kuai, hao, sheng* from Eighth Congress documents or joking about creating a committee for promoting retrogression. In this it might be said that Zhou was merely operating according to prevailing notions of Party democracy, particularly in that he was dealing with questions of economic policy rather than political line. Yet this is still perplexing for in 1953 Mao had transformed the technical issue of Bo Yibo's tax policy into a question of political line,[83] while in mid-1955 Deng Zihui's advocacy of a slower rate of cooperativization than what Mao desired was unilaterally declared a rightist deviation. Whether it reflected naïveté, an awareness that both Bo Yibo and Deng Zihui had been treated relatively leniently,[84] or some other consideration, Zhou's behavior could suggest considerable faith in formal Party norms or at least Mao's commitment to Party unity. Such faith is further suggested by the contrast of Zhou's behavior in this period with that following Mao's sharp criticism of him in early 1958: from that point on Zhou became very cautious and very seldom exhibited the degree of forceful advocacy he had shown concerning *fanmaojin*.[85]

None of this, however, is fully convincing in explaining the Premier's actions. Keeping in mind Shi Zhongquan's several assessments that Zhou and

---

[82]   While Mao would complain in 1958 that he had been insufficiently briefed, there is no reason to believe that he was not kept well informed about economic matters. Indeed, Bo Yibo, *Huigu*, vol. 2, p. 651, rejected Mao's claim with the comment that all major policies were reported and it was impossible to submit everything to him. Cf., however, the following discussion of whether Zhou Enlai reported to Mao with adequate sensitivity during this period.

[83]   See above, n. 63.

[84]   While Bo was forced to resign as Minister of Finance, he soon was placed in charge of industry and communications, and Deng continued as head of the Party Center's Rural Work Department, although his influence clearly declined.

[85]   On the changes in Zhou's behavior after early 1958, see Shi Zhongquan, *Zhou Enlai*, pp. 412-13.

others saw no opposition to Mao in their actions, it is at least plausible that he conceived of himself as trying to meet his leader's expectations for much of the time, and that he felt he had the Chairman's strong backing for measures he deemed essential for the remainder. Certainly, as in the case of his enthusiastic January remarks about the 40 articles, there are indications that for much of the first half of 1956 Zhou hoped the economy would speed forward at the same time as he addressed the problem of excessive targets. Perhaps most poignant was Zhou's April-May visits to steelworks in Anshan and Taiyuan as his awareness of the difficulties of the first leap grew. On these visits he both sought to encourage fulfilling the high targets that had been set but also saw first hand the difficulties in doing this, and upon his return to Beijing instructed his secretary to find a passage in Marx that could be used to attack adventurism.[86] Thereafter Zhou was clearly in *fanmaojin* mode and taking the lead rather than following the Chairman, but as demonstrated above he received Mao's concrete support on such occasions as the Eighth Congress and the Second Plenum. Nevertheless, despite Zhou's extremely Mao-sensitive political style both earlier and subsequently,[87] it appears that during the unfolding of *fanmaojin* the Premier, at least in the view of Shi Zhongquan, did not sufficiently initiate discussions with Mao before some important decisions, something which perhaps contributed to Mao's later irritation concerning opposition to rash advance. To the extent such behavior existed, given the realities of Mao's power, it is best understood as careless politics on Zhou's part.[88]

---

[86]   *Dang de wenxian*, no. 5 (1992), pp. 43-44; Shi Zhongquan, *Zhou Enlai*, p. 320; and Michael Schoenhals, *Saltationist Socialism: Mao Zedong and the Great Leap Forward 1958* (Stockholm: Institutionen for Orientaliska Sprak, University of Stockholm, 1987), p. 15.

   A similar intermediate position can perhaps be seen in Li Xiannian's (undated) April report to Mao on the financial situation. Li, apart from complaining about a tendency of some departments at the start of the financial year to seek more revenues than they expected to spend, called for tight expenditures but at the same time advocated doing more and producing more to develop the economy. See *Li Xiannian lun caizheng jinrong maoyi (1950-1991)* [Li Xiannian on Finance, Banking, and Trade, 1950-1991], vol. 1 (Beijing: Zhongguo caizheng jingji chubanshe, 1992), pp. 149-52.

[87]   On Zhou's sensitivity to Mao, see Frederick C. Teiwes with Warren Sun, *The Formation of the Maoist Leadership: From the Return of Wang Ming to the Seventh Party Congress* (London: Contemporary China Institute Research Notes and Studies no. 10, 1994), p. 46; and Teiwes, *Politics and Purges*, pp. xxvii-xxviii.

[88]   See Li Haiwen, ed., *Zhou Enlai yanjiu shuping* [Review of Research on Zhou Enlai] (Beijing: Zhongyang wenxian chubanshe, 1997), pp. 424-25; and Shi Zhongquan, *Zhou Enlai*, p. 343. Shi mentions the case of Zhou's report to the November 1956 plenum as an example of his failure to consult Mao, but bases this conclusion on Mao's angry comments *in early 1958*. In addition, several senior Party historians claim that Mao did not vet Zhou's report before the plenum, something difficult to understand given his practice of reviewing important documents prior to presentation in this period (see, e.g.,

Of the officials concerned with the economy under Zhou, Chen Yun was clearly the most significant. Chen, of course, must be regarded as more than an economic specialist given his status as a CCP Vice Chairman and his past leading role in the key area of Party organization work, but at the same time he clearly was the main architect of PRC economic policy over the entire 1949-57 period. According to the recollections of a former financial official, in this period Zhou normally chaired Politburo meetings dealing with economic policies and after hearing reports asked Chen for his views, saying comparatively little himself. Moreover, when Mao chaired Party conferences, after hearing Chen's views he would ask if anyone else had an opinion and, if not, Chen's view was accepted.[89] Thus among those concerned with the economy Chen's position was authoritative; it was natural that he was appointed head of the Party Center's economics work small group when it was set up in January 1957. To combine the views of several Party historians in interviews, Chen (subject to Mao's and Zhou's consent) formulated policy, while Li Fuchun, Li Xiannian, and Bo Yibo took charge of concrete implementation, and even if the others were unhappy with Chen's positions it was very hard for them to express their discontent given Chen's superior status.[90] Certainly Chen, whose prestige in the economic sphere also extended to the provincial level,[91] cannot be regarded as a mere representative of any particular institutional perspective: he played a key role in shaping both the FFYP with Li Fuchun and the SFYP with Zhou, as well as working closely with Li Xiannian and other financial officials in enforcing budget restraint.

In terms of *fanmaojin*, Party historians believe that there was little difference among Chen, Li Xiannian, and Bo Yibo. It is clear, however, that SPC head Li Fuchun was less involved in the policy than the others, and certainly he was blamed less by Mao. When Mao attacked *fanmaojin* with full fury at the start of 1958, he named Zhou, Chen, Li Xiannian, and Bo as

---

Mao wengao, vol. 6, pp. 136ff). There is, however, no evidence of any displeasure in this regard being expressed by Mao at the time; as we have seen (above, p. 40), he had declared his "complete agreement" with the results of the plenum. In any case, the analysis here is contrary to our speculation concerning frequent briefings in Teiwes with Sun, "The Politics of an 'Un-Maoist' Interlude," p. 168. Our revised view is also based on the testimony of a leading authority on Zhou Enlai, someone who should have access to records of the Premier's movements, that such contacts were not a regular thing. Interview, Beijing, 1997.

89   *Women de Zhou Zongli*, pp. 302-303.

90   Cf. Bo Yibo's comment in *Huigu*, vol. 2, p. 833, that after 1949 he worked under Chen Yun's leadership in economics work. On the small group, see above, p. 11n18.

91   Notwithstanding the conflict between *fanmaojin* and the desire of local leaders to spend more on their areas, our former provincial leader said most top provincial officials were greatly impressed with Chen's speeches on financial and economic matters which they usually found persuasive, although this did not include "people like Ke Qingshi." In contrast, our source described Li Fuchun's speeches as boring and uninspiring. Interview, Beijing, 1997.

culprits, but not Li Fuchun.[92] Moreover, while Li Fuchun had been involved in many of the key developments of the attack on rash advance, particularly in early 1956, he seemingly avoided the self-criticism ritual in the crucial period from the January Nanning conference to the Second Session of the Eighth Party Congress in May 1958.[93] Why, then, his easier time of it? Perhaps the most direct answer is that in policy terms Li apparently was less committed to the approach than the others, as reflected in his absence from accounts of developments for nearly all of the second half of 1956, which can only be partially explained by his time abroad. In this context it is worth noting Mao's January 1958 "factional" characterization of his leading planners: Li Fuchun assertedly represented the left, Bo Yibo the middle (zhongjianpai), and Jia Tuofu the right.[94] Various Party historians commented on Li's lower profile or comparatively ambiguous position, but this cannot be explained simply as the result of a planner's perspective since the other chief planner, Bo Yibo, was both deeply involved and criticized by Mao.

Other possibilities involve personal relations, personality, and bureaucratic considerations. In terms of individual relations, Li Fuchun was particularly close to Mao, being a personal friend as well as having a close political connection going back to the Jiangxi period. Thus Li was arguably in a better position than most to have a keen sense of Mao's preoccupations. Moreover, of special significance in our view, by dint of personality Li was not at all assertive in his relations with Mao. According to an oral source specializing in Li's career, Li always followed Mao very closely and wouldn't express a dissenting opinion even when he knew Mao to be wrong — something arguably at play when Li alone backed Mao's April 1956 proposal to increase capital construction spending.[95] Given occasional signs of Mao's possible ambivalence, Li may have concluded that a low profile was the best course of action. Yet there was also an institutional aspect, albeit one more specific than that of planner qua planner. The SPC, after all, formulated the 1956 plan and initial version of the new five-year plan which were both considered "rash," and thus was being held responsible for its errors by the fanmaojin drive, a factor leading an interview source to speculate about both the organization's role and especially Li's personal loss of prestige as explanations for his comparative quiescence. And in fact the SPC was slow to come around with its second version of the SFYP also judged maojin.

---

[92]   Women de Zhou Zongli, p. 303.

[93]   Although an oral source claimed Li did engage in self-examination at the Congress, written sources when discussing self-criticisms in this period do not mention Li. Moreover, a provincial leader present at the Congress has no recollection of Li undertaking self-criticism.

[94]   Zhou Weiren, Jia Tuofu zhuan [Biography of Jia Tuofu] (Beijing: Zhonggong dangshi chubanshe, 1993), p. 116.

[95]   Cf. Li's behavior during Mao's criticism of the SPC in 1963-64; Frederick C. Teiwes, "Mao and His Lieutenants," AJCA, nos. 19-20 (1988), pp. 28-29.

Additionally, the fact that the SEC and not the SPC was responsible for the contentious 1957 annual plan may have shielded Li from Mao's *ex post facto* anger.[96] But Li and the SPC did fall in line, bowing to the superior authority of Zhou and Chen — as backed, however tepidly, by Mao.

If, then, there was a basic consensus among China's top economic policy makers on *fanmaojin*, notwithstanding less wholehearted support on the part of Li Fuchun, there was nevertheless significant bureaucratic opposition from both the spending ministries and localities. Throughout the year-long struggle these organizations and their leaders continued to spend, demand more funds, and argue against the cuts being imposed in the name of opposing rash advance.[97] In this bureaucratic conflict the *fanmaojin* approach was pushed forward not only by the top officials of the CCP, including Zhou and Chen Yun as well as Liu Shaoqi and the ranking economic officials on the Politburo, but also by the peak institutions of both the planners and budgeteers. The SPC and especially the SEC (with its responsibility for the 1957 plan) as well as the Ministry of Finance were all deeply involved in the effort, for both planners and budgeteers, whatever the differences in their organizational missions, had overall responsibilities for providing some cohesion and balance to an economy which was supposed to work according to objective economic laws. In the case of *fanmaojin* there was a significant institutional component, but it was not that of conflict between planning and financial coalitions. Instead it was more a conflict of different levels in the economic structure, with the overall coordinating bodies attempting to discipline the specific task-oriented ministries and the localities wishing to fulfill their missions or encourage local development as rapidly as possible.

A special note should be made of the role of provincial-level leaders, not in terms of support for Mao (although this was willingly offered in their late 1955-early 1956 backing of the first leap), but through their opportunities to influence him. This was in large measure due to Mao's belief that the localities were close to reality, and his practice of touring the provinces to find out what was truly happening. Thus provincial leaders were well positioned both to add to Mao's enthusiasm for agricultural development and to seek his support for more funds in winter 1955-56, and also to continue lobbying for their needs during Mao's tours in May-June 1956. This does not mean that the provinces were unusually advantaged in this period — after all, Mao's mid-1956 tour came after his meetings with 34 ministries which preceded the drafting of the "Ten Great Relationships." Moreover, given his willingness to accept Zhou's policies, the efforts of the provinces had a decidedly limited

---

96 At a strictly personal level, Li may also have been shielded by the fact that Zhou Enlai took the leading role in drafting the final version of the SFYP.

97 This was especially emphasized in our interviews with the former central bureaucrat from the heavy industry sector. Cf. Bo Yibo, *Huigu*, vol. 1, pp. 554-55, for an account of how the SEC wanted to cut spending in the 1957 plan but various ministries and provinces still wanted high targets.

effect in combating the opposition to rash advance. Yet Mao's favorable bias toward local leaders was indicated in early 1958 when he declared one of the causes of *fanmaojin* was the failure of the responsible leaders to seek the opinions of provincial Party secretaries in advance.[98]

Two final considerations should be highlighted in the story of *fanmaojin*. First, as oral sources note, there was a deep desire for rapid economic development throughout the leadership, ordinary cadres, and indeed much of China's population. The idea of pushing a backward China forward was intensely popular, and even as sober-minded a leader as Zhou Enlai was genuinely enthusiastic about the prospect in late 1955 and into 1956. In this regard opposing rash advance went against the grain in a broader attitudinal sense: those who resisted *fanmaojin* were not simply reflecting a policy preference or a particular organization's interests, or even merely trying to avoid the dreaded right conservative label. Second, in 1956-57 the scope for internal debate and the airing of both dissenting opinions and concrete policy demands had reached arguably its high point in CCP politics during the Mao's lifetime.[99] This reflected not only the norm of inner-Party democracy but also the sense of victory in the socialist revolution. With class enemies defeated and the main task turning to the notionally nonpolitical area of economic construction, the opportunity for relatively forthright clashes of *legitimate* interests significantly expanded. Yet once again the overall trend was linked to Mao, although now in the sense of what the Chairman did *not* do. For while Mao backed *fanmaojin*, he did it in a distant sort of way. Those unhappy with the policy of the "Center" would have had no confident sense that the Chairman shared their views, but at the same time Mao was not applying personal pressure or making support of *fanmaojin* a matter of political line. When the Chairman, starting at the Third Plenum, and with particular ferocity from the January 1958 Nanning meeting, began to criticize opposition to rash advance, raising it to a question of a mistaken political line at Nanning, the Great Leap Forward inevitably followed.

---

[98]   Bo Yibo, *Huigu*, vol. 2, p. 640. In the same context, however, Mao mentions the divorce of the State Council from most of its departments, noting that industrial ministries wanted to do more and only the financial, banking, and trade system wanted to do less. Cf. below, p. 93n32.

[99]   See Roderick MacFarquhar's discussion of provincial economic demands on the Center at the Eighth Congress in *Origins 1*, pp. 130-33.

Chapter 2

THE ORIGINS OF THE GREAT LEAP FORWARD, 1955-58

While the Great Leap Forward emerged rapidly after Mao's rejection of opposition to rash advance at the Third Plenum, the origins of the movement are bound up in events stretching over the entire period from the second half of 1955. The crucial factor was the way in which these events were interpreted — above all by Mao — from the perspective of late 1957 and early 1958. As reflected in the imagery of U-shaped development and Mao's complaint that *duo, kuai, hao, sheng* had been "blown away," the rapid growth of cooperatives in 1955 was seen as evidence of what the mass movement could accomplish,[1] while the now discredited *fanmaojin* policies represented "cold water" dampening the enthusiasm of the masses. Together with the tension created by the Anti-Rightist Campaign in summer 1957 and the generally disappointing growth during the year,[2] the ideological, political, and economic conditions for a new developmental approach that did not rely on specialists or hew to concepts of balance had been laid.

Yet the question of "origins" requires further analysis in two important senses. The first is the issue of policy continuity, the fact that various policies which became important features of the Great Leap were evolving over the entire period as Chinese leaders began self-consciously to modify the Soviet model. While awareness of these developments and hypotheses concerning an incremental policy process predate Bachman's continuity argument,[3] his

---

[1] The general overestimation of past achievements during the early Great Leap was noted in the 1981 "Resolution on Certain Questions in the History of Our Party Since the Founding of the People's Republic of China," *Beijing Review*, no. 27 (1981), p. 19: "... Comrade Mao Zedong and many leading comrades ... had become smug about their successes, were impatient for quick results and overestimated the role of man's subjective will and efforts."

[2] The annual rate of growth in 1957 fell behind the growth rates for the whole FFYP in both value of industrial output (11.4 compared to 25.7 percent) and agricultural output value (3.6 to 3.8 percent). See Fang Weizhong, *Jingji dashiji*, pp. 182-83, 203-204.

[3] An early statement of the incremental policy thesis as applied to water conservancy is Michel C. Oksenberg, "Policy Formulation in Communist China: The Case of the Mass Irrigation Campaign, 1957-58," Ph.D. dissertation, Columbia University, 1969. For a brief mention of policies developed in 1956-57 that were subsequently extended during the Great Leap, see Frederick C. Teiwes, "Establishment and Consolidation of the New

analysis systematically makes the case that leap forward hallmarks, such as decentralization and the development of small and medium-scale industry, gradually took hold during the half year preceding the Third Plenum. The first part of this chapter, while affirming the conclusion of Chapter 1 that the fundamental change concerning the speed of economic growth only came *after* the fall 1957 plenum, examines the broader case for policy continuity with particular attention to the decentralization issue. Secondly, in the concluding section of the chapter, we address the *dynamics* of the Mao-centered political process which transformed the latent forces for policy change into a totally new and unanticipated economic strategy, while providing a new interpretation of the underlying reasons for Mao's actions. In this detailed analysis of the events of late 1957-early 1958, we illuminate the Chairman's unchallenged authority and how the overwhelming majority of the leadership fell in behind Mao with a remarkable degree of enthusiasm. As more than one Party historian has put it, it was a case of the whole Party following Mao.

Events and Linkages: Policy Issues and Political Developments, 1955-57

An important link between between events in 1955-57 and the Great Leap acknowledged in virtually all interpretations was the Anti-Rightist Campaign which unfolded from June 1957 to crack down on intellectual dissent which got out of hand during the Hundred Flowers experiment in the spring.[4] As one senior Party historian declared, the anti-rightist struggle "sowed the seeds for the Great Leap Forward." It created both a supercharged political atmosphere with strong overtones of class struggle[5] and doubts that China's intellectuals could perform the crucial role in economic and cultural development that had

---

Regime," in Roderick MacFarquhar and John K. Fairbank, eds., *The Cambridge History of China: Volume 14, The People's Republic, Part I: The Emergence of Revolutionary China 1949-1965* (New York: Cambridge University Press, 1987), p. 141.

[4]   Cf. Bachman's discussion of this linkage in the elite conflict literature and his adaptation in *Bureaucracy*, pp. 5-6, 93-95, 193-96. The Hundred Flowers, in turn, as well as the effort to modify the Soviet-style economic system, were influenced by the events threatening communist rule in East Europe in 1956. For a brief overview of the events, see Teiwes, "Establishment," pp. 133-42.

[5]   While a class struggle atmosphere was extended into the Great Leap and the "contradiction between the proletariat and the bourgeoisie" was officially declared the main contradiction at the Third Plenum, the full story was more complex. The main *task* remained economic development, and there was considerable theoretical ambiguity concerning the precise role of class struggle. See Teiwes, "Mao Texts." For a somewhat different view of this issue, see Keith Forster, "Mao Zedong on Contradictions under Socialism Revisited," *The Journal of Contemporary China*, Fall 1995.

been assigned to them following the "transition to socialism" in 1955-56.[6] More specifically, since some intellectuals during the Hundred Flowers period had adopted the *fanmaojin* perspective to criticize unrealistic official goals, the Anti-Rightist Campaign included denunciations for such sins as advocating economic balance and other moderate policies. This situation clearly was unfavorable to a program of relatively slow growth, and instead conducive to the emergence of a mass mobilization, nonexpert approach to economic strategy.

As inhospitable to continued policy moderation as the atmosphere created by the Anti-Rightist Campaign was, it was by no means inevitable that the Great Leap, or even a major shift of economic policy, would occur. As argued elsewhere,[7] not only did the June-September 1957 period see a continuation of moderate economic policies despite the harsh rhetoric of the movement, but the anti-rightist struggle was in fact quite compatible with their continuation over a longer period. Despite Mao's subsequent interpretation, the rightism of 1957 had little to with the rightist conservatism criticized in the first half of 1956 or the *fanmaojin* policies of 1956-57. The earlier "rightism" fitted the normal definition of the term — excessive caution, unwillingness to mobilize fully the masses, and failure to achieve rapid advance. Various policy preferences of the "bourgeois rightists" of spring 1957 notwithstanding, the essence of this rightism, according to Mao in mid-1957, was that mistakes outweighed achievements, the capitalist road was preferable to the socialist road, and the CCP was unfit to lead the country. Moreover, the basic aim of the Anti-Rightist Campaign was to restore Party control — an aim perfectly compatible with economic moderation. With Party control reestablished, concessions to intellectuals short of the leading role in Party rectification they were given in spring 1957 could again have been granted. That this did not occur, and the country instead veered off in radical new directions, was the result of both the objective conditions of a declining economic growth rate and some unique subjective conclusions drawn by Mao.

It is this usually ignored consideration — Mao's own interpretation of the meaning of the Hundred Flowers failure and the anti-rightist response — that we shall emphasize in our review of the post-Third Plenum period. But before turning to the political dynamics of late 1957-early 1958, we will first examine linkages between economic policy initiatives in 1956-57 and the Great Leap program. In the broadest sense this centered on the search for an alternative to the Soviet economic model which, by late 1955, was recognized as less than totally suited to Chinese conditions. This recognition led to Mao's

---

6   The January 1956 conference on intellectuals was the signal of intellectuals being assigned this role. Significantly, this was the occasion when Mao first proposed his "committee to promote progress." See Li Rui, *"Dayuejin" qinliji*, p. 204; and above, p. 22-23. For the keynote speech at this conference, see Zhou Enlai, "On the Question of Intellectuals," in *PDA*, pp. 128-44.

7   See Teiwes, *Politics and Purges*, pp. 226-27.

briefing by 34 ministries starting in February 1956 and thereafter in April to the "Ten Great Relationships," an effort to lay down broad guidelines for an adjustment of the Soviet model. This, in turn, gave rise to various efforts to develop concrete Chinese approaches in such areas as decentralization, the development of small and medium-scale industry, and providing inputs for agriculture through investment in industry, approaches which not only featured significantly during the leap, but in Bachman's institutional interpretation, represented the victorious platform of the "planning and heavy industry coalition."[8] In the analysis which follows, we both assess such measures with particularly detailed attention to the decentralization issue, and examine the roles of key actors at both the leadership and bureaucratic levels.

The reconsideration of the Soviet model began with leadership encouragement and bureaucratic studies in late 1955, with Liu Shaoqi first proposing a systematic review and Mao quickly taking up the idea which led to the "Ten Great Relationships." From the start there was a recognition of the need to alter the rigidly centralized economic system copied from the Soviet Union and to provide more scope for localities and enterprises under the state plan. This found expression in Mao's April speech in very general terms with the Chairman calling for adjustments favoring production units and even individual producers *vis-à-vis* the state and the localities *vis-à-vis* the Center. The planning of the necessary reforms then proceeded, with key roles played by Zhou Enlai, Chen Yun, and, to a lesser extent, Bo Yibo as the State Council met repeatedly from May to August 1956 to consider means of curbing the excessive centralization of the administrative system. Chen, moreover, made a number of proposals for structural reform at the Eighth Congress which gained Mao's approval, and experiments including enhanced enterprise autonomy and selective use of market mechanisms were carried out after the Congress. Meanwhile, the SFYP which Zhou Enlai had drafted with the assistance of Chen and SPC personnel, assigned more construction projects to local authorities. In January 1957, although the State Council, seemingly because of the complex administrative problems any change would require, effectively shelved market experiments by deciding that the basic pattern of planned allocation would continue for the year, the process of decentralization gained a further push as Chen again discussed the issues and won Mao's warm support at the conference of provincial secretaries. In addition, the newly established five-man small group on economics work consisting of Chen, Li Xiannian, Li Fuchun, and Bo Yibo as well as military leader Huang Kecheng was directed by Mao to study decentralization. The end product of this effort was several draft regulations which were presented to the Third Plenum in September, and

---

8   See above, p. 11, for a brief summary of Bachman's views concerning the bureaucratic forces assertedly involved in this policy struggle. The reported competing program of the "financial coalition," assertedly dominant until February 1957, included increased reliance on markets and greater investment in agriculture and light industry at the expense of the heavy industry sector, as well as an attempt to retain centralized financial control.

formally promulgated in November as the momentum built for a new production drive. While these measures were initially the formal principles for decentralization during the leap, they were soon pushed aside in practice.[9]

In this complex bureaucratic and political process Chen Yun clearly emerges as the architect of decentralization.[10] In this case, moreover, Mao and fellow generalist Liu Shaoqi were hardly ignorant and inattentive to the economic matters at hand; rather, they were deeply concerned that China find appropriate policies for her national conditions. While political considerations such as Khrushchev's denunciation of Stalin at the Soviet 20th Party Congress in February 1956 and Mao's undoubted feeling that he was the true leader of world communism surely contributed to his desire to change the Stalinist economic system,[11] he had demonstrated a keen interest in the economic issues as such since December 1955.[12] Finally, our analysis will once again reveal a clash of bureaucratic interests which had little if anything to do with alleged competing "coalitions," or with the clash of "radicals" and "conservatives" within the leadership.[13]

In the judgment of Bo Yibo, in the initial period of large-scale economic development during the FFYP both the central ministries and the provinces

---

9   Bo Yibo, *Huigu*, vol. 1, pp. 466-72, 478-82, vol. 2, pp. 780ff; *Dang de wenxian*, no. 6 (1989), pp. 32-33; Bachman, *Bureaucracy*, pp. 84-85; Peter N. S. Lee, *Industrial Management and Economic Reform in China, 1949-1984* (Hong Kong: Oxford University Press, 1987), pp. 51-55; Chen Yun's speech in *Eighth National Congress of the Communist Party of China*, vol. II (Speeches) (Peking: Foreign Languages Press, 1956), pp. 157-76; and oral sources.

10   This is contrary to Bachman's view which not only depicts the "planning and heavy industry coalition" as the advocate of decentralization in order to devolve unwanted tasks so that "modern heavy industry [could be further insulated] from the demands of the localities," but also argues that Chen was an opponent who "probably was pressured to authorize financial decentralization" against the interests of the "financial coalition" he headed. See *Bureaucracy*, pp. 86n, 125. In "Chinese Bureaucratic Politics," p. 47, Bachman further argues that "One simply cannot read Chen Yun's works in their entirety ... or his specific remarks ... to the Third Plenum ... and say that he supports decentralization" because "His words are redolent with caution and control...." The point, however, is that in 1956-57 Chen supported a variant of decentralization that both gained Mao's support and was, if anything, more pro-devolution than anything the planners were saying at the time.

11   While these factors have long been cited in the West, a recent PRC Party history article points to the significance of the Congress in "advancing [Mao's] independent thinking concerning socialism"; *Dangdai Zhongguoshi yanjiu* [Research on Contemporary Chinese History], no. 1 (1994), p. 16.

12   Cf. Bo Yibo's observation, *Huigu*, vol. 2, p. 785, that in the period leading to the "Ten Great Relationships" Mao paid unusual attention to analyzing Soviet and China's own economic experience.

13   For the "radicals" *v.* "conservatives" power politics interpretation of decentralization, see Chang, *Power and Policy*, p. 55.

supported the Soviet system — there were no differences. With the passage of time and especially the socialist transformation of industry and commerce, agriculture and handicrafts, however, rigid centralism began to grate on the localities and enterprises. These discontents were expressed to Mao by provincial leaders when the Chairman conducted investigations into the new situation in December 1955 and January 1956 and sought their views. In these meetings local officials complained that central control was choking productive activity, binding them hand and foot and leaving the localities no room for economic management, and they demanded a devolution of economic power. Anhui's Party leader, Zeng Xisheng, argued that central restrictions limited the development of local industry, while Guangdong's Tao Zhu and Party leaders from Tianjin complained that the state budget was denying their areas necessary funds. Mao, as on other occasions before and after,[14] appreciated the seeming enthusiasm of the provincial leaders for a greater role in development, and upon his return to Beijing spoke many times on the need to change the economic system and allow the localities more scope for their activities.[15]

In this period Mao directly pressed the central authorities. When, as part of the briefing process leading to the "Ten Great Relationships," the Chairman listened to the report of the Ministry of Heavy Industry on February 4, he noted that local cadres were very dissatisfied, and accused the assembled officials of ignoring requests from below and binding the localities.[16] In early March he sent a note to top leaders Liu Shaoqi, Zhou Enlai, Peng Zhen, and Deng Xiaoping observing that while the Party Center had been listening to the ideas of ministries concerning changes in the economic management system, from then on it was necessary to listen to the views of provincial, municipal, and other local Party committees. Such pressure quickly produced a bureaucratic response with Li Fuchun proposing that 200 to 300 important factories prepare reports for the Center. Then, when briefing Mao in the run up to the "Ten Great Relationships," the SPC noted the localities' requests for more factories and industries and strongly acknowledged the need to "release enthusiasm." The presentation of the State Council's Fifth Office, which was responsible for finance, also criticized the past overly centralized practices, although perhaps in less fulsome terms, thus providing some (inconclusive) evidence for possible differences along the planning/financial axis. The basic story, however, was one of both planning and financial authorities responding

---

14   The key case earlier in 1955, of course, concerned agricultural cooperativization; see Teiwes and Sun, *The Politics of Agricultural Cooperativization*, pp. 11, 19-20. For subsequent examples, see above, p. 22; and below, pp. 69, 72-74.

15   Bo Yibo, *Huigu*, vol. 2, pp. 781-82; and *Dangdai Zhongguoshi yanjiu*, no. 1 (1994), pp. 15-16, 18.

16   In addition to questions of central-local relations, in this period in another indication of his concern with improving on the Soviet model, as we have seen, Mao also pressed central bureaucracies to outstrip the Soviet Union's growth rate. See above, p. 25.

to pressure from the localities and, more importantly, Mao. In the event, Mao's systematic briefings by local leaders began in late April, and in May he personally drafted instructions on how these local Party authorities were to report to the Center on economic issues.[17]

In addition to supporting the provinces on these issues, Mao also supported increased enterprise autonomy to the extent of endorsing "semi-independent kingdoms" and asking Chen Yun to undertake research into the issue. All of this was on the agenda of the "national structure conference" convened by the State Council in May and concluding in August 1956. The conference consisted of two stages: 1) from late May to the end of June in Beijing concerning excessive centralization under the leadership of Zhou Enlai (who had been researching the question since March-April) and involving both central and provincial officials; and 2) an August session in Beidaihe again encompassing both central and local leaders, with Bo Yibo in charge of researching proposals that eventually produced a draft decision which was circulated for discussion at the end of October. In this process the main bureaucratic fissure was between central and local authorities. At the Beijing meetings provincial leaders "loudly cried out for more powers," but ministerial figures expressed many concerns, citing likely dispersionism and a negative effect on the state plan. Specifically, the greatest controversy concerned light industry[18] where central ministries argued there was already ample devolution. In this situation it was up to the top political figure present — Zhou Enlai — to insist on the need to divide administrative power in order to develop production and to point out the shortcomings of Soviet overcentralization, all the while bolstering his argument by citing Mao's authority as articulated in the "Ten Great Relationships."[19]

As indicated, the proposals emerging from this process in October were circulated for discussion and experimentation only, and much the same situation applied to Chen Yun's ideas at the Eighth Congress for restructuring the Soviet-style administrative system. The next major step came in January 1957 with the proposal for a five-man group to carry out further research on reforming economic management. This group, formally established on the 10th, became the Center's economics work small group which had overall responsiblity for economic affairs and was led by Chen, and Chen further

---

[17]   Bo Yibo, *Huigu*, vol. 1, pp. 480-81, vol. 2, pp. 783-84; *Dangdai Zhongguoshi yanjiu*, no. 1 (1994), p. 16; and *Mao wengao*, vol. 6, pp. 54-56, 116-17. In the period from November 1955 to April 1956 Mao had already heard reports from nine North China Party secretaries as well as the 34 ministries, while Liu Shaoqi heard from over 30 ministries. Zhou Enlai and other leaders also participated in the process. *Dang de wenxian*, no. 6 (1988), p. 34.

[18]   That is precisely the type of enterprises the planners should have been eager to jettison in Bachman's interpretation; see above, n. 10.

[19]   Bo Yibo, *Huigu*, vol. 2, pp. 786-87; and *Dang de wenxian*, no. 6 (1988), pp. 25-28, 36, no. 1 (1993), p. 31.

proposed six additional functional groups under the State Council to draw up sector-specific proposals — groups predominantly led by presumptive representatives of the "financial coalition."[20] Through this structure immediate research was conducted into ways to put into effect the draft proposals of the previous August, with Chen Yun and company urging the concerned ministries to propose concrete measures quickly. Meanwhile, when the conference of provincial secretaries met from January 18 to 27, Chen further argued the decentralization case, again earning Mao's approbation, and the Chairman urged the assembled local leaders to state their wishes which produced, in Bo Yibo's words, a "dynamic meeting." A key feature of this "dynamism" was provincial figures analyzing the faults of excessive centralism and demanding more power over enterprises and greater financial powers.[21]

In policy terms, at the closing session of the provincial secretaries conference on the 27th, Chen Yun responded to these developments with a position that both followed Mao's emphasis on decentralization and developed his own thinking on a more flexible system. As Bo Yibo put it, Chen went a step further than the "Ten Great Relationships" in arguing for a suitable division of power that avoided excessive centralization and devolved power in a gradual, step-by-step manner, views strongly endorsed by both Mao and all other Politburo Standing Commitee members. Chen apparently did not have everything his own way during the conference, however, with "some comrades" opposed to giving the localities a greater share of state finances, arguing, for example, that a dam the size of the Sanmenxia dam could be built using the money to be devolved to the provinces under Chen's proposal. Moreover, according to oral sources, the January conference saw relevant central and local organs engaged in a great deal of discussion and dispute over the division of power. Once again real bureaucratic conflict existed, but it was not between "planners" and "budgeteers"; instead, as in the case of opposing rash advance, it pitted high-level coordinators against central ministries, and — unlike *fanmaojin* — it also pitted those ministries against the localities. And regardless of any tension between Chen Yun as an architect of opposing rash advance and the desire of provincial leaders to spend more in their areas, on the issue of devolution they pushed in the same direction.[22]

---

20   Those groups and/or individuals assigned to the "financial coalition" by Bachman's schema were: agriculture and forestry (Deng Zihui), finance (Li Xiannian), commerce (Cheng Zihua), and [light] industry (Jia Tuofu). The sole representative of the notional "planning and heavy industry coalition" was Wang Shoudao, responsible for communications, while the last group, culture and education (Lin Feng), essentially stood outside the economic bureaucracies. See *Dang de wenxian*, no. 6 (1989), p. 32; and Bachman, *Bureaucracy*, pp. 48-49. In Bachman's terms the membership of the five-man group itself was balanced between "budgeteers" Chen and Li Xiannian and "planners" Li Fuchun and Bo Yibo, with military representative Huang Kecheng holding the balance.

21   Bo Yibo, *Huigu*, vol. 2, pp. 791-92.

22   *Ibid.*, p. 792; *Dang de wenxian*, no. 6 (1989), p. 34; and oral sources.

In any case, with Mao's and the Politburo's backing, an immediate decision was taken for Chen and the five-man small group to draft concrete decentralization measures. Moreover, in a move prefiguring much stronger action a year later, Mao both urged ministers and provincial secretaries to conduct their own investigations in the countryside and in factories, and expressed his discontent with their inadequate understanding of the grass-roots economic situation, declaring "Beijing is bad, they don't get hold of much knowledge, [but] the provinces are a bit better." While Mao was complaining about the shortcomings of both central and local officials, even at this stage his preference for provincial leaders with their presumed greater links to the grass roots was apparent.[23]

With this political momentum, moves toward decentralization developed more or less through regular administrative channels, even as other aspects of Chen Yun's overall vision fell by the wayside.[24] The five-man small group examined the proposals of the central departments and concluded that although these departments seemingly understood the faults of overcentralization and shared a common view with the localities in this respect, none of the proposals gave adequate consideration to the question of how to maintain comprehensive balance in the economy while devolving economic authority to lower levels. Such surprising proposals by central ministries suggest their bureaucratic interests were less important than the political need to respond to the forceful advocacy of devolution by Chen, especially Mao, and their leadership colleagues at the January conference. In any case, comprehensive balance was a particular concern at a time of strained resources and fears that a lack of control would lead to waste. While such a concern was central to Chen Yun's thinking then and later, it was not solely a personal concern, but something shared by all those responsible for overall economic coordination, "planners" and "budgeteers" alike. Thus Chen and Li Fuchun entrusted Bo Yibo with drafting the methods that would retain the necessary control while decentralizing, and after consultation with the concerned planning departments Bo reported to the five-man group at the end of August 1957. Bo's proposals aimed at retaining sufficient central powers under the slogan "big planning, small freedoms," a level-by-level responsibility system that required the carrying out of designated central plans and a simplification of planning procedures.[25]

---

23   Bo Yibo, *Huigu*, vol. 2, p. 792; and *Xuexi wenxuan*, vol. 1 [1949-July 1957] ([Beijing: 1967]), pp. 175-76, 186.

24   In addition to the sidelining of market mechanisms for the allocation of materials in January 1957 (see above, p. 56), the impact of the Anti-Rightist Campaign further inhibited discussion of the role of the nonstate sector. Cf. Liu Shaoqi's spring enthusiasm for Chen's ideas on the private economy which suddenly ended with the onset of the campaign; *Dang de wenxian*, no. 6 (1988), p. 36.

25   Bo Yibo, *Huigu*, vol. 2, pp. 792-94. This was similar to Li Xiannian's approach to financial decentralization at the NPC two months earlier: Li was concerned with setting

These proposals were approved by the five-man group and passed on to the State Council and Party Center. Chen Yun reported on decentralization to the Third Plenum in September in the same vein, linking the necessary decentralization to strengthening national balance work. On this occasion, much as he had supported *fanmaojin* virtually on the eve of Mao's rejection of that policy, on October 5 China's preeminent planner, Li Fuchun, endorsed Chen Yun's approach to decentralization, citing the need to strengthen planning so as not to lose control. The plenum as a whole "basically" approved Chen's specific draft proposals, proposals that were formally promulgated by the NPC Standing Committee in November as the Great Leap gathered political momentum.[26] These controlled decentralization measures — supported by planners and financial leaders alike[27] — were the official measures in place as the Great Leap developed. But rather than continuity, they had virtually nothing to do with the decentralization that emerged in the vastly different political and bureaucratic contexts to be discussed in the following chapters. In the end Chen Yun's proposals failed to last during the Great Leap not because of bureaucratic divisions, but due to Mao's growing impatience with what he considered their overly piecemeal approach which could not serve the rapidly evolving leap.

The continuity argument also fails for other aspects of the alleged program of the "planning coalition." Here we consider in more thematic and less detailed fashion the "planks" of simultaneous development of industry and agriculture, promoting industrial inputs for agriculture, emphasis on small and medium-scale enterprises, and lowering design standards for new construction. All of these measures, according to Bachman, furthered the institutional interests of the planning and heavy industry departments by increasing resource allocation to heavy industry.[28] In this view the various

---

limits to the process but nevertheless advocated redefining the jurisdiction of central and local financial authorities to increase the freedom of action of the localities. *CB*, no. 464, p. 29.

26 Bo Yibo, *Huigu*, vol. 2, pp. 794-95; *Dang de wenxian*, no. 6 (1989), p. 33; and *Li Fuchun xuanji*, p. 212.

27 In addition to the above evidence, Party historians in interviews claimed no knowledge of opposition within the leading group of economic policy makers to Chen's proposals, even though one well-informed source felt there was a "slight difference" between Li Fuchun who more strongly favored the Soviet model and Chen who gave greater attention to Chinese conditions. It is also of particular interest that when Xue Muqiao presented some ideas on reforming the planning system in September 1957 he claimed that his views drew on Chen Yun's ideas, while his actual suggestions fit well with those of Li Fuchun at the Eighth Congress. See Bachman, *Bureaucracy*, p. 128.

28 One of the problems for Bachman's argument, however, is that policies allegedly put in place by the planners actually *decreased* investment in machine building, certainly along with metallurgy (steel), the core of heavy industry. See *Bureaucracy*, pp. 118, 120, 126-27, 203. Bachman (pp. 108-109) also points to evidence of conflicting interests between the machine building and metallurgical ministries; while credible, this does little for the

measures protected heavy industry from demands for more funds to light industry and agriculture. On the contrary, more funds would go to the heavy industrial sector through its mission to support agriculture through such inputs as chemical fertilizer in particular and to become the "engine of agricultural growth"; simultaneous development of industry and agriculture thus meant both more investment in heavy industry, and light industry and agriculture relying on local financing outside the state budget and the mobilization of peasant labor. Similarly, much as with decentralization generally, emphasis on developing medium and small-scale plants off-loaded responsibility for meeting local needs on the local authorities who would be responsible for these plants; the planners and ministerial officials would retain control over large modern enterprises. Finally, lowering design standards and avoiding a one-sided emphasis on the most advanced technology would both speed up growth and limit funds allocated to nonessential construction, while the savings could be reinvested in priority projects.[29]

This package of policies was assertedly launched as a counterattack on the then dominant "financial coalition" from about March 1957, pursued brilliantly by Li Fuchun and Bo Yibo in the spring and summer, and finally emerged victorious at the Third Plenum. The argument fails, however, in terms of timing, the sponsorship of the program, and most significantly its meaning in the context of the time. The policy proposals at issue date from considerably earlier than spring 1957: the appropriate timing is clearly linked to the reconsideration of the Soviet model in 1956.[30] Thus the major reports of Liu Shaoqi and Zhou Enlai to the Eighth Party Congress urged the construction of small and medium-sized industrial enterprises throughout the country.[31] Moreover, the policies continued to be articulated throughout the asserted period of "financial coalition" dominance from the Congress through February 1957, with leaders presumptively aligned to that "coalition" prominent. Light industry specialist Jia Tuofu was already articulating in 1956 all of the ideas concerning small and medium industry that Li Fuchun and Bo Yibo advocated in spring and summer 1957,[32] but the most important figure in this regard was none other than Chen Yun.

In his major speech at the conclusion of the January 1957 conference of provincial secretaries, in addition to promoting decentralization Chen called for increased investment in heavy industry that served light industry and agriculture, warned against overreliance on advanced foreign equipment, and

---

notion of a strong "heavy industry coalition."

29   See *Ibid.*, pp. 117-19, 121-30.

30   Indeed, aspects could be seen even earlier as in Li Fuchun's July 1955 report on the FFYP which endorsed more attention to small and medium industries. *Li Fuchun xuanji*, p. 144. We do not, however, read this as uniquely the project of the "planners." Note especially Chen Yun's role in drafting the FFYP.

31   See Chan, "Leaders, Coalition Politics, and Policy-Formulation," pp. 68-69.

32   See Zhou Weiren, *Jia Tuofu zhuan*, p. 104.

advocated more medium and small iron and steel factories and coal shafts to obtain quick returns. This took place well before the March planning conference decision to develop medium and small (and locally administered) collieries, iron mines, and blast furnaces that Bachman regards as an early sign of the planners' fightback. Finally, at the symbolic level, Chen called for mainly relying on "self-reliance," thus raising the Yan'an slogan that would again become prominent during the Great Leap.[33] Clearly, these policies were hardly the sole preserve of the planners; moreover they were aimed at adapting economic policy to Chinese conditions, a project most firmly embraced by Chen Yun and, in the view of Party historians, least enthusiastically accepted by the SPC's Li Fuchun.[34]

Symbolic issues illustrate the flawed meaning assigned to these policies in the institutional interpretation as harbingers of the Great Leap Forward. As the above substantive policies unfolded several slogans and concepts appeared during 1957, matters which became prominent during the Great Leap — not only "self reliance," but also the 40-article Draft Agricultural Program. But as previously argued, this did not include the "blown away" *duo, kuai, hao, sheng*; the emphasis in spring and summer 1957 was on "better" and "more economically" to the virtual exclusion, a few rhetorical flourishes aside, of "more" and "faster."[35] The underlying message which echoed both Chen Yun and Mao, was not of rapid growth and leaping forward, but about thrift, modest investment, step-by-step industrialization, and comprehensive balance. Indeed, as Bo Yibo put it in his address to the NPC in July, "the basic way" to fulfill the plan was through increasing production and practicing economy[36] — i.e., the approach of avoiding waste advocated by Chen Yun since the winter. Similarly, "self-reliance" which Chen as well as the planners had been advocating, *in the context of 1957 before the Third Plenum* must be seen as a simple statement that where state finances were limited and foreign exchange for importing modern equipment was severely strained, China as a nation would have to rely on domestic resources, while lowering its sights in accord with the dominant *fanmaojin* program.[37]

---

[33]   Chen Yun, in Nicholas R. Lardy and Kenneth Lieberthal, eds, *Chen Yun's Strategy for China's Development: A Non-Maoist Alternative* (Armonk: M.E. Sharpe, 1983), pp. 56-57; and Bachman, *Bureaucracy*, pp. 117-18. Bachman oddly ignores this speech when claiming on the basis of a secondary source (p. 122) that Bo Yibo in May revived the "self-reliance" slogan for the first time since 1949.

[34]   See above, n. 27.

[35]   See above, pp. 44-45. It is also worth noting that "more economically" was Li Fuchun's contribution to the slogan in the first place; above, p. 23n10.

[36]   *CB*, no. 465, p. 21. For Mao, see his February 1957 comments in "On the Correct Handling of Contradictions among the People," *WM*, II, 337-38.

[37]   See Chen Yun's January 1957 speech in Lardy and Lieberthal, *Chen Yun's Strategy*, p. 57; and Chan, "Leaders, Coalition Politics, and Policy-Formulation," pp. 68-69. In his rebuttal of Chan, Bachman, "Chinese Bureaucratic Politics," pp. 47-48, argues that Chan

The story was similar with the 40-article draft, albeit with peculiarities of its own. As we have seen in the discussion of *fanmaojin*, the agricultural program had indeed been a symbol of leaping forward in early 1956, but it had been basically shelved by the time the "opposing rash advance" approach had taken hold in the middle of the year, notwithstanding some ongoing political genuflection.[38] Mao's dissatisfaction with the symbolic aspects of this was seen in his January 1957 chiding of Liao Luyan for his (Liao's) pessimism concerning draft targets, and, perhaps heeding the Chairman's lead throughout spring and summer 1957, a range of officials made approving references to the program. These included not only the planners, but also the chastised Liao, other members of the "financial coalition" such as Deng Zihui, and Liu Shaoqi.[39] Once again, moreover, it is the *meaning* of the 40 articles in this context which is crucial. Given both resource constraints and the continuing lag in agricultural production, not to mention the growing realization since the "Ten Great Relationships" of the importance of addressing the agricultural bottleneck, reliance on the various detailed measures of the draft program to increase production was a logical approach.[40]

The critical point is that references to the 40 articles were *not* linked to excessively ambitious production targets. Bo Yibo at the summer NPC session projected a healthy but still plausible agricultural growth of 4.9 percent in 1957, and virtually the same growth rate (4.8 percent) was adopted for 1958 at the August national planning conference. Moreover, in the lead up to the Third Plenum, a Central Committee directive approved by Mao and issued shortly before the meeting called for a *reduction* in the size of cooperatives, and Deng Xiaoping's major report early in the plenum, while citing the need to struggle

---

misses the point that "self-reliance" was rhetoric at variance with the Great Leap practice of actually increasing Sino-Soviet trade and China's trade-GNP ratio. This, however, truly misses the point that both the rhetoric and policy of most of 1957 was thrift and restraining imports, while the rhetoric and reality of the Great Leap was to leap forward by whatever means ("walking on two legs"), including both the modern sector which required imports and a vastly expanded traditional sector that would necessarily be reliant on internally mobilized resources. The best study comparing the Soviet-style and Great Leap economic strategies remains K. C. Yeh, "Soviet and Chinese Communist Industrialization Strategies," in Donald W. Treadgold, *Soviet and Chinese Communism: Similarities and Differences* (Seattle: University of Washington Press, 1967).

[38]   Thus while the famous June 20, 1956, editorial still called for the realization of the program, the reality was reflected in Zhou Enlai's observation to the November plenum that it was merely a proposal that required reexamination and revision. See *Renmin ribao* [People's Daily], June 20, 1956, in *SCMP*, no. 1321, p. 11; and *Selected Works of Zhou*, II, 238-39.

[39]   See Chan, "Leaders, Coalition Politics, and Policy-Formulation," pp. 70-71; and above, p. 43.

[40]   See, e.g., the *Renmin ribao* editorial of September 7, 1957, in *SCMP*, no. 1612, pp. 14-18.

for the realization of the 40 articles, advocated frugality and the gradual expansion of agricultural capital construction.[41]

To summarize, there clearly were continuities between elements of policy that surfaced in 1956-57 or even earlier and the Great Leap, but unlike their transformed versions during the leap they were relatively secondary to the overall economic strategy which remained firmly in the Soviet mold, notwithstanding adjustments to Chinese realities.[42] These adjustments, moreover, took place in the context of modest growth and comprehensive balance policies. As Party historians acknowledge, Mao borrowed some specific programs that had been earlier developed in the bureaucracy, but they do not believe these policies formed the essence of the Great Leap. That essence, which they characterize as breakneck speed generated by ideology and mass mobilization, stood in sharp contrast to the moderate economic growth constrained by objective laws approach which characterized the policy positions of *both* planners and budgeteers in 1956-57. Before the Third Plenum such policies as small-scale enterprises were clearly auxiliary programs designed to modify, but not challenge, the Stalinist economic structure. The changes beginning with that plenum, while reflecting several factors, fundamentally came from a single source — Mao Zedong.

The Political Dynamics Leading to the Great Leap: From the Third Plenum to Nanning, September 1957-January 1958[43]

The end of *fanmaojin* and the first rumblings of the Great Leap Forward came abruptly. Not only was Li Fuchun (as had Zhou Enlai earlier in the plenum) advocating opposition to rash advance only days before Mao launched his criticism of the whole program,[44] the entire Third Plenum which lasted from September 20 to October 9 was marked by sudden, unanticipated

---

[41] *CB*, no. 465, pp. 7-9; Ma Qibin, *Zhizheng sishinian*, p. 129; *Mao wengao*, vol. 6, pp. 572-73; and *PDA*, pp. 352-53.

[42] Consider, for example, the conclusion of Jean-Luc Domenach in his careful study of Henan that before the Great Leap the attention given to small-scale industry was a relatively unimportant innovation; *The Origins of the Great Leap Forward: The Case of One Chinese Province* (Boulder: Westview Press, 1995), p. 135.

[43] An earlier version of this section appeared as Teiwes with Sun, "The Politics of an 'Un-Maoist' Interlude," pp. 171-79. The present version is largely unchanged except for some corrections and additions resulting from further research. The most significant additions concern the Third Plenum, the Hangzhou meeting, and the Nanning conference; see below, pp. 69, 73ff.

[44] See *Zhou Enlai nianpu*, vol. 2, pp. 78-79; and above, p. 45. For further evidence of the planners' commitment to modest growth at an advanced stage of the plenum, see the report of a British politician who met Bo Yibo in what must have been the first week of October and received the impression that a downward revision of targets was likely; Desmond Donnelly, *The March Wind: Explorations behind the Iron Curtain* (London: Collins, 1959), pp. 228, 238-41. Cf. MacFarquhar, *Origins 2*, p. 342n58.

developments on several fronts. The original agenda had focused on Party rectification and rural policy, but not overall economic strategy. Indeed, even on the closing day Deng Xiaoping's speech summarizing the plenum, at least the available portion of it, called for great efforts in the spirit of the 40 articles in agriculture, but made no effort to link this to industry. These remarks, moreover, stood in sharp contrast to the moderate rural policies in evidence as late as Deng's earlier report to the meeting on September 23.[45] Clear signs of a Great Leap approach only emerged in Mao's final pronouncement, and even then the Chairman did not present a well-articulated economic strategy, despite his insistence on the absolute necessity for a comprehensive plan coordinating industry, agriculture, commerce, culture, and education. The key, however, was greater speed, an emphasis marking a clear break with *fanmaojin's* steady growth. As Mao forcefully put it, "There are at least two methods of doing things, one producing slower and poorer results and the other faster and better ones."[46] Finally, the major political issue of the nature of the main contradiction was unexpectedly foisted upon the plenum to the consternation of the participants, and in his final two talks on October 7 and 9 Mao overturned the Eighth Congress resolution and forced adoption of the class contradiction between the proletariat and the bourgeoisie as the main contradiction.[47] This had no logical implication for economic policy, but it contributed to the subsequent political tension which became critical to the evolution of the new approach to construction.

Mao's obvious dominance at the plenum, a fact which sits uncomfortably with both the leadership conflict and institutional interpretations, was nowhere clearer than in his attack on the opposition to rash advance and the absence of any protests by those present. In his concluding speech Mao declared that a rightist deviation had occurred in 1956, and he made his famous complaint about the 40 articles, the committee for promoting progress, and *duo, kuai, hao, sheng* being blown away. Moreover, he declared that the second half of 1956 saw the slackening of class struggle "that was brought about deliberately" and resulted in the attacks of the bourgeoisie and rich peasants on the Party during the Hundred Flowers period. This stopped short of linking the *fanmaojin* program to the rightist "attack"[48] and no names of erring

---

45   *Zhonggong dangshi jiaoxue cankao ziliao* [CCP History Teaching Reference Materials], vol. 22 (n.p.: Zhongguo Jiefangjun Guofang Daxue dangshi dangjian zhenggong jiaoyanshi, May 1986), pp. 312-14.

46   *SW*, V, 490.

47   On the main contradiction issue, see Bo Yibo, *Huigu*, vol. 2, pp. 624-67; and Teiwes, "Mao Texts," especially pp. 145-46. Unlike other issues, Mao clearly placed the new approach to the main contradiction on the agenda from the outset of the plenum, having raised it initially on the eve of the meeting.

48   In fact, at this stage it is likely that Mao was referring to the political policies adopted at and following the Eighth Congress, but the link to *fanmaojin* would be made at Nanning. See below, pp. 73-74.

leaders were mentioned, thus limiting the rejection of anti-rash advance at the plenum to the realm of economic policy. Yet the sense of the correct approach of the cooperativization high tide of 1955 having been wrongly derailed was heavy in Mao's comments, and he began to talk in terms of restoring the blown aside items. Later, conveniently overlooking his own acceptance of *fanmaojin*, he claimed that the Third Plenum had restored his position. Notwithstanding the distortion involved in this claim, as a provincial leader present at the plenum put it, "there would have been no Great Leap Forward without the Third Plenum."[49]

Clearly Mao's position had shifted both theoretically and economically by the end of the Third Plenum. Who influenced the Chairman in this process? The answer is not clear given the limitations on information about the plenum, including the fact that, according a senior Party historian, its records are closed to Chinese scholars. In contrast to the apparent passivity of central bureaucracies including the SPC at the alleged moment of victory for the "planning coalition,"[50] the limited information available suggests an important influence was exerted by local leaders. With rural policy a key agenda item, the meeting was an *enlarged* plenum, a gathering that included local officials from the provincial and prefectural levels. Moreover, in his comments Mao indicated that he had discussed issues — particularly the 40 articles — with provincial figures, and argued that conferences with their participation could play a key role in combating rightism. Indeed, at the Qingdao conference the previous July Mao had ended his main speech with a request that provincial and prefectural leaders study the 40 articles to see if any changes were needed.[51] While this was posed in a neutral manner and the main rural concern of such leaders for the remainder of the summer was to reestablish control in the countryside with little indication of any new production or investment upsurge,[52] arguably given the history of the 40 articles rather than their then current usage, as well as their interest in stepped-up local development, at least some came prepared to voice enthusiastic support for overfulfilling its targets. In any case, the Chairman did make seemingly positive references to local reports on this and broader matters in the outline for his October 9 speech.[53]

---

[49]   *SW*, V, 483, 491-93; *Dangshi wenhui*, no. 2 (1989), p. 8; and oral source.

[50]   Cf. below, p.80.

[51]   *SW*, V, 482, 483, 486-87. The 40 articles were also discussed at the highest level at an August Politburo meeting; *Zhou Enlai nianpu*, vol. 2, p. 70.

[52]   See the careful discussion of the summer's events in Henan, a pathbreaking province during the subsequent Great Leap, in Domenach, *Origins of the Great Leap*, pp. 123, 131-32. Domenach concludes that rural developments in the summer cannot be said to be preparations for what came later.

[53]   *Mao wengao*, vol. 6, pp. 592-98. Mao also noted the speeches of State Technological Commission head Huang Jing who discussed agricultural mechanization, and Politburo member Peng Zhen who concurrently held a local portfolio as leader of Beijing

Further information also points to the significance of local leaders, while at the same time indicating that the fundamental pattern of influence was from Mao to all other actors. According to an authoritative Party history, the raising of the *duo, kuai, hao, sheng* slogan *by local leaders* made the Chairman "very excited" (*hen xingfen*) at the plenum, while the leading provincial figure interviewed recalled Hebei's Liu Zihou and Hunan's Wang Yanchun as the key individuals concerned.[54] Whether these leaders were responding to Mao's cues, or simply using the opportunity to articulate again their jaundiced view of opposing rash advance, is unclear, but by this account they were influencing Mao in a way potentially threatening to his top colleagues and the key central bureaucracies responsible for coordinating the economy. Yet even more suggestive of the dynamics of the occasion were Mao's recollections at the March 1958 Chengdu conference.[55] This account suggests there was little attention to *duo, kuai, hao, sheng* at the plenum initially. In the Chairman's memory, hardly anyone spoke out for "more, faster, better, more economical"; he could only recall the historian Guo Moruo (his "only bosom friend" — and someone notorious for the ability to read his mind) addressing the question. Clearly, however, Guo was not alone as some provincial leaders also voiced support. But the turning point came when Mao pressed the issue forcefully in open session (presumably on October 9). The result was applause and

municipality.

54   Hu Sheng, *Gongchandang qishinian,* p. 414; and oral source. Another source, Gu Longsheng, *Mao Zedong jingji nianpu,* p. 404, quotes Mao in his October 9 speech as declaring himself happy that participants mentioned *duo, kuai, hao, sheng* at the plenum and that he had read an essay on the same question, while Xiong Huayuan and Liao Xinwen, *Zhou Enlai Zongli shengya* [Premier Zhou Enlai's Career] (Beijing: Renmin chubanshe, 1997), p. 237, also reports Mao's expression of pleasure on the same occasion. Neither source, however, gives any indication concerning who was involved.

55   See Li Rui, *"Dayuejin" qinliji,* p. 204. Mao's comments leave important uncertainties concerning timing. He claimed to have raised *duo, kuai, hao, sheng,* the committee for promoting progress, and the 40 articles to several Politburo Standing Committee members immediately "before convening the Third Plenum" (*sanzhongquanhui kaihui qian*), literally on September 20, and subsequently "disclosing" the matter at the plenum itself at some unspecified date. The implication is that this did not produce any particular reaction except from Guo Moruo. This sequence, however, seems unlikely to us in that had Mao raised "the three things" at the very outset of the plenum (although, of course, this could have been the most casual of references to his Standing Committee colleagues) it is unlikely that Zhou Enlai would have been pushing *fanmaojin* on September 26 or that Li Fuchun would have endorsed the approach on October 5 (see above, p. 45). Rather, we believe it likely that Mao did not raise *duo, kuai, hao, sheng* until late in the plenum, most probably not before the last session on October 9; in this interpretation "before convening the Third Plenum" could actually mean "before convening the closing session of the Third Plenum." Thus *all* of the activity concerning *duo, kuai, hao, sheng* (but not the 40 articles) could have taken place on the 9th, with Mao raising the slogan, others expressing support, and "the three things" then "restored." See also below, n. 56.

approval, not a single person expressed opposition, the three things were restored, and a legal basis had been established for subsequent developments at Nanning. Thus while Mao was arguably encouraged by expressions of local enthusiasm,[56] the direction of policy shifted in response to what most of his colleagues regarded as his sudden, unanticipated change of course.

With Mao's desire for greater speed understandable given the slow economic growth in 1957 and clearly articulated at the Third Plenum, a significant additional impetus for this approach developed out of his November visit to the Soviet Union to celebrate the 40th anniversary of the Bolshevik revolution. This must be seen in terms of the background currents in the Soviet camp; as one senior Party historian recalled, the question of the transition to communism had been raised by Stalin in 1952, and picked up in a more forthcoming manner by Khrushchev at the 20th Congress in early 1956. Khrushchev not only made the transition (albeit "gradual") to communism a current task, but in rhetoric that prefigured the Great Leap's claimed that the Soviet Union's present five-year plan would both be "a new great stride forward" for the economy and would make "a big new step forward in building up a ... basis for communist society."[57] Mao's own desire for China to find a way of developing even faster than the Russians was demonstrated by his interjections during the briefings by the 34 ministries which led to the "Ten Great Relationships," and by his comments at the Third Plenum.[58]

The Moscow meetings of 1957 added a new dimension. The sense of the imminent superiority of the socialist bloc, particularly in view of the Soviet sputnik and ICBM as well as the Soviet Union's general growth rate, created a climate of optimism which Mao seemingly felt even more strongly than his Russian comrades. When Khrushchev declared that the Soviet Union would overtake the United States economically in 15 years, Mao was "inspired" (*qifa*) and set his own goal for China to surpass Britain in the same period, a public declaration that arguably fueled both his insistence on faster growth in the immediate period and his subsequent resistance to retreating as difficulties became apparent. According to Hu Qiaomu's later recollection: "Mao was extremely satisfied with this conference. Along with the launch of the sputnik,

---

56   Conceivably, while Mao intended to use the October 9 session to press his point, he became more "excited" and went further in his actual speech than indicated in his outline (see *Mao wengao*, vol. 6, p. 594) in response to the views of "certain comrades."

57   As Peter Kuhfus has argued in a personal communication, this undoubtedly oversimplifies a far more complex process within the Soviet Party and other communist parties. The point, however, is that the issue of the transition to communism was a matter of discussion within the international movement. For Stalin's cautious outlook on the transition, see J. V. Stalin, *Economic Problems of Socialism in the U.S.S.R.* (Peking: Foreign Languages Press, 1972), pp. 66-71. For Khrushchev's 20th Congress views, see N. S. Khrushchov, *Report of the Central Committee of the Communist Party of the Soviet Union* (Moscow: Foreign Languages Publishing House, 1956), pp. 97, 137-39, 143-44.

58   Bo Yibo, *Huigu*, vol. 1, p. 528; and *SW*, V, 490-91. There arguably were also more narrowly political concerns; see above, p. 57; and below, n. 77.

[he] really felt that victory was ours, [and] proposed that the east wind was prevailing over the west wind.... Chairman Mao felt we could explore an even higher rate of development [and] if the masses were mobilized ... production could experience a Great Leap Forward." So aroused, Mao called China from Moscow, criticising the 1956 *fanmaojin* as wrong, saying that [it] should not be proposed again, and that building socialism must be a bit rash. Thus his Soviet visit left Mao encouraged by both the prospect of overcoming the imperialist enemy and the economic possibilities of the communist camp, and in the process further stimulated his considerable nationalist pride. More specifically, the Chairman was also impressed with Soviet advances in the heavy industry sector, and he returned to China even more obsessed with the development of the steel industry, an issue he had already stressed at the Third Plenum.[59]

The impetus of the Third Plenum as reinforced by Mao's visit to the Soviet Union began an important shift of policy, although in key respects initially it was more rhetorical and philosophical than substantive. In mid-November the *People's Daily* used the slogan "Great Leap Forward" for the first time in an editorial that closely followed Mao's remarks shortly after the plenum. In December Bo Yibo called for a Great Leap in production and enjoined cadres not to fear imbalance, and Li Fuchun argued for adjusting the Eighth Congress targets to "let heavy industry continue to expand rapidly." By this time similar rhetoric was being propagated by the SPC in the form of *relaying the instructions of Mao Zedong*, a clear sign that the Chairman's new orientation was having a direct impact on planning work. Yet the rhetoric was combined with a substantive caution, at least in Beijing. Speaking four days after the plenum Mao still endorsed the existing modest 15-year steel target. Moreover, a mid-December *People's Daily* editorial, while emphasizing *duo, kuai, hao, sheng*, declared that facts had proven the decrease in capital construction entirely correct. And until the end of the year both the SPC and SEC, perhaps influenced by the fact that Mao had advocated a *realistic* "more, faster, better, more economical" guideline at the plenum, still produced relatively restrained plans, with Li Fuchun's SFYP targets generally only marginally higher than those in the proposals put to the Eighth Congress by Zhou Enlai, and the targets for grain actually *lower*.[60] The new thrust had

---

59   Cong Jin, *Quzhe fazhan*, p. 105; *Bainianchao* [The Hundred Years' Tide], no. 6 (1997), p. 16; and *Mianhuai Mao Zedong*, pp. 67-68. Cong claims that Mao obtained the backing of "central leaders" in Beijing before unveiling the "overtake Britain" slogan in Moscow on November 18, but the individuals involved were not revealed. For overviews of the Moscow meetings and Mao's trip, see Donald S. Zagoria, *The Sino-Soviet Conflict, 1956-61* (Princeton: Princeton University Press, 1962), ch. 4; and MacFarquhar, *Origins 2*, ch. 1. Cf. Bo Yibo's discussion in *Huigu*, vol. 2, pp. 717-18, of the Chairman's late 1957 emphasis on the struggle with the imperialist camp following his return from Moscow. For Mao's concern with steel at the Third Plenum and subsequently before departing for the Soviet Union, see *SW*, V, 491, 512.

60   Ma Qibin, *Zhizheng sishinian*, pp. 135-37; *Mao wengao*, vol. 6, p. 594; Bo Yibo, *Huigu*,

apparently not yet worked its way through the key coordinating institutions even at the end of the year, although that would change abruptly in early 1958.

Meanwhile, however, the provinces (although apparently not yet the spending ministries[61]) responded more vigorously. At the practical level, the provinces convened conferences under the anti-right conservative banner in November-December, and approved ambitious plans for agricultural development with particular reference to water conservancy, some places even promising to meet the 40 articles' 12-year targets in two years. Symbolically, the provinces contributed greatly to the new atmosphere; for example, Henan produced the construction-oriented goal of "changing [China's] face in three years," while Zhejiang pushed Mao's new proletariat v. bourgeoisie formulation of the main contradiction. The spirit of the times was perhaps caught most succinctly in an early December Jiangsu editorial which declared: "On the agricultural front we should leap, we can leap, the question is whether we dare to leap." Three factors were arguably at work in these developments. First, it was an understandable response to the Third Plenum decisions to raise targets in the 40 articles and launch a water conservancy campaign. Second, the steps taken reflected the steady drumbeat of propaganda from the *People's Daily* and other organs in Beijing. Finally, there was the direct encouragement of Mao who, following his criticism of the economic policies of the Center at the plenum, reportedly felt the atmosphere in Beijing was depressed in comparison to the dynamic conditions in East China and undoubtedly conveyed that attitude in his late 1957 tour of the region. A case in point concerned Zhejiang's First Party Secretary Jiang Hua and then Shanghai leader Ke Qingshi using the proletariat/bourgeoisie formulation in reports to Party meetings. When Mao received a copy of Jiang Hua's report in mid-December he was reportedly "extremely happy," ordered Zhou Enlai and others to read it by the next day, assigned his leading secretaries Hu Qiaomu and Tian Jiaying to revise the report, and had it published in the *People's Daily* with an editorial note highlighting the main contradiction issue.[62]

---

vol. 2, p. 682; Cong Jin, *Quzhe fazhan*, pp. 106-107; *Zhonghuarenmingongheguo jingji dashiji* [Chronology of Economic Events in the People's Republic of China] (Changchun: Jilin renmin chubanshe, 1987), p. 138; Bachman, *Bureaucracy*, pp. 206-207; and oral sources.

61   Unlike the first leap, there is little information on ministries pushing for sharply increased targets before early 1958.

62   Bo Yibo, *Huigu*, vol. 2, pp. 629-31, 636-37, 680-81; Li Rui, *"Dayuejin" qinliji*, pp. 121-22; "unpublished Chinese document no. 2," pp. 179-80; Domenach, *Origins*, pp. 139-41; and *Mao wengao*, vol. 6, pp. 671-73. During his East China tour Mao met with provincial leaders from Shanghai, Shandong, Anhui, Jiangsu, Fujian, and Zhejiang in Hangzhou on December 16-17; *Bainianchao*, no. 6 (1997), p. 17. See Keith Forster, "Localism, Central Policy and the Provincial Purges of 1957-58: The Case of Zhejiang," in Cheek and Saich, *New Perspectives on State Socialism*, for a detailed analysis of the Zhejiang situation. The standard study of the water conservancy campaign remains

While the developments at and following the Third Plenum spelled the death of *fanmaojin* as a guiding economic program, a series of meetings, beginning in January 1958 with the Hangzhou conference and the crucial Nanning conference and extending to the Second Session of the Eighth Party Congress in May, marked a new stage which was crucial to the evolution of the Great Leap. These conferences raised the issue to a question of political line, saw the architects of the opposition of rash advance — particularly Zhou Enlai and Chen Yun — come under severe pressure that resulted in repeated self-criticisms and even an offer to resign on Zhou's part,[63] directed harsh criticism at the bureaucratic practices of the leading economic coordinating bodies, found provincial leaders exercising a crucial role, and, not least, demonstrated Mao's truly awesome power. This was nowhere more apparent than at Nanning.

Prior to the Nanning conference, however, the brief Hangzhou meeting from January 2 to 4 foreshadowed some of its key developments. In substantive terms, this small gathering with 14 mostly provincial leaders[64] addressed themes that would be stressed at the subsequent conference: the Party's methods for leading economic construction, the relationship between politics and administration (*zhengzhi yu yewu*), and technological revolution. More ominously, in a taste of things to come Mao not only criticized Zhou Enlai by name, but lost his temper. In his own subsequent words, "I set fire (*fang huo*) to Enlai, I had Old Ke [Qingshi] to back me up. In Hangzhou I really couldn't hold it back any longer [and] let off several years of anger at Bo Yibo [saying] I won't listen to your stuff, what are you talking about? I haven't read the budgets for the past few years, it's just been you pressing me to sign my name to them." Thus the stage was set for the Nanning meeting from January 11 to 22 where a fundamental change took place in the CCP's political processes.[65]

In an extraordinary outburst at Nanning, Mao seriously criticized two members of the Politiburo Standing Committee in Zhou and Chen Yun, as well as Li Xiannian and Bo Yibo, thus encompassing both financial and planning leaders; of these he regarded Chen Yun the principal culprit. Pinpointing June 1956 to January 1957 as the period of *fanmaojin* dominance, Mao circulated as negative materials the June 20, 1956, *People's Daily*

Oksenberg, "Policy Formulation in Communist China." There is confusion concerning responsibility for the "changing [China's] face in three years" slogan, with Bo (p.681) attributing it to Anhui, but more credibility must be given to Mao's 1958 attribution to Henan ("unpublished Chinese document no. 6," p. 143).

63 For the post-Nanning developments on these points, see below, pp. 92, 97-99. For a selection of self-criticisms by the concerned leaders, see Appendix 2.

64 See the list of participants in Appendix 1.1, pp. 233-34.

65 *Bainianchao*, no. 6 (1997), p. 17; Bo Yibo, *Huigu*, vol. 2, p. 637; and *Mao wengao*, vol. 7, p. 10. According to our interview with a leading provincial official, he did not think that Mao's criticism at Hangzhou was so serious, or that it had raised the matter to a question of "line."

editorial, Li Xiannian's speech to the NPC the same month, and Zhou's speech to the November 1956 Second Plenum. The Chairman also ordered the assembled officials never again to use the *fanmaojin* concept, explicitly linked opposing rash advance to stimulating the rightists' attacks on the Party, and most threateningly asserted that those guilty of the error stood "only 50 meters from the rightists." Despite the warning signals at Hangzhou, these developments clearly caught the affected leaders by surprise. Zhou Enlai was not entirely unprepared for Mao's criticisms, but their gravity was completely unexpected. Nearly every night, Li Xiannian and Bo Yibo would come to the Premier's place and talk until two or three in the morning, discussing how to make their self-criticisms. Thus Mao's actions sent shockwaves through the assembled participants and created the political pressure which drove the leap to such extremes. Indeed, Mao subsequently declared that without the Nanning conference there would have been no Great Leap Forward.[66]

Mao's performance at Nanning created a situation both at the conference and subsequently where it became impossible to say anything different. The Nanning meeting itself was a small gathering of 20-plus leaders, initially convened so Mao could hear reports from provincial leaders representing China's various regions and the provinces near Nanning. At the suggestion of Zhou Enlai, the 1958 plan was placed on the agenda and top economic officials Li Fuchun, Li Xiannian, Bo Yibo, and the Ministers of Metallurgy and Machine Building were summoned, although Chen Yun managed to stay away. The speeches of provincial Party secretaries were particularly influential in the heightened atmosphere, and several of these followed Mao's lead to make severe criticisms of the *fanmaojin* culprits; particularly notable were the direct attacks of Guangdong First Secretary Tao Zhu on Zhou Enlai and Shanghai's Ke Qingshi on the absent Chen Yun. Meanwhile Ke Qingshi, Hubei's Wang Renzhong, and Sichuan's Li Jingquan were singled out for the Chairman's praise. Wang Renzhong was lauded for Hubei's ambitious undertaking to complete its ten-year plan in six years, while Mao's favoritism toward provincial leaders generally was reflected in his comment that the *People's Daily* and the central organization and propaganda departments should learn from the localities. But pride of place went to Ke Qingshi, with Mao praising Ke's December report to a Shanghai Party conference, aggressively asking Zhou Enlai whether he could write anything as good, drawing the contrast with "central work comrades" who could hardly use their brains, and advising that "everyone must learn from Old Ke." Indeed, the contrast with Zhou could not have been greater, as shortly after the conference

---

[66]   *Dangshi wenhui*, no. 2 (1989), p. 8; Cong Jin, *Quzhe fazhan*, pp. 111-12; Li Rui, "*Dayuejin*" *qinliji*, pp. 219-20; Bo Yibo, *Huigu*, vol. 2, p. 639; *Bainianchao*, no. 6 (1997), p. 18; *Women de Zhou Zongli*, p. 303; *Mao Zedong sixiang wansui* [Long Live Mao Zedong Thought], vol. 2 [1958-59] (n.p.: n.d.), p. 223; *Hongqi* [Red Flag], no. 13 (1981), p. 66; and oral sources. For a brief excerpt from Zhou's self-criticism, see Appendix 2.1, pp. 245-46.

the Premier lost his "right to speak" on economic matters.[67]

The enthusiasm and influence of local leaders was undoubtedly largely due to the faith Mao had placed in them at a time of his alienation from his ranking colleagues and the economic bureaucracies; this was probably a more significant factor than any organizational interests. In contrast, the representatives from central government bodies reportedly said little during the meeting, although "a leading comrade of an industrial ministry" openly criticized Chen Yun as the representative of *fanmaojin* thinking.[68] The relative quiescence of such representatives is hardly surprising in that, apart from the individuals involved in *fanmaojin*, Mao also launched a wide-ranging critique of the central bureaucracies, including the SPC,[69] the Ministry of Finance, and the heavy industrial ministries, denouncing "these people who commit economic dogmatism" and were responsible for eight years of this erroneous work style, and complaining about their documents which couldn't be digested and the dispersionism of State Council organizations which prevented coherent Party direction of their activities.[70]

What is striking is that Mao's criticism included not only the central coordinating agencies — both planning and financial — which had enforced *fanmaojin* — but the spending ministries that had strained against the leash of "opposing rash advance." Equally significant was the comparative silence of the leaders of these ministries during the proceedings. Of particular note was Minister of Metallurgy Wang Heshou. Given Mao's preoccupation with steel

---

67   Bo Yibo, *Huigu*, vol. 2, pp. 637, 639; *Mao wengao*, vol. 7, pp. 11-12; "unpublished Chinese document no. 2," pp. 182, 185, 192, 194; Li Rui, *"Dayuejin" qinliji*, pp. 15, 73; *SS*, p. 394; Xiong Huayuan and Liao Xinwen, *Zhou Enlai Zongli shengya*, p. 243; and oral sources. With regard to Chen Yun, Chen was on Mao's original list of those who should participate, but in the event he did not turn up. Cf. the discussion in Teiwes, *Politics and Purges*, pp. xxviii-xxix, lxv, of Chen's propensity and the top leadership's ability more generally (although there is no firm evidence in this instance) to use sick leave as a convenient way of avoiding unpalatable political situations. For a complete list of participants, see Appendix 1.2, p. 234.

68   *Chen Yun yu jingji jianshe*, pp. 62-63; Sun Yeli and Xiong Lianghua, *Gongheguo jingji fengyun zhong de Chen Yun* [Chen Yun in the PRC's Economic Storm] (Beijing: Zhongyang wenxian chubanshe, 1996), p. 137; and interview with participant at Nanning. As to the identity of the industrial official who criticized Chen, the only possibilities present at Nanning were Wang Heshou (Metallurgy), Zhao Erlu (First Machine Building), and Huang Jing (State Technological Commission). We speculate that the individual was Huang Jing given apparent past differences with Chen; see below, n. 72.

69   A Party historian who has specialized on the conference knows of no statement at Nanning by SPC head Li Fuchun, the most prominent representative of the alleged "winning coalition."

70   "Unpublished Chinese document no. 2," pp. 186, 192; *Mao wengao*, vol. 7, pp. 24, 108, 112; Cong Jin, *Quzhe fazhan*, p. 130; MacFarquhar, *Origins 2*, pp. 24-26; and oral sources.

and Wang's prominent role as the leap shifted into high gear in the following months (see Chapter 3), one could expect strong advocacy from Wang and his ministry at the outset. But this does not appear to have been the case. According to an unusually well-informed source, at the Nanning conference Wang did not play a particularly big role; moreover, Wang's own recollection of the meeting emphasizes Mao's initiative in calling for expanded construction of smelting plants. The fact of being included in Mao's withering criticism was seemingly more significant than any possible institutional advantage, much as Wang's subsequent activism is more understandable as a response to the Chairman's advocacy than as the articulation of organizational interests.[71]

While the above indicates the tension and menace created by Mao's actions at Nanning,[72] it does not capture the full nature of the extraordinary relationship between the Chairman and his leadership colleagues as revealed at the meeting. According to a close student of this conference, apart from the shock of Mao's severe criticisms, the gathering had all the qualities of a big class. Mao was the teacher, lecturing his charges who sat passively in their seats striving to understand the meaning of their leader. Some of the most powerful leaders of the Chinese Party and state said little and mainly listened as the Chairman delivered four speeches and made extensive interjections on reports by local leaders. They, as well as their lower-ranking comrades in attendance, wanted Mao to talk more so that they could better understand his views. For Mao's part, he focused on theory and methodology[73] rather than concrete plans, attempting to infuse a new attitude that would cast aside conservatism and produce all-out efforts and innovation. He now emphasized "technological revolution" as the key task, thus fusing visionary economic goals with the political pressures he created at Nanning. The net result was not only to silence any doubts but also to generate real enthusiasm.[74]

---

71   *Mianhuai Mao Zedong*, pp. 69-70; and oral source.

72   In "The Politics of an 'Un-Maoist' Interlude," p. 175, we cited the example of State Technological Commission head Huang Jing sobbing and kneeling before the Chairman as indicative of this tension and menace. We now believe this must be modified due to evidence from an oral source that Huang was having psychological problems quite independent of developments at Nanning, although those developments seemingly exacerbated his problem. It further seems the case that Huang would not have been a major target of Mao's displeasure at Nanning given apparent differences he had with the Chen Yun approach. Thus Mao noted in March 1958 that, at the January 1957 conference of provincial secretaries where Chen Yun's ideas prevailed (see above, pp. 42-43), Huang had "different opinions" on economic questions, something which is consistent with our analysis of the tension between spending ministries and the push for *fanmaojin*; see Li Rui, *"Dayuejin" qinliji*, p. 248. Cf. above, n. 68.

73   See below, pp. 85ff.

74   This enthusiasm extended well beyond the actual participants at the conference; e.g., see below, pp. 84-85, 115. On the "technological revolution," see *Dang de wenxian*, no. 6 (1991), pp. 11-16.

Party historians in interviews unanimously see the origins of the Great Leap Forward in Mao, and advise studying Mao's thinking for an understanding of the leap since it was "fundamentally a product" of his thought. But in contrast to *fanmaojin*, the emergence of the Great Leap did not involve the same sort of complex interaction of supreme leader, top economic policy makers, coordinating bureaucracies, spending ministries, and localities. All were of course concerned with the process, but as all sources attest there was no expressed opposition to either the excessive charges against opposition to rash advance or the headlong drive to a new and unprecedented economic strategy. While provincial leaders enthusiastically led the charge, the planning bureaucracies scrambled to adjust,[75] and Zhou Enlai, Li Xiannian, and Bo Yibo at Nanning,[76] and later Chen Yun, engaged in self-criticism, it was, as a senior Party historian claimed, truly a case of the whole Party following Mao. The questions which remain are why the elite as a whole went along with the Chairman, and what led Mao to reject *fanmaojin* and subsequently opt for the Great Leap Forward.

To address the later question first, clearly a number of factors influenced Mao, some of which have been well covered in the existing literature. Undoubtedly the Chairman's oft-expressed desire, even when endorsing opposition to rash advance in 1956, for rapid growth was a fundamental consideration, one which perhaps became more salient by fall 1957 as the likelihood of continued slower growth sunk in. At this juncture Mao seemingly was at once impatient with slow growth, encouraged by the completion of FFYP targets ahead of schedule, and angry that, in his view, *fanmaojin* had prevented greater economic achievements. Belief in the inadequacy of the Soviet model — something shared by the key architects of *fanmaojin* as well as Mao — arguably prompted him to seek an even more radical Chinese alternative, while the unreliability of the "bourgeois intellectuals" who were to play such a key role in economic construction in the Eighth Congress vision but could no longer be trusted in the same way after the Hundred Flowers fiasco probably turned him toward the "masses" and away from the pro-bourgeoisie economic measures he had endorsed in late 1956. Also, looking back from the perspective of late 1957, the seeming ease of the victory of cooperativization in 1955 undoubtedly encouraged Mao to believe a similar mass mobilization approach could produce great achievements in construction. And international factors, both in terms of optimism resulting from the alleged new balance of forces in favor of the socialist camp and a nationalist pride to match if not surpass the deeds of the Soviet Union, were surely a contributing factor in Mao's intensified desire for rapid growth.[77]

---

[75]   See below, pp. 86-88.

[76]   *Bainianchao*, no. 6 (1997), p. 18.

[77]   See Teiwes, "Establishment," pp. 139-42; and MacFarquhar, *Origins 2*, pp. 3-4. Regarding the Soviet factor, Mao had long bridled at real and imagined Soviet slights,

Arguably, however, it was Mao's interpretation of political developments in 1957 which were crucial in his changing assessment. This had both positive and negative aspects, and reflected profoundly subjective judgments reflecting both history and personal psychology. On the positive side, from the time of the Third Plenum Mao interpreted the Anti-Rightist Campaign as completing the victory of socialist transformation on the political and ideological fronts, in contrast to the Party's (and his own) earlier conclusion that the transformation of ownership patterns in 1955-56 had secured that victory. The larger point was that the CCP was now truly in a position to shift work to economic construction and, to use one of the Chairman's favorite early 1958 concepts, the technological revolution. This, of course, confused cowing political dissidence with creating a genuine national consensus on a new program, but it fit Mao's preconception of the role of Party rectification. At the outset of the 1957 rectification he drew parallels with the Yan'an campaign, seeing both as movements creating a new unity of concept and will to achieve famous victories, in the then present context of national development. While the nature of the developmental effort was changing dramatically by the end of 1957, Mao insisted on the same notion that a unification of thought would in turn produce economic success. Significantly, he continued to emphasize the theme of rectification up to the May 1958 Congress, in this case to complete the process of unifying thought throughout the whole Party and especially among economic decision makers.[78]

This leaves the negative and more psychological consideration to be canvassed, a consideration at the heart of Mao's rationale for attacking *fanmaojin* and the generation of the pressure which gave shape to the Great Leap. This was Mao's linking of the serious political challenge to Party rule perceived by the leadership during the Hundred Flowers and the economic policies of opposing rash advance. While only making the case implicitly at the Third Plenum but explicitly at Nanning, the Chairman argued that *fanmaojin* encouraged bourgeois intellectuals to launch the rightist onslaught of 1957. This linkage was a gross exaggeration of reality as economic issues were only a minor part of the critical opinions offered by intellectuals in

---

even while accepting the Soviet Union's leadership of the international movement. According to senior Party historians, and consistent with much Western analysis, the death of Stalin greatly affected Mao in the sense of removing an obstacle to the greater pursuit of China's status *vis-à-vis* Moscow.

[78] See *Mao wengao*, vol. 6, pp. 651, 672, vol. 7, pp. 108, 202, 205; *Xuexi ziliao*, vol. 2, pp. 143, 148; "Dangdai Zhongguo de jingji guanli" bianjibu ["Contemporary China Economic Administration" Editorial Department], ed., *Zhonghuarenmingongheguo jingji guanli dashiji* [Chronology of Events in Economic Administration in the PRC] (Beijing: Zhongguo jingji chubanshe, 1986), p. 105; Li Chen, ed., *Zhonghuarenmingongheguo shilu* [True Record of the PRC], vol. 2, part 1, *Quzhe yu fazhan — tansuo daolu de jianxin* [Complications and Development — Hardships on the Path of Exploration] (Changchun: Jilin renmin chubanshe, 1994), pp. 102, 138, 148; and Teiwes, *Politics and Purges*, pp. 176-77, 261-62.

spring 1957, and especially since Mao's own efforts to promote "blooming and contending" had far more to do with the outpouring of criticism than any residual influence of *fanmaojin*.[79] Nevertheless this was a major preoccupation for Mao, one that seemed to intensify in repeated comments during the period from Nanning to the Second Session as he denounced the "bourgeois rightist" opinions of the Hundred Flowers period and apparently devised policies at least in part to refute such views. Thus, for example, he not only denounced rightist criticisms of the lack of separation of the Party and government, but used this to propose that Party first secretaries grasp economic work.[80] While the point remains speculative, Mao's anger at the "rightists" who caused the Hundred Flowers to blow up in his face apparently led to the spurious drawing of parallels between the views of bourgeois intellectuals in spring 1957 and those of his top colleagues throughout 1956-57, reinforced his impatience to break with the modest growth policies of the immediate past, and became an elemental force driving the process forward.[81]

As to why the elite followed Mao so comprehensively, it is, of course, impossible to determine precise motivations. Nevertheless, discussions with Party historians point to the two somewhat contradictory factors already noted — fear and belief. The systematic violation of inner Party democracy was traced to Mao's performance at Nanning,[82] and the impossibility of speaking out in the circumstances created where economic policy had been transformed into a question of political line was repeatedly emphasized by oral sources. Moreover, Mao's mobilization of provincial leaders against his central colleagues and their willing response, while not necessary for the Chairman's dominance, served to damage both inner Party norms and established status relationships. Yet at the same time various Party historians assert that collective leadership still applied in the early stages of the Great Leap because there was broad agreement. While Mao clearly pressured his colleagues into accepting the particular methodology of the leap, they appear to have been sympathetic to his goals and willing to be "persuaded"; as one participant in

[79]   See Teiwes, *Politics and Purges*, pp. 212, 226.

[80]   "Unpublished Chinese document no. 2," pp. 185-86, 195-96; and Bo Yibo, *Huigu*, vol. 2, p. 650. For other examples, see *Dang de wenxian*, no. 2 (1992), p. 54; and "unpublished Chinese document no. 4," p. 73. While the analysis here is our own, a senior Party historian made an unprompted statement pointing to the importance of Mao linking *fanmaojin* and the rightist "attack."

[81]   See the references to Mao's anger at Nanning and the Second Session in *Dang de wenxian*, no. 2 (1990), p. 10; and Bo Yibo, *Huigu*, vol. 2, p. 642. Other distortions from this period include Mao's claim that the "blowing away" of the 40 articles, etc. represented opposition activities against legal policies, and, similarly, his seeming sense that Zhou Enlai's effort at the November 1956 plenum to promote *fanmaojin* was an act of betrayal. See *Mao wengao*, vol. 7, pp. 204-205.

[82]   Cf. Liao Kai-lung (Liao Gailong), "Historical Experiences and Our Road of Development," Part II, *Issues & Studies*, November 1981, p. 90; and Teiwes, *Politics and Purges*, pp. l-lvi.

the meetings of the period observed, the belief that Mao had somehow discovered a new way to rapid development was paramount at this early stage of the Great Leap. In part, oral sources assert, such faith was due to the continuing high prestige of Mao who was seen, notwithstanding the hiccup of the Hundred Flowers, as having been consistently correct in leading the CCP from victory to victory.[83] Yet it also reflected a common desire for a strong and modern China, a genuine consensus on the desirability of rapid growth and the nation standing on its own feet — instincts similar to those which had gripped the leadership in late 1955 before excesses necessitated opposition to rash advance.

While there are similarities between the situations surrounding the first leap and Great Leap — political pressure for rapid growth following tense campaigns dealing with noneconomic issues, an anti-rightist guideline which made moderation difficult to achieve, criticism of high-ranking leaders for rightist deviations, and a widespread desire in the elite and population for economic development — there are also striking differences which contributed to curbing excesses in the former case and to allowing them to get totally out of hand in the latter. These differences had little to do with preexisting leadership conflict as Mao not only was unchallenged in either period, but also because a clear hierarchy and largely cooperative relations among other leaders kept elite politics generally harmonious and individual leaders' positions secure until Mao's onslaught of January 1958. Nor did the differences have much to do with organizational interests: in both periods spending ministries[84] and localities sought more resources which brought them into tension with the coordinating agencies, albeit with different manifestations as the leap developed.[85] As for the planning organs, which had joined in the enthusiasm for the little leap before implementing *fanmaojin*, their particular role in the origins of the Great Leap was succinctly summed up by a ministerial-level figure in the "planning and heavy industry coalition" who commented that "the SPC was absolutely passive."[86] In contrast, the

---

[83]   Cf. Bo Yibo's observation, *Huigu*, vol. 2, p. 652, that "Chairman Mao's prestige was so high that everyone respected him. When he said something, everyone acted accordingly." See also above, p.13.

[84]   Although seemingly slower off the mark (see above, n. 61), by early 1958 ministries were participating in the escalation of targets (see "unpublished Chinese document no. 3," p. 272) and, according to our central bureaucrat of the time (above, p. 17), were quite cognizant of the opportunities presented to fulfill their organizational missions.

[85]   For these manifestations, see below, pp. 114-15. Initially, however, the tension was quite similar to the earlier period. In a revealing incident at Nanning, Ke Qingshi complained to Mao that Chen was unduly tight with funds for provincial development, specifically citing Chen's refusal to approve a large gas project in Shanghai; Li Rui, *"Dayuejin" qinliji*, pp. 15, 57.

[86]   See Teiwes, "Leaders, Institutions, and the Origins of the Great Leap Forward," p. 244. When directly questioned concerning Bachman's argument that the leap originated in a bureaucratic struggle between the "planning and financial coalitions," both Party

activism of local leaders which set them apart from both the coordinating and spending bureaucracies at Nanning was seemingly rooted in Mao's perception and cultivation of them as closer to China's reality and their responsiveness to his encouragement.[87]

But the emergence of the Great Leap had everything to do with Mao's changing attitudes, concerning less — we would argue — his grand visions for China,[88] than his psychology and approach to leadership. In 1956 Mao was willing to listen to others, and he demonstrated considerable respect for the CCP's economic specialists. In 1958 he concluded running the economy was "no big deal" and took control himself.[89] In 1955 Mao had harshly criticized Deng Zihui over agricultural cooperativization, but this paled in comparison to the ferocity and sweep of his attack on the authors of *fanmaojin* which made impossible any reasoned response to excesses in 1958. Perhaps crucially, during the first leap Mao was building upon the perceived success of cooperativization, and while this encouraged unrealistic expectations it arguably left him in a secure frame of mind so that he could "cool down" in spring 1956 without self-reproach, or recriminations toward others. In contrast, as the Great Leap unfolded Mao lived with the memory of the Hundred Flowers failure, and he reacted with a passion that directed blame elsewhere and brooked no interference. While the widely shared desire for a rapidly developing China had inhibited the implementation of *fanmaojin*, it

---

historians and participants unanimously rejected this view. Such sources readily accept differences in the organizational missions of the two "coalitions" (although not the implication that these groupings operated as close knit bureaucratic alliances in competition with the "opposing coalition"), but they see a generally cooperative relationship between the leaders of the respective groupings and a basic agreement up to the Third Plenum of both planners and budgeteers on fundamental economic strategy. Moreover, as a bureaucratic participant at the time observed, there was no comparison in terms of bureaucratic clout between the Ministry of Finance and the planning organs. Under the Soviet-style arrangement (which did not change in this respect during the Great Leap) the planners reigned supreme while the financial officials were much less important, regarded, in the words of our source, as mere accountants.

[87]   Of course, not all local officials can be classified as fervent supporters of the leap forward, as the purge of significant numbers of provincial leaders beginning in December 1957 indicates. See below, p. 91.

[88]   Mao's changing thought is *the* explanation for the Great Leap as far as Party historians are concerned, but they tend to focus on various intellectual influences, such as Marxist theory, Mao's early interest in utopian writings, the legacy of traditional Chinese thought, and contemporary Soviet ideology, as well as on contextual factors, such as the struggle atmosphere generated by the Anti-Rightist Campaign, international developments, and the lack of sufficient experience to allow proper evaluation of exaggerated claims of production successes. Cf. Bo Yibo, *Huigu*, vol. 2, pp. 767-76.

[89]   *Mao Zedong sixiang wansui*, vol. 2 ([Taibei]: 1969), p. 192. Cf. Lee, *Industrial Management*, p. 61.

did not prevent the eventual success of that program given the energy and prestige of Zhou Enlai and Chen Yun, and Mao's willingness to support their efforts. But when this desire was linked to a headstrong Mao in a political context where *no one* was willing to attempt to ameliorate his passions, the result was inevitably excesses followed by disaster.

Chapter 3

POLICY MAKING WHILE LEAPING FORWARD, 1958

What was the nature of economic policy making and CCP politics more broadly once the Great Leap approach became unambiguously dominant by early 1958[1] through its utopian phase which began to wane in the late fall of the same year? The patterns revealed at the Nanning conference continued to prevail throughout this period — above all the dominance of Mao Zedong. Mao's exceptional authority was not unique to the new period, it rather reflected the fundamental leadership equation since 1949: whenever Mao forcefully expressed a preference he prevailed regardless of the forces arrayed behind contrary views, and extremely few actors ever contemplated opposing the Chairman in such circumstances.[2] Yet this authority *was* different in that it was now asserted in a manner which precluded discussion and brought enormous political pressure to bear on the (earlier) proponents of contrasting views; while Mao clearly gained the willing support of an overwhelming majority of the leadership, it was in essence a move to one-man dictatorship.

Apart from the new tone of Mao's overall political dominance, the situation in 1958 was also different because the Chairman now took direct managerial control of the economy. Mao could no longer swallow the view that only experts could manage the economy; in essence it became a case of the real commander taking over economic affairs. Mao's direct control was manifest throughout, whether initially when he saw running the economy as "no big deal," or at the time of the 1959 Lushan meeting when a somewhat chastened Chairman emotionally exclaimed that "in 1958 and 1959 I should

---

[1]   Party historians differ among themselves in dating the start of the Great Leap, with the fall 1957 Third Plenum as the earliest date and the January Nanning conference, the May Second Session of the Eighth Party Congress, and even the August 1958 Beidaihe conference also proposed. From our perspective, the decisive point was the Nanning conference, although the political momentum continued to develop and extend throughout the Party through to the Second Session, and the specific policies evolved over the nine months or so following Nanning.

[2]   The most noteworthy exception was Deng Zihui's brief argument with Mao over the speed of agricultural cooperativization in June-July 1955, an argument which led worried colleagues to fear that Deng would risk "bringing disaster" by continuing to argue with the Chairman; see Teiwes and Sun, *The Politics of Agricultural Cooperativization*, pp. 13-15.

take the main responsibility [for failures and shortcomings in construction and planning], you should blame me ... for I have indeed taken charge of a great many things...."[3] But while Mao was the central actor, of course he was not the sole story. Other leaders and institutions played their roles too, and bureaucratic tensions again became manifest. Once again, however, these tensions had little relation to competing planning and financial "coalitions" but more to do with the conflicting roles of spending and coordinating agencies, while the localities played a far more influential role in shaping economic policy than previously, and all actors fundamentally responded to Mao's cues — both explicit and imagined. All of these points will become clear as our discussion unfolds.

Although our analysis in this and the following chapter will refine existing understandings of Mao's dominance and role in the pre-Lushan stage of the Great Leap, the aim is broader, in accord with the overall design of this study. We seek to illuminate the roles of the key actors interacting with Mao under the transformed Great Leap policy process — the Chairman's leadership colleagues, members of his personal staff (uniquely accessible for this period in contrast to the preceding years), the central Party apparatus now exercising a major economic role for the first time, key central economic bureaucracies including both coordinating and spending agencies, and provincial leaders. In examining these actors in this chapter we consider the process leading to ever more radical objectives and increased targets from early 1958 well into the fall. Why did this process develop as it did, and who bore what responsibility? How were policy making and bureaucratic relationships transformed as a result?

Pursuing Utopia, January-November 1958

The Nanning conference set in motion a process of utopian dreaming and ever-escalating economic targets which reached a fever pitch by November 1958 when Mao began a "cooling down" process (see Chapter 4) at the first Zhengzhou conference.[4] Throughout this process a number of features present at Nanning or earlier were prominent: policy emerging from the dynamics of high-level Party meetings, Mao's method of using ideological concepts ("letting ideology loose" in the words of one senior Party historian) to create the circumstances for economic innovation, unrelenting although evolving political pressure, a widespread impatience for economic development among

---

3   *The Case of Peng Teh-huai* (Hong Kong: Union Research Institute, 1968), pp. 25, 411; and above, p. 81. While Mao claimed his directing role began in August 1958, in fact it had been apparent from the start of the year.

4   Bo Yibo, *Huigu*, vol. 2, p. 690, cites November as the time when the fever of escalating targets reached its high point, while later Bo (p. 806) designates September and October as the "peak" of the Great Leap.

high-ranking Party leaders[5] as well as ordinary cadres and the populace, a mix of belief and coercion motivating all levels of the Party, the prominence of provincial leaders in driving the movement forward, an impetus provided by nationalist sentiments, and disruption of the well-established bureaucratic procedures of the previous eight years.

While meetings were a familiar feature of CCP policy making, the early months of the Great Leap Forward saw a significant innovation. Previously, important policy-formulating meetings were largely formal sessions of established bodies such as the Central Committee or the State Council, or conferences organized by functional system (*xitong*) or administrative level. Now, starting with Nanning,[6] and lasting well beyond the "fever pitch" of the leap, Mao called a series of *ad hoc* conferences. He strictly controlled the agendas as well as the participants of these meetings, and personally dominated the proceedings of each. Participation normally reflected the agenda, and not all Politburo members attended the various conferences. (See Appendix 1 for lists of participants at various Party meetings in 1958-59.) Particularly significant participants were various combinations of China's provincial leaders which afforded Mao the opportunity to give direct guidance to these most active proponents of the leap forward, while at the same time giving them access to the Chairman. During the utopian phase of the leap, the most important meetings in addition to Nanning were the March Chengdu conference, the more formal Second Session of the Eighth Party Congress in May, and the August Beidaihe conference.[7]

These meetings saw the introduction of new ideological themes, the escalation of production targets, and the building of political pressure. At Nanning Mao articulated the "politics in command" approach to development,

---

5   According to the memoirs of Tao Lujia, then Party first secretary of Shanxi, *Yige shengwei shuji huiyi Mao Zhuxi* [A Provincial Party Secretary Remembers Chairman Mao] (Taiyuan: Shanxi renmin chubanshe, 1993), pp. 94-95, the absolute majority of leading cadres at and above the provincial department level were impatient with China's "poor and blank" situation and believed deeply in the prospects of changing it. A second book by Tao Lujia, *Mao Zhuxi jiao women dang shengwei shuji* [Chairman Mao Teaches Us Provincial Secretaries] (Beijing: Zhongyang wenxian chubanshe, 1996), largely covers the same material but organizes it differently.

6   Actually with the early January Hangzhou conference; see above, p. 73.

7   The most detailed studies of these meetings are found in "unpublished Chinese documents nos. 2-5." Other conferences convened by Mao in this period were the April Wuhan and Guangzhou meetings; see Li Rui, *"Dayuejin" qinliji*, pp. 262-76. Apart from the conferences themselves, during this period Mao further pushed ahead Great Leap themes through a series of *People's Daily* editorials and other articles he personally supervised or revised. See *Mao wengao*, vol. 7, pp. 6-7, 67, 110, 177-79, 302-303, 307-308, 434-35, 447-48; and Wu Lengxi, *Yi Mao Zhuxi — Wo jinsheng jingli ruogan zhongda lishi shijian pianduan* [Remembering Chairman Mao — Fragments of My Personal Experience with Certain Major Historical Events] (Beijing: Xinhua chubanshe, 1995), pp. 49-50, 57, 60.

with its emphasis on the human factor and enthusiasm from below, its call for amateurs to lead experts who in the past got lost in their own professions, its claim that the FFYP stress on economic laws and balance was mere superstition, and its dismissal of the entire "dogmatic" methodology of the central planners which was based on the Soviet model. A particularly major impact was created by Mao's theory of "uninterrupted revolution" (*buduan geming*) which, in the words of a leading Party historian, became "an ideological weapon for carrying out the Great Leap." This approach was codified shortly after Nanning in Mao's "60 Articles on Work Methods" which included the input of conference participants, most notably provincial leaders. Significantly, while Liu Shaoqi's contribution in drafting an "important" point on "rules and regulations" has long been noted, in the overall process the role of Mao's Politburo colleagues such as Liu was decidedly secondary to that of local leaders. While Liu did indeed draft the article on rules and regulations, it was apparently his only contribution and came "after consultations with comrades working in the localities." The experiences of "the localities and basic levels," moreover, provided a broader input into the document. And the ongoing role of provincial enthusiasm was seen in a report on the 60 articles by Henan's Wu Zhipu, who was fast becoming a Great Leap bellwether, which praised "uninterrupted revolution" as providing courage for leaping forward and destroying the *fanmaojin* viewpoint — a report Mao ordered distributed to the entire Party.[8]

Meanwhile, at a more elemental level, Nanning created the feeling that, in the words of Bo Yibo, "genuine left is better than right." In circumstances where everyone aspired to "genuine left" status but no one could be sure what degree of economic growth satisfied the requirement, upward pressure was manifest. This upward pressure, reflecting both the attacks on *fanmaojin* and discussions of the plan and budget at Nanning, nevertheless was not fully reflected in the first post-Nanning response of the planning authorities — the SEC's revised annual plan for 1958 which Bo presented to the NPC in early February. This draft was relatively restrained, with grain and cotton targets unchanged from December and steel targets only slightly raised, while the major change was a 17.8 percent increase in capital construction spending (see Table 1, pp. 36-39)[9]. The unchanged grain and cotton figures are especially notable, given, as Bo Yibo would observe in his memoirs, that the Great Leap had originated in agriculture with the Third Plenum's revised targets for the 40 articles and the decision for a mass water conservancy campaign (the "bugle

---

8   *Mao wengao*, vol. 7, pp. 30, 31, 46, 72-73; Cong Jin, *Quzhe fazhan*, pp. 109-10; "unpublished Chinese document no. 2," pp. 188, 192; Jerome Ch'en, ed., *Mao Papers: Anthology and Bibliography* (London: Oxford University Press, 1970), pp. 57, 61-64, 66-67; and Li Rui, *"Dayuejin" qinliji*, p. 86. For the text of the 60 articles, see Ch'en, *Mao Papers*, pp. 57-76; for analysis, see MacFarquhar, *Origins 2*, pp. 29-33, and Stuart R. Schram, "Mao Tse-tung and the Theory of the Permanent Revolution," *CQ*, no. 46 (1971).

9   This increase is based on Zhou Enlai's and the SEC's December 4, 1957, figure.

call" for the leap). That the key agricultural targets remained comparatively modest undoubtedly reflected the SEC's responsibility for annual planning. In a familiar pattern, however, following discussions of "the spirit of Nanning" in provincial and central units, various localities and now spending ministries presented leap forward projections in their reports to the NPC, while others quickly revised their plans. In particular, the "comparatively realistic" SEC grain and cotton targets were forced to much higher levels due to both the anti-right conservative atmosphere and the achievements of the water conservancy campaign conducted by the localities.[10] But arguably more important at this stage than the direct pressure on targets were several innovations in economic management.

In general terms, the Nanning emphasis on political leadership of the bureaucracy and criticism of the State Council's "dispersionism" stimulated the process of Party secretaries taking direct control of economic management at various levels of the system, an approach subsequently written into the 60 articles.[11] Administratively, local initiative was subsequently facilitated by a system of economic coordination regions (*jingji xiezuoqu*),[12] bodies that would play a critical role as the leap unfolded, while one of the leading bodies of the previous economic policy-making apparatus, the State Construction Commission, was abolished. But undoubtedly the most important innovation coming out Nanning was the adoption of multiple sets of plans. During the conference, after presenting the SEC's "not conservative" 1958 annual plan, Bo Yibo concluded that the "feverish" conditions of the meeting meant that it would be very difficult for the SEC proposals to satisfy the demands of local leaders for faster development. To deal with the situation and "in order to avoid being called conservative," Bo proposed to Mao a system of dual accounts (i.e., one set of targets that must be achieved and a second set that should be striven for). This did not fully satisfy Mao who criticized Bo as a

---

10   Bo Yibo, *Huigu*, vol. 2, pp. 679-82, 687, 692, 720-21; "unpublished Chinese document no. 2," p. 192; and "unpublished Chinese document no. 3," p. 272. For an earlier analysis which correctly captured both the relative sobriety and future implications of the NPC session, see MacFarquhar, *Origins 2*, pp. 33-34. Note that the SEC's performance better fits our interpretation of the coordinating role of the planners than Bachman's view of a "planning and heavy industry coalition" pressing for higher targets.

11   See "unpublished Chinese document no. 2," p. 194; and Ch'en, *Mao Papers*, pp. 60, 69.

12   Zhejiang province had proposed such coordinating regions in April 1957 and gained Mao's interest and a request for a report to the Center at the time. A report was circulated in May, but the proposal did not find its way into the decentralization measures approved in fall 1957. Nevertheless, at the close of the Third Plenum Mao wrote two comments on the report and mentioned the issue in his concluding speech, and the report was published in the *People's Daily* shortly thereafter. Now, in 1958, Mao raised the issue at the March Chengdu conference, and the regions were formally established on June 1st. See *Mao wengao*, vol. 6, pp. 594, 596-97, vol. 7, pp. 108, 111; *Xuexi wenxuan*, vol. 2, p. 75; and Fang Weizhong, *Jingji dashiji*, pp. 213-14. We are indebted to Keith Forster on this question.

"middle of the roader," but it did lead to the elaboration of the proposal, with profound implications for the leap. After study, Mao inserted into the 60 articles a proposal for three sets of targets, whereby the Center's second set became the first, publicly announced must be achieved targets for the provinces which in turn had their own second set of "strive for" goals. As the system evolved, each subsequent lower level replicated the provincial situation, with the result that altogether six or seven sets of plans existed which produced great level-by-level pressure for skyrocketing targets.[13]

At this early stage, however, the building pressure had not yet produced frenzy across the board; in early March many units reportedly had not yet started to leap forward and varying opinions existed concerning the movement within the Party as a whole. This, then, was the situation when Mao convened the next key conference at Chengdu which began on March 8 and lasted nearly three weeks. As at Nanning Mao again dominated the proceedings and personally drove the Great Leap process further.[14]

Developments at the Chengdu meeting have long been better known than those at Nanning.[15] New details, however, allow for a better understanding of its dynamics. Larger than Nanning with 39 participants, these included all Politburo Standing Committee members except Zhu De, the peak planning and financial coordinators, several of Mao's secretaries and propaganda officials, two military representatives, and (making up nearly half the total) 18 provincial leaders. The underrepresented group was the spending ministries, with only the Ministers of Metallurgy (i.e., steel), Railroads, the Chemical Industry, and Agriculture present.[16] Mao's domination was complete: he addressed the meeting six times, set an agenda of 24 problems to be dealt with, formulated what would in two months' time officially become the general line of "going all out, aiming high, and achieving greater, faster, better, and more economical results in building socialism," and articulated the conference's pervading themes of launching the technological revolution, continuing criticism of rightist ideology, and smashing superstitious belief in

---

[13]   Bo Yibo, *Huigu*, vol. 2, pp. 638, 682; Ma Qibin, *Zhizheng sishinian*, p. 139; and Ch'en, *Mao Papers*, p. 60. The importance of multiple plans has long been recognized, although previously they could only be traced to the 60 articles and the circumstances of their emergence at Nanning was unknown. See, e.g., MacFarquhar, *Origins 2*, pp. 31-32.

[14]   "Unpublished Chinese document no. 3," p. 274.

[15]   Due in particular to the Red Guard texts of several of Mao's key statements to the conference; see Stuart Schram, ed., *Mao Tse-tung Unrehearsed, Talks and Letters: 1956-71* (Harmondsworth: Penguin Books, 1974), pp. 96-124. A state-of-the-art summary of the meeting as of the early 1980s is MacFarquhar, *Origins 2*, ch. 3; a later analysis incorporating subsequent material is Schoenhals, *Saltationist Socialism*, pp. 25-33, 46-47.

[16]   See Appendix 1.3, pp. 235-36, for a full list of participants.

both experts and Soviet practice. The Chairman's key concern, and the core of the conference, was the need for greater speed in economic construction.[17]

Mao emphasized the *political* significance of the speed question by again harping on the *fanmaojin* issue — on this occasion contrasting the "anti-Marxist opposition to rash advance" with "Marxist rash advance." In addition to the Chairman, "various local comrades" also addressed the issue of the speed of construction. But perhaps the best sense of the urgency of the matter at Chengdu was provided by one of the conference's most prominent figures, Mao's secretary Chen Boda.[18] Chen told the meeting that under the new conditions created by the rectification campaign and anti-rightist struggle "one day was the equivalent of 20 years," and central and provincial leaders should act according to this situation — remarks which secured Mao's strong approval. This preoccupation was further manifested in significantly increased production targets, even if these were to pale in comparison with those of the following months. Here the multiple plans method produced its first dramatic results, with the conference approving the first "must achieve" targets approved at the February NPC which called for comparatively sober 1958 increases over 1957 in the output values of industry (14.6 percent) and agriculture (6.1 percent), but also a second set of "strive for" targets based on the proposals of the spending ministries and provinces, projected at 33 percent and 16.2 percent respectively. Moreover, as the Party groups of the SEC and Ministry of Finance emphasized when presenting these plans, even the second set was meant to be preliminary and could be raised further in the future.[19]

While Mao had clearly created an atmosphere where greatly higher targets were *de rigueur* politically, in a manner which would become increasingly familiar by the end of the year, he also occasionally warned of the need for realistic targets and "balance." Thus, in comments on March 9 that arguably only the Chairman could have made with any confidence, he criticized editorials for arguing the more imbalance the better, noting "we still must have a bit of balance," and he warned against empty catchcries and excessively high targets that could not be met. Nevertheless, these were not only passing comments, they were made in the context of a larger outlook which, despite similarities in Mao's statements, was considerably more sanguine than his subsequent attitude as an awareness of major problems

---

[17]   See "unpublished Chinese document no. 3," pp. 277ff; and Wu Lengxi, *Yi Mao Zhuxi*, pp. 60-61.

[18]   While a leading propaganda official and an alternate member of the Politburo, Chen's status as Mao's secretary was arguably his most important political asset.

[19]   "Unpublished Chinese document no. 3," pp. 277-79, 290; Ma Qibin, *Zhizheng sishinian*, p. 139; Cong Jin, *Quzhe fazhan*, pp. 120-21; and Schoenhals, *Saltationist Socialism*, pp. 45-47. Regarding the 16.2 percent figure, there is an inconsistency in the sources with "unpublished Chinese document no. 3," p. 290, stating this refers to agricultural output value, while in Cong Jin, *Quzhe fazhan*, p. 121, it refers to the output value of nongrain crops (*nongfuye*).

began to surface at the year's end. Thus he followed his comments on balance and unrealistic targets at Chengdu with the observation that "There's no great harm in this, there's no need to spank [the guilty] too harshly."[20]

Mao's occasional advocacy of "realism" notwithstanding, clearly the atmosphere at the conference was supercharged. In addition to the factors mentioned already, it was furthered by a number of factors, including Mao's references to class struggle[21] and two opposing lines, the emergence of the Chairman's personality cult, and strong nationalist overtones. Concerning the cult, Chen Boda again played a leading role with a long discussion of the need to uphold Mao's authoritativeness, while the speeches of various participants emphasized that they were not Mao's equals. According to a close student of the meeting, in addition to Chen the most prominent proponents of the cult were the heir apparent, Liu Shaoqi (who declared that Mao's brilliance far exceeded that of other leaders), and various provincial leaders, notably Ke Qingshi, Hubei's Wang Renzhong, and Guangdong's Tao Zhu. But clearly the key force behind the emergence of the cult was Mao himself who introduced the topic early in the conference, declaring the need to promote the "correct" cults of those who represented the truth (e.g., "Marx, Engels, Lenin, and the correct side of Stalin"), while opposing "the incorrect kind ... in which there is no analysis, only blind obedience," and later by interrupting Chen Boda with a blunter endorsement of cults than Chen was offering.[22]

Mao also stirred nationalist sentiments at Chengdu. This had several aspects. The Chairman again picked up the theme of Nanning on the need to eschew the "dogmatic" and "superstitious" copying of Soviet economic practice. While he observed that this was unavoidable in the early days of the People's Republic, it clearly was no longer suitable to the leap forward approach which promised greater results than the Russians ever achieved. Moreover, Mao mixed in a heady combination of politics and history with a long discussion of past Comintern mistakes concerning the Chinese revolution, Stalin's suspicious attitude toward the CCP and demands on China, and Khrushchev's bringing pressure to bear on the PRC through his mishandling of de-Stalinization, comments that clearly reflected a more deeply felt sense of patriotic resentment. This, in turn, involved attacks on his historic enemies within the CCP such as Wang Ming who assertedly had blindly followed Stalin's policies to the cost of the revolution, thus suggesting

---

[20]   Li Rui, *"Dayuejin" qinliji*, pp. 162-63; and below, pp. 126ff.

[21]   While "unpublished Chinese document no. 3," pp. 287-89, gives considerable emphasis to this point, it is not clear that this is entirely justified. It appears that Mao addressed the issue on only two occasions, and his available speech outlines for the conference largely avoided the subject. See Wu Lengxi, *Yi Mao Zhuxi*, p. 60; *Mao wengao*, vol. 7, pp. 108-119; and Teiwes, "Mao Texts," pp. 147-48.

[22]   "Unpublished Chinese document no. 3," pp. 286-87, 295; Li Rui, *"Dayuejin" qinliji*, pp. 195ff, 216, 224; Schram, *Mao Unrehearsed*, pp. 99-100; and oral source.

a connection between erroneous foreign methods and political opposition.[23] While the overall attitude toward the Soviet Union at the conference was more guarded than later in the year,[24] in stimulating national pride Mao struck a deep chord in his audience. Chen Boda characterized the FFYP as "lacking the independent language of the Chinese people," while Ke Qingshi's report declared that "now the question is the race against time with imperialism."[25] Such sentiments linked the Great Leap with both national creativity and China's position in the international scheme of things.

In addition to the political atmosphere created by the above factors, several developments at Chengdu brought even more direct pressure to bear on various actors. With regard to the provincial level that was so important to the leap, Mao pointed to a "class struggle question" within the Party and alleged that anti-Party cliques had appeared in several provinces, thus reflecting the ongoing provincial purges that were formally approved at the May Party Congress.[26] These complicated purges involved various factors, but past conservatism on economic questions was certainly among them. While various of the provincial leaders present clearly benefited from these purges, the larger message for cadres of their level was the need to toe the leap forward line ever more enthusiastically.[27]

---

[23] See Li Rui, *"Dayuejin" qinliji*, pp. 166, 170-77; Schram, *Mao Unrehearsed*, pp. 96-103; and MacFarquhar, *Origins 2*, pp. 36-40.

[24] Given the still cooperative state of Sino-Soviet relations at this point and continuing Chinese expectations of Soviet assistance in various spheres, this is hardly surprising. It was reflected in Deng Xiaoping's speech to the conference calling for a critical approach to the Soviet model, but one emphasizing "learning from the good experiences of the Soviet Union," a position consistent with the substance of Mao's position if not all of his emotional undertones. See Schoenhals, *Saltationist Socialism*, pp. 29-31. In addition, only 10 days earlier Mao had declared "complete support [for] every one of the recent foreign policy initiatives of the Soviet Union"; see the reference from Soviet archives in Odd Arne Westad, "Brothers: Visions of an Alliance," in idem, ed., *Brothers in Arms: The Rise and Fall of the Sino-Soviet Alliance, 1945-1963* (Stanford: Stanford University Press, forthcoming), section on 1958-60. See below, p. 110, for later attitudes.

[25] "Unpublished Chinese document no. 3," pp. 278, 280.

[26] *Ibid.*, pp. 288-89. The provinces named were Guangdong, Guangxi, Anhui, Zhejiang, Shandong, Xinjiang, Gansu, and Qinghai, all of which had purges confirmed at the May Congress, along with Zhejiang, Yunnan, Hebei, and Henan. At Chengdu Mao also referred to another type of inner-Party class struggle, that involving "rightist activities" in places like Sichuan. The phraseology here, however, suggests the issue had more to do with criticism during the Hundred Flowers than issues relating directly to the leap.

[27] For an early assessment of these purges emphasizing economic conservatism in 1956-57, see Teiwes, *Politics and Purges*, pp. 273-93. Subsequent research, however, suggests the key may lie in long-standing conflict between different factions within provincial leaderships, with various factions able to use the emerging leap to eliminate their opponents. See Forster, "Localism, Central Policy and the Provincial Purges"; and Domenach, *Origins of the Great Leap*, especially ch. 4. While these studies refer to

If either provincial leaders or top national figures needed any further reminder of the need to toe the line, this was provided at the very end of the conference when Mao proposed that the remaining days be devoted to rectification seminars. Absenting himself, the Chairman turned the proceedings over to Liu Shaoqi who convened a large meeting of virtually all the participants. The speeches of these leaders focused on the lessons of *fanmaojin* and amounted to self-criticisms, with Liu, Zhou Enlai, Chen Yun, and Deng Xiaoping all making offerings and Peng Dehuai commenting on the exemplary nature of the experience. Peng, notwithstanding some initial skepticism about the leap, reportedly was persuaded of Mao's vision at Chengdu and became a Great Leap enthusiast. Among the self-examinations provided orally but not in written form by top leaders (see Appendix 2.2 for excerpts) there were some variations. Zhou Enlai identified his shortcomings in the more philosophical manner of Mao ("failed to see the human factor," etc.), Liu Shaoqi, apart from emphasizing his inferiority to Mao, harked back to his early 1950s "errors" that had been singled out by the Chairman in 1953,[28] while Deng Xiaoping seemingly gave a very general self-criticism that did not touch upon *fanmaojin*. But perhaps most interesting was Chen Yun who had tried to introduce some cautionary notes earlier in the conference, and now assumed the main responsibility for opposing rash advance at the 1956 Second Plenum. Chen's offering was couched in fairly technical terms, seemingly reflecting the observation of a conference participant that he was never one for excessive self-criticism. Nevertheless, he concluded with some procedural comments which were in harmony with Mao's themes and the new reality of economic policy making: separate direct reporting to Mao by ministerial leaders, all financial and economic documents to go through the Secretariat (which had already been strengthened by the *de facto* addition of Li Fuchun and Li Xiannian), advocacy of brief reports and less formal, smaller meetings, and emphasis on the economic coordination regions. The assembled local leaders also contributed to the self-criticism, with only Ke Qingshi — described as playing a dynamic role — seemingly able to ignore this aspect. But it was the architects of *fanmaojin* who were clearly under particular political pressure — none more so than Zhou Enlai, who had already been stripped of economic authority after Nanning, and now submitted a letter of resignation to Mao not long after the March conference.[29]

Zhejiang and Henan respectively and their leaders were not at Chengdu, the top Party officials of Xinjiang, Gansu, Yunnan, Hebei, and Qinghai were.

28   Cf. Teiwes, *Politics at Mao's Court*, pp. 41-44.

29   Wu Lengxi, *Yi Mao Zhuxi*, pp. 64-65; Li Rui, *"Dayuejin" qinliji*, pp. 221-24; *Peng Dehuai zhuan* [Biography of Peng Dehuai] (Beijing: Dangdai Zhongguo chubanshe, 1993), p.572; oral sources; above pp. 74-75; and below pp. 98-99, 246-50. Chen Yun, of course, was responding to Mao's wishes, it is particularly noteworthy that this is the first known mention of the specific institutionalization of such measures, including personnel arrangements in the assignment of Li Fuchun and Li Xiannian to the Secretariat which was approved in May at the Second Session of the Eighth Party Congress.

As already indicated in several respects, provincial leaders played a critical role at Chengdu. The key, as before, was Mao's partiality toward these officials. This could be seen in his behavior in attending sessions of the conference when various local leaders spoke, drawing interjections from the Chairman, interjections that were especially long during the undoubtedly enthusiastic performances of Sichuan's Li Jingquan, Tao Zhu, Ke Qingshi, and Liaoning's Huang Oudong. In contrast, Mao was absent during large group meetings when Liu, Zhou, other central leaders, and various ministers gave speeches.[30] The Chairman also stated explicitly the reason for his local bias: "At the local level the class struggle is more acute, closer to natural struggle, closer to the masses. *This gives the local comrades an advantage over those at the Center.*"[31]

Yet if Chengdu again emphasized the unusual significance of provincial leaders in the unfolding of the Great Leap, it also marked an enhanced role on the part of spending ministries as they too now earned Mao's favor. In part, this was a due to their earlier resistance to the *fanmaojin* policies, a resistance which, ironically given that these ministries had systematically implemented Soviet methods during the FFYP, was linked to their response to Mao's ongoing theme of the need for new work methods. Thus the Chairman claimed that the opposition to rash advance was a result of faulty methods whereby the top authorities failed to consult not only provincial secretaries but also the opinions of "various ministries" which had wanted to do more.[32] Beyond this he praised the efforts of several ministries to develop new methods. A particular favorite was the Ministry of Metallurgy's Wang Heshou whom Mao praised for writing an essay that "dared to criticize dogmatism" and whose ministry convened meetings with "a different atmosphere" that were able to solve important problems, grasp guiding principles, and talk about ideology and theory. Further praise was directed at Minister of the Chemical Industry

---

The issue of Zhou Enlai's resignation is played down in Party history sources, but a historian reported seeing Zhou's letter which was written about two months before the Politburo dealt with the matter on June 9; interview, Tianjin, 1998.

30   Li Rui, *"Dayuejin" qinliji*, p. 177. While the radicalism of Li, Tao, and Ke can be taken for granted, Huang's case is peculiar in that he was downgraded from first to second secretary when Liaoning was purged in fall 1958.

31   Mao on March 22 in Schram, *Mao Unrehearsed*, pp. 114-15 (emphasis added). Ironically given past differences over de-Stalinization and the future schism of the international movement, Mao's comment reflected favorably on Khrushchev as he noted that "Khrushchev came from a local area."

32   Li Rui, *"Dayuejin" qinliji*, pp. 247-48. Mao distinguished between industrial ministries that wanted to do more and the financial and trade ministries that wanted to do less. While this is compatible with Bachman's interpretation, we believe it more fundamentally reflects the conflict between spending ministries and coordinating agencies.

Peng Tao and Minister of Railways Teng Daiyuan for also writing good essays on how their ministries were leaping forward.[33]

The Chengdu meeting then was an important step toward the Second Session of the Eighth Party Congress in May which formally launched the Great Leap by further increasing political pressure and involving ever expanding sections of the elite in the methodology of the leap. It also provided preparation for the Congress by stimulating extensive propaganda on the new approach to socialist construction and the mobilization of cadres and masses alike. Concretely, the period between the two meetings saw various localities pledge new construction projects and output targets, while the amalgamation of agricultural cooperatives spread quickly following the Chengdu conference's opinion calling for larger cooperatives.[34] While this much was predictable under the circumstances, several other features of the period deserve comment.

First, similar to various comments at Chengdu and in a manner that would become familiar throughout 1958-59, Mao expressed doubts about the specifics of the more ambitious proposals advanced by local leaders, something once again only he could safely do. A case in point was the grandiose plans of Henan, a pacesetter throughout the leap whose ranking leader, Wu Zhipu, had been a student of Mao's at the peasant academy in Guangzhou during the 1920s.[35] Henan proposed to complete provincial irrigation during the year, to eliminate the "four pests,"[36] to achieve the 12-year target for grain production per *mu* in one year, and to eliminate illiteracy by the end of the year, goals which left Mao with reservations. In April he expressed those reservations not merely regarding Henan's specific plans but also its slogan of "striving hard for three years to change fundamentally the face of the whole country," asking whether it was opportunism to extend the period a bit longer and declaring that "this type of opportunism is what I want." His doubts notwithstanding, the Chairman was basically supportive, considered the risks in Henan's program "not large," and sanctioned a year's experiment in the province, with the proviso that even if Henan failed other provinces could attempt a big movement the following year. Far more relevant for officials at all levels than such tepid reservations were both the general pressure for faster construction and specific demands such as Mao's late April letter requiring provincial secretaries to bring a schedule for local

---

33   *Ibid.*, pp. 166, 197, 231, 248-49, 252. High steel targets proposed at the May Party Congress by Wang Heshou also earned Mao's praise; see below, p. 100.

34   See "unpublished Chinese document no. 3," pp. 293-95.

35   Henan's importance in the evolution of the Great Leap has long been emphasized in the literature. See Chang, *Power and Policy*, pp. 40-46, 80-82, 84-85. The most sophisticated analysis of both Henan's role and the personal impact of Wu Zhipu is Domenach, *Origins of the Great Leap*, part 3.

36   Rats, sparrows, flies, and mosquitoes. Subsequently sparrows were removed from the list after it was explained to Mao that they played a key role in environmental balance.

industrialization over the next five years to the Second Session in less than two weeks' time.[37]

While the political and administrative pressures on Party leaders at all levels are abundantly clear, it nevertheless is essential to emphasize another aspect of the situation at this juncture — the critical importance of belief on the part of actors at all levels of the system. This involved a utopian conviction that China would soon become a communist society where problems of scarcity and exploitation had disappeared. According to a senior Party historian who worked in a provincial committee during this period, most people felt everything was possible, ordinary cadres and populace alike believed Chen Boda's equation of one day being the equivalent of 20 years. Only later, in the light of practical experience and difficulties, did different and more sceptical attitudes emerge. Similarly, the ministerial-level official we have interviewed at length believes that up to the Second Session belief and a sense of Party discipline rather than coercion were the main forces motivating the circles in which he circulated.

The extremes to which belief could take diverse individuals, and the dynamics involved, were graphically illustrated by a remarkable encounter at the Guangzhou railway station in late April, an encounter that was to have a bearing on the emergence of the people's communes. At a time when Mao's stipulation that local industrial value should exceed agricultural value over several years created a need to reconsider both the name and functions of basic-level rural organizations (the agricultural producers' cooperatives), Liu Shaoqi came to Guangzhou to report to Mao on preparations for the Second Session. Together with Zhou Enlai, propaganda chief Lu Dingyi, and Liu's secretary Deng Liqun, Liu received the Chairman's comments on the situation. Seemingly inspired, the four officials repaired to the railway station where they engaged in excited discussions about communes, utopia, and the transition to communism. They boasted about popularizing education, collectivizing living, kindergartens, factories running schools, and schools running factories. These flights of fancy stimulated experiments and, of course, most of the features discussed became aspects of the leap. That experienced officials including the practical Zhou Enlai would be caught up in such dreams speaks of the power of the vision, but even more tellingly of its source. As Bo Yibo commented in his memoirs, when Lu Dingyi told the Second Session of the views of "Chairman Mao and Comrade Shaoqi" concerning "communist communes" in China's villages, what was important was less the contents of the boasting at the Guangzhou railway station than Mao's preceding words to the four.[38]

---

[37]   Bo Yibo, *Huigu*, vol. 2, pp. 682-83, 692-93; Wu Lengxi, *Yi Mao Zhuxi*, pp. 63-64; and "unpublished Chinese document no. 5," pp. 143-44. Cf. Schoenhals, *Saltationist Socialism*, p. 48.

[38]   Bo Yibo, *Huigu*, vol. 2, pp. 730-33. While this account traces the concept of the commune to an earlier point and more directly to Mao than was previously known (cf.

While as a major formal Party gathering of over 1,300 people from the 5th to 23rd of May the Second Session of the Eighth Party Congress had a decidedly different character from the Nanning and Chengdu meetings, it fundamentally extended the process set in motion by those conferences.[39] As has long been known, the key features of the Congress included the formal adoption of the new general line and the launching of the leap, highlighting the project of overtaking Britain, threatening political pressure as seen in talk of Party splits, dealing with "accounts settlers" and "tidewatchers" sceptical of the new program, and the ratification of the purges in nearly a dozen provinces, developing further the theme of the superiority of the poorly educated masses over experts, criticism of "revisionism" (i.e., Yugoslavia) internationally, and new appointments to the Politburo, Secretariat, and Central Committee. In addition, a number of less frequently commented upon continuities were present: flights of utopian fantasy as in Ke Qingshi's projection that within 15 years each village would have its own university; further discussion of the personality cult; and the expression of nationalist sentiments as in statements by various provincial representatives complaining of other countries looking down on China in the past, and of the need to dare to surpass not only Britain but the Soviet Union as well.[40]

What is more clear now than earlier is Mao's absolute dominance of the proceedings.[41] Not only did the Chairman address the meeting four times, but he vetted and altered the reports and speeches of his top colleagues, including Liu Shaoqi's keynote report. While the public press highlighted Liu's report, as Michael Schoenhals has pointed out, internal Party communications focused almost exclusively on Mao's speeches, and the situation was succinctly summed up by Ke Qingshi's comment that "now that we've heard the Chairman's reports, our orientation is even clearer.... [F]rom now on, the world is [ours]!" It was, of course, Mao who emphasized the themes of Party splits and the wisdom of the uneducated, and he who in inner-Party speeches developed nationalist pride with even more outlandish goals than the 15 years to overtake Britain that had been formally restated in Liu's report. Mao not

---

MacFarquhar, *Origins* 2, pp. 77-82), it does not gainsay the importance of Henan in developing the new rural organization from an early stage. Indeed, after traveling from Guangzhou and alighting in Zhengzhou, Liu reported the railway station discussions of the four to Wu Zhipu, who excitedly strove to find ways of realizing the vision; see Bo, p. 732. Another indication of Mao's early involvement in the commune concept was discussions he held with Chen Boda in February and March 1958 on combining cooperatives and local government; *Dang de wenxian*, no. 5 (1993), p. 46.

[39]   The best existing accounts of the Congress are MacFarquhar, *Origins* 2, ch. 4; and Schoenhals, *Saltationist Socialism*, pp. 52-59. A listing of Congress Presidium members and delegation leaders is given in Appendix 1.4, pp. 236-37.

[40]   See "unpublished Chinese document no. 4," pp. 81, 83-85, 87-88.

[41]   This contrasts with MacFarquhar's view, *Origins* 2, pp. 51, 57-58, of the Congress as the "high point of the Mao-Liu alliance" and an occasion where Mao had to consider carefully personnel arrangements in order to protect his own position.

only reduced the time necessary to catch Britain to seven years, but seemingly influenced by Wang Heshou he also argued that China could become an industrialized nation as powerful as the United States in a further eight years.[42]

Mao's hand also determined the direct political pressure brought to bear on his leading colleagues and the final laying to rest of the *fanmaojin* issue.[43] Although Mao declared that the Congress would be a rectification meeting with a "save the patient" approach, it was nevertheless the Chairman who especially criticized "tidewatchers" and "accounts settlers" and linked the behavior of such types in 1956-57 with the current leap forward situation. Moreover, it was Mao who had directly brought to bear pressure on his colleagues since Nanning, a situation which still left them feeling the need to make amends, notwithstanding self-criticisms over the intervening months. Liu Shaoqi's criticism of *fanmaojin* in his report (which had, of course, been vetted by Mao) simply reflected this situation; moreover, various local representatives felt it was not tough enough on the proponents of *fanmaojin* and called for more serious criticism, particularly of those responsible at the Center, even accusing them of attacking the Party.[44]

The key proponents of *fanmaojin,* including Chen Yun, Li Xiannian, and Bo Yibo, but seemingly not Li Fuchun, all made new self-criticisms at the Congress, but the situation facing them was most graphically illustrated by the case of Zhou Enlai.[45] As the most important architect of *fanmaojin,* Zhou, who had already submitted his letter of resignation, had to assume the greatest responsibility. In the period after the Chengdu conference and well into the Congress, Zhou and the others had to prepare their self-examinations in considerable uncertainty as to what would be sufficient to satisfy Mao who remained unhappy with Zhou's and presumably others' Nanning and Chengdu offerings. From the account of his secretary, Fan Ruoyu, this process caused the Premier considerable distress. While Zhou, on the basis of a personal conversation with Mao, apparently accepted the view that the basic cause of his errors was that his thought had not kept up with the Chairman's, the actual drafting of the self-criticism was a painful experience which revealed

---

[42] *Mao wengao,* vol. 7, pp. 194-211, 218-28, 234; Li Rui, *"Dayuejin" qinliji,* pp. 302-304; and Schoenhals, *Saltationist Socialism,* pp. 52, 54-56. Wang's speech to the Congress, "Overtake America in 15 Years," claimed that such a goal for steel production was realistic. This, in turn, was assertedly based on enlightenment received from Mao's thinking, especially his criticism of *fanmaojin.* Cf. below, pp.100-101.

[43] The following contrasts with the interpretation of MacFarquhar, *Origins 2,* pp. 55-59, which argues that in order to strengthen his position Mao protected the leading figures of "opposing rash advance," while Liu Shaoqi wished to treat them more harshly in order to consolidate his position *vis-à-vis* Zhou Enlai.

[44] *Mao wengao,* vol. 7, p. 202; and "unpublished Chinese document no. 4," pp. 79-80.

[45] For an overview of these self-criticisms, including that of Zhou, see Cong Jin, *Quzhe fazhan,* pp. 123ff. Cf. Teiwes, *Politics and Purges,* pp. xxvii-xxviii; and the excerpts provided in Appendix 2.3, pp. 250-57. On Li Fuchun, see above, pp. 49-51.

"contradictions in his heart." A possibly revealing incident during the process occurred when Chen Yun rang Zhou, perhaps reminding him of the reasons for *fanmaojin*, and afterwards, seemingly given pause, the Premier lapsed into five or six minutes of silence.[46]

In another incident during the Congress itself, while Zhou struggled to formulate his self-examination Fan Ruoyu added a passage claiming that Zhou had "shared the boat through many storms [with the Chairman], always remaining together." When he discovered this indiscretion, the Premier, on the verge of tears, angrily rebuked Fan for knowing too little about Party history, since he and Mao had not always stood together during the CCP's revolutionary struggle. In the event, whatever his reservations, Zhou produced an excessive self-criticism in the same style he had shown during the Yan'an rectification in the 1940s. He not only took the main responsibility for the errors committed which he characterized as mistakes of guiding principle (*fangzhen*), endorsed Mao's view that such mistakes had been used by non-Party rightists in 1957 to launch a serious class struggle against the CCP, and equated opposing rash advance with government work breaking away from Party leadership, but he also devoted a special section of his speech to "learning from Chairman Mao." In this lavish praise, which prefigured Lin Biao's notorious January 1962 paean to the Chairman,[47] Zhou held that experience showed Mao represented the truth, good results were inseparable from Mao's correct leadership, and on the contrary mistakes and losses occurred when the Party became divorced from his leadership and directives — something assertedly demonstrated by the Premier's own case.[48]

Even this abject self-criticism did not fully settle Zhou's situation as the issue of his resignation as Premier was considered by the Politburo at a meeting shortly after the Congress on June 9. Although there was also a perception at the time that Mao was considering Ke Qingshi for the position, the status quo was maintained. When Zhou asked whether it was suitable for him to continue as Premier, Mao was present but said nothing, while Deng Xiaoping produced an outline stating that no change was necessary — an outline which Mao accepted. Indeed, it would seem Zhou's position and those of the others had been already secured by Mao's actions at the Congress. Once the self-criticisms had concluded, and notwithstanding the baying of local

---

[46]   *Bainianchao*, no. 6 (1997), p. 19; *Renwu* [Personalities], no. 1 (1986), pp. 175-76; and Cong Jin, *Quzhe fazhan*, p. 127.

[47]   On Lin's 1962 speech, see Teiwes, *Politics and Purges*, pp. xxxix-xl; and Frederick C. Teiwes and Warren Sun, *The Tragedy of Lin Biao: Riding the Tiger during the Cultural Revolution, 1966-1971* (London: C. Hurst & Co., 1996), p. 196.

[48]   Cong Jin, *Quzhe fazhan*, pp. 123-28; and *Bainianchao*, no. 6 (1997), pp. 21-22. On Zhou's excessive self-criticisms during the Yan'an rectification, see Teiwes with Sun, *Formation of the Maoist Leadership*, p. 46. In contrast, Chen Yun's self-criticism (see Appendix 2.3, pp. 251-52) was considerably more restrained, although he too characterized his mistakes as ones of guiding principle.

leaders, Mao declared that they were good comrades who he wanted to help and, rather contradictorily given his views on experts, there was still a need to rely on these people for economic construction. The Chairman now declared that the *fanmaojin* question had been settled, and unity at the Center was reestablished. But as a Party history account from the reform era would observe, it was Mao's repeated references to Party splits at the Congress which had damaged inner-Party democracy. In any case, Zhou's position had been precarious in the period since Nanning, but Mao was now willing to move on.[49]

At least two of the architects of *fanmaojin*, Li Fuchun and Li Xiannian, were indeed placed in key economic roles by the personnel changes made at and immediately following the Congress. As indicated by Chen Yun in his self-criticism at Chengdu, both now formally became secretaries in the Party Secretariat in addition to their State Council positions, and it would be from their new Party posts that they would carry out many of their leading functions. This now replicated at the central level the increasing dominance of the Party apparatus in economic affairs which had been developing in the localities with decentralization, the development of local industry, and the emphasis on Party secretaries taking command. The trend was further reflected in the election of new alternate members of the Central Committee predominantly from the provinces, and the promotion of Secretariat member Tan Zhenlin, now China's top agricultural official, and Shanghai's Ke Qingshi and Sichuan's Li Jingquan to the Politburo.[50] Oddly, the most spectacular promotion, that of the ill Marshal Lin Biao to Party Vice Chairman and member of the Politburo Standing Committee, while undoubtedly reflecting Mao's personal favoritism as well as Lin's historic prestige, seemingly had little bearing on the Great Leap.[51]

For all of the political and ideological pressure generated by the Congress, the economic targets endorsed by the SPC at the meeting did not represent a quantum jump over what had emerged at Chengdu, even though various spending ministries had set out ambitious Great Leap plans. In reporting to the Second Session on the SFYP, Li Fuchun projected average annual increases in industry of 26 to 32 percent (compared to Chengdu's second set of targets of

---

[49]   *Mao wengao*, vol. 7, p. 205; *Zhou Enlai nianpu*, vol. 2, p. 147; Li Ping, *Kaiguo Zongli*, p. 362; Shi Zhongquan, *Zhou Enlai*, p. 412; Ye Yonglie. *Chen Yun quanzhuan* [Complete Biography of Chen Yun] (Taibei: Zhouzhi wenhua chubanshe, 1995), p. 147; *Dang de wenxian*, no. 2 (1990), p. 10; and oral sources. According to a senior Party historian, at this juncture Peng Dehuai also raised the issue of retirement, in his case due to declining health since the Korean war and the heavy workload at the Ministry of Defense.

[50]   Cf. MacFarquhar, *Origins 2*, pp. 59-62; and Donald W. Klein, "The 'Next Generation' of Chinese Communist Leaders," in Roderick MacFarquhar, ed., *China Under Mao: Politics Takes Command* (Cambridge: The M.I.T. Press, 1966), p. 79.

[51]   See Teiwes and Sun, *The Tragedy of Lin Biao*, pp. 18, 179-81; and Teiwes, "Mao and His Lieutenants," p. 48n.

33 percent for 1958) and 13 to 16 percent (compared to 16.2 percent) in agriculture.[52] The truly remarkable jump in targets took place between the Congress and the August Beidaihe conference. The escalation of steel targets, where upward pressure had already been greater than in other areas, was undoubtedly one of the most dramatic cases, and one illuminating the transformed economic policy-making process under the leap forward. A crucial aspect of the new process was the interaction among Mao, Minister of Metallurgy Wang Heshou, Bo Yibo's SEC, and local leaders. Table 2 (pp. 102-104) summarizes this escalation against the background of steel targets since mid-1956 and also includes the initial retreat in late 1958.

Although Mao's obsession with steel production had intensified since the November 1957 Moscow meeting, the steel target for 1958 approved at the February NPC represented only a 17 percent increase over the actual 1957 output of 5.35 million tons. This 6.24 million tons was increased under the second set of targets submitted by the SEC to the Chengdu conference to 7 million tons, a further 12 percent. During the conference, moreover, pressure for still higher targets developed as a result of interaction between Mao and Wang Heshou, an interaction we have already noted with regard to Great Leap methodology. Reflecting Mao's ongoing criticism of *fanmaojin*, in early March Wang organized a meeting of the ministry and some large steel enterprises to consider plans, and he authored two reports on the results. Apart from also proposing the 7 million figure for 1958, in one of the reports Wang stated that with all-out efforts the SFYP steel plan could be realized in three years, with British production overtaken in 10 years and U.S. production in 20 years or a bit more. These optimistic projections were well received by Mao who praised the report three times as pointing the way for metallurgical work and called on other ministries to emulate Wang's organization and overcome their doctrinairism, empiricism, and other faults. The Chairman's enthusiasm was even more sharply expressed two months later when he referred to the report as "lyric poetry."[53]

The pressures intensified by developments at Chengdu led to additional increases over the next two months. In mid-April the SEC, significantly on the basis of local reports, reported a further small increase of 110,000 tons in its second set of steel targets to the Center. But the next major step came at the Second Session of the Eighth Congress in May. Early during the Congress on the 7th Mao again emphasized his desire for rapid growth of steel production, while invoking the nationalist factor by calling for greater speed in this area than that achieved by the Soviet Union. With Mao having spoken, Wang Heshou addressed the conference in a talk mixing higher steel targets and

---

52   "Unpublished Chinese document no. 4," p. 85; and Li Rui, *"Dayuejin" qinliji*, pp. 302-12. The ministries setting out high Great Leap targets at the Congress included, in addition to metallurgy, petroleum, railroads, state farms and land reclamation, communications, textiles, and forestry.

53   Bo Yibo, *Huigu*, vol. 2, pp. 693-95; and above, p. 93.

ambitious rhetoric. In his speech entitled "Overtake America in 15 Years," Wang reported that his ministry, on the basis of Mao's thinking and after localities had conducted research on the pace of development of the steel industry, concluded that targets of 12 million tons in 1959, 30 million by the end of the SFYP in 1962, 70 million by the end of the Third FYP in 1967, and 1.2 billion by the end of the Fourth FYP in 1972 were completely reliable, of great political significance, and would hasten the collapse of capitalism internationally. Moreover, overtaking America in 15 years and the 1962 target of 30 million tons was realism, and if romanticism were mixed in then 35 to 40 million tons could by achieved by 1962. The competitiveness of the situation was reflected in a speech by Li Fuchun which not only forecast similar (if slightly lower) production of 25 to 30 million tons by the end of the SFYP, but also advocated overtaking Britain in 7 years and the U.S. in 15 — goals endorsed by Mao on the 18th. As for the effect of these developments on the current year's tasks, the Politburo at the end of May following the Congress endorsed a 1958 target of 8 to 8.5 million tons, up by 12.5 to 21.4 percent over the Chengdu figure.[54]

While the 1958 steel target had now increased by 28 to 36 percent in the four months since the start of February, over the next three weeks the target would explode by a further 31 to 37.5 percent. Bo Yibo would argue over three decades later that this process owed much to his own hot headedness and Wang Heshou's various presentations, but what was decisive (leaving aside, of course, Mao) was the role of Ke Qingshi and the economic coordination regions. Whether Bo's assessment of responsibility is strictly correct, Ke and the regions did play a key role. From May 19 to early June regional metallurgical conferences were held to consider steel targets. Emphasizing new local production, Ke Qingshi's East China conference produced very high

---

[54]   See Bo Yibo, *Huigu*, vol. 2, pp. 693, 695-96; and Li Rui, *"Dayuejin" qinliji*, pp. 302-304.

Another version of developments in April and May advanced by Jiang Huaxuan *et al.*, eds., *Zhongguo Gongchandang huiyi gaiyao* [Outline of CCP Meetings] (Shenyang: Shenyang chubanshe, 1991), p. 407, is dubious. According to this source, in mid-April a local metal work conference, organized by Wang's ministry and the SEC, concluded that present capacity could not produce enough steel to double output and new factories would not become productive in time; the solution assertedly advocated was the construction of small furnaces. A further conference organized by the ministry and the SEC in mid-May reportedly concluded that the use of such locally produced steel would produce a total of 18 to 20 million tons by the end of 1959. Meanwhile, at some undefined time "after Chengdu," Ke Qingshi allegedly proposed a 1958 target of 11 million tons, while Wang Heshou told Mao it was possible to reach 8 million tons in 1958, but when Mao asked whether the 1957 figure couldn't simply be doubled, Wang indicated this would be difficult, although he promised to undertake more research. Apart from the fact that no other source confirms these developments, they must be regarded as highly unlikely since the best evidence indicates Mao only advanced the idea of doubling the 1958 target on June 19. Cf. the following account.

Table 2: EVOLVING STEEL TARGETS, AUGUST 1956-DECEMBER 1958

Date/Occasion	Proposed by	1957	1958	1959	1960	1962	1967	1972
August 30, 1956	Mao	5				10	20[a]	
September 16, 1956	Zhou Enlai					10.5-12		
July-August 1957	SEC		5.78[b]					
October 13, 1957	Mao	5.2				11.5	20[c]	
November 18, 1957/Moscow	Mao	5.2				12	20-25	40-45
November 28-	Bo Yibo		6.1/6.19[d]					
December 12, 1957	Li Fuchun					12		40
January 15, 1958/Nanning	Bo Yibo		6.2					
January 19, 1958/Nanning	Wang Heshou					15		
January 25, 1958	SEC		6.24					
January 28-30, 1958	Mao		6.24					40
February 3, 1958/NPC	Bo Yibo		6.24			15	30	
February 18, 1958	Zhou Enlai Metallurgy		7					
March 7, 1958	SEC		7[e]					
March 20, 1958/Chengdu	Wang Heshou		7.11[f]			17-20	35-40	
April 14, 1958	SEC		7.11					
May 6, 1958	Party Center							
May 5-23, 1958/	Mao (May 8)			11	17	40[g]		
2nd Session of the	Li Fuchun[h]					25-30		100
8th Party Congress	Wang Heshou[i]			12		30	70	112
May 26-31, 1958	SEC		8.5					
	enlarged Politburo		8-8.5[j]					
	Ke Qinshi[k] (East China alone)			8				
early June 1958	North China			6				
	Northeast			11				
	Southwest			3.1				
	Northwest			1.5				
	Central China			5				
	Total (incl. East but not South China)			34.6				
June 4, 1958[l]	SEC			15				

Date	Source					
June 6, 1958	Wang Heshou[m]	8.2				
June 12, 1958	SEC		16-17			
June 16, 1958	Li Fuchun[a]	8.5-9	20-25			100
June 17, 1958	Bo Yibo	9	20			
June 18, 1958	Bo Yibo	10	25			
June 19, 1958	Mao/Wang Heshou	10.7-11				
June 21, 1958	Metallurgy/localities		30		80-90	
July 17, 1958	Secretariat[c]		25/27/28			
July 28, 1958	Zhou Enlai		27/30			
August 21, 1958/Beidaihe	Mao	11	30	50		
	Mao to Chen Yun	11.5[p]				
August 23, 1958	SPC/Li Fuchun		27-30		80-100	
August 28, 1958	SEC/Bo Yibo		27-30		80-100	
August 30, 1958	Party Center		27-30	50	80-100	
September 5, 1958	Mao	11	30	50		
October 18-30, 1958	localities at nat'l planning conference		39			400
November 2-10, 1958	1st Zhengzhou conference					
November 17, 1958	Chen Yun		30			
November 21-27, 1958	Mao[q]		18-22	30	50	
before 6th Plenum	SPC		20			
November 28-	Li Fuchun		18-20			
December 10, 1958/	Zhou Enlai		18-20			
6th Plenum	plenum resolution		18/20.5-22.1[r]			

Unit: million tons

Sources: Bo Yibo, Huigu, vol. 2, pp. 692-97, 699-700, 703-705, 709; Chen Xuewei, Mao Zedong yu dangdai Zhongguo jingji [Mao Zedong and China's Contemporary Economy] (Henan: Zhongyuan nongmin chubanshe, 1993), p. 113; Cong Jin, Quzhe fazhan, pp. 107, 117, 119-20, 130, 132-33, 152-53, 167, 171; Fang Weizhong, Jingji dashiji, pp. 202, 222-23; Gu Longsheng, Mao Zedong jingji nianpu, p. 429; Lin Zhijian, Xin Zhongguo yaoshi, p. 234; Ma Qibin, Zhizheng sishinian, pp. 129, 145-46, 156; Mao wengao, vol.7, pp. 226, 274, 279, 281-82, 382, 394, 549-50; Su Donghai, ed., Zhonghuarenmingongheguo fengyun shilu [True Record of the PRC's Storms] (Hebei: Hebei renmin chubanshe, 1994), vol. 1, pp. 505, 520, 542-43, vol. 2, pt. 1, pp. 146, 155, 163, 188; "unpublished Chinese documents" no. 2, p. 180, no. 3, p. 290, no. 4, p. 70, no. 5, pp. 105-107, 115-15, no. 6, p. 135; Zhou Enlai nianpu, vol. 2, pp. 124, 145, 156, 192; Xuexi ziliao [Study Materials], vol. 4 [1949-67], xuyi [Supplement 1]([Beijing: 1967]), p. 73; Zhao Dexing, Jingji zhuanti dashiji, pp. 178, 542, 544-45; ZGDSRWZ, vol. 44, p. 80; Guomin jingji he shehui fazhan jihua dashi jiyao, p. 111; Zhou Weiren, Jia Tuofu zhuan, p. 139; and in Chongji, Zhou Enlai zhuan, vol. 3, pp. 1410-11.

Notes:

a In early 1956 Mao had proposed a target of 30 million tons by 1967; Bo Yibo, vol. 1, p. 529.

b Our calculation based on the SEC's projected growth rate of 16.1 percent.

c Mao also indicated this target on September 9 at the Third Plenum.

d Presented at the 6th national planning conference. Su Donghai, p. 509, and Ma Qibin, p. 135, give the 6.19 figure. Zhao Dexing, p. 542, Fang Weizhong, p. 201, and *Guomin jingji he shehui fazhan jihua dashi jiyao*, p. 111, report 6.1.

e Prepared for the Chengdu conference; approved at the conference on March 21 and subsequently by the Politburo on April 5.

f This figure was forced on the SEC by the localities. It was formulated after Nanning, presumably on the eve of Chengdu, and was taken by the SEC as the "second account" for the 1958 national target.

g This figure from "unpublished document no. 4," p. 70, is doubtful as a target for 1962. It is more likely that Mao's ambiguous statement referred to 1964.

h Li Fuchun's target had not only been discussed with the central financial and economics small group, it was also based on plans proposed by localities and various central departments. See Cong Jin, p. 132.

i Wang Heshou's new target was reached after "consulting the localities"; Bo Yibo, vol. 2, p. 695.

j This target would be severely criticized at Beidaihe; see *Guomin jingji he shehui fazhan jihua dashi jiyao*, p. 112.

k At enlarged Politburo meeting.

l After localities industry conference of May 19-24. Ma Qibin (p. 145) gives June 4, while Bo Yibo (vol. 2, p. 697) dates the proposal as June 12. The most likely reconciling of these dates is that the SEC's report was made on June 4 and approved by the Party Center on the 12th; see Li Chen, *Zhonghuarenmingongheguo shilu*, vol. 2, part 1, p. 199.

m After consulting Hebei First Secretary Lin Tie. Bo Yibo, vol. 2, p. 696, put Wang's report on June 7, but this clearly was similar to the one given on June 6. Cong Jin, p. 134, wrongly placed it in "mid-June." Between this time and June 19 Wang's ministry increased this figure to a "preliminary estimate" of 9 million tons, but no precise date is available.

n Representing the reorganized central financial and economics small group.

o Three sets of targets were proposed by the Secretariat.

p In view of his recent revelation of the steel target to the visiting Khrushchev, Mao rang Chen Yun and ordered him to increase the target by an extra 500,000 tons in order to create a safety margin for guaranteeing that 11 million tons would be met.

q Part of Mao's effort to "cool down" the Great Leap.

r 18 million tons was the publicized figure, 20.05 and 22.1 were internal targets.

targets for 1959, claiming the region by itself could realize 8 million tons, and the other regions subsequently followed suit in the intense competitive atmosphere. On the basis of such projections the SEC reported to the Party Center that *the next year's* steel output could be doubled, but the *1958 projection* offered by Wang Heshou remained within the range of the late May Politburo decision at 8.2 million tons. The competitive situation was further seen when Li Fuchun presented a range of 8.5 to 9 million tons on June 16 and Bo upped his figure to 9 million tons at a June 17 Politburo meeting not attended by Mao. Rivalry between the two planning bodies was also suggested by Li Fuchun's new projection of overtaking Britain in five years which — to Mao's great pleasure — was topped by Bo Yibo's estimate of two years the next day. Meanwhile, Ke Qingshi had arrived in Beijing in mid-June, and Ke's enthusiasm for local steel production apparently influenced Mao, who had a fondness for doubling steel output in any case,[55] in the decision to double the target *for 1958*. This unfolded when the Chairman met his leading colleagues face-to-face over the next few days.[56]

In a conversation with Bo Yibo on the 18th during a meeting at the Chairman's temporary residence at the Zhongnanhai swimming pool attended by top economic officials including the recently downgraded Chen Yun (see below),[57] Mao observed that the grain problem had been solved (the optimism

---

[55] In 1956 Mao called for the doubling of steel production every five years; Bo Yibo, *Huigu*, vol. 2, p. 691.

[56] *Ibid.*, pp. 696-98, 700-701; Ma Qibin, *Zhizheng sishinian*, pp. 146-47; Cong Jin, *Quzhe fazhan*, p. 155; "unpublished Chinese document no. 5," p. 95; and oral sources. Cong Jin (p. 136) gives Bo's June 17 figure as 10 million tons, but as the following account suggests, this seems to confuse developments on the 17th with those on the 18th.

There are also uncertainties concerning the precise role of the regions and Ke Qingshi in that much of Bo Yibo's argument (pp. 700-701) is based on Mao's *ex post facto* comments, not the most reliable of indicators. Also, the report of the Ministry of Metallurgy drawing on the regional projections in glowing terms to set a *1959* target in excess of 30 million tons (more than double the SEC's early June target) was only sent to the Center a few days after the decision to double the *1958* goal. Thus Mao may not have had all the information about regional projections at the time of the June 19 decision, but he almost certainly would have been aware of local enthusiasm through the SEC's earlier report and (most likely) Ke's arrival in Beijing. In any case, the June events clearly indicate that even relatively enthusiastic central actors such as the Ministry of Metallurgy, which had increased its June 6 projection of 8.2 million tons for 1958 to 9 million tons by the time of the June 19 meeting, were caught between pressure from Mao above and the localities below, while also having to take into account the competitive bidding of other central players such as Bo Yibo and Li Fuchun. See also Jin Chongji, *Zhou Enlai zhuan*, vol. 3, pp. 1410-11.

[57] Those present included key economic figures Bo, Chen, Li Fuchun, Li Xiannian, Liao Luyan, and Wang Heshou, as well as Peng Zhen and Huang Kecheng; Sun Yeli and Xiong Lianghua, *Gongheguo jingji fengyun zhong de Chen Yun*, p. 148. Chen's participation in this crucial meeting indicates a degree of involvement in the emerging Great Leap in sharp contrast to our previous understanding; see Teiwes, *Politics and*

concerning this alleged development seemingly was another factor contributing to the fixation with steel production) and he asked what the people in industry were doing, wanting concrete plans for overtaking Britain. Bo, acutely aware of his self-examination regarding *fanmaojin* at the May Congress, in addition to increasing the target again to 10 million tons, responded with the concept of "taking steel as the key link" and earned Mao's approving "correct, very correct!" The next day, the 19th, center stage fell to Wang Heshou as top leaders again gathered at the swimming pool, this time minus Bo who was busy trying to convert the previous day's commitments into a concrete plan. At the new gathering Mao asked Wang: "Last year [the target] was 5.3 million, can this year's be doubled? Why can't we double it?" Wang, while indicating this would be difficult, could only reply "it should be all right" (*haoba*)! This reflected a certain uncertainty over the proposed objective, but also a recognition that the Chairman's wishes were decisive. Thus the 1958 target was set at 11 million tons, although publicly announced as 10.7 million — exactly double the actual 1957 figure.[58]

The *ad hoc*, personally driven nature of these momentous developments was further indicated by the reaction of Li Fuchun. While Li, by now both China's top planner and also holding a position in the Party Secretariat which had suddenly become a critical economic policy organ, had played his role in the ratcheting up of steel targets in June, he was apparently in the hospital around the time when the decision to double the 1958 target was taken. As at the Third Plenum, the role of the SPC was essentially passive, or more accurately in this case reactive; rather than institutional interests, Mao-initiated political pressure ruled the day. This was graphically reflected in Li's reaction when he emerged from his sick bed: he commented in disbelief that "While staying away in the mountains for seven days, one thousand years have passed in the outside world."[59]

In the midst of the steel drama important organizational changes took place in the economic sphere which reflected the attacks on *fanmaojin* that had reached their conclusion at the May Congress. The most well-known measures were the policy supremacy of the Secretariat and the cooption of Li Fuchun

---

Purges, pp. xxvi-xx-ix. For even more dramatic evidence of Chen's activeness, see below, p. 110.

58   Bo Yibo, *Huigu*, vol. 2, pp. 698-700; and *Mianhuai Mao Zedong*, p. 73. According to Wang's recollection in the latter source, he initially told Mao that 8 million tons could be achieved in 1958, something difficult to understand given developments of the previous days, not to mention his own projection of 8.2 million on June 6.

There is a tension between Bo's account and that of Cong Jin, *Quzhe fazhan*, pp. 136-37, which seems to place Bo at the meeting on the 19th. More generally, while hardly denying his own faults in the overall process at the time, Bo tends to emphasize the role of Wang Heshou while Cong paints a picture suggesting Bo must share the "blame" with Wang.

59   Xue Muqiao, *Xue Muqiao huiyilu* [Memoirs of Xue Muqiao] (Tianjin: Tianjin renmin chubanshe, 1996), p. 255.

and Li Xiannian to that body, both of which had been mentioned by Chen Yun in his self-criticism at Chengdu. A little known but very significant measure, however, was the reorganization of the Party Center's five-person small group for economics work which had been exercising overall leadership in this area since being set up in January 1957. This body had been led by Chen Yun and included the other key practitioners of "opposing rash advance," Li Xiannian, Bo Yibo, and the less committed Li Fuchun, as well as the army's Huang Kecheng. In his Chengdu self-criticism Chen realized that the role of this body would have to change and he proposed that its members should participate in meetings of the economic coordination regions, but the actual changes went considerably further. Now a new body, the Center's financial and economics small group, was set up on June 10. There was considerable continuity in membership, with Chen Yun again designated group head. However, the group was leavened with new additions — Secretariat member and agricultural czar Tan Zhenlin, Wang Heshou, and Minister of First Machine Building Zhao Erlu, while only Huang Kecheng, who became People's Liberation Army (PLA) Chief of Staff later in the year, dropped out. But more significant than the expansion of membership was the drastic reduction of the group's power in comparison to that of its predecessor. The fundamental change was the elimination of the group's decision-making power; Mao personally inserted in the document announcing the new body that it would have only "the power of making proposals," and not "the power of making decisions." It had become, as the group's full time secretary, Xue Muqiao, later recalled, a body whose functions had been limited to "consultation and research investigation."[60]

Mao further stipulated that the small group would report directly to the Secretariat, a new arrangement which now made the CCP's previous economic architect and Party Vice Chairman Chen Yun accountable to the lower-ranked Deng Xiaoping. This, of course, reflected the well-known shift of economic authority to the Party apparatus when it had always previously been centered in state organs, with the small group a kind of gathering of leading government policy makers wearing their Party hats. Now, Mao emphasized, the Yan'an principle of "unified leadership" (*yiyuanhua*) would be applied: there would only be one "political design body," no longer two. A sign of the times was the fact that the following day, June 11, Li Fuchun, rather than Chen Yun, convened a joint meeting of the SPC and SEC. Li, the least capable of all the top CCP economic officials but the one least compromised by *fanmaojin*, was functioning as the leader in this area, notwithstanding Chen's position as small group head.[61]

---

[60] *Mao wengao*, vol. 7, pp. 268-69; Xue Muqiao, *Xue Muqiao huiyilu*, p. 258; and Li Rui, *"Dayuejin" qinliji*, p. 224. Also formally approved at the same time were political and legal, foreign affairs, science, and culture and education small groups. Cf. below, n. 62.

[61] *Mao wengao*, vol. 7, pp. 268-69; and Chen Zhiling, "Li Fuchun," in *ZGDSRWZ*, vol. 44 (Xi'an: Shaanxi renmin chubanshe, 1990), p. 80.

This completed the humiliation of Chen Yun who, following months of criticism and self-criticism culminating in the very public forum of the Second Session of the Eighth Party Congress, was now formally stripped of the authority to make major economic decisions, much as Zhou Enlai's economic function and perhaps his key foreign policy role had been diminished earlier in the year. In Zhou's case the denouement came on June 9, the day after Mao issued the order for the new financial and economics small group, when the Politburo considered the Premier's resignation, although as we have seen this course was rejected after seemingly extended discussion.[62]

These organizational changes and the escalation of steel and other targets in June and July set the stage and the tasks necessary for the August Beidaihe conference. (See Table 1, p. 37, for the rapid growth of capital construction goals in this period.) This involved the feverish drawing up of plans with, in sharp contrast to the usual prolonged process, officials of the SEC and SPC preparing the 1959 plan and revised SFYP in five days' time — the five-year projections setting annual growth rates of 53 percent for industry and 30 percent for agriculture. It also involved finding ways to meet these fantastic goals: regarding steel the emphasis was on local production, including the use of the disastrous backyard furnaces. At the same time, the utopian pursuit of a transition to communism became prominent, with the concept and organizational forms of the people's commune quickly evolving under the impetus of the central propaganda organs, notably Chen Boda's new *Red Flag* magazine, local experiments particularly in Henan, and not least Mao's approving comments.[63]

Of particular note in this process was wild optimism concerning grain. As we have seen, when Mao asked whether steel production could be doubled, he claimed that the grain problem had already been "solved." This came against the background of other developments in June. In the middle of that month the new economic coordination regions convened conferences on agriculture, and Ke Qingshi's East China called for a 70 percent increase compared to the previous year; about two months later, seemingly before the convening of the Beidaihe conference, Ke would advocate free meals. In these circumstances the role of Tan Zhenlin, the Secretariat member responsible for agriculture who, along with Ke and himself, Mao would nominate a year later as among those most responsible for leap excesses, became particularly significant. Tan

---

62   See Ma Qibin, *Zhizheng sishinian*, pp. 140, 146; and   above, pp. 74-75, 98-99. Regarding foreign policy, Zhou had been replaced by Chen Yi as Minister of Foreign Affairs in February, and then on March 6 Mao set up a foreign affairs small group excluding the Premier. The relationship of this group to the foreign affairs group established on June 10 is unclear. While these changes arguably reflected Mao's dissatisfaction with Zhou, it is important to note that he continued to play a foreign policy role, not only meeting foreign representatives as Premier, but also reporting on foreign affairs to the Chengdu conference. See *Zhou Enlai nianpu*, vol. 2, p. 133.

63   "Unpublished Chinese document no. 5," pp. 96-99, 114-16; MacFarquhar, *Origins 2*, pp. 77-82; and Schoenhals, *Saltationist Socialism*, pp. 62-63.

had been especially active in promoting the winter 1957-58 mass water conservancy campaign which played such a key part in launching the Great Leap. Now, after spring investigations of leap forward progress in various provinces, on June 26 Tan highlighted East China's "flying leap," and this in turn led other economic coordination regions to raise their aspirations. In July the Ministry of Agriculture, undoubtedly reflecting the influence of Tan and Minister Liao Luyan, reported sharp increases in grain already harvested, while at Beidaihe in August the ministry estimated that 1958 grain output would exceed 800 billion catties, more than double the actual 1957 output, and it set the 1959 figure at more than 1,000 billion catties, 2.7 times 1957 output. Throughout the summer and extending past the Beidaihe conference Tan became increasingly "hot-headed," praised local claims of immediate entry into communism, and took responsibility for ensuring that production targets were met, encouraging communes to knock down anyone who dared "raise the white flag." Such projections and enthusiasm led an elated Mao to ask in early August what should be done with so much surplus grain.[64]

Against the backdrop of such political pressure and utopian hopes, the Beidaihe conference in 1958 was much more than the usual summer gathering of top leaders at the seaside resort. It involved two overlapping meetings, an expanded Politburo meeting from August 17 to 30 incorporating provincial first secretaries and responsible personnel from central Party and state organs, and a conference of provincial industrial secretaries and other relevant local leaders from the 25th to the 31st. Notwithstanding some later disingenuous remarks to the contrary,[65] once again the proceedings were utterly dominated by Mao. The Chairman set the agenda from the outset, addressed the meeting repeatedly, and intoned the visionary goals that would become even more prominent after the conference. Highly optimistic about grain production and agriculture, Mao designated industry as the key topic, with both the 1959 plan and the SFYP requiring attention. But also demanding priority attention was meeting the current year's doubled steel target, a project he came back to repeatedly and feared might not be met.[66]

Industry generally and steel particularly raised much concern among conference participants as to whether the goals laid down in the previous months could be realized. In the recollection of Bo Yibo, everyone felt steel targets were not being met due to administrative preoccupation with the

---

[64]   Bo Yibo, *Huigu*, vol. 2, p. 688; Cong Jin, *Quzhe fazhan*, pp. 140, 143-44; Ma Qibin, *Zhizheng sishinian*, pp. 148, 150; and Jiang Weiqing, *Tan Zhenlin zhuan* [Biography of Tan Zhenlin] (Hangzhou: Zhejiang renmin chubanshe, 1992), pp. 318-22.

[65]   In 1959 Mao claimed to have been preoccupied with the Taiwan crisis during the Beidaihe conference and to have had little influence on its resolution; "unpublished Chinese document no. 6," pp. 157-58.

[66]   "Unpublished Chinese document no. 5," pp. 100, 102, 105 and *passim*; Bo Yibo, *Huigu*, vol. 2, p. 706; and *SS*, p. 427. For an incomplete list of participants in the Beidaihe conference, see Appendix 1.5, p. 237.

changeover from central to local control of factories, shortages of supplies, and because officials were attending excessive meetings and neglecting production. Mao himself emphasized the need for firm control and tight planning on the steel front, and turned to a familiar but surprising source of assistance — Chen Yun. In a broad-ranging directive to Chen, Mao ordered the reorganization of administrative responsibilities, with the SPC regaining annual planning, the SEC given responsibility for "grasping production," and a new State Capital Construction Commission (a body formally set up in September) established under Chen to provide control over China's rapid construction program. Chen was also handed the task of overseeing the fulfillment of steel plans at the conference. The way had already been laid down by Mao on the eve of the meeting — a mass movement with "the whole people making steel" and Party secretaries grasping leadership. But ironically it was Chen Yun, one of the two main architects of *fanmaojin*, who became Mao's messenger on the absolute importance of steel, personally assured Mao that the doubled target could be met, devised methods to that end, and invoked the threat of harsh Party discipline to make sure the goal would be fulfilled. Clearly Chen was deeply involved in creating the unprecedentedly heated campaign for steel production over the following months.[67]

At Beidaihe Chen Yun was joined by Bo Yibo and Li Fuchun in pushing the Chairman's solution. Chen faithfully echoed Mao by proposing to the assembled industrial secretaries that the way out of the predicament, the way to meet the targets demanded by Mao, was by relying on Party committees and launching the masses to run small-scale native furnaces. Bo Yibo put the matter even more directly, declaring that "the Chairman directs us to have faith in native furnaces." In the course of the conference, an incident illuminated the nationalist passions which bolstered the whole leap forward venture. When, at a time of building foreign policy tensions with Moscow,[68] Chen noted that Khrushchev didn't believe in the 11 million ton steel target, and that the Soviet representative in China also indicated disbelief, the entire audience of top-level leaders became indignant. National pride was also involved in the decision to publish the 10.7 million ton target, a target the Chairman said could not be reduced because it was already known abroad.

---

67   Bo Yibo, *Huigu*, vol. 2, pp. 703-704; Sun Yeli and Xiong Lianghua, *Gongheguo jingji fengyun zhong de Chen Yun*, pp. 152-57; *SS*, pp. 405-406; and interview with participant at Beidaihe.

68   The Chinese leadership had clearly been unimpressed with the Soviet response to the Middle East crisis in July, while the Taiwan Straits crisis which was underway during the Beidaihe meeting produced unease in each leadership over the performance of its partner. Also of major significance, following the May-July Military Affairs Committee meeting where he had emphasized combating dogmatism and excessive reliance on the Soviet Union, Mao rejected a number of Russian proposals for defense cooperation. See Zagoria, *Sino-Soviet Conflict*, pp. 195-221; Teiwes, *Politics and Purges*, pp. 294-96; and Westad, "Brothers," section on 1958-60. It is unclear, however, to what extent these matters were known by the participants at Beidaihe.

Finally, at the end of the conference Bo brought all the regional secretaries responsible for steel to meet Mao, and one by one they guaranteed fulfillment of their individual targets. Mao still expressed doubts, referring to himself as a tidewatcher and accounts settler. But unlike later and even earlier,[69] Mao was not indicating any need for greater realism, only his fears that his cherished steel target might go unfulfilled.[70]

Mao's imprint was also clear in other aspects of the conference, notably the well-known utopian currents that escalated over the following two to three months. In particular, the Chairman spoke of the need to eradicate the ideology of bourgeois right, the transition to communism, the gradual introduction of free meals, and the possible elimination of wages.[71] But perhaps less well known is the Chairman's role in an important but little commented upon shift in emphasis occurring over the summer and manifest at Beidaihe — the increased importance of coercive discipline. Specifically, Mao decreed that Party disciplinary measures including expulsion should be used against those who failed to meet the required targets. While this may not yet have represented a marked shift away from belief despite growing scepticism in some quarters[72] as targets escalated after the May Congress, it did involve a decided intensification of harsh administrative measures to guarantee plan fulfillment. Both at Beidaihe and in four telephone conferences following the meeting, a particular role was played by the Party Secretariat and General Secretary Deng Xiaoping personally. According to a significant figure of the period, Deng was even harsher than Mao, declaring that even one catty of grain short of the target would not be tolerated. Whatever Deng's responsibility, the true source of this as all other developments was Mao.[73]

Roles and Responsibility: The Actors during the Upsurge

Clearly, in reviewing the entire period through fall 1958, Mao stands at the center of all radical developments. While his claim that the people's commune was unanticipated and "the creation of the masses" (more accurately, lower-level Party leaders) is not without some rationale, here as with the escalation of targets, the fixation with steel, and the transition to communism, the

---

[69]   See above, pp. 89-90, 94; and below, pp. 126ff.

[70]   Bo Yibo, *Huigu*, vol. 2, pp. 704-707; and "unpublished Chinese document no. 5," pp. 106-107.

[71]   Bo Yibo, *Huigu*, vol. 2, pp. 741-45; *SS*, pp. 405, 414, 426; and "unpublished Chinese document no. 5," pp. 110-12.

[72]   See below, p. 115.

[73]   Jiang Huaxuan, *Dang huiyi gaiyao*, p. 408; and oral source. Cf. Mao's November 1958 comment that the steel campaign had "something coercive about it," and had been "rammed through at the Beidaihe conference and the four telephone conferences"; *SS*, p. 515.

Chairman's hand can be seen from an early stage.[74] While there was nothing new about Mao's ability to dominate the scene, his involvement in the details of economic policy and the extreme positions he adopted were major departures. Also new was his style of interacting with his colleagues: from Nanning on he attended Politburo meetings even more rarely than previously and instead stood aloof from routine procedures, considering the recommendations of the collective which only came into effect if he agreed.[75]

As for other actors, however much they may have contributed specific slogans or practical innovations, or added to the pressure driving the process further, they all fundamentally followed Mao. But what further can be said of the roles of each? Considering the Chairman's top colleagues first, it is clear none offered any opposition to his course. Liu Shaoqi, as has long been known,[76] was a firm supporter, although the evidence now available suggests he was less a major driving force behind the leap than someone striving to catch up with developments unfolding around him. Deng Xiaoping's critical organizational role, particularly from the time of the Beidaihe conference, is now equally clear. Of particular interest, among those enthusiastic about the leap in this period were Peng Dehuai and Zhang Wentian, the "right opportunists" who would be dismissed at the Lushan conference in summer 1959 for their growing doubts about the program.[77] As for Zhou Enlai, there is little to indicate that his backing was anything other than unstinting. Even though the Premier "no longer had any right to speak" on economic matters following the conclusion of the Nanning meeting, in the view of one of the leading specialists on Zhou, throughout this period he shared the common desire to speed up socialist construction and initially believed in Mao's line, only beginning to sense problems in summer 1958. At the same time, as Party historian Shi Zhongquan has observed, following the events of January-May Zhou became very cautious politically — he had learned the lesson of *fanmaojin*, never again acting as boldly as in 1956 and taking recourse in studying Mao whenever difficult situations emerged.[78]

---

[74] See Bo Yibo, *Huigu*, vol. 2, pp.740-41; and above, p. 95.

[75] "Unpublished Chinese document no. 2," p. 195. This is undoubtedly more accurate than Liao Gailong's claim, "Historical Experiences," II, 90, that Mao completely ceased attending Politburo meetings. Even in the pre-Great Leap period, however, Mao was not a regular participant in Politburo meetings.

[76] See especially MacFarquhar, *Origins 2, passim.*

[77] The enthusiasm of Peng and Zhang was apparent to an oral source with access to the top leadership. On Zhang's positive attitude, see also Zhang Peisen, ed., *Zhang Wentian yanjiu wenji* [Collected Research on Zhang Wentian] (Beijing: Zhonggong dangshi ziliao chubanshe, 1990), p. 351.

[78] Shi Zhongquan, *Zhou Enlai*, p. 413; *Selected Works of Zhou*, II, 406; Xiong Huayuan and Liao Xinwen. *Zhou Enlai Zongli shengya*, p. 243; and oral source. Seemingly during the last days of the Nanning conference, however, Zhou indicated some unease with the new policy orientation by inserting amendments to the draft 1958 budget. He added "or a

But of all the top leaders the most interesting case is that of Chen Yun, with Zhou the main architect of *fanmaojin*. While it previously appeared that Chen had little or no policy role before late 1958, whether as a result of being shunted aside by Mao or at least partly due to his own volition,[79] developments at Beidaihe where he both received new administrative responsibilities from the Chairman and became a key proponent of small-scale steel furnaces indicate this can no longer be maintained; moreover, at Chengdu, although clearly a marginal player, his procedural comments were in line with Mao's wishes and he was at least present during a key discussion which furthered the process of exploding steel targets in June. Nevertheless, the dominant view of Party historians is that Chen harbored unique doubts about the Great Leap at this early stage. As a figure with personal and professional links to Chen put it, while having some belief in the leap forward, he was not entirely convinced. Whether Chen at any time expressed any reservations to Mao privately is not known, but he certainly observed the self-criticism ritual, if in a more restrained manner than Zhou Enlai. In any case, whatever his reservations, Chen Yun actively carried out the Great Leap line even where it most directly contradicted his long-standing economic philosophy. This was nowhere clearer than in his performance as head of the new State Capital Construction Commission where he argued that the scale of capital construction did *not* have to be proportional to the nation's resources, illustrating the situation by citing the Red Army's victorious crossing of the Yangzi despite chaotic conditions. Perhaps the key to Chen was his strict observance of discipline, a factor Mao later commented on and which arguably made it easy, together with political prudence, to enlist his help in summer 1958.[80]

While the role of Mao's personal staff would only become especially significant with the process of "cooling down" later in the year, a development at Nanning was revealing about the potential influence of such figures and the contrast in their situation to that of top leaders. An item on the agenda of the conference was proposals for a dam at the Three Gorges, a proposal known to be strongly favored by Mao. Naturally no leader would take a contrary position, but Bo Yibo was opposed to the proposal and prevailed upon Mao to hear both sides as articulated by junior officials. To argue the negative case an official from the Ministry of Water Conservancy, Li Rui, was summoned to Nanning, and his presentation not only won over the Chairman but so impressed him that he invited Li to become one of his secretaries. The larger

---

bit longer" to the proposal to overtake Britain's steel, iron, and other industrial production in 15 years, and he deleted "or even a bit less" from the pledge to realize the targets of the 40-article agricultural draft within 10 years; Xiong and Liao, p. 242.

[79] See the successive treatments in Teiwes, *Politics and Purges*, pp. 268-71 and xxvi-xxxi, 499-500n54.

[80] See Cong Jin, *Quzhe fazhan*, p. 580; Sun Yeli and Xiong Lianghua, *Gongheguo jingji fengyun zhong de Chen Yun*, p. 161; and above, pp. 92, 105, 110.

lesson of the experience, according to someone familiar with Mao, was that he would be prepared to listen depending on the source. By this time at least, those close in rank to Mao had to be very cautious in expressing themselves, but it was much easier for low-ranking officials to speak up — a situation which seemingly applied especially to the Chairman's secretaries.[81]

Turning to institutional actors, the central coordinating agencies, specifically the SEC and SPC,[82] were frantically busy drawing and redrawing plans, but they were essentially reacting to events rather than performing anything like their traditional organizational roles. Not only were planning leaders, as candidly detailed in Bo Yibo's memoirs, forced into advocating policies and targets they were unsure of in order to avoid charges of rightism, but the very process of planning was undermined as a result. Ironically, while Mao became obsessed with the need for planning at Beidaihe and later complained bitterly that the SPC had abdicated its function from the time of the conference,[83] it was precisely the type of demands placed on the planning system at that time which made such "abdication" inevitable.

The frenzied process of drawing up new plans, raising targets, and then doing it all over again made impossible the careful preparation and substantial consultation under the auspices of the SPC and SEC which had marked past practice. Now ministries produced programs without comprehensive coordination by the planning bodies, and they did not seriously consider problems of coordination with other ministries. Plans were drafted very quickly with only a rudimentary exchange of information with the ministries on whose supplies the feasibility of plans hinged. At the same time the activism of the localities produced an additional pressure on the central organs concerned, ministries and planning bodies alike. While pressure had initially come downward from Mao, soon the enthusiastic local response placed pressure on the central agencies as soaring targets were well beyond anything these agencies had planned or could rationally handle, but they were targets which had to be adopted given Mao's immense enthusiasm for them. Beijing's economic bureaucracies were caught between Mao's demands from above and the wild claims of the localities from below.

Of particular interest was a form of inversion in the bureaucratic politics of central economic organs resulting from the leap. As argued in our analysis of opposition to rash advance, before the leap the main friction had been

---

81   Li Rui, *"Dayuejin" qinliji*, pp. 15ff; and oral source. Li did not fully take up Mao's offer, electing to stay in his bureaucratic post while assuming the status of "corresponding secretary" (*tongxin mishu*) which gave him occasional access to the Chairman. Another indication of the capacity to speak out during this period was also illustrated by Li Rui's July 1958 letter to Mao describing the problems caused by East China's plan for 6 million tons of steel in 1959 and warning against crude, preemptive work styles; *Bainianchao*, no. 4 (1997), p. 8.

82   Little attention is given to the Ministry of Finance in the available accounts.

83   See *Case of Peng*, p. 411.

between the planning agencies and the spending ministries. There was constant bickering over money and projects, but according to a source involved in the process it was one where the planners clearly had the upper hand. Now, however, although in formal terms a great deal of power was exercised by the planners in setting targets and pressing for their realization, in fact, as already noted, their essential coordinating function had become impossible. The key relationship was between the SEC and the SPC on the one hand and the Ministry of Metallurgy on the other. Given that steel was declared the key link, the planning organs were dependent upon Wang Heshou's ministry achieving its tasks. The result was rather than acting as a comprehensive planner which could maintain balance by rejecting the excessive demands of ministries as in the past, the planners had no choice but to satisfy the Ministry of Metallurgy and supply whatever resources it demanded while neglecting other sectors, thus causing a loss of control over the economy. Moreover, while the case was extreme with metallurgy, given the political imperative of rapid growth, the SEC and SPC had to follow the initiative of other ministries as well as that of the localities or risk the dreaded label of *fanmaojin*.[84]

Despite their new bureaucratic clout and their adaptation to the situation by proposing ambitious goals, the spending ministries were also placed in a difficult situation by the need to pursue highly dubious targets. Comparatively speaking, leaders of the industrial spending ministries knew how the modern economy worked and were aware of how difficult the accelerating targets would be to achieve, and thus they had doubts about the achievability of the new program especially after the May Congress. But the thinking of officials in these ministries was complex and not devoid of either faith in Mao or calculation based on their organizational missions. According to a high-ranking ministerial official from one of these ministries, he was doubtful in early 1958 that the targets in his specific sector could be met, but at the same time he saw the opportunity to promote needed projects. As for the overall program he was not sure, but he held out some hope that the targets could be achieved notwithstanding (unexpressed) doubts. Westerners cannot understand, he observed, how high Mao's prestige was from past victories, or how much enthusiasm could be generated by a mass campaign atmosphere. This most cool-headed of officials, and top ministerial personnel more generally, were caught up in the high hopes of the leap at the outset despite lingering uncertainty.

The opportunities and dilemmas of the spending ministries can be seen in the performance of their outstanding representative — Wang Heshou and the Ministry of Metallurgy. Wang's prominence was preordained by Mao's obsession with steel, but he made the most of it with his rhetorical and writing skills, particularly his ability to excite the Chairman's mood with talk of new

---

84   The two preceding paragraphs are substantially based on discussions with a participant in the bureaucratic politics of both 1956-57 and 1957-58.

work methods and overtaking the steel output of foreign countries. This, of course, allowed the promotion of the ministry's pet projects, as when Wang pushed construction of the Juji Huagang iron and steel plant in his report to Mao at Chengdu. Nevertheless, he exhibited a certain caution and hesitation at various junctures before succumbing to the pressure of the moment. Thus, concerning a situation similar to the doubling of the steel target in June, many years later Wang recalled dealing with pressure from above at Beidaihe: "Although the targets were proposed by Comrade Mao Zedong, in our estimates we did indicate difficulties, but subjectively we wanted to rely on the urging and support of Comrade Mao Zedong and the Party Center to make the iron and steel industry develop somewhat faster." But overambitious plans ran the risk of failure, as in the case of the Juji Huagang plan which was abandoned in the subsequent chaos of the leap. In any case, the initiative fundamentally came from Mao rather than from institutional interests; Wang and his organization were forced into exemplary roles which would also be reflected in their postures once the leap began to encounter difficulties.[85]

In contrast to the spending ministries which, whatever their organizational interests, had been among the economic organs criticized at Nanning for following Soviet methods and were largely responding to pressures, throughout this period provincial leaders continued to play the dynamic role they had assumed since the Third Plenum in pushing the leap forward. These leaders were clearly the most forceful critics of *fanmaojin* throughout the first half of 1958, they retained their fundamental interest in local development, and the emphasis on local industry and the innovation of the economic coordination regions placed them in a crucial position to force targets to ever higher levels. The dynamics of the situation, moreover, meant that provincial figures competed among themselves for Mao's favor and approval. This was not only seen in the competitive regional steel targets of late May-early June, it had been graphically illustrated at Nanning where, following Mao's praise of Ke Qingshi, Ke became the number one model, leading Tao Zhu and others to observe that they had to catch up to Old Ke.[86] It could also be the case that local leaders' fervor for pleasing Mao was in some measure due to their relative physical distance from the Chairman, that they had a stronger urge to worship him than those in closer proximity.

There may also be some limited force in the argument put strongly in interviews by our high ministerial official that the generally low educational level of provincial officials and their lack of understanding of the modern economy explains the intense enthusiasm generated in the localities.[87] But it must be noted that not all provincial leaders were blind to the difficulties involved, particularly as doubts set in after the May Congress. Thus not only were local officials caught up in the purges ratified at the Congress, but a new

---

85   *Mianhuai Mao Zedong*, pp. 73, 75; above, pp. 93,100; and below, pp. 158, 172.

86   See Li Rui, *"Dayuejin" qinliji*, p. 73; and above, p. 74.

87   The counterargument is presented below, pp. 175, 197.

purge of the Governor of Liaoning in September seemingly resulted from his effort to give some realistic priorities to the leap in his province.[88] In any case, provincial leaders as a group had a disproportionate influence throughout this period of utopian expectations, a situation that was fundamentally due to the same reason as earlier — Mao's propensity to viewing them as fresh forces, close to the masses and unfettered by the negative bureaucratic practices of the capital.

Finally, the Party apparatus as such requires comment. To a significant extent the most important aspect of the Party as an institution has already been covered in the discussion of provincial leaders whose power came primarily from their leadership positions in local CCP committees. The dominance of the Party was also thoroughly reflected in the basic leap forward ideological principle of political leadership of the bureaucracy. It has further long been argued that the organizational and personnel changes at the Center enhanced the Party's institutional position through the Secretariat,[89] a development which can now be seen in greater detail through the replacement of the existing economics work small group with a new, less powerful body subordinate to the organ in charge of all Party work. Moreover, events before and during the Beidaihe conference illustrate that the Secretariat, Secretary Tan Zhenlin as agricultural overlord, and Secretary General Deng Xiaoping all exercized great power. Indeed, Deng Xiaoping's support of the Great Leap has been in part explained in Western analyses by how much he had to gain from the program as a Party organization man.[90] Yet it must be questioned to what extent the power gained by Deng and others represented the institutional interests of the Party. Under Great Leap conditions, Secretariat officials wearing Party hats[91] fundamentally reacted to pressures coming from all sides — metallurgy and other spending ministries, the planning commissions, the localities, and above all Mao himself. While able to strike fear in the hearts of

---

[88]   See the analysis in Alfred L. Chan, "The Campaign for Agricultural Development in the Great Leap Forward: A Study of Policy-Making and Implementation in Liaoning," *CQ*, no. 129 (1992), pp. 61ff. It is important to emphasize that Liaoning Governor Du Zheheng's problem apparently concerned managing the demands of the leap rather than opposing the program, while those ousted in the earlier provincial purges had generally been involved in "right conservative" activities in 1956-57 and not direct opposition to the Great Leap. On the latter point, see Teiwes, *Politics and Purges*, p. 274.

[89]   Cf. MacFarquhar, *Origins 2*, pp. 60-61.

[90]   E.g., Kenneth Lieberthal, "The Great Leap Forward and the Split in the Yenan Leadership," in MacFarquhar and Fairbank, *The Cambridge History of China*, vol. 14, p. 307. Lieberthal similarly described Liu Shaoqi's pro-leap stance as reflecting his work primarily in Party affairs, as well as the calculation that such support would sustain Mao's support of Liu as his successor.

[91]   These officials, of course, also had government hats, with Li Fuchun and Li Xiannian in particular having much stronger ties to government bodies. Tan Zhenlin and Deng Xiaoping also held significant government posts.

subordinate officials throughout the system, the wielders of power in the central Party apparatus were no more able to shape policies supporting a coherent set of organizational interests than any other official body.

By fall 1958 all actors were advocating ever higher targets and ever more fanciful dreams. Whatever doubts may have existed within the top leadership, economic coordinating agencies, spending ministries, and provincial Party committees, they were largely unexpressed in the face of Mao's agenda. This flight from reality, however, could not exist indefinitely. In the resultant process of "cooling down" Mao once again was crucial in contradictory ways, while the ostensibly common view of 1958 up to that point gave way to increasingly discordant voices. It is to this complex situation that we now turn.

1 The Architects of Opposing Rash Advance, 1956

1a Zhou Enlai, the most forceful advocate of opposing rash advance throughout 1956, makes the first major statement criticizing "the mistake of blind rash advance," January 30, 1956. At the time, this involved only a scaling down of spending requests from ministries and provinces, and although subtly different from the views of Mao (seated behind Zhou), there was no conflict between the Premier and Chairman.

1b Li Xiannian addresses the NPC, June 15, 1956, laying down a more systematic and far-reaching statement of opposing rash advance. This speech was attacked by Mao at the January 1958 Nanning conference as one of the key examples of the "erroneous" approach. In June 1956, it represented not only an effort to wind back excessive spending, but also to shift the overall policy context from "anti-right conservatism" to a more centrist position.

1c Zhou Enlai further articulating the *fanmaojin* approach in his report on the SFYP to the Eighth Party Congress, September 16, 1956. That this report had Mao's firm backing was indicated by the Chairman's careful vetting of the speech, his restoration of Zhou's "conservative" grain target after an attempt to have it increased, and his overall comment that the report was "very good."

1d The official Eighth Congress photo of Chen Yun, the PRC's economic czar before the Great Leap Forward. Chen was not only the architect of the Soviet-style FFYP, but the main economic thinker behind both the opposition to rash advance and the effort to modify the Soviet model in 1956. From the time of the Eighth Congress through early 1957, Mao singled out Chen for high praise.

1e SPC chief Li Fuchun at a Beijing electrical tube factory, October 5, 1956. While a participant in the *fanmaojin* effort, particulary in the first half of 1956, Li was the least committed architect. There is little record of any role by Li during the extensive efforts of the second half of the year, and in January 1958 Mao declared Li the representative of the "leftist" faction of the PRC's planners. Alone of the anti-rash advance architects, Li was apparently spared self criticism in 1958.

1f SEC head Bo Yibo (right). Although categorized by Mao in early 1958 as representing the "middle" faction of planners, Bo had been fully committed to curbing rash advance, particularly in winding back excessive spending demands from ministries and provinces in the second half of 1956. In this May 1959 photograph, Bo attends an athletics event with (to his right) He Long and Liu Shaoqi. By this time, Bo was again advocating a moderate course during Mao's "cooling down" phase, after having contributed significantly to wild targets in spring and summer 1958.

2 From Opposing Rash Advance to the Great Leap Forward, Fall-Winter 1957-58

2a Mao on the rostrum at Tiananmen, October 1, 1957, during the September-October Third Plenum. The plenum marked a sudden turnaround in economic policy, with Mao, to everyone's surprise, articulating his dissatisfaction with opposing rash advance on October 9. Only four days before, the "leftist" planner Li Fuchun restated the *fanmaojin* approach. At this point, however, the "error" was treated as one of "policy" rather than of "line."

2b The opening ceremony at the trade union congress where Liu Shaoqi made the initial public announcement of Mao's slogan of "overtaking Britain in 15 years," December 2, 1957. This slogan arose during Mao's November visit to the Soviet Union where he was inspired by Khrushchev's pledge to overtake the U.S. in 15 years. From the left: Zhu De, Liu, Mao, Zhou Enlai, Mme. Sun Yat-sen, Deng Xiaoping.

2c Mao with Khrushchev and members of the Chinese delegation during celebrations of the 40th anniversary of the Bolshevik Revolution, Moscow, November 4, 1957. Mao's visit to the Soviet Union not only led to the "overtake Britain" slogan and intensified his commitment to rapid growth, it also greatly enhanced his fixation with steel production. From the left: Ulanfu, Peng Dehuai, Deng Xiaoping, Mme. Sun Yat-sen, Mao, Khrushchev, Guo Moruo, Li Xiannian, Shen Yanbing, Yang Shangkun, Saifudin.

2d The winter 1957-58 water conservancy campaign, a precursor to Great Leap mass mobilization, in the suburbs of Zhengzhou, Henan. Following the Third Plenum the provinces approved ambitious agricultural development plans, with special emphasis on water conservancy projects. The mobilization of labor required larger rural organizations, a process which led to the people's communes.

3 Party Meetings and Central Leaders during the Pursuit of Utopia, January-August 1958

3a Mao receiving representatives of national minorities during the Nanning conference, January 1958. A pivotal moment in the history of the PRC, Mao now declared the *fanmaojin* "errors" mistakes in "political line," harshly criticized Zhou Enlai, Chen Yun, Li Xiannian, and Bo Yibo by name, and rejected the entire Soviet-style economic approach as "dogmatism." The result was to create a situation "where no one could say anything different."

3b Mao viewing a model of an irrigation project during the Chengdu conference, March 1958. The conference continued the impetus of Nanning with the theme of smashing superstitious belief in both experts and Soviet practice, while Zhou, Chen, Li, Bo, and other leaders were forced to offer self-criticisms. Also notable at Chengdu were the first dramatic increase in economic targets, the key role of provincial leaders in pushing the "leftist" tide, and the emergence of Mao's personality cult.

3c A self-satisfied Mao in complete domination of the Second Session of the Eighth Party Congress, May 1958. The Congress formally launched the Great Leap, promoted provincial Party leaders to the Politburo and Central Committee, and saw the completion to Mao's satisfaction of further self-criticisms by Zhou, Chen, Li, and Bo, whom he now declared "good comrades" worthy of help.

3d Chen Yun (left) shortly after the Second Session on May 30, 1958. Although having successfully passed the self-criticism process, Chen was soon formally stripped of his key economic authority with the reorganization of his central small group responsible for the economy on June 10. Now Chen's group was restricted to advisory functions, with decision-making authority transferred to the CCP Secretariat under Deng Xiaoping (second from right, rear). To Chen's left are Lin Boqu and Zhu De.

3e Zhou Enlai (center) on June 1, 1958, shortly before the Politburo considered his resignation as Premier on June 9. Zhou had already been denied "the right to speak" on economic questions after the Nanning conference, and there was now a perception that Mao was considering Shanghai leader Ke Qingshi as Zhou's replacement, although in the event no change was made. Zhou is flanked by Zhu De (left) and Chen Yi.

3f SEC Vice Chairman Jia Tuofu (third from the right), considered by Mao to represent the "rightist" faction of planners, in a 1958 group photo. Jia was a strong advocate of opposing rash advance in 1956, and again came to the fore in the May-June 1959 effort to reduce steel targets. To Jia's right: Zhu De and Chen Yun.

3g Chen Yun (center), usually thought to have been inactive during the utopian phase, inspects the Wuhan steelworks in July 1958. Despite the loss of his status as economic czar, Chen remained active throughout the utopian phase, and by the time of the Beidaihe conference received important assignments from Mao concerning steel production and capital construction.

3h Mao on an inspection tour, Xushui county, Hebei, August 4, 1958. During his inspection of this model area, Mao responded with delight to the inflated production claims of the county Party leader, asking what should be done with so much surplus grain beyond what the local peasants could eat, and he also proposed setting up people's communes.

3i Deng Xiaoping (center, weraing hat) viewing high-yield sorghum in a Hebei commune, August 1958. In this period Deng assumed a critical role in driving Great Leap targets ever higher, declaring that even one catty of grain short of the target would not be tolerated. This, in combination with the enthusiasm of provincial leaders, provided an irresistible force for fanciful goals.

3j Mao speaking at the Beidaihe conference, August 1958. The conference marked the height of unrealistic targets, the decision to establish communes nationwide, priority attention to industry and especially steel now that the grain problem was "solved," and projections of an early transition to communism. Liu Shaoqi is to Mao's left.

4 People's Communes and Rural Fantasies, 1958

4a Following the Beidaihe decision, people's communes were set up throughout the country within a few months, with most provinces claiming 100 percent compliance by the end of September, regardless of whether local conditions existed for such large-scale undertakings. Pictured here is a mass meeting establishing a commune in the suburbs of Changchun, Jilin.

4b One of the most radical features of the communes was the communal mess halls, as in this Guangdong commune. Involving both a strategy to increase female field labor and a collectivist ideology, by 1959 the communal mess halls were creating widespread peasant dissatisfaction, and became a factor in the developing famine conditions.

4c "Gray power" as old peasants in a Shaanxi commune organize an "overtake Britain battalion" for collective labor. An example of the Great Leap approach of mobilizing labor of all ages, these agricultural endeavors were an incongruous response to Mao's slogan aimed at outstripping an advanced industrial nation.

4d Zhu De (left) displays giant winter mellons he assertedly grew in his own garden. This reflected claims during the Great Leap concerning new methods of cultivation and scientific innovations which allegedly produced both unprecedented crop yields and huge agricultural products.

Chapter 4

THE POLITICS OF "COOLING DOWN," 1958-59

While the immediate post-Beidaihe conference period saw intense pressure from the top, further escalation of targets and claims of unprecedented production achievements at all levels, the spread of collectivized living including communal mess halls, and fervent efforts to jump stages to realize communism in the near future,[1] the same period saw the seeds of an eight-month effort to "cool down" (*lengjingxialai*). Mao inevitably stood at the center of both processes. While he did not unambiguously endorse every specific proposal to smash "bourgeois right,"[2] as we have seen the Chairman created the passion for the effort at Beidaihe. Yet by October 1958 he was receiving feedback on the situation and became the first leader, if not to become aware of significant problems with the Great Leap, to begin to address them openly. From the time of the first Zhengzhou conference in early November to the eve of the July-August 1959 Lushan conference[3] the

---

[1]   For an overview of this period, see MacFarquhar, *Origins 2*, ch. 6. The flavor of the time is captured by Liu Shaoqi's late October claim that with hard work "we will be able to build communism in no time at all"; see Schoenhals, *Saltationist Socialism*, p. 43.

[2]   For example, in September the idea of "settling accounts without cash" spread and "central responsible comrades" drafted a document supporting this method. Although the document was not approved by Mao, it was nevertheless distributed to various local units in the name of the Anhui provincial authorities. Bo Yibo, *Huigu*, vol. 2, p. 753. In any case, on a tour of Anhui in this same period, Mao not only declared that communes with the appropriate conditions could have free food, but also that in the future free clothing could be provided as well. Cong Jin, *Quzhe fazhan*, p. 157.

       But perhaps the best example of Mao's slight standoffishness is the case of Shanghai propagandist Zhang Chunqiao's October article attacking "bourgeois right" in the form of the wage system. Zhang, who also had the benefit of a rural inspection in Mao's company just prior to the Beidaihe conference, began work on his essay after Ke Qingshi returned to Shanghai from Beidaihe in early September and reported the Chairman's comments concerning "bourgeois right." It was reprinted in the *People's Daily* on Mao's orders and with his comment that it was correct but a bit onesided. See Bo, p. 752; MacFarquhar, *Origins 2*, pp. 104, 106-107; and Schoenhals, *Saltationist Socialism*, pp. 135-38.

[3]   During this period the Great Leap process of policy making by high-level Party meetings continued. The first Zhengzhou conference was followed by the Wuchang expanded

Chairman repeatedly addressed the excesses of the leap and called for greater realism. But despite various policy adjustments China remained firmly on the radical course set in the first half of 1958, and thus on the road to disaster.

Developments over this crucial period raise a number of key questions. First and foremost, if Mao was the all-powerful figure we have been portraying, how was it that his efforts to "cool down" had such a limited impact, even to the extent that he complained that others failed to understand what he was driving at and treated his efforts as "rightist and retrogressive."[4] Other related questions include: Why was Mao the first to address the serious problems emerging? What was the nature of his effort to "cool down," i.e., how serious was he about this undertaking? Why did various actors not only persist with policies profoundly damaging to the nation but also to the local and organizational interests of those concerned? Which individuals or groups were most culpable in resisting the "cooling down" process, and which contributed most significantly to the effort to bring realism to CCP policy?

Both Western and official Chinese sources have noted the effort to rein in excesses from the time of the first Zhengzhou conference, and the central role of Mao in that effort. While Western analyses have emphasized the crucial point that Mao never retreated from the fundamental correctness of the leap forward, they still credit him with "[leading] the effort to bring greater rationality and efficiency to the program," while resistance to this course is sometimes attributed to those, particularly local cadres, "who had inherited greater power during 1958."[5] PRC sources, for their part, portray the period from Zhengzhou to Lushan as a systematic effort to "rectify the 'left'" led by Mao, although there are signs recently that many Party historians no longer consider this characterization adequate.[6] And at least some of the Chairman's former colleagues go even further, as in Bo Yibo's claim that Mao worked day and night from mid-October 1958 to the end of the year to correct the excesses

---

Politburo meeting and Central Committee plenum (known as the Wuhan plenum) in late November and early December, a Beijing meeting of provincial secretaries in late January and early February 1959, the second Zhengzhou conference in late February and early March, the Shanghai expanded Politburo meeting and Central Committee plenum in late March and early April, and finally the pivotal Lushan conference and plenum in July-August.

4   "Unpublished Chinese document no. 1," p. 152. See also *Xuexi ziliao*, vol. 3 [1962-67] ([Beijing: 1967]), pp. 39-40.

5   Lieberthal, "Great Leap Forward," pp. 294-95. On Mao's leading but ambivalent role in the effort to curb excesses, see Teiwes, *Politics and Purges*, pp. 306-10.

6   See, e.g., Liu Wusheng, "Cong diyici Zhengzhou huiyi dao Lushan huiyi qianqi dui Mao Zedong jiu 'zuo' de lishi kaocha" [A Historical Investigation of Mao Zedong's Rectifying the "Left" from the First Zhengzhou Conference to the Early Stage of the Lushan Conference], *Zhonggong dangshi ziliao* [Materials on CCP History], no. 48 (1993). In a recent interview (Beijing, 1997) a historian specializing in the period noted the trend to scepticism concerning the official view within his profession.

of the leap.[7] The evidence now available clearly indicates that these views have exaggerated Mao's dedication to greater realism. At root, at least initially Mao saw "cooling" as little more than a necessary adjustment of work style that would allow a continuing leap forward. In this sense many of his efforts were rhetorical or cosmetic; indeed, his statements involved the same enjoinders to leave a margin for safety, be realistic, reduce excessive targets, etc., that he had articulated in spring 1958 as his political pressure drove targets ever higher.[8] Yet there was now, unlike in the spring and increasing as time went on, a sense not simply that proposals might be too optimistic and specific targets could not be met, but a concern that significant dislocation might result from overheated efforts, and with it a willingness to entertain some significant adjustments. In this Mao was anything but consistent, and this inconsistency lay at the heart of the failure of "cooling down."

Both the centrality of the Chairman in starting "cooling down" and the inherent limitations imbedded in this fact are illustrated in the initial raising of the issue. While Bo Yibo and other sources routinely state that Mao was the first leader to understand more fully the problems created by the new reality,[9] in fact other leaders were also well aware that something was amiss. The difference was that unlike Mao they did nothing. A case in point was Zhang Wentian, an early Great Leap enthusiast and later one of its most trenchant critics. According to an oral source specializing on Zhang, in October, at about the same time as Mao, Zhang formed a more or less clear view of the left errors of the Great Leap, but owing to his lesser status he couldn't initiate proposals to deal with them.[10] Over the preceding months two leaders in a vulnerable position because of *fanmaojin* — Zhou Enlai and Chen Yun — had also become aware of the problems being created for the economy, but they took no action. In Zhou's case, although the Premier was increasingly concerned with the potential damage caused by the leap, he could not air his misgivings for fear of being again criticized by Mao.[11] The situation was revealed even more starkly in mid-1958 when Chen, being urged by subordinate officials to offer advice to Mao on the problems he (Chen) sensed, responded by saying that "the timing is not right, I still want to keep my Party membership, we must wait for the time he [Mao] himself makes the turn."[12] Meanwhile, Bo Yibo participated in a visit by delegates to the Beidaihe conference to nearby Xushui county where they viewed bountiful cotton

---

7   Bo Yibo, *Huigu*, vol. 2, pp. 817-18.

8   See above, pp. 89-90, 94-95.

9   See Bo Yibo, *Huigu*, vol. 2, pp. 807, 817.

10   Cf. Teiwes, *Politics and Purges*, pp. lii-liii.

11   Tong Xiaopeng, *Fengyu sishinian*, p.363.

12   According to a reliable oral source reading from Party history materials. For accounts of a somewhat less dramatic expression of the same sentiment by Chen, see *Chen Yun yu jingji jianshe*, p. 37; and Sun Yeli and Xiong Lianghua, *Gongheguo jingji fengyun zhong de Chen Yun*, p. 150.

fields. Bo was pulled aside by "a comrade" who told him it was a false model, something which Bo's detailed examination confirmed. Yet like Zhang, Zhou, and Chen, Bo seemingly was silent as Xushui became a national model.[13] Clearly, without Mao's imprimatur, no one was game to address the problems before their eyes.[14] The situation had changed dramatically from pre-Great Leap days when, although Mao had the unchallenged last word in disposing of issues, now the Chairman had to be the first to propose a course of action.

While Mao's colleagues suppressed their concerns, the Chairman himself seemingly became aware of problems through two time-tested devices — sending individuals close to him, particularly from his personal staff, to conduct investigations, and especially his own inspection tours of the country.[15] Notwithstanding his infatuation with utopian visions, Mao retained a political sensitivity to events unfolding around him as well as a shrewd understanding of the system's capacity to generate false reports. In this context, personal staff such as secretary Tian Jiaying were in effect commissioned to uncover problems, so it was no surprise that they did, although they always had to be wary of finding *too many* problems and thus drawing the Chairman's displeasure. This was graphically illustrated by a late October conversation Mao held with Tian and *People's Daily* chief editor Wu Lengxi before sending them off to conduct investigations. Mao urged them to be open and candid, but also to be "calm promoters of progress" (*lengjing de cuijinpai*), a phrase he subsequently repeated on several occasions, the implication being that they were to avoid becoming "promoters of regress." And while local leaders and basic level cadres finding themselves face to face with Mao often distorted the truth, others under his prompting revealed glimpses of the real situation; moreover, some local leaders provided unsolicited reports of dire situations through regular channels to the Chairman and the Center, as in cases of starvation in summer 1958 in Anhui and Yunnan. As Party historians today put it, Mao's own discoveries were the primary factor in changing his views, but local figures in particular abetted the process by revealing difficulties.[16]

---

[13]   Bo Yibo, *Huigu*, vol. 2, p. 751.

[14]   Another example at a somewhat lower level concerned State Statistical Bureau head and SPC Vice Chairman Xue Muqiao (one of those who had urged Chen Yun to speak out) who advised his colleagues to desist from complaining about patently false production figures. Xue Muqiao, *Xue Muqiao huiyilu*, p. 256.

[15]   The importance of local tours in altering Mao's perceptions was earlier illustrated by the case of cooperativization in 1955; see Teiwes and Sun, *The Politics of Agricultural Cooperativization*, pp. 10-13.

[16]   Wu Lengxi, *Yi Mao Zhuxi*, pp. 93-96; *Mao wengao*, vol. 7, p. 436; Dali L. Yang, *Calamity and Reform in China: State, Rural Society, and Institutional Change Since the Great Leap Famine* (Stanford: Stanford University Press, 1996), p. 44; and oral source. In the case of Anhui the situation was drawn to Mao's attention early in the day, no later than October 2nd, but he does not appear to have learned of the Yunnan difficulties until late November during the Wuchang conference.

In mid-October, from the 13th to the 17th, Mao left Beijing to clarify the actual situation by touring nearby areas of North China. On the 14th and 15th he visited Tianjin where he discussed problems of the people's communes with Huang Huoqing, Huang Oudong, Wu De, Lin Tie, and Wan Xiaotang, leading cadres of Liaoning, Jilin, Hebei, and Tianjin. On the 16th he expanded the range of those consulted to higher and lower levels, including Politburo member Peng Zhen, alternate member (as well as his own leading secretary) Chen Boda, Shanghai propagandist Zhang Chunqiao, and various prefecture and county secretaries, in addition to Lin Tie and Wan Xiaotang in further discussions of commune problems. On the 17th he reportedly discovered significant "ideological confusion" in the communization movement through talks with Hebei Secretary Liu Zihou and responsible officials of the Party committees of Hebei and several of its prefectures and counties. On this occasion Mao instructed Liu Zihou to carry out investigations in Xushui county, causing Liu to organize promptly a 70-person work team to go to Xushui.[17]

Xushui was particularly significant as a national model, a status conferred after Mao's enthusiastic if not completely unsceptical visit in August. Apparently suspicious as a result of his discoveries during the October tour, Mao now received a report on the 18th revealing subjectivism, commandism, and false claims at Xushui from one of the organs closest to his household, the confidential office of the Central Committee's General Office, and on the 21st Liu Zihou reported to the Chairman in Beijing, revealing false reporting and systematic deception. Subsequently, Mao again visited Hebei where in exchanges with Lin Tie and Liu Zihou he heard more about serious commandism on the part of the Xushui county authorities who refused to listen to the instructions of their higher local levels, a phenomena which earned the county his criticism as an independent kingdom at the first Zhengzhou conference. Thus it appears that the Hebei leaders, rather than taking the initiative to bring problems to Mao's attention, like the Chairman's secretaries were responding to his cues. Meanwhile, on the 19th the Chairman spoke twice with Chen Boda and ordered Chen and Zhang Chunqiao to conduct investigations of so-called satellite communes, to include Hu Sheng and Li Youjiu, two intellectuals, or *xiucai*,[18] in their group, and to report their

---

Another method of uncovering problems also reflecting local input in this period were reports by ranking figures who had attended work conferences in the localities, as in the case of deputy rural work chief Chen Zhengren who reported to Mao on problems of transition to state ownership in the communes following an October 10-18 conference on inter-provincial agricultural cooperation in Xi'an; see Schoenhals, *Saltationist Socialism*, pp. 151-52. Note that by the time Chen would have reported, the Chairman's concern for greater realism was known within the top circles.

[17]   Bo Yibo, *Huigu*, vol. 2, p. 807; and Liu Zihou, "Huiyi Mao Zhuxi zai Hebei de jige pianduan" [Some Recollections of Chairman Mao in Hebei], in *Mianhuai Mao Zedong*, vol. 1, pp. 250-51.

[18]   This loose category can be regarded as intellectuals with access to Mao. The most

findings to him at the Zhengzhou meeting. Then on the 23rd he telegraphed Chen who was already in the field concerning issues he wanted addressed. Subsequently, on the 26th Mao talked with Wu Lengxi and Tian Jiaying prior to dispatching them to the countryside for investigations, and two days later he again telegraphed Chen Boda.[19]

Moreover, throughout this last part of October the Chairman involved several high-ranking leaders and especially the CCP's leading economic officials, talking with Zhou Enlai, Chen Yun, Peng Zhen, Chen Yi, Li Fuchun, Bo Yibo, Wang Heshou and First Machine Building Industry head Zhao Erlu. Finally, on the 31st while traveling to Zhengzhou Mao met with local officials and heard reports from officials of the provincial, municipal, prefecture, and county levels. As Bo Yibo would comment, "not a few people" were unable to overcome their leftism and truthfully reflect the situation, but the experience was still of some use.[20]

What bears comment is the range of people being consulted about problems, and thus made aware of Mao's concern with defects in the Great Leap program. Clearly the most numerous and seemingly first involved were local officials, particularly leading provincial secretaries from North China and the Northeast, but also leaders from lower levels. Another significant group was those from Mao's personal coterie, whether Chen Boda who also had high-level positions or Tian Jiaying whose position was limited to that of the Chairman's secretary. An interesting aspect of this was that these figures were more concerned with ideology than practical administration; it is also notable that those such as Chen Boda and Zhang Chunqiao (who was not from Mao's household but who apparently had come to the Chairman's attention in the summer) were proponents even in this period of some of the most radical aspects of the leap. Finally, what is striking in existing accounts is the relative underinvolvement or comparatively late involvement of both top leaders and representatives of the key coordinating economic bureaucracies and spending ministries, a fact undoubtedly at least partially due to their preoccupation with meeting Mao's industrial — and especially steel — targets, while Mao's main focus was on the communes.[21] In any case, during the first signs of "cooling down," as with the emergence of the leap, the core economic organizations were lagging behind.

---

important individuals in this group were the Chairman's secretaries and the term was sometimes used as synonymous with them, but others were included who had virtual secretarial status. A case in point was Wu Lengxi who held leading posts in the *People's Daily* and the New China News Agency, but was seemingly regarded by Mao as an *ad hoc* secretary. See Wu Lengxi, *Yi Mao Zhuxi*, p. 54. Cf. below, p. 131.

19   Liu Zihou, "Huiyi Mao Zhuxi," pp. 250-51; Bo Yibo, *Huigu*, vol. 2, pp. 751-52, 807-808; and Wu Lengxi, *Yi Mao Zhuxi*, pp. 93-97.

20   Bo Yibo, *Huigu*, vol. 2, p. 808.

21   For example, from September to early November Zhou Enlai and others were engaged in a series of meetings and activities to fulfil the steel target; see *Zhou Enlai nianpu*, vol. 2, pp. 169, 186, 188.

This, however, is not to say that economic officials, who by dint of expertise should have had a greater sense of realism, did not find some benefit from Mao's new attitude. Thus when Wang Heshou reported on the steel situation to Mao on October 29, he presented two likely possibilities concerning the goal of doubling production. The first was that with every province and major factory meeting their targets the goal could be achieved. The second was that although the goal might be achieved on the surface in terms of quantity, the output might be short on quality, and while he hoped to realize the first result it was likely the plan would not be met. Mao was impressed, underlined Wang's conclusion, and declared it a good document to be circulated. He further commented that "this is what I want Wang Heshou to write," and he had the Secretariat invite other leaders to come up with similar documents.[22] The stage was thus set for the initial effort to "cool down" in the first of a series of major Party conferences at Zhengzhou.

Zhengzhou and Wuchang/Wuhan, November-December 1958: Initial Steps and Theoretical Muddle

When Mao arrived in Zhengzhou at the start of November he was ready to make a concerted attempt to introduce more realism into high Party circles. But at the same time he manifested attitudes that consistently undermined his efforts over the next eight months. These involved not only his long noted refusal to contemplate any change to the basic line of the leap,[23] something which had an undoubted impact on Party leaders who had been exposed to the Chairman's harsh strictures against *fanmaojin* at the start of 1958,[24] but equally significantly his views on leadership methodology. While his now comparatively more cautious views placed greater emphasis on achieving *what was possible*, he remained committed to promoting activism and not "pouring cold water" on either the masses or the cadres. The resultant ambiguity not only meant other leaders and lower officials had considerable leeway to continue pursuit of unrealistic goals if so inclined ideologically, but even if they held reservations about the course of the leap the approach of "better left than right" still seemed prudent. Finally, Mao's approach to securing greater realism bore a striking similarity to his initial efforts to promote the leap: theory and ideological persuasion were to do the trick. In early 1958 "letting ideology go" did indeed drive the new movement to ever more incredible heights; now theoretical argument and exhortation was to encourage the necessary corrections. The crucial difference, however, was that

---

22   *Mao wengao*, vol. 7, pp. 474-76.

23   See Teiwes, *Politics and Purges*, pp. 306-10; and Schoenhals, *Saltationist Socialism*, pp. 167-68.

24   See Bo Yibo's comment explaining the difficulty of getting people to admit leftist mistakes as due to the Great Leap emerging in the course of Mao's personal criticism of opposing rash advance; *Huigu*, vol. 2, p. 813.

new ideological themes were not linked to political attacks and harsh discipline. All of this can be seen at the first Zhengzhou conference.

As Bo Yibo later observed, the first Zhengzhou conference which was held from November 2 to 10 marked the highest fever of the leap forward, as well as the initial effort to cool the movement down. With regard to fevered imaginations, at the meeting discussions were conducted on surpassing Britain *in per capita production* within 15 years. The conference also heard enthusiastic advocacy of abolishing the commodity economy and speeding the transition to communism, with some participants apparently opposing drawing a clear demarcation between socialist and communist stages. Moreover, optimism concerning production goals remained very high, with steel output for the end of the Sixth FYP in 1972 set at 400 million tons, four times the target proposed by Li Fuchun at the May Party Congress.[25]

In this context Mao's efforts to "cool down" the leadership covered a broad front. He found various economic targets dubious, notably the 1972 steel projection, and concerning steel he called for lengthening the period to achieve targets and only to seek to surpass Britain, not the U.S. As a result he stopped distribution of the conference's 40-article document on socialist construction[26] setting out the various production goals, allowing it only to go to leading cadres for their information rather than being formally transmitted to the coming Wuhan plenum for discussion, and inevitably approval. Mao also saw the need for planning and a responsibility system in agriculture so that "chaos [does not] reign," warned against a onesided emphasis on steel to the neglect of agriculture, and insisted that responsible leaders pay attention to "objective [economic] laws," especially the "law of balanced development." Moreover, the Chairman was aware and critical of practices common in the pursuit of exaggerated targets such as beating, cursing, and subjecting people to struggle meetings, and of course the widespread phenomena of false output reports. Thus he concluded that of the reported 900 billion catties of grain for the current year, only 740 billion at most could be considered real. And Mao pointed out to those in attendance that in at least some places the situation was dire indeed, noting for example (with some hyperbole) that "in Shanghai and Wuhan there is nothing to eat."[27]

But Mao's major concern, and undoubtedly in his mind the source of the most serious problems facing the nation, was the confusion created by the headlong rush toward "communism." This was seen in his insistence on the idea that there was a clear demarcation between socialism and communism, and China was still properly in the socialist stage. Thus a commodity economy

---

[25]   Bo Yibo, *Huigu*, vol. 2, pp. 708-709; and "unpublished Chinese document no. 6," pp. 129, 131, 134-35.

[26]   This document must be distinguished from the famous 40 articles on agricultural development with which it has sometimes been confused; see *SS*, pp. 451n23, 459n43, 460n45, 466n62, 470n74, 485n20, 493n44.

[27]   Bo Yibo, *Huigu*, vol. 2, pp. 709, 809; and *SS*, pp. 452-54, 460, 468, 470, 471.

was appropriate for the current situation and had to be protected and developed, rather than treated as a pernicious force that led to capitalism. While much of his concern was directed at the people's communes in the rural areas where he also spoke of the need to retain small freedoms within the collective and some family functions, Mao was also aware of "big chaos" in the cities and observed that perhaps urban communes could not be achieved. Moreover, notwithstanding Zhang Chunqiao's strictures against "bourgeois right" that had received his (basic) approval only the previous month, the Chairman now spoke of the need for unequal wages to remain for the time being. He also reserved some barbs for Chen Boda's advocacy of doing away with money, something which had a particular irony as we shall see. Basically, Mao regarded plans for a very rapid transition to communism as too ambitious, citing the proposals of various localities for a transition to ownership by the whole people (a necessary preparatory stage) in two to six years, or ten years to communism, as too short a period. Even a transition to communism in 15 years which he seemingly regarded as feasible was not to be published, presumably to avoid excessive pressure for that goal. And as he had done earlier in the year but now with new significance, the Chairman depicted his own position as somewhat to the "right" in the alignment of forces within the Party.[28]

In the process of attempting to enforce his comparatively sober view, Mao provided profoundly ambiguous signals to those gathered at Zhengzhou.[29] Apart from the inherent ambiguity created by his continuing commitment to the correctness of the general line, the Chairman also regarded as "realistic" grain production reports in excess of his own projections at the heated Beidaihe conference, called for instituting the supply system in the cities and, his doubts notwithstanding, ordered the organization of urban communes, stipulated the abolition of "the patriarchal [family] system," and affirmed that "bourgeois right has to be demolished in part." Perhaps most difficult to fathom, for all of his advocacy of commodity production, Mao argued that it was necessary to develop in two directions, allocation and transfer — the very antithesis of commodity exchange by his own account — as well as commodity production. Moreover, while the law of value that underpinned commodity exchange was important, the "main regulator" was not only planning but also its Great Leap variant of the Party secretary (and politics) "taking command."[30]

---

[28]   Bo Yibo, *Huigu*, vol. 2, pp. 808-10; *SS*, pp. 444, 455, 459, 465, 478; and MacFarquhar, *Origins 2*, pp. 130-31.

[29]   On Mao's proclivity toward ambiguity throughout the pre-Cultural Revolution period, see the introduction to the second edition of Teiwes, *Politics and Purges*, especially pp. xvii, xx, xxii-xxvi, xxxii, xxxvi, xxxix, xliii-xlv, liii, lvii-lviii, lx-lxi.

[30]   *SS*, pp. 449, 451, 454, 456, 457-58, 460, 463; and "unpublished Chinese document no. 5," p. 101.

While all of this would have been perplexing enough for the assembled leaders, in turning to theory to help them clarify their thinking and by extension to proceed with the leap in a more realistic mode Mao's prescription was also inherently confusing. Mao stipulated that Party committee members from the central to county levels read two books, Stalin's 1952 treatise, *Economic Problems of Socialism in the USSR*, and *Marx, Engels, Lenin and Stalin on Communism*, a collection of writings prepared by CCP propaganda authorities during the Great Leap and published in August. The strange choice of the later is suggested by the fact that it originated with fervid discussions in the spring, including the utopian dreaming at the Guangzhou railway station in April, as well as its publication during the upsurge of enthusiasm in the summer. How could such a compilation be a reliable guide for "cooling down"? But equally perplexing is Mao's use of Stalin's famous *Economic Problems of Socialism*.[31]

Mao's discussion of Stalin's treatise was profoundly ambivalent. Certainly on the main points of what he was trying to get across — the importance of commodity production in the current stage and the need to observe objective economic laws, Mao was clearly positive in his assessment of Stalin's views. Ironically, Mao used Stalin's authority to refute Chen Boda's views on abolishing money when Chen himself had used the Chairman's enthusiasms of the summer to bolster his own case. Yet even in these core areas Mao hedged his bets in a way that would give uncertain cadres food for thought; thus after approving of Stalin on the need to make use of commodity production and exchange and the law of value, he challenged his audience with "Are there no negative aspects? Refute him!" More directly, he declared parts of Stalin's book "entirely wrong," accused him of establishing a "rigid framework," failing to acknowledge "dialectical laws," and making the transition to communism "hardly possible." Of particular concern, and forcefully rejected, was Stalin's overemphasis on heavy industry (although heavy industry still had priority in Mao's view) with the result that the Soviet Union "walks [with] one leg long, one leg short" producing an unbalanced economy, and his allegedly exclusive focus on the economy, technology, and specialists without any interest in the masses or politics. In short, the Chairman's extended commentary highlighted the differences between the (flawed) Stalinist and (fundamentally correct) Great Leap approaches at the very moment when he was attempting to enlist the dead Soviet leader's authority to moderate the leap.[32]

---

31   On the CCP collection, see *Dang de wenxian*, no. 5 (1993), pp. 46-47. Cf. above, p. 95. Concerning Stalin's book, writing more than a decade ago Roderick MacFarquhar reasonably concluded that Mao's many remarks about it were an attack on Stalin and by extension the Soviet Union; *Origins 2*, pp. 134-35. Bo Yibo, however, makes clear that Mao's intention in stipulating *Economic Problems of Socialism* as required reading was for the purpose of clearing up confused leftist thinking; *Huigu*, vol. 2, p. 810.

32   *SS*, pp. 444, 446, 448, 455-56, 461-64, 469-74, 476; and *Xuexi ziliao, xuyi*, pp. 184-92.

Whether Mao was moved by a self-proclaimed theorist's desire to sort out the positive and negative aspects of Stalin's thinking, his own complex feelings toward the dead dictator, or — very likely — by the nationalist pride evident throughout the leap that the Chinese could do things better than the Russians,[33] his theoretical ruminations were not the only factor causing uncertainty among his colleagues and lower officials as too how much "cooling down" was really required. Particularly instructive are Mao's interactions with other individuals and categories of participants at Zhengzhou. Examining these interactions, moreover, allows us to deepen further our understanding of the actors around Mao.

During the conference Mao sought to enforce his views (or perhaps for once his self-characterization as engaging in "persuasive work toward some comrades" was adequate) through a series of private meetings as well as speeches to plenary sessions. Over the nine days he met with provincial leaders repeatedly, as befit the primary concern with production relations in the countryside. In these discussions the Chairman "began to lower the temperature of work," consistently taking a more cautious line than his interlocutors. When Henan's noted radical Wu Zhipu and Hubei's Wang Renzhong, also generally regarded as a Great Leap enthusiast, informed him on November 4 of plans for a 10-year transition to communism, Mao not only indicated that he did not agree with the period but also that socialism, not communism, was still the matter of concern. Similarly, at this time when Shandong's Tan Qilong reported on a county's plan to achieve communism in 2 years, Mao asked Chen Boda, Zhang Chunqiao and Li Youjiu to investigate. On their subsequent report he commented that adding a "0" (i.e., 20 years) would not even be long enough. Then on the 5th, when Ke Qingshi reported on ideological confusion in Shanghai, Mao took a bleaker view of conditions than Ke. Ke had responded to Mao's question concerning fear of communism with an estimate that less than 30 per cent of local cadres had such an attitude; the Chairman's rejoinder was that while this might be so at the county and lower levels, he believed it was more at the provincial and municipal levels. And seemingly on the same day, he remarked to Wang Renzhong and the only central official reportedly involved, Li Fuchun, that he lagged four years behind their steel targets and therefore had a bit of a rightist tendency. In all this Mao seemingly was the moderating force now claimed.[34]

---

[33] Note his comment that "The Soviet Union also brags [about entering communism] but you only hear a noise on the staircase, you don't see anyone coming down"; *SS*, p. 446. Cf. MacFarquhar's discussion of Sino-Soviet tensions in this period; *Origins 2*, pp. 132-35.

[34] Bo Yibo, *Huigu*, vol. 2, pp. 808-10; and Tan Qilong, "Jianchi shishi qiushi shenru diaocha yanjiu" [Uphold Seeking Truth From Facts, Immerse Oneself in Investigation and Study], in *Mianhuai Mao Zedong*, vol. 1, p. 239. In addition to Wu Zhipu, Wang Renzhong and Ke Qingshi, other provincial leaders involved in private discussions with Mao at the conference were Zhou Xiaozhou, Shu Tong, and Zeng Xisheng (see below), as well as Gansu's Zhang Zhongliang, Shaanxi's Zhang Desheng, Hebei's Lin Tie, and

Yet other aspects of this situation should be noted. First, in contrast to earlier in the year when provincial leaders, at least those visible in the process, seemed to be critical forces pushing the leap ahead, now — although to the left of Mao — a degree of concern on their part can also be sensed. These leaders were, after all, responsible for implementing the Great Leap, and even such a prominent radical as Ke Qingshi felt the need to report on ideological confusion, although in Ke's case one always wonders about the degree to which he may have been responding to Mao's cues.[35] In addition, Hunan's Zhou Xiaozhou, Shandong's Shu Tong and Anhui's Zeng Xisheng, the last of whom was a particularly well known Great Leap radical, also expressed concerns over such matters as runs on banks and panic purchasing to the Chairman.[36]   Second, while Mao positioned himself to the "right" of these leaders and sought to instil greater moderation in their behavior, he brought no particular pressure on them to achieve that goal. Thus his remark in plenary session that Wu Zhipu was imbued with "too much Marxism" was hardly a withering critique such as Zhou Enlai, Chen Yun *et al.* had suffered at Nanning and thereafter.[37] And however much provincial leaders may have been enlightened (or otherwise) by Mao's discussions of Stalin's theories, the Chairman's continuing commitment to rapid growth, profound social transformation and activism to achieve these ambitious goals was clear to all. The prudent as well as genuinely enthusiastic provincial officials were thus encouraged to do their best to achieve leap forward objectives. For them, as well as Mao, "cooling down" was completely different from "pouring cold water" on the masses.

Also of interest is the apparent minor role at Zhengzhou of top central leaders and responsible economic officials who were seemingly consulted less than in the period immediately preceding the conference. Only Li Fuchun is known to have had an audience with Mao, Deng Xiaoping's presence at Zhengzhou is indicated by an interjection during the Chairman's talk on the 9th, while Zhou Enlai and others were seemingly absent from the meeting.[38]

Shanxi's Tao Lujia. As for Tan Qilong, Zhang Chungqiao, and Li Youjiu, it is not entirely clear they actually attended the meeting; see below, p. 238n2.

35   See below, pp. 196-97.

36   Bo Yibo, *Huigu*, vol. 2, p. 809.

37   *SS*, p. 478.

38   "Unpublished Chinese document no. 6," p. 128, only states that a portion of central leading comrades, economic coordination region leading comrades, and a portion of provincial Party secretaries attended the conference without providing any names. Our knowledge of who was definitely there largely comes from Bo Yibo, *Huigu*, pp. 808-10. According to Kenneth Lieberthal, *A Research Guide to Central Party and Government Meetings in China, 1949-1975* (White Plains: International Arts and Sciences Press, 1976), pp. 123-24, based on appearances elsewhere it is likely that Zhou, Zhu De, Chen Yi, He Long, Peng Zhen, Dong Biwu, *Tan Zhenlin, Li Xiannian, Bo Yibo*, Lu Dingyi, Luo Ruiqing, Nie Rongzhen, and Ye Jianying (key economic officials in italics) did not attend, while it is reasonable to conclude from Bo's discussion that Chen Yun, Wang

As for his attitude toward those responsible for the economy, Mao was somewhat contradictory. On the one hand he not only placed himself to the right of Li Fuchun (along with Wang Renzhong) on steel targets, he also rather sharply criticized "economists" as "leftists" who "get by under false pretences." At Zhengzhou Mao also showed concern over the breakdown of planning, although at the time this seemed a broad complaint against authorities from the central to local levels and only later did he allege that the SPC had abrogated its responsibilities after the Beidaihe conference. On the other hand, he gave credit to the unlikely couple of Chen Yun and Li Fuchun as more knowledgeable than himself in economic matters. Perhaps the Chairman was becoming aware of the need for some professional help, but there is little to indicate that such leaders played a key role (or in most cases were even present) at the Zhengzhou meeting.[39]

Finally, Mao's concluding remarks to the conference concerning *xiucai*, scholars or skillful writers — literally holders of the first imperial degree, a term often used to refer to the Chairman's secretaries, bears comment. In complaining about people who refused to acknowledge a demarcation line between socialism and communism, the Chairman explicitly referred to *xiucai* who "all can't agree [and] want to rebel."[40] While these individuals were not identified, they can safely be taken to include Chen Boda who suffered Mao's criticism over the abolition of money, and Zhang Chunqiao who, although not Mao's secretary, had gained his attention and had become the spokesperson for opposing "bourgeois right." They might also have included Mao's other secretaries, Hu Qiaomu and Tian Jiaying.[41] What is striking here is that all of the above, with the exception of Hu Qiaomu, are known to have been dispatched by Mao on investigation trips to uncover problems in this very period. Arguably, it was their radical tendencies as well as, in most cases, their closeness to the Chairman, that made them acceptable representatives for discovering the "truth." Moreover, it is also possible that their ideological preferences colored the picture they presented to their master.

In any case, following the conclusion of the Zhengzhou conference Mao brought his senior colleagues into the process. Two days after the meeting broke up, he wrote to Deng Xiaoping proposing that the Zhengzhou document on people's communes be discussed before the forthcoming Wuchang

---

Heshou, and Zhao Erlu were also absent. Further indication of the absence of Zhou, Wang Heshou, Zhao Erlu, and other central economic officials is provided by *Zhou Enlai nianpu*, vol. 2, pp. 187-88. See Appendix 1.6, p. 238, for an incomplete list of those attending.

39 Bo Yibo, *Huigu*, vol. 2, pp. 809-10; *SS*, pp. 465, 469, 471-72; and *Case of Peng*, pp. 411-12.

40 "Unpublished Chinese document no. 6," p. 129. On the usage of *xiucai*, see above, n. 18.

41 While Tian Jiaying later became a voice for moderation as a result of his investigations (see below, pp. 168, 224ff), his radical tendencies were apparent earlier in his 1957 criticism of the Eighth Congress formulation of the main contradiction. Cong Jin, *Quzhe fazhan*, pp. 74-75.

conference, especially asking that Deng consult with "Beijing comrades" in order to make sure that consideration of the document by provincial officials not be hindered. On the following day, November 13, the Chairman wrote to Deng and Liu Shaoqi proposing that the Politiburo and Secretariat convene three or four meetings within a few days to discuss the Zhengzhou documents and Stalin's book in order to prepare for the coming conference. As a result, from the 13th to 19th Politburo and Secretariat members carried out discussion and study according to Mao's directive.[42]

But more important to unfolding developments were Mao's own activities. In the by now familiar pattern, he continued his investigation and research in Henan and Hubei (the provinces of Wu Zhipu and Wang Renzhong), holding discussions on the commune supply system with prefecture, and county Party secretaries on November 11. On the 12th, the Chairman, who was accompanied on his trip by Wu Lengxi and Tian Jiaying, met with 18 cadres from organs in Zhongnanhai (thus involving people either in or in proximity to his own household) who had been sent down to the countryside, as well as with the same prefecture leaders for the second time. Over the next two days he met with commune, district, county, prefecture, and provincial officials, sessions where he placed avoiding breaking up the family and guaranteeing peasants sufficient rest high on his agenda. Mao finally arrived in Wuchang on the 14th when he heard Wang Renzhong's report on local conditions and communization in Hubei.[43]

From the time of his arrival to the eve of the conference (which ran from November 21 to 27, to be followed by the Wuhan plenum from the 28th to December 10) Mao had Wu and Tian participate in a seminar run by Wang and fellow Hubei secretary Zhang Pinghua. Various county and commune Party secretaries, heads of iron and steel works, and sent-down cadres reported to the seminar, and Wu and Tian regularly reported to the Chairman on the views expressed, emphasizing contradictions between rich and poor brigades within the communes, popular objections to "militarization" and communal mess halls, the low proportion of "good" output resulting from the steel drive, and cadre bragging and brutal behavior. Meanwhile, on the 16th and 17th Mao met with key central agricultural officials Tan Zhenlin and Liao Luyan, with local host Wang Renzhong also in attendance. On the 19th he received mayors and prefecture Party secretaries from the area, and the following day on the eve of the conference he held discussions with influential provincial secretaries Zhou Xiaozhou, Tao Zhu (Guangdong), Li Jingquan (Sichuan), and Tao Lujia, followed by top central figures Chen Yun, Deng Xiaoping, Peng Zhen, and Party Center General Office Director Yang Shangkun, again with

---

42   "Unpublished Chinese document no. 6," pp. 135-36; and Bo Yibo, *Huigu*, vol. 2, pp. 811-12.

43   Bo Yibo, *Huigu*, vol. 2, p. 812; and Wu Lengxi, *Yi Mao Zhuxi*, pp. 105-106. Bo has Mao arriving in Wuchang on the 15th, but as someone accompanying the Chairman, Wu's account is preferred.

Wang Renzhong in attendance.[44] Clearly the Chairman's main source of information was still local officials and his personal staff played a key role, but as in October several central leaders also had an opportunity to provide input.

While the precise influence of these various encounters cannot be gauged, according to Mao's account over six years later he was disturbed by a county official's report on how terrible local conditions were, including people having nothing to eat, and he arrived in Wuchang deflated. Notwithstanding this and other evidence that he was aware of starvation conditions in some localities, once the conference started on the 21st the Chairman displayed the same contradictory mix of enjoinders for greater realism and continued attachment to the programs and methods of the leap forward that he had shown at Zhengzhou. Thus on the one hand he could warn that continuing in the same manner as at present could result in half of China's population dying, but go on to say that Anhui, which he classified elsewhere as extreme and where starvation had already occurred, could more or less continue on its course as long as the province "[made] it a principle to have no deaths." Similarly, Mao professed a relaxed attitude toward the transition to communism, even allowing that the Soviet approach might be more prudent than China's, but he still endorsed measures to develop communal mess halls and the supply system. As to production achievements, he indicated scepticism about claims concerning 1958 grain output and called for attention to the serious problem of false reports, yet at the same meetings projected very fast agricultural growth including overproduction of grain so that peasants could soon take a year off. And he attempted to encourage moderation by remarking that rural cadres should not be branded with the dreaded "right conservative" label if they pushed the masses a little less hard, although elsewhere he suggested that regions with larger percentage increases in steel production had shown more Marxism-Leninism.[45]

The last matter went to the heart of Mao's dilemma, both at Wuchang and throughout the entire effort to "cool down." More realism, yes, but also continuing activism was what the Chairman wanted. Statements that he doubted this or that target were accompanied by observations that if they could nevertheless be achieved, that was all for the good and indeed cause for celebration. Put more abstractly, Mao insisted that the principle of *duo, kuai, hao, sheng* accorded with objective law, meaning that what could not be done should not be forced, but also that "Where acceleration is possible, [then] accelerate.[46] More reliable plans simply meant scaling back targets to still

---

44 *Ibid.*

45 Gu Longsheng, *Mao Zedong jingji nianpu*, p. 624; *SS*, pp. 484, 494-95, 503-504, 507-508, 512; *Mao wengao*, vol. 7, p. 436; "unpublished Chinese document no. 6," pp. 138-39; Bo Yibo, *Huigu*, vol. 2, p. 813; and Schoenhals, *Saltationist Socialism*, p. 167. Cf. above, n. 16.

46 *SS*, pp. 484, 504, 512. Bo Yibo's account of Mao's view on the objective law question in

incredible levels. When observing that the doubling of steel output in 1958 he had insisted on was risky and distorting the economy, Mao now applied pressure to reduce the outlandish 30 million tons target for 1959, "suggesting" that "we don't triple [output] next year, but just double it." The Chairman also used a number of metaphors and references to past developments to get his point across, but these inevitably muddied the message of moderation. Thus Mao called for "compressing air" (*yasuo kongqi*), i.e., the "leftist air" dominant in Party circles according to Bo Yibo, but he also declared that *yasuo* was not the same thing as *jianshao* despite the fact that both verbs carry the same connotation of reduce, cut down, retrench. Mao's usage had a special twist: he argued that "compressing air" did not mean reducing its amount, only to compress it into the liquid form of oxygen. While Bo Yibo in his memoirs and arguably various leaders (including Bo) at the conference might see an anti-left intent in the Chairman's imagery, many would not hear that message but instead, and more accurately, heed his insistence that the general line remain in place. [47]

Another more familiar reference touched on a particularly sensitive matter. On November 23 Mao now revived the notion of rash advance, saying that "In the past you all opposed my *maojin*, [but] I'm not opposing anyone's [rash] advance here today."[48] As Bo Yibo reflected decades later, Mao's treatment of the *fanmaojin* effort of 1956 left an implicit threat for any leaders or cadres who may have had more fundamental reservations about the leap. This implication was emphasized in Mao's references to the key sin of opposing rash advance: "pouring cold water on the masses." While the Chairman claimed that his own efforts to instil greater realism might produce resentment from low-level cadres who perceived them as "cold water," his main point was that "cooling down" efforts had to be done with great care.

Huigu, vol. 2, p. 813, only includes the cautious injunction.

[47]   *SS*, p. 502; Bo Yibo, *Huigu*, vol. 2, pp. 813, 815; *Mao Zedong sixiang wansui* [Long Live Mao Zedong Thought] (n.p.: September 1967), p. 87; *Xuexi ziliao, xuyi*, p. 207; and Li Rui, "Zhonggong zhongyang Wuchang huiyi he bajie liuzhong quanhui" [The CCP Central Committee's Wuchang Conference and the Sixth Plenum of the Eighth Central Committee], *Zhonggong dangshi ziliao*, no. 61 (1997), pp. 55-56.

[48]   *SS*, p. 502. There is a direct clash between this and other Cultural Revolution texts of Mao's comment and those in post-Mao accounts (e.g., Bo Yibo, *Huigu*, vol. 2, p. 816; and "unpublished Chinese document no. 6," p. 138) which render his remark as he *would* criticize others for their rash advance. We favor the Cultural Revolution version for several reasons. First, it can be found in a number of disparate collections (see *Xuexi wenxuan*, vol. 2, p. 230; *Xuexi ziliao, xuyi*, p. 209; and *Mao Zedong sixiang wansui* [September 1967], p. 89) that are not mere reproductions of a single original source, suggesting that various members of the audience perceived Mao as still articulating anti-*fanmaojin* attitudes, while post-Mao sources may have settled on a conventional wisdom concerning what transpired. Second, even later when there was much more reason for Mao to reconsider the verdict on opposing rash advance he remained negative despite some concessions; see below, p. 152.

Pouring "buckets of cold water" in 1956 was a serious mistake, this time it was necessary to "draw a lesson from 1956" and make sure not to "dampen the enthusiasm of the masses." When added to a ringing affirmation of the general line and the methods of "politics in command" and the mass line, such reminders of the central political "error" of the recent past could only argue for circumspection when it came to correcting Great Leap excesses.[49]

In fact, this message came through loud and clear to those assembled at Wuchang. Remarkably, given signs of serious dislocation and human tragedy in the country, there is little evidence of *anyone* taking a position to the "right" of Mao at these meetings. While being somewhat more forthcoming about his own "adventurism" earlier in the year than he had been at Zhengzhou, it was now the Chairman who seemingly dragged other radicals to more "reasonable" positions: Chen Boda's investigations debunked claims of fantastic crop yields, while Wu Zhipu now allowed the road to communism would take "a bit longer." Meanwhile, although many top leaders were present, and at least Liu Shaoqi, Zhou Enlai, Chen Yun, Deng Xiaoping, Peng Zhen, Li Fuchun, Tan Zhenlin, and Bo Yibo are known to have met with Mao during the meetings, there is little to indicate any forceful advocacy on their part, with the very partial exception of Bo noted below. However useful the Politburo and Secretariat members' study of the Zhengzhou documents and *Economic Problems of Socialism*, it seemingly had not emboldened them to move faster than Mao.[50]

Sketchy information also sheds some light on central ministerial officials and local leaders. Mao's speech at the November 23 plenary session where he commented favorably on reports prepared for the conference by 12 ministries (including metallurgy, railroads, and water conservancy and electric power), suggests ministerial leaders firmly endorsed Great Leap orthodoxy. The

---

[49]   Bo Yibo, *Huigu*, vol. 2, p. 813; *SS*, pp. 496, 501; and Mao's comments of November 30, 1958, cited in Schoenhals, *Saltationist Socialism*, p. 167. Officials could also ponder the Chairman's discussion of comrades whose brains were too hot or too cold. The former were enjoined to pay attention to their problem while the latter were to have their brains gradually heated up; Bo, pp. 816-17.

[50]   *SS*, pp. 486, 489; Bo Yibo, *Huigu*, vol. 2, pp. 815-16; and Schoenhals, *Saltationist Socialism*, p. 169. Our information on who from this group met with Mao is largely from Bo's reflections. Bo also placed Ke Qingshi and Li Jingquan, both Politburo members since the May Party Congress, at a discussion with Mao, but for our purposes they are better considered as provincial leaders. For an incomplete listing of participants in the Wuchang conference and the immediately following Wuhan plenum, see Appendices 1.7 and 1.8, pp. 239-41.

Our conclusions regarding the lack of forceful advocacy by central leaders is largely based on inference from Bo Yibo's account. Bo is normally quick to point out anything striking in exchanges with Mao, and particularly to emphasize those actions by his leadership comrades that fit into behavior approved by post-Mao orthodoxy, as standing out against leap excesses certainly would. But here he only lists their presence at a meeting which seemingly endorsed Mao's drift toward "cooling down."

Chairman expressed pleasure that these ambitious reports showed that the "line is still that line; the spirit is still that spirit," but linked this to the mild criticism that "the bases for the plan targets are not fully substantiated" and asked for more reliable revised targets. Judging from this, central bureaucrats, i.e., those officials presumably with the technical knowledge to understand better than anyone the outlandishness of Great Leap targets, seemingly had adopted a "safe" approach of expressing fidelity to the line and setting overambitious goals, while Mao pulled them back toward greater realism at Wuchang.[51]

As for the localities, serious difficulties were increasingly in evidence as the conference convened. These difficulties, which provincial leaders seemingly eschewed discussing at least initially,[52] can be seen in Alfred Chan's fine account of Liaoning where, by the end of 1958, provincial leaders had to contend with the Center hurling contradictory demands at the province, they themselves were increasingly "unable to set priorities and make real decisions," lower levels engaged in a range of defensive behavior including false reporting and ritual compliance, and strong grass-roots resistance had appeared.[53] Nevertheless, there is little sign of such matters being forcefully addressed by the responsible provincial officials at Wuchang. On the contrary, when key leaders of the economic coordination zones Ke Qingshi, Li Jingquan, Wang Renzhong, Tao Zhu, Ouyang Qin (the Northeast), Zhang Desheng, and Lin Tie joined Mao and other top central leaders[54] at a small evening discussion on the 22nd, they were reluctant to admit problems. In Wu Lengxi's account, while the Chairman was keen to discuss lowering production targets and to persuade these local chieftains of this view, the result on the contrary was that they sought to persuade him to preserve the Beidaihe targets. As Mao remarked with some scepticism, the regions and provinces lacked a basis for their projections, with some regions calling for a doubling of steel in 1959 while various provinces aimed to increase output by four times, more than 10-fold, or even 30-fold.[55]

The evidence from Bo Yibo's memoir account suggests that a greater degree of initiative, although again under Mao's prodding, came from some members of a group that had seldom played a key role in shaping policy since the discarding of *fanmaojin* — key economic officials at the Center. From the

---

51   *SS*, pp. 499-500; and Wu Lengxi, *Yi Mao Zhuxi*, pp. 107-108.

52   After praising the ministries for their optimistic reports, the Chairman went on to complain about the failure of provincial secretaries to mirror their central comrades: "it just won't do for not a single one of you to write a report.... None of you is saying a word"; *SS*, p. 501. While this could have several interpretations, it does suggest local leaders did not come to Wuchang armed with detailed reports on the problems facing them.

53   Chan, "Agricultural Development in the Great Leap Forward," pp. 69-71.

54   Liu Shaoqi, Chen Yun, Deng Xiaoping, Peng Zhen, and Tan Zhenlin.

55   Bo Yibo, *Huigu*, vol. 2, pp. 815-16; and Wu Lengxi, *Yi Mao Zhuxi*, p. 107.

very outset of the meetings Mao, for reasons which remain unclear,[56] focused on the issue of steel targets, clearly feeling they were too high. At the opening session, after complaining generally of people being out of touch with reality, expressing doubt over claims for the 1958 grain crop, and declaring that publicly announcing the Zhengzhou document's projected 400 million tons of steel by 1972[57] would be "very bad" (presumably because it would expose China's ambitions to the outside world including the critical Russians), the Chairman asked whether the 1959 steel target should be set at 30 million tons as proposed at Beidaihe. Bo reports that he interjected, saying that the large mass mobilization on the steel front naturally had its good points but that a tense situation existed in many places. Bo claimed that the 11 million tons guaranteed for 1958 at the August meeting could still be met or overfulfilled, but there was a serious issue concerning quality. He further argued that different methods would have to be used in 1959, proposing "fixed points" in order to determine where conditions were suitable and to disband operations that were unsuitable. Mao's reaction to Bo's interjection was largely positive: he floated the idea of setting the 1959 figure at 22 million, although he "humorously" added that this was a bit of "cold water" and "right opportunism."[58]

Mao's continuing pursuit of the steel issue, and diverse positions among several economic officials, was apparent over the next few days. On the afternoon of the 21st Li Fuchun, who had overall responsibility for the economy, took charge of discussions on the 1959 steel target involving the central ministries represented at the conference. That evening Mao called in Li, Bo Yibo, Minister of Metallurgy Wang Heshou,[59] and First Ministry of Machine Building chief Zhao Erlu to consider the same issue, thus consulting

---

56 MacFarquhar, writing more than a dozen years ago in *Origins 2*, pp. 129-30, speculated that Mao's "awakening" on the steel question might have been due to new estimates on the worth of backyard steel, awareness of the transport crisis caused by the need to ship coal all over China in support of the steel drive, and/or by hints from officials at the major Wuhan steel works who had been emboldened to tell the truth. We find all of these suggestions plausible, but further argument concerning the possible moderating influence of Zhou Enlai, Wang Jiaxiang, and Li Fuchun is less persuasive. Clearly Li was not a moderating force (see below), while Mao seemingly resented Wang's sober observations at the Central Committee plenum; see Cong Jin, *Quzhe fazhan*, p. 188. As for Zhou, while a senior Party historian reports that he started to express doubts after the first Zhengzhou conference, it is our view that after the criticism of *fanmaojin* his propensity to follow Mao as closely as possible makes it unlikely that he was playing a forceful role at this juncture.

57 Mao, in Bo Yibo, *Huigu*, vol. 2, p. 813, mentioned "40 articles" by which he clearly referred to the Zhengzhou document. On the confusion between this document and the more famous 40-article draft agricultural program, see above, n. 26.

58 Bo Yibo, *Huigu*, vol. 2, pp. 814-15.

59 Bo does not mention Wang in his account of those present, but subsequently quotes Mao who indicated Wang was there. *Huigu*, vol. 2, p. 815.

both leading planners and the heads of key spending ministries. Li Fuchun typically was the most optimistic of the group, nominating 25 million tons as possible; just over a week later Mao would dress down Li in the presence of Zhou Enlai, telling him to "cool off." On this occasion Zhao Erlu was more cautious about what could be achieved, (apparently) only offering the comment that 16 million tons was about the maximum that could be produced. Bo also felt that 16 million was about the limit, but seemingly fearing Mao might regard this as too conservative, he suggested that 18 million be set as the internal target while 16 million tons was the publicly announced goal. As for any opinions expressed by Wang Heshou, these were not reported.[60]

Two days later Mao described himself as unable to sleep after this encounter as he went over what they said in his mind, and despite still floating the possibility of again doubling output to 22 million tons, he concluded that the issue was not whether 30 million was uncertain, but whether even 18 million was reliable. He also mentioned a discussion on the evening of the 22nd with 12 "big region" and central comrades[61] which seemingly concluded that there was an insufficient basis for guaranteeing 18 million tons. Mao's continuing discussion noted that the amount of good steel being produced in 1958 was only 8.5 of the 11 million ton target, so that doubling it would only produce 17 million tons in 1959. In the course of his comments, moreover, the Chairman offered the lowest projection on record at the meetings, but at the same time maddeningly suggested that almost anything was possible: "[If there is no assurance of success the target] will have to be lowered further — 15 million tons would be all right. If there is an assurance, make it 18 million tons; and if there is still more assurance [of success], make it 22 million tons; and if still more, then 25 or 30 million tons are all fine with me."[62]

A brief footnote on yet another group of actors, Mao's secretaries, is in order. While there is little to indicate that these *xiucai* as a whole departed significantly from the radical tendencies criticized by Mao at Zhengzhou, in one case the possibilities for such personal staff to be (relatively) candid with the Chairman was manifested at Wuchang. At least in his own account, during the conference Li Rui discussed with Mao several of the problems created by the Great Leap, and when the issue of unrealistic grain production claims came up, Li asked the Chairman how, as someone who had grown up in the countryside and had lived there for a long period, he could believe the astronomic production claims then current. In response Mao said he had read noted scientist Qian Xuesen's essays, and believed the word of scientists. While there clearly is the possibility of exaggeration here, the incident

---

[60] *Ibid.*

[61] Liu Shaoqi, Chen Yun, Deng Xiaoping, Peng Zhen, Tan Zhenlin, Ke Qingshi, Li Jingquan, Wang Renzhong, Tao Zhu, Ouyang Qin, Zhang Desheng, and Lin Tie. By "big region" Mao referred to the economic coordination regions set up earlier in the year.

[62] Bo Yibo, *Huigu*, vol. 2, pp. 815-16; *SS*, pp. 502-503; and Schoenhals, *Saltationist Socialism*, p. 169.

seemingly again indicates the ability of such lower ranking but ostensibly trusted figures as Li Rui to raise sensitive issues with the Chairman.[63]

The Chairman's many ambivalences and the political caution of seemingly all actors at Wuchang notwithstanding, by the end of the Wuhan plenum on December 10 his message that some "cooling" was required made an impact. While Western characterizations of this development as a "withdrawal" or a sign of "disillusionment" are greatly overstated, the plenum's resolution did moderate policy concerning the people's communes, placed the transition to communism in the more distant future, and lowered various industrial targets set at Beidaihe, including a reduction of the 1959 steel target to 18 to 20 million tons (the published and internal targets respectively) and a cut in capital construction from ¥50 to ¥36 billion, although agricultural targets were increased. Moreover, both during the plenum and immediately thereafter various provinces began to take measures to implement the more prudent approach, despite the radical stand taken by leading local figures at the outset of the Wuchang gathering.[64]

Importantly, the developments at the plenum encouraged two leaders who had over the years demonstrated a keen sensitivity to the Chairman's wishes and moods. Premier Zhou Enlai, whose policy role in the economic sphere since the criticism of opposing rash advance had been limited, apart from loyally carrying out Mao's directives concerning the steel campaign, now actively articulated the "realistic" approach. Soon after the meetings Zhou told officials from the Ministry of Foreign Trade that there had to be a limit in striving for high targets, and he drove his point home by quoting the Chairman on not pursuing things that were not there. On December 24, when visiting Xushui and another Hebei county, the Premier called for realism and complained that the slogan of "food for free" was a "vulgarization of Marxism." Then on the 25th, after viewing a play seemingly about armed struggle, he emphasized that managing industry could not be treated as if it were a military campaign, enthusiasm was not enough, and it was necessary to have a scientific basis. Also in December Zhou dispatched his secretary Gu Ming, a former official in a major steel complex, to investigate the small furnaces, a mission which concluded that the claims for such furnaces were false. And finally in this period, while on a visit to a commune in the company of North Korean leader Kim Il Sung, the Premier ordered the commune authorities to stop making steel because they lacked iron ore and sufficient techniques. While it is easy to believe that these actions corresponded to Zhou's own beliefs, it was only with Mao's authority that he began to speak out.[65]

---

63 *Bainianchao*, no. 4 (1997), p. 8; above, pp. 113-14; and below, p. 151.

64 Bo Yibo, *Huigu*, vol. 2, p. 817; Ma Qibin, *Zhizheng sishinian*, p. 156; Cong Jin, *Quzhe fazhan*, p. 171; MacFarquhar, *Origins 2*, pp. 136-37, 140; and *PDA,* pp. 24ff.

65 *Dang de wenxian*, no. 5 (1992), p. 44; Li Ping, *Kaiguo Zongli*, p. 369; Cheng Hua, *Zhou Enlai he tade mishumen* [Zhou Enlai and his Secretaries] (Beijing: Zhongguo guangbo

Of particular interest, especially in view of developments over the following months, was the role of another architect of *fanmaojin* — Chen Yun. Chen like Zhou had been largely bypassed in economic policy since the start of the year, apart from his Beidaihe and post-Beidaihe efforts to meet Mao's steel targets and to provide some coherence to the rapidly developing capital construction front. At Zhengzhou, however, he had received a favorable mention from Mao for his economic knowledge, albeit along with the less accomplished and less realistic Li Fuchun. But given that the Chairman remained fundamentally committed to the broad thrust of the Great Leap, Chen had to proceed with great caution and he began to speak up about the time of the Wuhan plenum. In one of his first moves he drafted a proposal not to publish the still ambitious grain target that was being pushed by Tan Zhenlin and Minister of Agriculture Liao Luyan, but Mao's secretary, Hu Qiaomu, in an apparent effort to shield Chen, failed to pass on his opinion to the Chairman. Mao, however, although allegedly only aware of Chen's proposal the following April when he criticized Hu for his temerity in pigeonholing the opinion of a Party Vice Chairman, nevertheless seemed inclined to give Chen some room to air his views. Later in December, at a conference convened by his new State Capital Construction Commission in Hangzhou where Mao was also staying, Chen raised some "serious mistakes and shortcomings" and called for more attention to the quality of output as opposed to the current obsession with quantity. That Mao was not particularly displeased is perhaps suggested by the invitation Chen received to the Chairman's birthday party a few days later, an occasion Chen used to air his concerns directly to Mao. While Mao did not accept Chen's views, he left the door ajar with the comment that they should let practice judge the matter. Later Mao would comment that at this time he came to share some of Chen's opinions, and Chen began to voice them more openly over the next few months. In any case, in the absence of a clearer signal from Mao, Chen's efforts were not taken seriously within the Party as a whole and "no one listened to him."[66] This situation was played out against the background of the next set of leadership meetings beginning in Beijing in late January.

---

dianshi chubanshe, 1992), p. 19; *Zhou Enlai nianpu*, vol. 2, pp. 194, 197-98; MacFarquhar, *Origins 2*, pp. 129-30; oral source; and above, pp. 74-75.

[66]   Cong Jin, *Quzhe fazhan*, pp. 188, 256; *Chen Yun wenxuan (1956-1985 nian)* [Selected Works of Chen Yun, 1956-1985] (Beijing: Renmin chubanshe, 1986), pp. 96-99; *Hongqi*, no. 13 (1986), p. 13; MacFarquhar, *Origins 2*, pp. 163-65; "unpublished Chinese document no. 6," p. 156; Bo Yibo, *Huigu*, vol. 2, pp. 711, 828; oral sources; and above, pp. 107, 110, 113. While the source on Mao's birthday party (Cong Jin) is highly reputable, a Party historian specializing in the period is dismissive of this account.

Beijing, Zhengzhou, and Shanghai, January-March/April 1959:
Practical Concerns and A Mercurial Chairman

As events unfolded around the turn of the year, it became clear that the problem facing Chen Yun, as well as other leaders seeking to further the "cooling down" process, was not limited to the failure of the Chairman to provide clear signals. With conditions further worsening, Mao, who conducted additional investigations in Hubei and Hunan after the Wuhan plenum before stopping at Hangzhou and then returning to Beijing at the end of December, and other leaders gained increasing understanding of the depth of the problems facing the country. In particular, the realization dawned that despite a bumper 1958 harvest, state grain procurement targets were not being met. Moreover, during January and February of the new year, with the Chairman as well as both central and local officials involved, still greater knowledge of serious difficulties accumulated in the period leading to the second Zhengzhou conference in late February and early March. These investigations were interrupted by a meeting of provincial Party secretaries from January 26 to February 2 in Beijing that was called by Mao to consider the 1959 plan. In this difficult situation Mao's behavior became even more erratic and threatening.[67]

These developments can be seen most clearly in Chen Yun's situation. Chen continued to call for "cool heads" in the context of his ongoing capital construction meeting and articulated again his view at the Wuhan plenum that the ambitious targets decreed then would be difficult to achieve. Also, at the start of January both Zhou Enlai and Deng Xiaoping "touched on" planning, and after the 8th when Li Fuchun, still the most important economic official, returned to Beijing, discussions began on the 10th where the steel target was a key issue that generated different views. About this time, probably on the 8th, 9th, or 10th,[68] Mao called in Li, Chen, Bo Yibo, and Li Xiannian, thus involving the four top planning and financial officials, as well as Peng Dehuai, to discuss economic and industrial questions. Although Mao would claim on various subsequent occasions that he shared Chen Yun's views and wanted to lower targets but could not do anything about it in the atmosphere of the time, the available detailed accounts tell a different story.[69]

67 Bo Yibo, *Huigu*, vol. 2, p. 819; MacFarquhar, *Origins 2*, pp. 140-42, 144-45; Gu Longsheng, *Mao Zedong jingji nianpu*, p. 624; and *Mao wengao*, vol. 8 (January-December 1959) (Beijing: Zhongyang wenxian chubanshe, 1993), pp. 17-18. Specific examples of "moderate" efforts include investigations carried out by the Guangdong authorities, a warning by the Party Center's Industrial Work Department against indiscriminately treating technical and administrative personnel as "white flags," and Chen Boda's report on village investigations that sought to rectify the left.

68 According to Bo Yibo, *Huigu*, vol. 2, p. 828, this occurred during the first part of January (*Yiyue shangxun*), i.e., the first 10 days of the month. Since Li returned to the capital on the 8th, the likelihood is that the gathering took place during the last three days of the period.

69 *Ibid.*, pp. 711, 828; and Gu Longsheng, *Mao Zedong jingji nianpu*, pp. 471, 606, 608,

During this meeting Chen, who earlier had felt the time was not right to offer advice to Mao, now responded to the Chairman's request that he express his views on four key targets with the opinion that the 1959 targets would be difficult to fulfil. In the discussions of the period on the steel target, in speeches to the SPC and SEC small groups Chen intimated that difficulties would be a bit too much, while to Mao he expressed fears concerning achieving 18 million tons of good steel. Mao responded with "Drop it, this even goes to whether the general line in the end is correct or not, [and] I am still watching it," a response indicating the utmost sensitivity of the issue. Such a reaction undoubtedly encouraged those who opposed lowering targets (perhaps Li Fuchun and Tan Zhenlin[70]) to criticize Chen as a "rightist" and contributed to the situation where no one took seriously Chen's efforts. Chen himself, clearly unnerved by the Chairman's reference to the line, the very perspective which justified the onslaught at Nanning and thereafter, concluded his speech on February 1 to the provincial secretaries conference with a self-criticism. Later Mao would say (and decades after Bo Yibo would also claim) that he (Mao) wanted Chen to speak out but Chen had misunderstood him, but given the tenor of his remark and recent history it was a perfectly understandable "misunderstanding."[71]

In this context, it is also understandable that the Beijing conference found it hard to alter targets, and the meeting basically supported those set by the Wuhan plenum. This was further due to Mao's contradictory performance at the conference itself. In the by now familiar manner, on the one hand he voiced some "moderate" sentiments, calling for reducing the capital construction "a little," and particularly by acknowledging that there were objective economic laws that he still didn't understand and that the leadership collectively was like small children playing with fire. He also subsequently claimed his aim in convening the conference was to lower targets, and implied he had to badger the participants to stay on in pursuit of this goal, although to no avail in the end. Nevertheless, as MacFarquhar's analysis has noted, the predominant tone adopted by the Chairman was one of pushing forward again. Although he had allowed that people should not feel bad if their efforts came up short, in his concluding speech on February 2nd Mao emphasized that the general line could not be changed, defects were only one finger out of ten, every effort for "more, faster, better, and more economical" results must still be exerted, there would be a leap forward every year, and what had happened over the past two months was a short rest, but *now* the time had come to press

---

624.

70   These two leaders were identified by a junior historian specializing in the period on the basis of what he was told, and the identifications are credible given Li's and Tan's general performances in the period.

71   Bo Yibo, *Huigu*, vol. 2, p. 828; Gu Longsheng, *Mao Zedong jingji nianpu*, p. 624; "unpublished Chinese document no. 6," p. 156; *Chen Yun yu jingji jianshe*, p. 294; Tao Lujia, *Yige shengwei shuji*, p. 81; oral source; and above, p. 121 .

ahead again.[72]

In the period both before and especially after the Beijing conference, however, Mao seemingly was exposed to some particularly strong currents indicating the need for a reassessment which apparently came largely from the provinces. In a letter to Liu Shaoqi and Deng Xiaoping on March 1, the Chairman claimed his current (more restrained) thinking had gradually developed during January and February, particularly when not long after the conference he visited Tianjin, Jinan, and Zhengzhou and held discussions on commune issues with provincial and lower-level leaders, including Tianjin's Wan Xiaotang, Hebei's Liu Zihou, and Shandong's Shu Tong and Tan Qilong, which "greatly enlightened" him. In this same period he had been paying considerable attention to developments in the south and, notwithstanding some critical comments at the second Zhengzhou conference, he later singled out for praise two most unlikely forerunners of greater moderation, Tao Zhu and Wang Renzhong. As he put it, "As early as the start of 1959 there were two provinces making self-criticisms [i.e., revealing serious problems] to the Center. They were Guangdong and Hubei."[73]

With the Chairman's "new thinking" developing, the period immediately prior to the convening of the second Zhengzhou conference from February 27 to March 5 saw contrasting developments. There was still no retreat on production targets, with the Party Center on February 15 approving SPC estimates concerning what would be necessary to guarantee the Wuhan plenum's 20 million ton steel target and other high targets. On the 24th, however, Bo Yibo reported to the Center that there was insufficient

---

72   Bo Yibo, *Huigu*, vol. 2, p. 819; Gu Longsheng, *Mao Zedong jingji nianpu*, p. 606; "unpublished Chinese document no. 6," pp. 146-47; and MacFarquhar, *Origins 2*, pp. 145-46. Schoenhals, *Saltationist Socialism*, p. 168, quotes similar sentiments to those expressed on the 2nd in Mao's speech of February 1. For a very incomplete list of participants in the Beijing conference, see Appendix 1.9, p. 241.

73   Bo Yibo, *Huigu*, vol. 2, pp. 819-20; "unpublished Chinese document no. 6," pp. 147-48, 152; Zheng Xiaofeng and Shu Ling, *Tao Zhu zhuan* [Biography of Tao Zhu] (Beijing: Zhongguo qingnian chubanshe, 1992), p. 263; and MacFarquhar, *Origins 2*, pp. 140-42, 145. Tao Zhu's and Wang Renzhong's radical proclivities throughout 1958 are clear (see, e.g., above, pp. 74, 90, 93), but efforts to depict Wang in particular as continuing to push the radical course throughout 1959 go against the existing evidence. Cf. Li Zhisui's flawed recollections concerning Wang, *The Private Life of Chairman Mao: The Memoirs of Mao's Personal Physician* (London: Chatto & Windus, 1994), pp. 299-300, 307, 308.

With regard to Tao Zhu and Guangdong, MacFarquhar's analysis (pp. 137ff) not only points to Mao's criticism of Tao at Zhengzhou but argues that a conflict existed between Mao (on the "right") and Tao over handling "departmentalism," i.e., peasants hiding grain and financial resources from the authorities. While this is clearly true in the sense that the position adopted by Mao at Zhengzhou rejected Guangdong's effort to uncover such hidden resources, we believe the more important aspect of developments in this period is that the Guangdong authorities were moving in a "moderate" direction overall and thus reinforced the Chairman's own drift in that direction, something suggested by his subsequent praise seemingly offered around May.

distribution of steel products and equipment to realize the plans of the key Ministries of Metallurgy, Machine Building, and Coal, and he recommended a telephone conference of provincial first secretaries to deal with the problem since under the arrangements of the time power was shared by central and local authorities and the SEC was not empowered to act on its own. Bo's view was endorsed by the Center shortly after the conclusion of the meeting and, moreover, the SEC was now given responsibility for industrial production. This concern for greater order and comprehensive planning was also seen in the emergence of the "whole nation as a chessboard" concept, a policy enunciated at Wuhan by Mao and now receiving prominence in the press after first coming to note in an article by Shanghai's Ke Qingshi.[74] But clearly the issue of greatest concern as the conferees gathered was the question of commune organization, the matter dominating Mao's inspections of Hebei, Shandong, and Henan.

The centrality of the commune issue was also reflected in the composition of the participants at Zhengzhou: 29 provincial-level Party secretaries with primary responsibility for the rural areas, plus 18 leaders from the Center. Of the central leaders in attendance, Deng Xiaoping appeared to play a particularly important role, usually chairing meetings when Mao was not present; in addition, Party leaders Liu Shaoqi and Peng Zhen were among those present from the outset. In contrast, key economic officials Li Fuchun, Bo Yibo, and Chen Yun, in addition to Premier Zhou Enlai and others,[75] were only summoned to the meeting by Mao at the halfway point, arriving on the afternoon of March 2. In terms of contact with Mao, he met with smaller groups of up to 29 people on his train on six occasions. Those mentioned as attending such gatherings were top Party leaders Liu, Zhou, Deng, Chen Yun, and Peng Zhen, agricultural chief Tan Zhenlin, and provincial secretaries Wu Zhipu and Shi Xiangsheng from the host province, plus Ke Qingshi and Li Jingquan. Of course, the full group having the possibility of exchanging views with the Chairman was considerably larger, and these listings may reflect little more than the tendency of Party history sources to observe official status. Nevertheless, it is striking that key central Party leaders Liu Shaoqi, Deng Xiaoping, and Peng Zhen, whose names rarely surface in available accounts of earlier "cooling down" efforts, keep reappearing at these gatherings, and also that they seemingly assumed prominent roles at meetings where Mao was not present during the conference. On a purely speculative basis, it might be the case that Mao, in taking a more systematic view of the problems facing the CCP, felt a need to enlist the aid of hardened central leaders in curbing the excesses of lower-level officials.[76]

---

[74]   Bo Yibo, *Huigu*, vol. 2, pp. 828-29; and MacFarquhar, *Origins 2*, pp. 142-44.

[75]   The others summoned were Chen Yi, Peng Dehuai, Xiao Hua, Lu Dingyi, and Kang Sheng. The remaining key economic official, Li Xiannian, was present throughout. *Dang de wenxian*, no. 6 (1992), pp. 91-92; and *Mao wengao*, vol. 8, p. 87.

[76]   *Dang de wenxian*, no. 6 (1992), pp. 91-92; and *Mao wengao*, vol. 8, p. 91. Liu, Deng,

Whatever the role of Liu, Deng, and Peng, the available records of Mao's speeches at the second Zhengzhou conference indicate a performance that was, in comparison to his efforts at the first Zhengzhou and Wuchang meetings, considerably more consistent in its "anti-left" posture. As MacFarquhar has commented, although Mao repeated the standard emphasis on the successes of the leap forward (nine out of ten fingers), in terms of his concrete discussions of rural policy and the communes his talks "contained little but criticism." The Chairman's observations were also more practical than earlier, with little of the theoretical preoccupations of late 1958. Since MacFarquhar has ably summarized these speeches, their critical message will be summarized briefly here.[77]

The Chairman focused his attack on the "communist wind" (*gongchan feng*) that had arisen since the previous autumn, a "wind" that forced egalitarianism on the peasantry, arbitrarily transferred resources from actual production units to the commune and from rich to poor brigades, utilized excessive amounts of corvée labor, enforced high levels of accumulation, and collectivized household items and private plots and animals. He further attacked the large-scale transfer of resources from agriculture to industry, both in terms of labor power and the practice of calling in bank loans to communes in order to support industrialization. More generally, and in direct contrast to his call only four weeks earlier for a fresh exertion of efforts, Mao advocated going at a somewhat slower, more relaxed pace. Perhaps most striking was the severity of much of the Chairman's language. Mistakes were attributed to "adventurism committed by us in the upper ranks," "our leadership does not have the support of the masses," the transfer of wealth amounted to "banditry," and efforts such as those by the Guangdong Party apparatus to extract hidden grain from the peasants in the name of combating

---

and Peng were listed at four of the six discussion sessions with Mao, and they were all present at another six meetings (five chaired by Deng, one by Liu). In addition, Peng Zhen chaired a meeting where the other two were apparently not present, while Deng chaired his sixth meeting with Peng but seemingly not Liu in attendance.

While the sources refer to 20 central leaders at Zhengzhou, this figure is apparently arrived at by including Politburo members Ke Qingshi and Li Jingquan as central representatives. Of the true 18 central leaders, all Politburo Standing Committee members except for Zhu De and Lin Biao were included, while 9 of the remaining 17 (non-local) full and alternate Politburo members (excluding Party elders Lin Boqu and Dong Biwu, Marshals Luo Ronghuan, Liu Bocheng, and He Long, Vice Minister of Foreign Affairs Zhang Wentian, and surprisingly Chen Boda) were present. This central group also included Mao's secretary Hu Qiaomu and military figures Tan Zheng, Huang Kecheng, and Xiao Hua. Cf. Appendix 1.10, pp. 241-42.

[77]   See *Origins 2*, pp. 146-55. MacFarquhar largely relied on the Red Guard collection *Mao Zedong sixiang wansui* [Long Live Mao Zedong Thought], vol. 2 ([Taibei]: 1967), which has been available since the late Cultural Revolution period. Subsequent information has done little to change the impressions conveyed by this source. See *Mao wengao*, vol. 8, pp. 61-75, for a speech outline and the text of Mao's February 27 talk which is virtually identical to the Red Guard text.

"departmentalism" were denounced while the peasants' actions were defended as "basically reasonable and legal." The overall policy response was to curb commune overcentralization and the extraction of village resources by introducing a policy of "three levels of ownership and accounting with the brigade as the basic unit." But again it was the force of the rhetoric that was most notable: "I say — thoroughly implement right opportunism, thoroughly and to the end. If you don't follow me then I'll do it on my own — even to the lengths of abandoning my Party membership."[78]

Clearly Mao's criticism of "left adventurism" at Zhengzhou achieved some results. The conference officially accepted Mao's opinions, adopted policies to decentralize the communes, and drafted regulations on commune management, although the issue of defining what was meant by "the brigade as the basic [accounting] unit" would still be thrashed out over the coming weeks. As we have seen, relative realism surfaced in other areas, as in the development of the "chessboard" concept and the fixing of authority for industrial issues in the SEC. On the other hand, the question of production targets was not addressed, and Mao's treatment of the "departmentalism" issue still seemingly assumed that the high estimates of 1958 grain production were correct.[79] But there is a mystery in developments at Zhengzhou which goes beyond the signs of continuing optimism on the part of Mao and others: why, if Mao was so forceful, were there signs of resistance to the views the Chairman now put forth? Concretely, what do we make of such evidence as the claim that "some comrades" didn't understand his views and considered them "somewhat off the track" and even "rightist and retrogressive"?[80]

While any answer must be to some extent conjectural, it would seem to lie in familiar waffle and contradictions on the Chairman's part despite his many criticisms of "leftism," together with a combination of belief and timidity on the part of "some comrades." Bo Yibo would reflect many years later that notwithstanding the acceptance of Mao's opinions on the "communist wind" the conference did not alter the Wuhan resolution's stipulations for a rapid completion of the transition to ownership by the whole people, and that for all of Mao's warnings against excessive urgency for the transition to communism he only moved back a bit and did not basically change his position. Apart from the ambiguity in strict policy terms, what was arguably more significant was his sharp warning to those harboring doubts about the communes: "[If] one still has problems about such a basic question, then he is entirely mistaken and

78   MacFarquhar, *Origins 2*, pp. 146-55; and *Mao wengao*, vol. 8, pp. 61-75.

79   See MacFarquhar, *Origins 2*, p. 157. It is also instructive that Chen Yun, in his article on capital construction that was published while the conference was in session, although attempting to highlight the importance of quality and nationwide coordination, neverthless found it necessary to reiterate such Great Leap themes as *duo, kuai, hao, sheng*, the importance of ideological work, the mass line, and Party leadership. See Lardy and Lieberthal, *Chen Yun's Strategy*, pp. 88-111.

80   "Unpublished Chinese document no. 6," p. 152; and *Mao wengao*, vol. 8, pp. 85-86.

must be a right opportunist." This was classic Mao — while he could rhetorically apply "right opportunist" to himself to define the issue against "leftist" trends, when the label was used relative to others it became profoundly threatening. So too was his subsequent comment that "the broad masses" would surely rise up and smash the sarcasm of backward elements."[81]

But perhaps a keener sense of the matter can be seen through the interaction of the Chairman and reluctant "leftists" at Zhengzhou. Mao's account of unconvinced "leftists" comes from a letter to Liu and Deng on March 1 where he notes that he had met with 10 comrades the previous day, seemingly local leaders including Ke Qingshi and Li Jingquan plus Tan Zhenlin, the radically inclined leader responsible for rural affairs who had shortly before the conference called for an even greater leap forward in agriculture,[82] but not involving the otherwise active trio of Liu, Deng, and Peng Zhen. Among them were the comrades who allegedly suspected rightism in and harbored reservations about Mao's views. Yet in contrast to the rhetorical strength of his speeches, Mao's letter indicates a much softer approach to his "critics." After referring to their doubts about his opinions, the Chairman said: "Naturally [we] can still discuss [these matters]. I can say this, the thought of these comrades has some correctness, but I think my observations and basic thought are not bad. But they are still not completely perfect. Some [of my] viewpoints need the help, supplementation, revision, and development of [other] comrades." Here Mao, as ever concerned with not "pouring cold water" on enthusiastic leaders, seemed to be pulling back from any sweeping condemnation of "left" views. As for the participants at the conference who would have heard the contents of the letter when it was read out to them by Hu Qiaomu on the Chairman's orders, those genuinely convinced of the desirability of pushing ahead without letup had license to stick to their guns and try to convince Mao, while those trying to catch the political wind could still believe that "left" was safer than "right." As an interview source with access to Mao in this period put it, provincial leaders such as Wu Zhipu dared to express doubts because "[mistakes from] the left were not a problem."[83]

---

[81]   Bo Yibo, *Huigu*, vol. 2, pp. 764, 766; and *Chinese Law and Government*, Winter 1968/69, pp. 23-24. While the backward elements referred to were landlords, counter-revolutionaries, etc. presumably outside the Party, this would give little solace to Party leaders and cadres.

[82]   Tan's advocacy came in a February 17 *People's Daily* article. Reportedly, however, "in the [presumably second] Zhengzhou conference [Tan] was *brave enough* to raise with Mao the problems which the mass smelting campaign was causing for the grain and cotton harvests"; Jin Ye, ed., *Huiyi Tan Zhenlin* [Remember Tan Zhenlin] (Hangzhou: Zhejiang renmin chubanshe, 1992), p. 378 (emphasis added). Even in this case Tan's action can be seen as less reflecting doubts concerning the Great Leap than the fact that the leap's visionary goals for the countryside were being impeded by the iron and steel drive.

[83]   "Unpublished Chinese document no. 6," pp. 152-53; *Mao wengao*, vol. 8, pp. 85-86;

In the weeks immediately following the Zhengzhou meeting multi-level cadre conferences were held throughout the country to consider the readjustment of commune management. As these conferences sought to give definition to Mao's vague guideline that the brigade (*dui*) should be the basic accounting unit of the communes,[84] evidence of divisions among provincial leaders — which were already implied by the early self-criticisms of their "leftist" behavior by Guangdong and Hubei — began to surface. As Mao monitored these cadre conferences while he traveled south from Henan to Hubei, he discovered the varying interpretations being proposed by different provinces. The most radical approach, taking *dui* to mean the large brigade (*shengchan dadui*), i.e., an area larger than the former higher-level cooperative, was adopted predictably by Wu Zhipu's Henan, and ironically — in view of his designation as a leading "right opportunist" a few months later at Lushan — Zhou Xiaozhou's Hunan. The more moderate interpretation that the (smaller) brigade (*shengchan dui*), the equivalent of a cooperative, was adopted by Hubei and supported by Guangdong, the provinces of the erstwhile radicals Wang Renzhong and Tao Zhu who had already "cooled down" before Zhengzhou. In considering these approaches Mao made clear his preference for the Hubei plan, but consistent with his unwillingness to "pour cold water" he allowed Henan to proceed, provided its plans were acceptable to the province's basic-level cadres. For all his strictures against "leftism" at Zhengzhou, the Chairman now concluded that "whatever the method, as long as it meets the demands of the masses, then it can be carried through."[85]

Thus, once again, there was a lack of clarity when the expanded Politburo met for the Shanghai conference from March 25 to April 1, followed on April 2-5 by a Central Committee plenum at the same venue.[86] As at Zhengzhou, several top central Party leaders were particularly prominent at Shanghai. Most significant was Liu Shaoqi whose long foreshadowed elevation to the chairmanship of the state, along with Mao's retirement from the post, was formally endorsed by the Central Committee.[87] Perhaps more provocatively,

---

Dang de wenxian, no. 6 (1992), p. 91; and oral source. In his letter Mao also asked the participants in an apparently nonthreatening manner to read the record of the six-level cadre conferences held in Henan on February 27 and 28 which assertedly contained "much criticism of my rightist and retrogressive views."

[84]   See MacFarquhar's excellent discussion of the terminological confusion in *Origins 2*, pp. 161, 181-84.

[85]   *Ibid.*, p. 162; "unpublished Chinese document no. 6," p. 153; Ma Qibin, *Zhizheng sishinian*, p. 162; and *Mao wengao*, vol. 8, pp. 93ff.

[86]   Unlike various other conferences from the period, no information is available concerning the numbers participating in the expanded Politburo meeting, but it is recorded that 81 full Central Committee members and 80 alternates, or more than 80 percent of the total, attended the plenum. Ma Qibin, *Zhizheng sishinian*, p. 162. Cf. Appendices 1.11 and 1.12, pp. 242-44, for incomplete information on those present at Shanghai.

[87]   For a review of the steps leading to Liu's elevation, as well as the larger question of Mao's "retreat to the second front," see MacFarquhar, *Origins 1*, pp. 152-56.

Mao also referred to one of his long-term favorites, Deng Xiaoping,[88] with the comment that while he himself was the "main marshal," Deng was the "vice marshal." In Bo Yibo's account of the meetings, both Liu and Deng, along with Zhou Enlai, were involved in efforts to promote a more realistic course.[89] As we shall see, provincial leaders also played a major role in developments at Shanghai, as did at least some key central economic officials.

In policy terms the contradictory strands of the previous months were present. Progress of sorts in "cooling down" was made with the adoption of 18 articles on commune management which stipulated the (small) brigade as the accounting unit,[90] steel (as well as other) targets were somewhat lowered, in this case from 20 to 18 million tons in the published target to be "striven for" while 16.5 million tons was circulated internally as a "reliable" target, Deng and Zhou clearly argued that plans must be dependable while Liu noted that there were many problems with achieving even the internal steel target, and nine points were proposed which subsequently became 16 articles on work methods stressing flexibility and listening to different opinions. As for Mao personally, he was the author of the nine (and later 16) points, he now clearly endorsed Chen Yun's sober views of the winter as correct, and, using the Ming official Hai Rui who had criticized the emperor as a model, he called on officials to speak out. But by emphasizing work methods, even if they were significantly different in substance from those advocated in the 60 articles at the start of 1958, Mao in effect upheld the general line — at one point rhetorically asking "is our general line correct or not," a question brooking only one answer — and reduced the massive problems facing the nation to questions of work style.[91] His attitude toward his leading colleagues during the meetings would be even more unsettling.

Mao's mercurial moods at Shanghai — and the roles of various other actors — are apparent in his interactions with such actors during the meetings. The more benign, albeit obscure Mao can be seen most clearly in events involving provincial leaders. The memoirs of Tao Lujia, the first secretary of Shanxi at the time, discuss the question of industrial and agricultural targets. Notwithstanding Mao's greater "realism," at the start of the expanded Politburo meeting unnamed "central leading comrades" responsible for

---

88   The evidence suggests that of all top leaders Deng and Lin Biao were Mao's personal favorites. See Teiwes and Sun, *The Tragedy of Lin Biao*, p. 20.

89   Bo Yibo, *Huigu*, vol. 2, pp. 830-32; *Mao wengao*, vol. 8, p. 196; and MacFarquhar, *Origins 2*, pp. 173ff.

90   "Unpublished Chinese document no. 6," pp. 155-56. This document also mentioned the still smaller production team (*shengchan xiaodui*) which was to be assigned various management functions.

91   *Ibid.* pp. 155-58; Bo Yibo, *Huigu*, vol. 2, pp. 830-32; and MacFarquhar, *Origins 2*, p. 172. For the nine points and 16 articles, see *Xuexi ziliao*, vol. 3, pp. 368-79; and *Miscellany of Mao Tse-tung Thought (1949-1968)*, part I, *Joint Publications Research Service*, no. 61269-1, February 20, 1974, pp. 178-81.

industry and agriculture — who most likely included Li Fuchun and Tan Zhenlin[92] — proposed maintaining the targets approved by the Wuhan plenum. Moreover, to the consternation of Tao and others, these leaders had not discussed the matter beforehand with their provincial colleagues, and moreover they demanded that each local leader clearly indicate his attitude on the matter. This, as Tao complained, created an oppressive atmosphere; in his recollection the great majority of provincial officials believed the targets were too high but felt it was "inconvenient" to take a clear stand.[93] There is no indication in Tao's memoirs, however, that any of these officials reflected on the exceptional pressure *they* had placed on the central figures responsible for the economy the previous year.

Unnamed central officials were not the only culprits, however. When pressure was brought to bear on the reluctant provincial leaders, two of their own number, Ke Qingshi and Li Jingquan (both also Politburo members) sought to "persuade everyone" to accept the targets. Li reportedly stepped forward to say that if provinces could not meet their individual grain targets, Sichuan (which was actually facing severe shortages) would step in to help, while Ke made a similar offer on Shanghai's behalf concerning steel. This, as Tao recalled, presented other local leaders with "two hardships": if they did not accept the targets they ran the risk of "rightism," but if they did accept them it would be difficult to achieve the goals. This difficult situation was perceived by "central leading comrades," and some of them came to small group meetings to persuade local leaders of ways to meet the targets. The delegation to persuade Shanxi, consisting of Shanxi native Peng Zhen, Tan Zhenlin, and Li Fuchun, was not successful, and after phoning his provincial Party standing committee which was unanimous that the 1959 targets could not be met, Tao proposed that the Center reduce its targets. Tao soon discovered that all of the other provincial leaders at Shanghai with whom he came into contact shared the same outlook.[94]

The divisions among the provincial leaders soon became sharper. During the expanded Politburo meeting Mao called in leaders of the six economic coordination areas for a discussion. Tao Lujia was late and arrived for the

---

92   Li and Tan were the officials primarily responsible for industrial and agricultural targets. On Tan, see below, p. 173. As for Li, although eventually on April 4 proposing a reduction in steel (to 18 million tons) and other targets, he seemed less involved in pointing out difficulties than other leaders; see Bo Yibo, *Huigu*, vol. 2, pp. 831-32. One top economic official who can be safely excluded is Li Xiannian, not only because of his financial responsibilities and track record in supporting *fanmaojin*, but in view of his March 1959 financial and economics work report emphasizing difficulties; see Zhou Weiren, *Jia Tuofu zhuan*, pp. 152-53.

93   Tao Lujia, *Yige shengwei shuji*, pp. 81-82. While, according to his recollections of Shanghai, Tao consistently advocated the "realistic" course, it is of interest that shortly before the meeting Mao had criticized Tao for Shanxi's refusal to pay compensation to brigades for expropriated property; MacFarquhar, *Origins 2*, p. 162.

94   Tao Lujia, *Yige shengwei shuji*, pp. 82-83; and oral source.

afternoon meal, whereupon he was seated facing Mao. Tao took the opportunity to express his reservations, particularly concerning the grain and steel targets. Before he had finished the Chairman turned to Wang Renzhong and observed that Wang too had the same attitude. Tao soon discovered that before his arrival Wang had spoken out against high targets, clashing with Ke Qingshi and Li Jingquan. Ke Qingshi now pressed Tao, saying that lofty ambitions and high ideals were what was required, leading Tao to reply that in the view of Shanxi peasants "[you can] speak big words and make empty talk, [but] a yield of 1,000 catties per *mu* can't be done." Li Jingquan also pressured Tao with entreaties to jump for results, but Tao answered that jumping high again would not produce the desired results. Anhui's Zeng Xisheng also joined in by remarking that his province's targets could be realized as long as everyone went all out. During all this Tao observed Mao smile; the Chairman's only comment was that they had different opinions and could discuss the matter again. He seemed relaxed and to have enjoyed the discussion.[95]

Another instance where Mao at least ostensibly took a relatively open-minded view concerning the raising of Great Leap shortcomings concerned his secretary Li Rui. During early spring 1959 Li wrote to Mao about steel targets and the difficulties in realizing them based on a conversation with Liao Jili of the SPC, who had told Li that it would be impossible to reach the target of 20 million tons. Li's letter to Mao argued that the target had to be reduced. When he met Li Rui during the Shanghai conference, Mao complained that the letter failed to point out the reasons why the 1959 target could not be reached and the problems that it would create. After this meeting, Li wrote another letter, again raising in a fairly blunt way the problems of realizing the production targets for 1959 and the SFYP. Mao's reaction now was to praise Li on the last day of the conference. Once again Mao seemed comparatively receptive to opinions from this junior figure.[96]

A less open and receptive Chairman was on display on other occasions during the Shanghai gathering, however. His dissatisfaction with the situation outlined in Bo Yibo's report on industrial production and basic construction was expressed sharply at the outset of the meetings. On the eve of the gathering on March 25, Bo submitted a letter and speech outline to Mao describing three possibilities (that the goals would be completely met, basically met, or there would be economic dislocation), and proposing to "shorten the front." When Bo spoke on the next day Mao interrupted with

---

[95] Tao Lujia, *Yige shengwei shuji*, pp. 83-84; and oral source. In the provinces themselves during this period, Dali L. Yang argues, considerable diversity was emerging in response to the rural crisis both between and within provinces, with some even facing leadership splits over contracting output to individual households. See his "Surviving the Great Leap Famine: The Struggle over Rural Policy, 1958-1962," in Cheek and Saich, *New Perspectives on State Socialism*, pp. 267-69.

[96] *Bainianchao*, no. 4 (1997), pp. 9-10. While once again this is Li Rui's own account, it is backed up by the text of the second letter.

criticisms of economics work that had some echoes with the Nanning conference, even if the substance was considerably different. The Chairman complained that although various ministries responsible for industry had ten years' experience they still had few achievements and didn't know what to do. In pithy language he asked "who is running this, [you're] only dandies," and declared what was needed was someone tougher, a Qinshihuang. Toughness, in this case, ostensibly meant being more ruthless in cutting back unrealistic projects; Mao declared that if there were too many capital construction projects, then cut them by 500 or even 600 items. Yet his position was ambiguous in the sense that if officials were able to achieve the industrial goals he would be happy, if they failed he would not be particularly impressed. This, at least, is the implication of Bo and Li Fuchun writing to the Chairman shortly after the plenum and reporting that his criticism left them both depressed and joyful — depressed that they performed badly and thus disappointed the Chairman, joyful that they now had a better idea of what to do.[97]

Mao's threatening ambiguity also was expressed in other public and private settings. At the concluding session of the Central Committee plenum on April 5, Mao claimed that while he favored reducing production targets, he still could not agree with opposing rash advance. While he acknowledged that specific cutbacks in 1956 including those authorized at the previously disgraced Second Plenum had received his approval and that U-shaped development would happen again, he rejected the publicizing of *fanmaojin* and concluded with the warning "do not oppose rash advance, opposing rash advance is no good." While Mao's approval of reducing targets suggests moderation in a policy sense, his rejection of *fanmaojin* could not have been reassuring in a political sense.[98]

The double-edged nature of Mao's remarks on the 5th can also be seen as he again commented on a lack of guts on the part of his comrades, and invoked the Hai Rui spirit, claiming that "if you don't oppress me I won't be stimulated." That this did have an impact in encouraging people to speak out was attested to in an interview with a participant at Shanghai who cited his own (relatively) candid approach and that of Peng Dehuai at Lushan as a consequence of the Chairman invoking Hai Rui. But who could possibly take up the injunction for bravery *vis-à-vis* the Chairman himself? Such entreaties as "Now there's a tendency not to criticize seriously my shortcomings [but] you can attack me by innuendo.... Look how pointed Hai Rui was, that letter he wrote to the emperor was very blunt, extremely blunt," were bound to fall on deaf ears. As Mao privately confessed during the meetings, while he wanted Hai Ruis to appear he feared he might not be able to bear criticism if it

---

97   Bo Yibo, *Huigu*, vol. 2, pp. 830, 832; and Gu Longsheng, *Mao Zedong jingji nianpu*, pp. 459-60.

98   *Mao wengao*, vol. 8, p. 196; Shi Zhongquan, *Zhou Enlai*, p. 354; and *Dang de wenxian*, no. 2 (1992), p. 50.

was offered. He also noted that even "[Liu] Shaoqi doesn't dare to speak to me frankly," and that although he was now notionally on the "second front" (as reflected in his retirement as head of state), he was not completely confident of others and thus would still be active on the "first front." This side of Mao was well understood by at least some of those close to him. Thus in the evening following his talk Li Rui discussed Mao's extraordinary performance with Tian Jiaying. Apart from suspecting that the Chairman had taken too many sleeping pills, Tian also told Li that Hu Qiaomu believed Mao's purpose in raising Hai Rui on several occasions was not to create "Hai Ruis" but rather to ensure that they didn't appear.[99]

But perhaps above all, what would have been disconcerting to the leaders assembled at Shanghai were signs of the Chairman's sheer bad temper, whether due to too many sleeping pills or a purposeful effort to warn his colleagues to adhere to the general line. One of Mao's outbursts at the meetings was the claim that "Peng Dehuai hates me," something perhaps linked to Peng's alleged opposition at the meeting to Mao "personally taking command," but arguably a comment out of the blue. But most chilling would have been a remarkable speech during the Shanghai meetings which has been ignored, or to put it more bluntly suppressed, by the Party history establishment but verified by both a participant at Shanghai and a historian who has read the document.[100] In this speech Mao launched a wide-ranging attack on Party leaders who had disagreed with him at some point in the Party's history. Apparently in a bad mood because of the setbacks to the leap, in the name of preventing a Party split he criticized nearly 20 top Party leaders for such past indiscretions, including Liu Shaoqi, Zhou Enlai, Chen Yun, Zhu De, Lin Biao, Peng Dehuai (especially harshly), Liu Bocheng, Chen Yi, and even the long-deceased Ren Bishi — in fact, virtually every Party Center leader except Deng Xiaoping. The participant on the occasion described his shock at Mao's outburst and his inability to understand the reasons behind it, but the historian concerned saw it as another reflection of Mao's real intention in raising the Hai Rui analogy — to warn others of the need for loyalty to the emperor. Be that as it may, it was not a performance to further the spirit of fearlessly dealing with problems that Mao claimed he was seeking at Shanghai.

---

99 "Unpublished Chinese document no. 6," p. 158; *Dang de wenxian*, no. 1 (1989), p. 96; and *Bainianchao*, no. 4 (1997), pp. 10-12. An interesting example of Mao's declared impatience with those who hesitated to speak out ironically concerned Li Rui's letter expressing doubts about the steel target. Li had sent this letter to Chen Yun, someone clearly of like views, but sought to cover himself by sending a copy to Li Fuchun. Mao complained that Li's ploy showed that he "feared ghosts." *Mao wengao*, vol. 8, p. 197.

100 There is no published version of this speech, or even a reference to it, insofar as we are aware. We are, however, convinced of its existence given the independent accounts of these two reliable oral sources. It is, moreover, possible that Mao's comment concerning Peng's "hatred" of him came in this speech.

Thus when Party officials left Shanghai a number of contradictory tendencies were at work. Mao, arguably, felt that the attention to work style could provide the necessary ingredient to get the leap forward back on track, but at the same time that both encouragement to candor and warnings against it had to be impressed on the Party. Some responsible leaders like Bo Yibo, while recognizing the danger of underperforming, seemingly felt some leeway to push the cause of realism further, although apparently little impetus to moderation was felt by others — particularly certain provincial leaders. Finally, the degree of political tension introduced by Mao must have left a residue of trepidation for all concerned. These contradictory tendencies would play themselves out in the period up to and into the Lushan conference in the summer.

After Shanghai, April-June 1959: Greater Compromises and Continuing Unreality

The Chairman's ill temper and inevitable hesitations among his colleagues notwithstanding, the Shanghai meetings did give a boost to efforts to introduce greater realism into CCP policy. Mao personally continued the effort on the rural front with an April 29 letter to rural cadres denouncing "mere bragging" and demanding that production targets be based on reality, an effort that allegedly further displeased the Chairman's "left"-inclined colleagues at the provincial level.[101] Meanwhile, the chastened Bo Yibo and Li Fuchun at least had a clearer direction as they convened a two-day conference of planners in mid-April. But undoubtedly the most significant development was the newly authoritative role of Chen Yun who "no one had listened to" in the months leading up to Shanghai. Now Chen had the benefit of Mao's clear and repeated statements at the meetings that his (Chen's) cautious views during the winter had been correct, and he began to influence policy. At Shanghai he acted on the request of Hunan's Zhou Xiaozhou who even after the second Zhengzhou conference had been on the radical side of rural policy but now wanted Chen to approach Mao about reducing the density of planting, an approach the Chairman had been identified with. Chen agreed with Zhou Xiaozhou's view, discussed the matter with agricultural czar Tan Zhenlin, and wrote Mao accordingly — with the result that the recommendation was endorsed in the Chairman's April 29 letter. But clearly the most significant indication of his growing importance was that, sometime after the conclusion of the plenum, Mao entrusted Chen with investigating the increasingly serious situation concerning steel production.[102]

---

[101]   *Mao wengao*, vol. 8, pp. 235-40; and MacFarquhar, *Origins 2*, pp. 170-71. According to Cultural Revolution sources, Li Jingquan strongly disagreed with this letter to the point of appending a different view when it was distributed in Sichuan; see Teiwes, *Politics and Purges*, p. 309.

[102]   Bo Yibo, *Huigu*, vol. 2, pp. 832-33; Sun Yeli and Xiong Lianghua, *Gongheguo jingji*

While the story of Chen's involvement in, and the general process of the revision of steel targets, has long been known,[103] greater detail is now available which allows a more refined analysis of the politics of the situation. Chen's efforts came against a background where three views had been expressed on targets at Shanghai. One view, that of a "small group," felt that since the Wuhan targets for 1959 had been publicized, it was necessary to strive to achieve those targets. A second opinion held by "most" at the time was that these targets could hardly be achieved and if they were pursued at any cost great political and economic costs would result, and this apparently led to the 16.5 million internal steel target. Finally, a "minority" believed that even the low 16.5 million target could not be accomplished and should be revised further.[104] What is striking in the events following Shanghai is not only the sharp drop in the steel target and Chen Yun's critical role in pushing the project forward, but also the seemingly widespread central bureaucratic support for the move. This can be seen in Table 3 (p. 156) which indicates the proposals of various actors.[105]

Following the Shanghai plenum the SPC became involved in the steel question with Vice Chairman Jia Tuofu, the "rightist" of the planning leaders in Mao's early 1958 assessment, calling in various officials to check the actual steel output for 1958. This resulted in the conclusion that only 8 million tons of quality steel had been produced in 1958, and that as a result 18 million tons, still the official published target for 1959, was clearly not possible. The same conclusion emerged when in April Zhou Enlai instructed SPC Vice Chairman Xue Muqiao, the PRC official who had exercised the greatest responsibility for economic statistics after 1949, to go to the State Statistical Bureau and scrutinize the production figures for 1958. When he reported back, Xue not only informed Zhou that the steel production was 8 million tons, not 11 million, he also estimated 1958 grain production at 500 billion catties, not 750 billion (and subsequently this estimate was reduced to 400 billion), a report leaving the Premier decidedly uneasy. When the planners gathered by Jia Tuofu met, Song Ping, who was in charge of the SPC's annual planning and coordination bureau, asked what could have caused such a critical situation, and all those present agreed a sharply reduced figure of 12.5 million tons would be more realistic. This was reported to the full SPC chaired by Li

---

fengyun zhong de Chen Yun, pp. 173-74; and *Miscellany of Mao Tse-tung Thought*, I, 170. Chen Yun was also active on other fronts, particularly through an April letter dealing primarily with consumer supply and markets. See Lardy and Lieberthal, *Chen Yun's Strategy*, pp. 112-16; and MacFarquhar, *Origins 2*, pp. 164-65.

[103] See especially the fine discussion in MacFarquhar, *Origins 2*, pp. 165-70.

[104] *Chen Yun yu jingji jianshe*, p. 294. This account differs from Mao's claim that "many" at Shanghai resisted changing the Wuhan targets, although "some" were for changing them; Gu Longsheng, *Mao Zedong jingji nianpu*, p. 483.

[105] This table extends that compiled in MacFarquhar, *Origins 2*, p. 167.

Fuchun, but Li characteristically avoided a bold stand and only commented that the proposal was worth studying.[106]

Table 3

READJUSTMENT OF THE 1959 STEEL TARGET, APRIL–MAY 1959

Date	Proposed by	Reliable target	Strive for target
December 1958	Wuhan plenum[a]	18	20
April 4, 1959	Li Fuchun	18[b]	
April 2-5, 1959	Shanghai plenum[c]	16.5	18
after Shanghai	SPC officials group	12.5	
early May 1959	SPC heavy industry bureau	12.5/13	14
early May 1959	SPC annual planning & coordination bureau	12/12.5	
early May 1959	SEC metallurgy bureau	13	15
early May 1959	Ministry of Metallurgy[d]	13/14/15/16[e]	
May 11, 15, 23, 1959	Chen Yun	13	
May 23, 1959	Secretariat[f]	13	
June 13, 1959	Politburo[g]	13	

Unit: million tons

Sources: MacFarquhar, *Origins* 2, pp. 165-69; Bo Yibo, *Huigu*, vol. 2, pp. 832-33, 836; *Chen Yun yu jingji jianshe*, pp. 279-80, 292-95; *Dang de wenxian*, no. 5 (1992), pp. 44-45; Wu Lengxi, *Yi Mao Zhuxi*, pp. 132-34; Lardy and Lieberthal, *Chen Yun's Strategy*, pp. 118-19; and *Zhou Enlai nianpu*, vol. 2, p. 237.

Notes:
[a] Formally internal and published targets.
[b] Of which 16.5 million would be "good steel."
[c] See a above.
[d] No indication given which figures regarded as "reliable"or "strive for" targets.
[e] According to Chen Yun, the 16 million tons figure was "not carefully explained."
[f] On the proposal of Chen Yun representing the central financial and economics small group.
[g] Mao, Zhou Enlai, and Li Fuchun all endorsed Chen Yun's proposed target.

---

106   Zhou Weiren, *Jia Tuofu zhuan*, pp. 141, 143; *Chen Yun yu jingji jianshe*, pp. 294, 296; *Huainian Zhou Enlai* [In Memory of Zhou Enlai] (Beijing: Renmin chubanshe, 1986), p. 37; *Dang de wenxian*, no. 5 (1992), p. 44; Xue Muqiao, *Xue Muqiao huiyilu*, pp. 255-56; *Zhou Enlai yanjiu xueshu taoyunhui lunwenji* [Collected Conference Papers on the Study

This concern, as well as an awareness that a 20 percent shortfall in the rolled steel target for the second quarter of 1959 was inevitable, now animated a conference convened by the Party Secretariat on April 29-30. This conference asked whether the steel target should be divided into "reliable" targets and those to be "striven for," whether the distribution of rolled steel should be based only on the reliable figure, and if the rolled steel target had to be reduced should capital construction projects be cut as well. While the Secretariat was continuing to play the critical role in economic policy making that it had assumed during the Great Leap, it now turned to the organ that had been placed in a marginal position since its reorganization in June 1958, the central financial and economics small group headed by Chen Yun. In addition to the more important personal commission from Mao, Chen now received Secretariat authority through its request that the small group investigate the problems raised at the conference. In the fortnight which followed Chen clearly took the lead, with other small group members Li Fuchun, Bo Yibo, and Zhao Erlu definitely involved.[107]

With Chen Yun in overall charge, various bureaucracies undertook studies to answer the demands of the small group, studies which, except for that from Wang Heshou's Ministry of Metallurgy, all resulted in estimates for reliable output in the 12 to 13 million ton range, i.e., roughly the amount advocated by the group assembled by Jia Tuofu. Within the SPC itself, Song Ping's annual planning and coordination bureau held a sharply reduced figure of 12 to 12.5 million tons would be more realistic, while the heavy industry bureau gave a slightly higher range of 12.5 to 13 million tons. The SEC's metallurgy bureau was also at the slightly higher end of the spectrum, advocating 13 million tons. These figures from within the planning agencies provide a mild echo of the different bureaucratic pulls evident during the *fanmaojin* period. The bureau most concerned with overall planning and coordination was on the low side, while those responsible for specific sectors, and thus analogous to spending ministries, were on the high side. Moreover,

---

of Zhou Enlai] (Beijing: Zhongyang wenxian chubanshe, 1988), p. 350; and above, p. 50. Xue Muqiao had been head of the State Statistical Bureau since 1952 before being replaced by his deputy Jia Qiyun in November 1958.

[107] MacFarquhar, *Origins 2*, p. 166; Bo Yibo, *Huigu*, vol. 2, p. 833; and above, p. 107. Of the others noted, Li Fuchun and Bo Yibo were of course the CCP's most prominent economic officials, although one might speculate as to whether Li, whose "lack of zest" for "cooling down" Mao was soon to allude to at Lushan (see *Chinese Law and Government*, Winter 1968/69, p. 40), had much stomach for the project. As for Zhao Erlu, who had earlier shown signs of boldness on the side of moderation (see above, p. 38), and was arguably even braver in this period as he submitted a turn-of-the-year investigation report to Mao in late May, he of course represented the vitally concerned First Ministry of Machine Building and had been a member of the small group since its reorganization the previous year; see Bo Yibo, p. 711. MacFarquhar, p. 166, speculates that Zhao was included in the current discussions to safeguard the interests of the defense industries.

the organization which stood out in its apparent reluctance to cut as deeply as the others was one of those spending ministries, the Ministry of Metallurgy.[108]

The interaction of Chen Yun with Wang Heshou's ministry and other economic units demonstrated Chen's meticulous methods that MacFarquhar has described so well. Drawing in more technically competent people to examine the situation and demanding concrete, detailed, and comprehensive information, Chen received six briefings from the Ministry of Metallurgy in early May. In "face-to-face" encounters with Chen, metallurgy officials advanced three different projections of 13, 14, and 15 million tons, each argued on the basis of an economic rationale and with a preference for 15 million, as well as a fourth proposal for 16 million tons that was "not carefully explained." This comparatively "leftist" posture can perhaps be explained to some degree, as intimated above, by the undoubted interest of the ministry in maximum resources, but such a bureaucratic explanation must be tempered by the fact that the ministry was arguing for targets it would most likely be unable to meet. Earlier behavior on Wang Heshou's part had shown that he was aware of technical problems but chose to go with the political wind, seemingly more readily than at least some of his colleagues in the industrial ministries. Arguably it was the political calculation that "left" was still better than "right," as well as the historical baggage of his own prominent role in the explosion of steel targets in the first place, that was telling.[109]

Indeed, the central argument made by Wang Heshou's ministry, an argument unpersuasive to Chen Yun, was political. The ministry argued that if the target was too low it would cause people to lose heart, a view that would draw Liu Shaoqi's retort at the May 11 Politburo meeting, which considered Chen's report, that setting the target too high and not reaching it would be even more demoralizing. Chen's report on this occasion, which he stated reflected the agreement of Li Fuchun, Bo Yibo, Zhao Erlu, and himself, rejected the metallurgy view and advocated a reliable target of 13 million tons, which was linked to a guaranteed 9 million tons of rolled steel and a proposal to cut back on capital construction. What was significant about this report, in addition to Chen's noted meticulous argument, was his equally characteristic political sensitivity. Leaving aside the Ministry of Metallurgy, Chen's recommendation was at the higher end of the options offered by the economic departments for reliable steel. Moreover, in making his recommendation Chen still hedged, noting that he had not heard from other ministries besides metallurgy and asking that the small group be given more time to study Wang Heshou's proposal for 15 million tons. Most significantly, in his crucial May 15 letter to Mao outlining his position and (according to Bo Yibo's reflections) "bravely" expressing doubt concerning the argument about the demoralization resulting from a lower target, after noting different opinions

---

[108]   *Chen Yun yu jingji jianshe*, pp. 279-80, 295, 296-97.

[109]   *Ibid.*, pp. 64, 279-80; Bo Yibo, *Huigu*, vol. 2, p. 833; Lardy and Lieberthal, *Chen Yun's Strategy*, p. 118; MacFarquhar, *Origins 2*, pp. 167-69; and above, pp. 115-16.

both in Beijing and "every province and city," he expressed the hope that "several comrades of the financial and economics small group, including Comrade Heshou, will report to you soon." As a participant in the process would recall, given the atmosphere at the time, and existing research suggesting 13 million tons was achievable if everyone worked hard, no one (presumably at the top) would have accepted any lower target. But reducing the figure to even this level clearly would require Mao's blessing.[110]

That blessing apparently came quickly as further efforts to establish the new low target (albeit one, we should recall, that was still higher than the projections made in the heated atmosphere of the May 1958 Party Congress) appeared during the following days and weeks. Shortly after Chen's letter to Mao, on the 16th or 17th, Zhou Enlai submitted a report calling for investigations of nine key iron-producing areas by eight vice premiers as well as himself,[111] and asked Deng Xiaoping to circulate it to Mao and other members of the Standing Committee plus Peng Zhen. The State Council leaders were to leave about May 20 and return around the middle of June, and their efforts resulted in the closing down of some small blast furnaces. On May 23 Chen Yun proposed and the Secretariat accepted submitting to the Politburo a lowered 1959 steel target of 13 million tons, while on the 28th Deng Xiaoping lectured a Secretariat conference in broadly philosophical terms on the need to avoid fixation with the 18 million ton target, an attitude he argued would lead to the loss of the overall situation, including the support of the people. Then on the 30th Bo Yibo spoke more concretely that the steel task had not been met over the past five months, that 18 million tons was an "empty wind" that diverted resources, with the result that some places were without food and there was nothing to buy in the stores in Beijing's main shopping area, and that this was his responsibility. And on June 11 after his return to Beijing, Zhou Enlai criticized the subjectivism of the 1958 leap forward. In view of all this, it is clear that the June 12-13 Politburo meeting, where Mao, Zhou, and Li Fuchun all emphasized the importance of comprehensive balance in the economy, simply endorsed Chen Yun's 13 million figure which had already been decided.[112] At almost precisely that time, in another familiar development, Chen went on extended sick leave.[113]

---

[110] Lardy and Lieberthal, *Chen Yun's Strategy*, pp. 124, 126, 127-28; *Chen Yun yu jingji jianshe*, pp. 279-80, 294, 297-98; Bo Yibo, *Huigu*, vol. 2, p. 833; and MacFarquhar, *Origins 2*, p. 169.

[111] The personnel involved and their inspection areas were: Zhou (Hebei), Chen Yi (primarily Shanxi), Tan Zhenlin (Shandong), Xi Zhongxun (primarily Henan), He Long (primarily Sichuan), Luo Ruiqing (primarily Hunan), Lu Dingyi (primarily Jiangsu), Nie Rongzhen (Anhui), and Ulanfu (Baotou). Bo Yibo, *Huigu*, vol. 2, pp. 835-36; Tong Xiaopeng, *Fengyu sishinian*, pp. 364-65; and *Zhou Enlai nianpu*, vol. 2, p. 228.

[112] Bo Yibo, *Huigu*, vol. 2, pp. 835-39, 845; *Dang de wenxian*, no. 5 (1992), pp. 44-45; and MacFarquhar, *Origins 2*, pp. 169-70.

[113] On June 8 Mao approved a three-month sick leave for Chen. About this time Deng

While Chen Yun's efforts and the Chairman's assent had a significant effect in the industrial sector, Mao still muddied the waters with comments such as the observation at the June Politburo meeting that "[we] can still carry out *duo, kuai, hao, sheng*, but too much *duo* and *kuai* is not on."[114] The contradictory nature of his attitudes and their impact can be seen most clearly in developments concerning the countryside. Following Shanghai the Great Leap radical Tan Zhenlin, whose moderating steps can usually be traced to Mao, now toured rural areas, affirmed the achievements of the leap but warned of the dangers of exaggeration and false production figures, acknowledged that he bore responsibility for the errors now being corrected, and indicated that, as Mao had instructed, he was studying the works of Mao, Marx, and Lenin, as well as those on political economy.[115] The contrast between this and not only the unreconstructed views of some provincial leaders but, significantly, also the Chairman's continuing emotional attachment to incredibly ambitious leaping forward, was particularly revealed in a conversation shortly after the Politburo conference between Mao and Henan's Wu Zhipu, a consistent Great Leap radical who not long before had been unable to answer Chen Yun's concrete questions about the food situation in his province. This exchange underlined the Chairman's ambivalence about the economy generally as well as concerning rural policy. Despite the "low key" he had adopted toward the communes, particularly since his late April letter to the Party, not to mention his many specific demands for greater realism, Mao remained profoundly unwilling to apply the pressure needed to produce the needed rectification of "leftist" practices in the countryside or elsewhere.[116] All this and more was apparent in his talk with Wu Zhipu.

The encounter of Mao and Wu[117] on June 22 covered a broad front and certainly had philosophical overtones that would have been missing in any meeting of Wu and Chen Yun. Mao affirmed his acceptance of lower steel targets, now envisaging a downward revision of the 1960 target to 13.5

Xiaoping (who had broken a leg) also went on sick leave. See *Mao wengao*, vol. 8, pp. 294-95, 303. While Chen, who genuinely had fluctuating health (see Sun Yeli and Xiong Lianghua, *Gongheguo jingji fengyun zhong de Chen Yun*, pp. 132, 184), might have been exhausted from his exertions of the previous months, his ability to avoid difficult meetings (e.g., Nanning) is worth noting, although in this case it is difficult to believe that even Chen could have sensed what was coming at Lushan. Cf. Teiwes, *Politics at Mao's Court*, p. 29; and idem, *Politics and Purges*, pp. xxviii-xxix, lxv, 511n184. In any case, we have considerable sympathy with Bo Yibo's view (*Huigu*, vol. 2, p. 833) that over a long period Chen emerged at the critical moment with real knowledge and genuine insight into economics work.

114   Wu Lengxi, *Yi Mao Zhuxi*, p. 134.

115   Jiang Weiqing, *Tan Zhenlin zhuan*, p. 323; and Jin Ye, *Huiyi Tan Zhenlin*, p. 500.

116   See Teiwes, *Politics and Purges*, p. 309; and MacFarquhar, *Origins 2*, pp. 171-72.

117   Actually five Henan leaders were present. In addition to Wu, provincial secretaries Shi Xiangsheng, Zhao Wenfu, Yang Weiping, and Dai Suli attended. *Dang de wenxian*, no. 4 (1995), p. 36.

million tons, only a slight increase over the new 1959 figure. More philosophically, in contrast to his past criticism of "U-shaped development," he now reiterated his Shanghai remark that such a pattern was inevitable, but insisted this still meant increased production. Again jumping to the concrete, the Chairman addressed comprehensive balance in a fashion that Chen Yun would have approved, noting the various interrelated factors involved and the need for quality, realizing for example that sorting out the steel question required a good job on the coal front. But while calling for greater attention to quality he still insisted on the importance of quantity. While acknowledging that the capital construction plan had clearly been too ambitious, he nevertheless declared ambition a good thing. And throughout this discussion the Chairman, again as at Shanghai, touched on unsettling matters: while shrinking the capital construction front in 1956 was quite acceptable, *fanmaojin* was still the main mistake of that year, the aim of surpassing Britain in 15 years or a little less remained a viable slogan even if it had gone out of fashion, and the (implicitly threatening) question was asked whether the Great Leap slogan itself would be abandoned the next year.[118]

With regard to the countryside where Chen Yun had failed to get satisfactory answers from Wu Zhipu, Mao was considerably encouraged by Wu's report, despite his indications over the previous months that Henan had been too far to the "left." Wu gave a rosy picture indeed, claiming that the rural high tide in 1959 was better than the previous year, food production was significantly up and the only problem was short supply of a few items in the cities, 90 percent or more of communal mess halls could be maintained, and the province was confident of achieving its grain target of 25 million tons. Mao responded to the last claim by saying they could then do slightly better the next year. Later in the conversation the Chairman gave an even more expansive version of what was possible. When Wu reported that grain production was up 25 percent in the current year, his response was "only 25 percent"? He then observed that with a further 25 percent increase they could reach 50 to 60 percent, and added that he still wanted to achieve the goals of the 40-article agricultural program and raise its targets a bit higher.[119]

But arguably more significant than any of the above is the simple fact of the sheer encouragement Mao drew from Wu's hollow claims. While Peng Dehuai and others were forming a bleak picture of the countryside in the period leading up to Lushan on the basis of their local investigations, the Chairman was hearing a much more congenial voice from below. While enjoining everyone to consider whether the situation was good or not and to act accordingly if they believed the government was about to collapse, he clearly drew the conclusion from Wu that this was not the case, conditions "are still very prosperous, there are only a few waves, I don't believe it's a big

---

[118]   *Ibid.*, pp. 36, 40-42.

[119]   *Ibid.*, pp. 38, 42, 44, 45.

deal."[120] The effect of Wu Zhipu's representations were most succinctly captured in another of the Chairman's comments:

> Your material is very useful for me, especially concerning the general situation [which is] stable, developing, and prosperous. The whole province is without any panic over grain, ... the whole situation looks good, public feeling is stable. Now in taking stock ... [we can see] the people providing such support and that the cadres are united.... [I] can still uphold the [communal] mess halls. I don't want them to collapse, and I'm hopeful they can be maintained.[121]

Armed with such encouragement, Mao asked Wu to prepare materials on the province's achievements concerning mess halls to show to people at Lushan. He further indicated that he would go to Hubei and invite Wang Renzhong and Tao Zhu, two erstwhile "leftists" who had recently earned his praise for greater realism, to consider the matter. Also to be invited was Hunan's Zhou Xiaozhou who was apparently still in something of a "leftist" phase a few short weeks before Lushan, identified by Mao as, along with Li Jingquan, a supporter of the communal mess halls. The presumed backing of such people led him to conclude that if a few provinces could maintain the mess halls the overall situation would be very good. Against such a background Mao's famous statement on the eve of Lushan is easily understood: "Our achievements are great, problems are quite a few, and the future is bright."[122]

Yet Mao also expressed much more gloomy views in this same period, and fault can be found not only with the Chairman's mercurial feelings and the encouragement of radical provincial leaders, but also in the timidity, albeit understandable timidity, of some key actors at the Center. This can clearly be seen in the events surrounding the June 12-13 expanded Politburo conference where not only was the steel target cut, but Liao Luyan proposed lowering the 1959 grain target from 800 to 600 billion catties. On that occasion Mao gave what amounted to the most forthright self-criticism he had ever given. Noting that he had started to conduct economic construction and especially industry the previous year, Mao acknowledged three big errors: overambitious plans and targets that produced economic dislocation, excessive decentralization that resulted in chaos and waste, and overly rapid communalization that caused the "communist wind" and a tense food supply situation. He further acknowledged that it was the first time he was in charge of industry and also the first time he had suffered a defeat, although his illustration of the seriousness of the setback by comparing it to the 1927 failed August Harvest Uprising indicated it was not truly his first defeat. As was always the case when the Chairman made a self-criticism, other leaders felt it imperative that

---

120   *Ibid.*, p. 44.

121   *Ibid.*, pp. 43-44.

122   *Ibid.*, pp. 44, 45; and *Chinese Law and Government*, Winter 1968/69, p. 63.

they too should shoulder responsibility — Zhou Enlai and Li Fuchun in particular stressed their share. This sombre mood, together with concrete steps, such as the reduced steel and grain targets, clearly required a change of direction. The question was how to achieve this, and the area now coming under scrutiny was propaganda work.[123]

Mao himself demanded a new orientation for propaganda, telling Wu Lengxi that the previous year's publicity for good news only, which included publishing false production claims, had to be changed, but leaving it to the Secretariat to determine how. The Secretariat duly met on the 14th, now chaired by Peng Zhen in view of Deng Xiaoping's recently broken leg. Notwithstanding the gloominess of Mao's words or the severity of the actual situation, the meeting felt the change should not be too drastic and advocated a slower, more gradual turn. The revelation of problems in the public media should be partial, with only certain difficulties publicized. The meeting then instructed propaganda department leaders Hu Qiaomu, Zhou Yang, and Wu Lengxi to draft a document to this effect which was sent to Liu Shaoqi on the 17th after revision by the Secretariat. Liu concluded that the draft was basically all right, but since the issue was so crucial it had to receive Mao's approval. Mao then chaired a Politburo meeting on the 20th which heard a systematic speech by Liu, a speech reflecting Mao's consistent approach of avoiding a negative impact on the people while exposing problems, i.e., making sure not to "pour cold water on the masses." Mao agreed to the draft, but wanted it issued in the names of Hu Qiaomu, Zhou Yang, and Wu Lengxi rather than the Party Center, with a covering notice that the Center agreed, a move presumably designed to distance the Center and Chairman from any unpalatable aspects of the decision.[124]

After the meeting Mao asked Liu and Wu Lengxi to stay. The Chairman told Liu that his views on propaganda work were very good, and asked him whether he would take charge of *People's Daily* while it implemented the new direction. Liu demurred, saying he had so much on his plate and it would be better if Mao took direct charge. Mao seemed somewhat disappointed, and told Wu to remember that in the future he should "report more often to Shaoqi and the Premier." Of course Wu could still report to Mao, but he was to report to the other two more often.[125] The degree to which Liu's reluctance largely reflected what was undoubtedly a full work load or the kind of caution indicated in Mao's remark at Shanghai that "Shaoqi doesn't dare to speak to me frankly" is a matter for speculation. But clearly several factors were involved in the cautious turnaround of propaganda policy. The reluctance of leaders of an ideological state to admit that they could have possibly made far-reaching mistakes was an obvious consideration. So too was the fact that there was no consensus yet within the leadership on how serious those errors were.

---

[123] Wu Lengxi, *Yi Mao Zhuxi*, pp. 134-36.

[124] *Ibid.*, pp. 136-41.

[125] *Ibid.*, pp. 141-42.

But for actors at the center of the system the fact that Mao himself was not only unwilling to approve a sharp turn of policy, but also that his underlying views were in a constant state of flux, was undoubtedly decisive.

The volatile mix in Mao's thinking was visible right up to, and indeed during the first stage of, the Lushan conference. If Wu Zhipu's encouragement contributed to expectations of future brightness, dealing with problems still dominated Mao's activities over the entire half month leading up to Lushan. On June 15 he convened a conference of central leaders where he again emphasized comprehensive balance. Mao returned to the same theme when addressing a seminar of economic coordination area leaders on June 29 and July 2. On this occasion he once again affirmed that the realistic Chen Yun had been right about economic management, specifically singling out the relationship of markets to construction. But even on this occasion his "guiding thought" remained the affirmation of the "three red banners." Last year's leap had been very good although a bit of blindness emerged and now the situation was turning for the better with such blindness reduced. And even during the comparatively relaxed first stage of the Lushan meeting before it exploded with Peng Dehuai's letter and Mao's reaction, the Chairman remained unwavering in his commitment to the notion that achievements were nine fingers out of ten.[126] Such a position to a large degree rendered meaningless the efforts of the previous eight months — both in terms of Mao's intellectual and emotional capacity to approach the unfolding disaster in truly realistic fashion, and in terms of political opportunity for other actors to come to grips with the actual situation.

The Actors: "Hot" and "Cool" Heads

Although the eight-month effort to "cool down" clearly produced some results including a more gradualist conception of the transition to communism, attention to various problems in the management of the communes, a significant degree of recentralization in running the economy, and three separate reductions of production targets, with the steel target cut by more than half, in a fundamental sense the Great Leap Forward was not altered. Huge increases in production were still sought, the mass mobilization of labor remained the basic approach, a far-reaching change of social relations remained high on the agenda, and the "three red banners" remained politically sacrosanct. Who were the "hot" heads whose activities contributed to the efforts of these months falling so short of the needs of the situation? Who were the "cool" heads who used the limited opportunities available to bring some measure of realism, however inadequate, to the economic policy-making process? And what factors influenced the actions of each?

Before turning to the individuals and groups concerned, a number of broader contextual factors should be noted. First, and paramount, throughout

---

[126]   "Unpublished Chinese document no. 6," pp. 160-61, 164.

the "cooling down" period China remained in the grip of a mass movement. This, of course, was an approach tested in revolutionary struggle and repeatedly used since 1949 in many areas, particularly political campaigns and the countryside. It was thus linked to past successes in the minds of most CCP leaders and cadres, but it also imparted the visceral understanding that unwavering support of the official line was a matter of both Party discipline and political prudence — that "left" was indeed to be much preferred to "right," an attitude reinforced by intimidating challenges from radicals such as Ke Qingshi. Quite apart from the pressure created by a mass movement, it is also clear that a genuine degree of ideological commitment — of faith — was involved. Earlier we reported the testimony of participants and Party historians that a wide segment of the Chinese population from top leaders to ordinary people both shared the desire for a modern, prosperous China and the belief that somehow Mao had found a way to achieve that goal more quickly than previously imagined possible. While the growing problems emerging with greater clarity from fall 1958 clearly dented that faith, it would be foolish to ignore the undoubted fact that it remained a potent factor for many actors. Indeed, a key provincial official who by summer 1959 was deeply disturbed by some of the consequences of the leap has recalled his own continuing belief in the general line throughout this period.[127]

Another general consideration is the imperfect understanding of the situation throughout the official apparatus, and particularly at higher levels. Indeed, in one of his many blasts at false reports, Mao singled out the fact that several (higher) levels starting with the prefecture, and especially "central comrades," actually "believed these things" as the real problem and source of danger.[128] Given both the insufficient technical understanding of (in particular) the modern sector that nonspecialist cadres were responsible for overseeing, and the flood of misleading reports from below,[129] it is not surprising that recognition of the depth of the crisis was slow in coming. In addition, although we do not find it the most telling factor, particularly in our account of specific decisions and events, oral sources have pointed to the concrete interests of various actors as a factor in the resistance to "cooling down." This will be seen in the following discussion of several official groups, but here we note the reluctance of new workers to return to their former peasant status when policy demanded a reallocation of labor back to

---

[127] Interview, Beijing, 1997.

[128] "Unpublished Chinese document no. 6," p. 138. This happened early in the "cooling down" process at the Wuchang conference.

[129] That such imperfect understanding was a real factor and not simply a cover for political timidity is suggested by the behavior of even specialist officials at the time of the May 1959 downward revision of the steel target (see above, pp. 155ff). Here not only the political calculation that "no one would have accepted any lower target" applied, but the officials concerned believed on the basis of existing research that 13 million tons was possible.

agriculture. Finally, the factor of nationalism and national prestige which was noted in connection with the utopian phase of the leap in 1958 also seemingly played a part. This was evident in Mao's ambivalent attitude toward Stalin and the Soviet Union as seen in his speeches at the first Zhengzhou conference in particular, and in the involvement of the leap forward as an issue in the worsening state of Sino-Soviet relations during this period. More specifically, in the view of Shanxi leader Tao Lujia, while the Chairman was resolute from November 1958 in "correcting the left," his efforts were nevertheless offset by "a certain contradictory attitude" which Tao thought was linked to his 1957 Moscow speech that boasted of China's developmental ambitions on an international stage and was so important in the process leading to the Great Leap.[130]

General considerations do not provide an answer to the question of responsibility, however. The starting point is the Chairman himself who was ultimately responsible for both "hot" and "cool" heads. Mao clearly opened the door to a reassessment, not because he was particularly realistic in his assessment of the situation or (contrary to official claims[131]) the first to sense something was amiss, but because his initiative was necessary before *anyone else* could do anything effective to deal with the difficulties encountered by the leap. Yet Mao was also, and more profoundly, responsible for the "hot" heads. His unwillingness to "pour cold water," his delight in the efforts of local leaders in particular to accomplish great things, meant there was no truly effective political pressure on "left" inclined officials to moderate seriously their overly ambitious efforts. Indeed, it may not be going too far to say that those who "resisted" his efforts to "cool down" were the best readers of the Chairman's mind. And Mao's ideological confusion, perhaps seen most strikingly in his treatment of Stalin's *Economic Problems of Socialism*, his penchant for allowing the lower levels to devise their own methods even when he ostensibly favored a more moderate approach, vagueness over precisely what targets should be reduced and by how much, and the very changeability of his views left leaders and officials of various levels unsure of what he really wanted and, crucially, of what efforts were safe to undertake.

---

130   Tao Lujia, *Yige shengwei shuji*, pp. 92-93; Teiwes, *Politics and Purges*, pp. 310-11, 327-29; and above, pp. 128-29. For reviews of deteriorating Sino-Soviet relations including the significance of the Great Leap factor, see Zagoria, *Sino-Soviet Conflict*, chs. 3 and 9; and Westad, "Visions of an Alliance," section on 1958-60.

131   Note particularly the favorable gloss put on Mao's efforts in memoir literature, such as that of Tao Lujia and Bo Yibo. Bo in particular makes great efforts to assert both Mao allegedly being first to recognize the problems and his "day and night" efforts to rectify them, as well as to sing his praises as "higher than us" in his understanding of the situation, but he nevertheless points to such factors as the Chairman's encouraging of activists and his insistence on the correctness of the "three red banners," which engendered fear of being considered a "tidewatcher," "accounts settler," or even a "hostile element" and prevented a thorough rectification of "left" errors. *Huigu*, vol. 2, pp. 807, 817-18, 833, 840; and MacFarquhar, *Origins 2*, p. 146.

This was perhaps most clearly seen in the behavior of Chen Yun who would not act "until the time was right," then started to articulate his views cautiously as Mao started the "cooling down" process in late fall 1958, but quickly engaged in self-criticism after "mistakenly" believing that the Chairman's patience had been tried in January 1959. These events also indicate another aspect of Mao's behavior — his increasing arbitrariness and inability to accept genuinely as opposed to rhetorically his own mistakes. There had been a development in the Chairman's "realistic" side throughout 1958. Although similar expressions of the need to "compress air" and avoid "unrealistic high targets" could be found as early as the Chengdu conference when he was clearly applying pressure for ever more ambitious goals,[132] by late 1958 it was linked to a recognition that some correction of course, however poorly understood, was required. At that juncture, however, Mao was both sanguine in his expectations and seemingly unperturbed about both the "left" he was mildly chastizing and the "right" he was tepidly encouraging. But with his January outburst that frightened Chen and his Shanghai speech sweepingly criticizing a range of Party leaders, this equanimity seemed lost. While it is not the aim of this study to reduce explanation to an analysis of the Chairman's psychology, there is nevertheless a striking similarity to Mao's extraordinarily heated turn against *fanmaojin*. In both cases he seemed unable to cope with his own failures. Then, we have argued, it was the failure of the Hundred Flowers which led him to find scapegoats in the CCP's top economic officials. Now, arguably, it was accumulating evidence of *serious* problems with *his* Great Leap that led him to lash out ever more erratically.

Clearly, then, Mao's behavior created critical problems for the other actors in the system. How did they react? Starting with those closest to him — his personal staff and particularly his secretaries — we can see some of the paradoxes of the situation. First, it is necessary to observe that in *relative* terms these so-called *xiucai* could be frank with Mao. They were completely dependent on him and with some exceptions (notably Chen Boda) not of particularly high rank. As with Li Rui and the Three Gorges project at Nanning, the Chairman apparently felt comparatively little threat to his prestige, and certainly none to his power, in listening to the opinions of such figures. Indeed, according to Li Rui's account, during the early stage of the Lushan conference only Mao's secretaries apparently feared nothing and had the freedom to speak out. Moreover, in spring 1958 Mao remarked that Hu Qiaomu was particularly daring in arguing with him, often cornering him into a "defenseless position." While clearly a gross exaggeration, this remark and the behavior of the *xiucai* at Lushan nevertheless did reflect a certain leeway on their part. Moreover, other leaders clearly perceived the secretaries as having a special understanding of the Chairman, a perception expressed in Zhou Enlai's early 1960 observation that to understand Mao's thinking it was

---

[132] See Wu Lengxi, *Yi Mao Zhuxi*, pp. 63-64; Gu Longsheng, *Mao Zedong jingji nianpu*, pp. 414-15; and above, pp. 89-90

necessary to rely on the *xiucai*, although more importantly on Liu Shaoqi, the designated successor, and Deng Xiaoping, the "vice marshal."[133]

How did Mao's secretaries use their ability to interpret Mao and their relative freedom to speak out? Clearly their investigations at Mao's behest from October 1958 did discover problems which were reported back to the Chairman and contributed significantly to his launching of the "cooling down" effort. Yet these secretaries, with the apparent exception of Li Rui who, at least in his own account, made several modest cautionary efforts during 1958-59,[134] were hardly overly realistic as the views of Chen Boda concerning the abolition of money and the apparent opposition of the *xiucai* as a group at the first Zhengzhou conference to the idea of a clear demarcation between socialism and communism indicates. Even more revealing is the case of Tian Jiaying, whose later estrangement from Mao led to his suicide on the eve of the Cultural Revolution and whose doubts about the Great Leap have been approvingly portrayed in post-Mao accounts. It is important to note not only Tian's earlier radical tendencies but also his warnings about decollectivization measures well into the deep crisis of 1961-62. Moreover, in the incident singled out as evidence of Tian's realism during 1959 — his clash with Li Jingquan over communal mess halls and close planting following his investigations in Sichuan — it appears he exercised the caution so common in CCP circles. While the investigations in Sichuan took place over the March-June period, it seemingly was only during the early stage of the Lushan conference when Mao was particularly encouraging of critical views that Tian reported on the Sichuan situation thus engendering Li's sharp retort.[135]

---

133   *Dang de wenxian*, no. 4 (1993), p. 74; Li Rui, *Lushan huiyi shilu* [True Record of the Lushan Conference] (Beijing: Chunqiu chubanshe, 1989), pp. 82, 87, 90, 152, 212, 352; and oral source. Further evidence of the special position of the secretaries can be seen in Zhou Enlai's envy in April 1959 when Li Rui told Zhou that the secretaries could speak to Mao without fear or constraint, and in Liu Shaoqi's approach to Hu Qiaomu at Lushan concerning how to curb leftist excesses, apparently to gauge through Hu how far he could go in raising issues with the Chairman; Li Rui, pp. 86, 351-52.

134   See above, pp. 138-39, 151. Li, in any case, was not a true secretary to Mao, having gained the status after Mao was impressed with his performance at Nanning, but continuing to work as a central bureaucrat. He was the only secretary to have suffered severely at Lushan, being dismissed from his posts and sent to the countryside.

135   See the essay by Tian's subordinate Pang Xianzhi, "Mao Zedong he tade mishu Tian Jiaying" [Mao Zedong and His Secretary Tian Jiaying], in Dong Bian, Tan Deshan, and Zeng Zi, eds, *Mao Zedong he tade mishu Tian Jiaying* [Mao Zedong and His Secretary Tian Jiaying] (Beijing: Zhongyang wenxian chubanshe, 1990), pp. 31, 32, 34, 36; and Li Rui, *Lushan shilu*, p. 50. The timing of the Tian-Li clash is not given explicitly in these accounts, but we conclude it occurred during the first week of the Lushan conference since Tian personally reported to Mao after arriving in Lushan, he came under attack in Li's Southwest group meetings by June 10 (the same time when Chen Boda and Hu Qiaomu were attacked for similar findings in Fujian and Anhui respectively), and Pang knew nothing of any clash until August 9. This timing is also supported by the often unreliable memoirs of Li Zhisui, *Private Life*, pp. 307-309, 319. On Li Zhisui's

Overall, the paradox of the "left" inclined *xiucai* is that they became a force for "moderation" precisely because Mao required them to find problems. By the time of the Lushan conference at least some of them had moved significantly to the "right," even advocating giving Chen Yun overall responsibility for the economy.[136] Yet throughout they moved with circumspection, and had no unusual impact on the limited "cooling down" which did occur.

After his immediate household, the group "closest" to Mao would be the top Party leadership — i.e., those Politburo leaders at the Center with overall authority for running the country according to the Chairman's wishes. This particularly refers to his "close comrades-in-arms" on the Standing Committee of the Politburo (Liu Shaoqi, Zhou Enlai, Chen Yun, and Deng Xiaoping[137]) as well as Peng Zhen who, as second in command in the central Secretariat as well as a leading Politburo member, clearly had a major role to play under Great Leap arrangements. (While it could also include Politburo members, such as Li Fuchun and Tan Zhenlin, with direct economic responsibilities, these figures shall be considered separately.) We have already commented on Chen Yun's cautious style in getting the timing right; the same could be said even more so for Zhou Enlai who, in his post-Nanning mode of maximum attention to Mao's meaning, only ventured forth to push moderation when the Chairman seemed relatively clear that this was what he wanted. And Liu Shaoqi, who didn't "dare to speak to [Mao] frankly," also exhibited caution. A striking case of the timidity affecting top leaders was an incident concerning Wang Jiaxiang. During the Wuchang meeting Wang Jiaxiang was unhappy with the lack of candid discussion of the problems of the leap and approached Liu Shaoqi with his misgivings. While apparently reluctant to approach Mao directly, Wang "earnestly requested" Liu to pass on his views to the Chairman and the other members of the Standing Committee. On learning of Wang's views, an angry Mao reportedly said: "Not one of all these Standing Committee members dares dissent, only Jiaxiang gives a different opinion."[138]

---

memoirs, see Frederick C. Teiwes, "Seeking the Historical Mao," *CQ*, no. 145 (1996). On Tian's role in 1961-62, see below, pp. 219, 224-225.

[136] Cong Jin, *Quzhe fazhan*, p.418; and Li Rui, *Lushan shilu*, p. 50. Cf. the discussion below, pp. 208-209, of the collective shock of the *xiucai* at Lushan when Mao turned on Peng Dehuai.

[137] This excludes the comparatively inactive Zhu De and Lin Biao. On Lin's activities over this period, see Teiwes and Sun, *The Tragedy of Lin Biao*, pp. 181-82.

[138] Xu Zehao, *Wang Jiaxiang zhuan* [Biography of Wang Jiaxiang] (Beijing: Dangdai Zhongguo chubanshe, 1996), pp. 539-41; and Cong Jin, *Quzhe fazhan*, p. 188. Mao's anger seemed at least partially directed at Wang, but clearly also involved disdain of his timid Standing Committee colleagues. It is technically in error to consider Wang himself a "top leader" given his status as merely a Central Committee member and Vice Minister of Foreign Affairs, but justified in terms of his historical position in the Party. On Wang's historical role, see Teiwes with Sun, *Formation of the Maoist Leadership*, pp. 47-52.

High rank clearly was no guarantee of boldness; on the contrary, the closer to Mao in rank the more wary leaders seemed to be.

Another notable aspect of the role of top Party leaders is their low profile during the "cooling down" process prior to the second Zhengzhou conference. While these leaders, or some of them, were present on many of the key occasions, accounts of interaction between Mao and various officials give little indication of a prominent role before late February 1959. Here there seems to be a parallel with developments during the upsurge in 1958. Then top leaders were relatively mute at the critical Nanning conference, and they only became prominent in pushing the leap ahead once its direction had been set there. Liu Shaoqi, as the presumptive successor, then played a significant role in elaborating ideology as well as in undertaking a multitude of organizational tasks, Deng Xiaoping brought immense pressure on lower levels politically and administratively, and Chen Yun, reflecting Mao's subsequent comment about his strong sense of Party discipline, came off the sidelines to attempt to find suitable methods for achieving the Chairman's goals concerning steel production and capital construction. Now, fairly late in the "cooling down" process, Liu, Deng, and Peng Zhen emerged to provide some central muscle behind Mao's various calls for more realism. Their role, unlike that of Chen Yun who obviously did have a major hand in shaping policy, is less clear, but again it appears largely one of implementing a new direction than being forceful advocates of new departures.[139] While the information is incomplete, it appears that Mao looked elsewhere for policy input, but turned to his top Party colleagues for support in carrying out his wishes.

A further step away from Mao were the major economic coordinating bodies and their leaders. As head of the central financial and economics small group Chen Yun overlapped with this group, although as throughout the entire period since late 1955 we regard him more as a top leader standing above bureaucracies. Clearly his drastically fluctuating fortunes as someone "nobody listened to" when Mao's disfavor was widely perceived in early 1959 to someone who, before Peng Dehuai's letter, was regarded by Mao at Lushan as the "good general" who could lead the country out of chaos,[140] owed nothing to bureaucratic clout and everything to the Chairman's attitude. Of the remaining former advocates of *fanmaojin*, relatively little has been uncovered concerning Li Xiannian, something which may reflect little more than the

---

While it should be noted that a respected senior Party historian claims that "many senior leaders dared to report the truth to Mao," our own belief is that although such cases did occur in response to positive signals from the Chairman, the predominant tendency was caution, even timidity.

[139]   Arguably, an exception was support of Chen Yun's reduced steel target at the May 11, 1959, Politburo meeting by Liu, Zhou, and Deng before the matter was submitted to Mao for decision, but given Mao's recent indications they may already have known the Chairman's answer. See Wu Lengxi, *Yi Mao Zhuxi*, p. 133.

[140]   Cong Jin, *Quzhe fazhan*, p.418; and Li Rui, *Lushan shilu*, p. 80.

inappropriateness of financial constraints during the leap forward and/or the traditional lesser role of financial as compared to planning organs, but what is known suggests an advocacy of "realism" when the circumstances allowed.[141] As for the leading planners, there was a clear distinction between Li Fuchun and Bo Yibo. Li, analogous to his role in opposing rash advance, seemed the most reluctant to "cool down." Indeed, it was more than that, as seen at Wuchang where Li proposed a steel target more than a third greater than what was felt feasible by Bo. Clearly the difference was not one of bureaucratic function but of individual proclivity. In fact, it could be argued that Li, the "leftist" planner in Mao's assessment who held the greatest economic responsibility prior to Chen Yun's return in spring 1959, was irresponsible toward his organizational interests while the "centrist" Bo, and particularly the "rightist" Jia Tuofu, in pushing (cautiously) for lower targets and greater coordination, much more reflected institutional roles. In any case, it is clear that China's planners were not monolithic during the effort to "cool down."

As argued in chapter 3, the organizational role of the planning bodies had been so bent out of shape by the pressures of the Great Leap that they could no longer perform their coordinating functions adequately. While Mao had notionally placed great power in the hands of Li Fuchun in particular, in fact this amounted to little more than adding another voice to the chorus demanding ever higher production targets, while the injunction for Party secretaries to "take command" clearly undercut the role of the planning committees. Only as his awareness of the need to "cool down" grew did Mao begin to focus on the dangers of the situation. By the time of the first Zhengzhou conference he noted the need for planning (albeit by organs from the provinces and "each level" as well as the SPC) in conjunction with the economic law of balanced development, and by spring 1959 he was flailing the planning authorities for having abdicated their role after the Beidaihe conference and lacking resourcefulness. At the same time he sought the advice of Li Fuchun and Bo Yibo along with other central economic officials in his efforts to cope with the growing chaos, but it was only with the March decision to give Bo's SEC clear authority regarding industrial policy that a more effective institutional role was possible. The activities of the SPC and the SEC during the effort to reduce steel targets in April and May also suggest a greater degree of meaningful organizational activity than was previously possible. None of this, however, prevented Mao from again attacking the SPC at Lushan for not taking care of planning, and having used "planned directives, which is equal to no planning." That this was widely perceived as unfair given that the planners had performed in an impossible environment created by Mao was of no consequence; even as the planning agencies regained some degree of their normal functions they remained exposed to the

---

[141]   Regarding Li Xiannian, see Bo Yibo, *Huigu*, vol. 2, pp. 828, 830; and above, n. 92. Oral sources specializing in the period, moreover, identify Li's Ministry of Finance as one of the more sceptical ministries concerning the leap.

will and whims of the Chairman.[142]

As problems with the modern economy became apparent Mao also drew in people from the spending ministries to deal with the issues. The main individuals mentioned in the available documentation are Minister of Metallurgy Wang Heshou and head of the First Machine Building Ministry Zhao Erlu. Zhao was the "cool" head of the two, arguing in November 1958 that the 1959 target of 16 million tons of steel would be difficult to achieve, and backing Chen Yun in arriving at the 13 million ton figure the following May. Wang, in contrast, was "warm" if not necessarily "hot," apparently reluctant to offer a figure in November and holding out for 15 million tons in May. Arguably a bureaucratic factor was involved. As a user of steel Zhao's ministry needed quality products which could only be guaranteed if the fixation with quantity was overcome, while Wang's ministry was judged on the basis of total output. But, as already suggested, Wang's position seemed more politically based, argued in the terms loved by Mao of not discouraging the masses and defending the established position of his ministry as a Great Leap pacesetter. While organizational function may have played some role in the positions adopted by different ministries, political calculation and personal proclivities seemingly provide a stronger explanation.[143]

Nevertheless, both political caution and organizational interests contributed to the reluctance of many spending ministries to "cool down." Both can be seen in the ambitious reports prepared by 12 ministries for the Wuchang conference, while the assessment of a Party historian that in early 1959 ministerial leaders "just tried to figure out what Mao wanted and said nothing" suggests the growing role of political caution as perceptions of difficulties increased. Such caution arguably was well founded in that despite the huge efforts made by these ministries in 1958-59 Mao never completely

---

[142]   See *SS*, p. 471; "unpublished Chinese document no. 6," pp. 157-58; and *Case of Peng*, pp. 24, 411. The ironies of the Lushan situation were that the planners were first attacked by Peng Dehuai who nevertheless indicated that external pressures made it difficult for them to perform their role properly, Mao compared the SPC's neglect of the balancing function unfavorably to the approach of the architect of *fanmaojin*, Zhou Enlai, and all the industrial ministers paid a visit to Li Fuchun at Lushan to comfort him, notwithstanding the fact that he was probably more guilty than most of those on the receiving end of Mao's ire. *Dang de wenxian*, no. 5 (1990), pp. 22-23; *Case of Peng*, pp. 26, 412; and oral source.

[143]   When asked in general terms to identify notably sceptical ministerial officials, historians specializing in the period named Zhao Erlu and Vice Minister of Water Conservancy and Electric Power Liu Lanbo. A "hotter" ministerial leader was undoubtedly Vice Minister of Railroads Lü Zhengcao who proposed at Wuchang a 1959 target for new tracks equal to the entire SFYP target approved at the Eighth Congress in 1956 and again at the Chengdu conference. Typically, Mao "greatly enjoyed" Lü's "daring" report, but also expressed scepticism. See Wu Lengxi, *Yi Mao Zhuxi*, p. 107; and *SS*, pp. 485n19, 505-506.

retreated from his suspicion of central bureaucrats and their work methods.[144] As for institutional interests, Party historians note that with the leap forward an investment thirst was stimulated and projects started, and few leaders wanted to retreat from what had been promised their organizations. Thus the thirst for investment led to conflict among ministries, as each of them sought maximum funds and attempted to protect every new factory. Although various high-level ministerial officials may have understood the unreality of their targets, the combination of pressure from within their organizations to hold on to gains, the mass movement atmosphere, and Mao's lingering suspicion of "those people in Beijing" all contributed to making the spending ministries a comparatively marginal player in the process of "cooling down."

Another key central leader responsible for the economy, in this case agriculture and thus with it the profound social transformation involved in setting up the people's communes, was Party secretary and new Politburo member Tan Zhenlin. Tan's major radical role throughout the leap has long been recognized by Western analysts and most graphically in Mao's comment at Lushan that Tan, along with Ke Qingshi, Wang Heshou, Li Fuchun, and especially himself, was one of those most responsible for Great Leap disasters. Overall, post-Mao sources do not alter this assessment; their vagueness concerning Tan's role in this period is merely suggestive of an effort to lessen his culpability. Indeed, recent biographical and memorial accounts try to portray Tan as having a "cool" as well as "hot" side, citing such instances as his "bravery" in raising with Mao the problems which the mass smelting campaign was causing for agriculture at the (presumably second) Zhengzhou conference. But such "cool" moments notwithstanding, moments which arguably usually reflected a desire to achieve radical Great Leap goals in the area of his responsibilities, the overall impression is less of someone whose views moderated with time, although this may have happened to some degree, than of a radical leader whose more moderate positions owed most to dealing with concerns raised by Mao since, in Tan's words, "we must adopt the same attitudes as primary school children [would], doing just as [the Chairman] says."[145]

In contrast to top leaders and bureaucrats in Beijing, Mao clearly retained his enthusiasm for provincial leaders throughout the period. While individual local officials received his criticism, this group was consistently consulted as Mao attempted to come to grips with what was, and in his eyes was not, going wrong with the leap. As a result they were well placed both to further the

---

[144] E.g., at Wuchang Mao complained that "The Center can talk big, but the burden eventually is on the shoulders of the regions" (SS, p. 506), while in April 1959 he again criticized the previous way of doing things which had only started to be replaced by the mass movement in the second half of 1958 (Gu Longsheng, Mao Zedong jingji nianpu, p. 464).

[145] See Jiang Weiqing, Tan Zhenlin zhuan, p. 323; MacFarquhar, Origins 2, pp. 82-85, 127, 221; and above, n. 82.

"cooling down" process and to hinder it. Much of the impetus for the Chairman's efforts to get a better grip on reality came from his investigations normally conducted in the presence of provincial Party secretaries, even if one suspects that it was lower-level officials also present on those occasions who provided the most telling input to the Chairman.[146] Yet, on the whole, at least early in the period, provincial leaders continued the "leftist" posture that had been their calling card as the Great Leap unfolded, something clearly seen in their efforts to dissuade Mao from reducing targets at Wuchang. Yet it was also voices from the provinces at Shanghai that encouraged the Chairman in his new effort to lower targets.

In considering the strength of the "leftist" tendency among local leaders which included some prominent figures (especially Ke Qingshi and Li Jingquan) right through the early stage of the Lushan conference, Party historians and participants from the period have noted various factors. Apart from ideological commitment and sheer opportunism ("many local leaders belonged to the wind faction and raised targets to please Mao"), the critical factors appear to have been "a question of recognition" with many leaders believing they could indeed achieve high targets, and, as with the ministries, a sense of their own interests. Investment thirst existed in the localities as well as in the central bureaucracies, and provinces and counties sought maximum funds in order to boost local economic development. Indeed, one senior Party historian noted, even today leaders from the time, such as Anhui's Zeng Xisheng, still insist on the achievements of the leap forward. He further described the reaction to a lecture to an audience of local officials outlining the disasters caused by the leap: he was handed a note refuting his analysis as untrue since "we developed here."

But as discussed above, there were significant differences among provincial leaders, differences which led to sharp conflict by the time of the Shanghai conference. Of course, various individuals changed their positions as events unfolded and their understanding of the situation changed — perhaps most notably Hunan's Zhou Xiaozhou.[147] The most famous "hot" heads were

---

146 It is difficult to get a fix on subprovincial leaders as a group, but as Dali Yang, "Surviving the Famine," pp. 268-69, argues, there was considerable variation, with substantial numbers opting for significant concessions to the peasants. Our general feeling, however, is that overall these officials carried out the official line with all its radical overtones, even at the cost of causing great havoc in their areas and villages. Cf. Thomas Bernstein's excellent study, "Stalinism, Famine, and Chinese Peasants."

147 As previously indicated, Zhou took a comparatively radical view on commune organization before becoming a critic of the leap at Lushan. Other notable cases are Tao Zhu and Wang Renzhong, "hot" in 1958 before turning "cool" in early 1959 (even if Mao still identified Wang's Hubei as "leftist" at Lushan). Even Tao Lujia received Mao's criticism for excesses shortly before he articulated the moderate position. Moreover, the same province could have "hot" and "cool" leaders. Hebei would be a case in point if the identification by a significant participant in the meetings of the period of Lin Tie as advocating the radical position at the second Zhengzhou conference is

Ke Qingshi (Shanghai), Li Jingquan (Sichuan), Wu Zhipu (Henan), and Zeng Xisheng (Anhui), while their main protagonists in inner-Party debate apparently were Tao Lujia (Shanxi) and Wang Renzhong (Hubei) who seemingly spoke for a much larger "cool" group from spring 1959. The differences cannot be attributed to regional variations if neighboring provinces Sichuan/Hubei and Henan/Shanxi are considered. Moreover, despite the importance of "recognition," the proposition advanced by our central bureaucrat that the low educational level of provincial leaders was responsible for their "leftism" cannot be sustained. As a senior Party historian noted, leading radicals Wu Zhipu and Shandong's Shu Tong were Party intellectuals, while leaders of worker-peasant background such as Jiangxi's Yang Shangkui were much more "unexcited" in their attitude to the leap.[148] Although as several oral sources have pointed out, central economic officials had a more profound understanding of problems in the modern sector, lower educational levels *per se* do not explain provincial radicalism.

The reasons for different views were basically practical, political, and ideological. While the provinces as a whole started the leap as strong supporters of the program, after dealing with practical problems views began to diverge. The impact of actual experience can be clearly seen in the case of a leading provincial secretary who, as part of the information-gathering process prior to the Lushan conference, investigated communal mess halls and concluded that without a change of policy the peasants would rebel.[149] Undoubtedly ideological predispositions were a considerable influence,[150] but as with Wang Heshou's Ministry of Metallurgy one's previous position as a pacesetter seemingly sustained radical inclinations — Ke Qingshi, Li Jingquan, Wu Zhipu, and Zeng Xisheng all illustrate this point. In addition, the promotion of Ke and Li to the Politburo in May 1958 arguably added to their intense backing of the new general line adopted at that time. In any case, Mao clearly listened to both sides, sometimes taking heed of the views of a Tao Lujia, and other times drawing sustenance from the claims of a Wu Zhipu.

Finally, a likely a factor in the equation was that, like the *xiucai*, local leaders for all *their* caution had a certain leeway in expressing their opinions. As someone with a close connection to Mao's household during the period put it, key local leaders could dare to push for unchanged targets at Shanghai not

---

correct since Mao praised the more moderate position of Liu Zihou at the same meeting. See *Case of Peng*, p. 23; and MacFarquhar, *Origins 2*, pp. 156, 162.

[148] This historian, who worked in Liaoning at the time, described that province as "midstream." In a separate interview, other historians specializing in the period identified Shaanxi's Zhang Desheng and Heilongjiang's Ouyang Qin as among the more realistic provincial leaders. Concerning "our central bureaucrat," see above, p. 17.

[149] Interview, Beijing, 1997.

[150] Interestingly, when asked to identify local leaders who resisted "cooling down," a Party historian pointed to ideological orientation by saying it was not a question of "resistance" but rather a case of the concerned people having different ways of thinking (*xiang butong*).

only because being on the "left" did not raise serious problems, but also because by the very fact of being provincial figures they were not so "important." That is, by being relatively low in the hierarchy, they could not be imagined by Mao to be a threat. In any case, being further from the Chairman physically and in status, together with Mao's preference for a group notionally closer to the masses, was a distinct advantage which allowed provincial leaders of sharply contrasting views to have an influence on him. But it was entirely up to Mao to decide which proposed course of action he would heed.

In the end, the various "hot" and "cool" attitudes on display from November 1958 to early July 1959 must be explained in terms of individual preferences rather than structural factors or organizational interests. Most groups had their clearly identifiable radicals and "realists" — e.g., Li Fuchun v. Bo Yibo and even more so Jia Tuofu for the economic coordinators, Wang Heshou v. Zhao Erlu for the spending ministries, and Ke Qingshi, Li Jingquan, Wu Zhipu *et al.* v. Tao Lujia and others among provincial leaders. All actors regardless of functional group or political persuasion were, in a profound sense, engaged in a competition to pledge loyalty to Mao, but, given his mercurial performance, they had to proceed with considerable caution. The least "cautious" were those on the "left" who could take heart from the notion that "left is better than right," not to mention some encouragement from the Chairman. On the "right" far-reaching caution ruled: even those with the clearest insight such as Chen Yun and Tao Lujia moved with circumspection. Of the various actors vying for Mao's attention certain groups and individuals were favored: provincial leaders as closer to the grass roots, the *xiucai* as closer to (and more dependent on) him personally, and Chen Yun, when the situation demanded it, because of his undoubted expertise and firm Party discipline. But for all the diverse pulls on Mao, with *his* general line in place and his stubborn unwillingness — indeed incapability — to address fundamental problems, genuine retreat was impossible until a far graver crisis faced the Chinese nation.

5 The Frantic Striving for Mao's Steel Target, 1958

5a Communes smelting steel in Hebei's acclaimed Xushui county. Following the rapid escalation of the 1958 steel target in June 1958, it became apparent that this could not be met by modern steel plants. By the time of the Beidaihe conference, Mao determined that a mass steel-making campaign using native methods--the famous backyard furnaces--would be necessary to achieve the goal, and assigned Chen Yun to oversee the effort.

5b Shanghai workers celebrating the fulfilment of Mao's 10.7 million ton 1958 steel target. Mao set the target in June with the simple demand to double actual 1957 production, and continued to insist on its achievement, at least in part because it was known by foreigners. In fact, the amount of up-to-standard steel produced in 1958 was only 8 million tons.

6a Mao addressing the Sixth Plenum, which reduced various key targets, relegated the transition to communism to the more distant future, and authorized commune readjustment, November-December 1958. The plenum followed the first Zhengzhou and Wuchang conferences where Mao launched the "cooling down" theme, with particular emphasis on obeying "objective economic laws." Mao, however, was profoundly ambivalent, continuing his commitment to mass enthusiasm and still supporting wild targets. From the left: Lin Biao, Zhu De, Liu Shaoqi, Mao, Zhou Enlai, Chen Yun, Deng Xiaoping.

6b With provincial leaders of both radical and comparatively moderate inclination at the second Zhengzhou conference, February-March 1959. While Mao was comparatively consistent in his criticism of "left" excesses during the conference, he failed to apply the kind of pressure that would curb radically-inclined local leaders. From the right: Shanghai's Ke Qingshi, Mao, Liu Shaoqi, Sichuan's Li Jingquan, Guangdong's Tao Zhu, Hubei's Wang Renzhong, Hunan's Zhou Xiaozhou, agricultural czar Tan Zhenlin, Anhui's Zeng Xisheng, Shanxi's Tao Lujia, and Mao's secretary Hu Qiaomu.

6c Deng Xiaoping (center), accompanied by Li Fuchun (far left), inspect a heavy industry plant under construction in Heilongjiang in 1959. In this year central leaders carried out inspection tours as awareness of Great Leap problems deepened. At various points, Deng contributed to the "cooling down" effort, but Li tended to maintain a "leftist" posture.

6d Chen Yun (left) and Peng Dehuai at the Shanghai conference, March April 1959. During the conference Chen received Mao's praise for his cautious economic views, and shortly thereafter was assigned responsibility for bringing greater realism to steel targets. Peng, however, suffered Mao's severe criticism for unclear reasons, and was accused by the Chairman of "hating me."

6f Mao chatting with relatives in his native village, Shaoshan, Hunan, late June 1959. Mao's rural investigations had been a major aspect of his policy making throughout the leap, both stimulating his enthusiasm as at Xushui in August 1958 (photo 3h) and contributing to the "cooling down" effort since fall of that year. Mao heard peasant grievances at Shaoshan, but headed for the Lushan conference declaring that while "problems are quite a few, the future is bright."

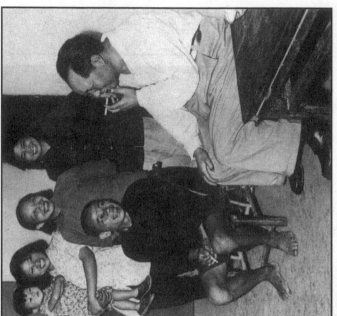

6e Mao and Liu Shaoqi in April 1959, when Liu assumed the post of state chairman. While this move had long been planned as part of Mao's move to the "second front," he still emphasized concentrating power under his supreme command. Although encouraging other leaders to criticize "the emperor" at this point, Mao privately acknowledged that he might not be able to tolerate such criticism, and commented that Liu "doesn't dare to speak to me frankly." Zhu De is to the rear.

7 Mao and Provincial Leaders, 1957-62

7b With Sichuan First Secretary Li Jingquan (holding cigarette), another key provincial radical, carrying out rural investigations, March 1958. Li, who with Ke Qingshi was promoted to the Politburo in May 1958, claimed high grain yields and strongly advocated communal mess halls, but agriculturally-rich Sichuan suffered severe and long-lasting famine conditions under his leadership.

7a With Shanghai First Secretary Ke Qingshi viewing wall posters, Shanghai, on the eve of the Third Plenum, September 1957. Ke, the leading provincial radical throughout the Great Leap, had influenced Mao during the 1955 agricultural cooperativization campaign, and conceivably had a role in Mao's turn to the "left" at the plenum. He was of great importance from late 1957 through spring 1958, as reflected in Mao's call for everyone to "learn from Old Ke." Later, at the 1959 Lushan conference, Mao identified Ke as one of the leaders most responsible for the failures of the leap.

7c With Hunan First Secretary Zhou Xiaozhou (left), apparently in summer 1959 shortly before the Lushan conference. Zhou, who had been one of Mao's secretaries in the 1930s, was relatively "leftist," notably on commune organization, well into 1959. But at Lushan he expressed views similar to those of Peng Dehuai, and was purged as part of Peng's "anti-Party clique." Arguably, however, Zhou's downfall had less to do with his views than with coincidences, such as fellow Hunanese Peng having gathered critical materials in Hunan.

7d With Hubei First Secretary Wang Renzhong (to Mao's right), March 1962. A radical during the early stages of the Great Leap, by 1959 Wang adopted a moderate position and clashed with Ke Qingshi and Li Jingquan in Mao's presence. Here Wang poses with Mao and the investigation group for neighboring Hunan. Three months later Wang and Tao Zhu, both Mao favorites, advocated a type of household responsibility system that briefly appealed to Mao before he sharply reaffirmed collective agriculture.

8a Peng Dehuai receiving PLA literary and artistic workers shortly before the Lushan conference, June 20, 1959. Although Peng had undertaken rural investigations since the previous winter and was deeply concerned with the consequences of the Great Leap, he was largely involved in military affairs. He sought to avoid going to Lushan and only responded to Mao's urging to come, thereafter writing his private letter criticizing leap policies and suffering Mao's unanticipated ferocious response. Peng, in front, is followed by Xiao Hua, to his right.

8b Zhang Wentian, arguably the bravest "member" of "Peng Dehuai's anti-Party clique," with staff during the Lushan conference, July-August 1959. While Peng sought to have his letter withdrawn as indications of Mao's possible displeasure appeared, Zhang determined to support Peng's views, making a systematic argument on July 21 despite prior warnings and a hostile reception.

8c Mao addressing the Eighth Plenum at Lushan, August 1959. The plenum was convened following Mao's insistence on removing Peng, Zhang, Zhou Xiaozhou, and Huang Kecheng from office, despite the hopes of other leaders that his anger would diminish short of such a step. The plenum dutifully approved the ouster of the "anti-Party clique" and launched a campaign against right opportunism that had the effect of greatly exacerbating famine conditions. Mao is flanked by Liu Shaoqi on his right, and Zhou Enlai.

8d Guangdong First Secretary Tao Zhu and family during the Lushan conference. At Lushan, despite strong reservations about the leap after initial enthusiasm, Tao was significant as one of the leaders persuading Peng Dehuai to yield to Mao's pressure and make a self-criticism. Tao employed the feudal analogy that serving the emperor is like a wife or concubine serving her husband or master, the overriding virtue being loyalty and submissiveness.

8e Mao presiding at the Guangzhou conference, March 1961. The conference adopted the 60 articles on people's communes which liberalized commune management. While Mao took the leading role on the 60 articles, others, such as his secretary Tian Jiaying, seated to Mao's right, influenced him to limit further concessions. From the right: Zhu De, Dong Biwu, Mao, Tian, Liu Shaoqi, Zhou Enlai. Peng Zhen is at the rear of the table; on the opposite side from the rear are Deng Xiaoping, Chen Yun, Lin Biao.

8f Tian Jiaying (left) carrying out rural investigations, Zhejiang, April 1961. Tian and Mao's other secretaries, whose input into the Chairman's perception of reality throughout 1958-62 was only surpassed by his own investigations and perhaps the views of local leaders, now acted under Mao's injunction that 1961 would be a year of investigation and research, a major shift from the ideology-driven politics of the leap. A year later, new investigations would lead Tian to a position less supportive of collective agriculture, thus earning Mao's displeasure.

8g Liu Shaoqi at the 7,000 cadres conference, January-February 1962. At the conference, Liu offered a systematic critique of Great Leap errors with Mao's encouragement, but at the same meeting he echoed Mao's criticism of the Anhui responsibility system. Although supporting further retreat including responsibility systems as assessments of the situation became even more dire over the following months, Liu sharply reversed course in July when Mao turned decisively against such measures. From the left: Liu, Chen Yun, Deng Xiaoping, Peng Zhen, Li Fuchun.

8h Mao presiding at the Tenth Plenum, September 24-27, 1962. The plenum marked a decisive rejection of the policies of retreat as Mao attacked economic retrenchment, concessions to individual peasant production, and the rehabilitation of "right opportunists," and criticized Liu Shaoqi, Zhou Enlai, and Chen Yun among others. Although economic and rural policies remained cautious, Mao introduced a significant change in ideological direction under the slogan "never forget class struggle." From the left: Liu, Deng Xiaoping, Mao, Zhou, Zhu De. Note that Chen Yun, present at all plenums since the start of the Great Leap except for Lushan when he was ill, is absent.

Conclusion

POLITICS AND PLAYERS UNDER MAO, 1955-59

Much is known about the course of CCP economic policy from late 1955 to mid-1959 which placed China on the brink of disaster. The changes in policy and their rationale have long been clear: the attempt to accelerate economic growth by applying mass mobilization techniques within the framework of the Soviet model in late 1955 and early 1956, the effort to curb the resultant "rash advance" from spring 1956 to fall 1957 in the name of "comprehensive balance" while making marginal adjustments to the Soviet strategy, the rejection of this balancing approach as well as Soviet-style methods and the initial moves toward a distinctive Chinese model from fall 1957 to early 1958, the further elaboration of a Chinese way together with an unprecedented explosion of economic targets from spring to fall 1958, and the abortive effort to curb excesses, to combine the basic thrust of the Great Leap Forward with more realistic approaches from fall 1958 to mid-1959.

In general terms the different policy processes before and after the start of 1958 are also well known. In the earlier period, even including the politicized atmosphere of the debate leading to the "little leap" of the first months of 1956, economic policy making was by and large rational, and when problems arose they were quickly dealt with by the top leadership and coordinating economic bureaucracies with Mao's assent. The key policy makers were those Party and state officials with formal authority for the economy: in Mao's words at Lushan, "the responsibility could be laid to others — [Zhou] Enlai and [Chen Yun]."[1] Mao himself was vitally interested in economic questions in this period, but he basically limited himself to oversight and approval, with limited personal input.[2] In comparison, the Great Leap Forward was marked by a situation where unrealistic plans and utopian goals fed upon one another and only the most dire of economic conditions could terminate the program after two and a half years of growing chaos (see Epilogue 2). Moreover, the terms of elite interaction had changed drastically from one where Mao largely allowed his leading colleagues and the relevant bureaucracies to get on with

---

[1]   *Chinese Law and Government*, Winter 1968/69, p. 39. Chen is identified as "XX" in this text. Cf. the first quotation on p. 3, above.

[2]   The main exception was his April 1956 "Ten Great Relationships," but even this was based on the reports of central economic bureaucracies.

the job of running the economy and normal bureaucratic conflict was a natural feature of political life before the Nanning conference. As the leap unfolded, in contrast, policy relevant actors expanded to include Party bodies and lower-level organs that had been comparatively peripheral to the process previously, Mao was in direct command of the economy,[3] and unprecedented political pressure prevented real debate.

It is also well understood — and with increasing clarity with the passage of time — that the new policies and processes which marked the Great Leap produced an enormous tragedy for the Chinese people, with at least 15 million and perhaps upwards of 40 million perishing as a result of starvation and undernourishment.[4] How could such a man-made disaster occur? Again, some answers have long been known. The inherent pressures of mass mobilization, false reporting of production achievements and goals and the belief placed in those reports by Party leaders, intense political and administrative pressure from the top, equally intense competition by local organs vying for the Center's and Mao's approval, and the impact of nationalist sentiments as reflected in emerging Sino-Soviet tensions were all apparent at the time or soon after. Less well integrated into the accepted wisdom is the fact of the widespread acceptance of, and impatience for, rapid economic development, something affecting the general population and ordinary cadres, local leaders, and central bureaucrats, and even such normally sober-minded leaders as Zhou Enlai, a phenomenon present throughout the 1955-59 period but whipped into a frenzy during the leap. Such considerations, however, only take us part of the way to an understanding of how a disaster of such proportions could have developed and — importantly — continued effectively unchecked.

There is also much that has not been known, or only inadequately dealt with in the existing literature. Above all there is the question of political dynamics: What were the politics of the dramatic changes of course over the larger period? What roles were played by various individuals and groups in the process? How was the power and influence of these political players affected, and why? As has been argued throughout this study, the existing literature offers two approaches — elite conflict and bureaucratic politics — which in their present form do not explain the course of developments even though both elite differences and bureaucratic conflict repeatedly surfaced in the events in question. The bureaucratic approach has only been systematically developed for the *fanmaojin* period where it *does* have relevance. In contrast, relatively little analysis of this type has been applied to the Great Leap where, particularly during its utopian stage from spring to fall 1958, a truly unique policy process emerged in which, as one participant put it, Mao had broken all regulations and systems and *People's Daily* editorials

---

3   See above, n. 1. In a famous line from the same passage, Mao said that "in 1958 and 1959 the main responsibility has fallen on me and you should take me to task."

4   See above, p. 5.

had greater influence than Central Committee directives.[5] But even for 1956-57 the preeminent statement of the institutional interpretation[6] both gravely underestimates the independent role of CCP leaders whose authority derived fundamentally from revolutionary status rather than institutional affiliation, and misinterprets the basic bureaucratic cleavage which did exist. Rather than a struggle between "planning and heavy industry" and "financial" coalitions based on their allegedly clashing organizational missions, our analysis has shown the basic conflict was between those bodies — both planning and financial — responsible for overall coordination of the economy and more task-oriented and parochial organizations, the spending ministries and the localities. Simply put, the latter asked for more, while the coordinating bodies sought to restrain their demands before the onslaught of the leap forward. But even in this "bureaucratic" period, policy approaches reflected the views of leaders standing to a substantial extent "above" institutions, such as Zhou Enlai and Chen Yun, while the opinions of Mao — whether expressed or anticipated — were *always* a crucial factor in the evolution of policy.

While the dynamic of policy change clearly originated within the top elite, existing elite conflict interpretations also fail to explain adequately the developments of the period. The crucial problem with these interpretations, whether crude adaptations of "two line struggle" or more sophisticated analyses, is their treatment of Mao as to some degree a *politically* constrained actor, as someone either beset by potential challengers or at least repeatedly required to make political assessments in order to make sure that his support within the elite was sufficient to achieve his ends. This is not only at variance with evidence of the Chairman's overall dominance, as succinctly summed up in the view of a Party historian that "Mao had absolute power over the Center,"[7] but it also cannot explain how the comparative weakling of 1956-57 came to so dominate his colleagues in 1958-59. Moreover, political calculation on the part of other leaders, e.g., Liu Shaoqi's presumptive desire to secure his anointment as head of state, is not sufficient to explain the slavishness which so marked leadership attitudes to Mao even as the severe problems caused by his policies became increasingly apparent in the first half of 1959.

The ultimate test of Mao's dominance comes not in such dramatic images as those at Nanning where the top leaders of the Party and state sat like school children striving to understand every nuance of his meaning, or of the procession of leaders to his Zhongnanhai swimming pool residence five

---

5   The significance of the *People's Daily* was dramatically seen in Mao's instruction summoning leaders to the Nanning conference. Mao placed the paper's editor-in-chief Wu Lengxi first on the list above both Politburo members and local leaders, something which surprised Zhou Enlai, Liu Shaoqi, and Wu himself. *Mao wengao*, vol. 7, p. 11; and Wu Lengxi, *Yi Mao Zhuxi*, pp. 46-48.

6   Bachman, *Bureaucracy*, which basically stops with the fall 1957 Third Plenum.

7   See above, p. 13.

months later where they projected totally unprecedented steel targets in order to accommodate his mood. It comes rather in those periods and instances where policy clearly did *not* reflect his greatest passions and/or explicit proposals. First, Mao was clearly disappointed that a retreat from the "little leap" of 1956 was necessary, and he even floated the idea of an increase in capital construction in April of that year when his colleagues almost unanimously argued for holding the line or for cutbacks. While the information concerning this specific incident is too sketchy for sweeping conclusions, it does seem that Mao in the end was persuaded by Zhou Enlai's argument for cutbacks. What is clear is that throughout 1956-57 Mao provided general and specific support for the policy of opposing rash advance, regardless of any reservations he may have harbored. Even those Party historians who argue — with the benefit of hindsight — that Mao and Zhou *et al.* represented two different approaches to the economy during this period, conclude that other Politburo leaders did not believe they were contradicting the Chairman's wishes. And such a belief was rational given his careful vetting of Zhou's report on the SFYP to the Eighth Congress, his "complete agreement" with the *fanmaojin* measures introduced at the November 1956 Second Plenum, and his several statements lauding the economic leadership of Chen Yun.

But what is striking in this case is not simply that, in contrast to stereotypes of a radical Mao thwarted by a conservative opposition, he actually supported opposition to rash advance, but even more revealing are a number of crucial implications for the policy process. One is that a *relatively* healthy "inner-Party democracy" did exist in this period as claimed by official sources. This, of course, was not the formal "rule of the majority" or "collective leadership" laid down by Party norms.[8] It rather reflected Mao's willingness to consult and be guided by those with a greater knowledge of economic affairs than himself. The most dramatic results can be seen in the behavior of Zhou Enlai, forceful in both word and deed during the *fanmaojin* interlude despite more than a decade of showing great sensitivity to Mao's power and preferences. Zhou pushed the cautious economic line in repeated bureaucratic discussions, was able to joke about such sensitive matters as the "committee for retrogression," and in the April 1956 incident argued his case directly with the Chairman. Clearly he believed there were no fundamental differences with Mao, and more importantly that it was possible to be a forceful advocate in his presence. This behavior, as leading Party historian Shi Zhongquan has observed, was completely at odds with that Zhou adopted following Mao's severe criticism of himself and others at Nanning. From then on Zhou eschewed vigorous advocacy and devoted his efforts to being sure he understood what the Chairman wanted.[9] Yet even within the "vigorous

---

[8]   On Party norms, see Teiwes, *Leadership*, especially ch. III; and idem, *Politics and Purges*, especially pp. xliv-lxii.

[9]   See Shi Zhongquan, *Zhou Enlai*, p. 413; and above, p. 112.

democratic life" of the earlier period, Mao's perceived views were critical. Notwithstanding the Chairman's support for *fanmaojin*, the fact that this support was rather distant and impersonal, and that his "anti-rightist conservative" line from 1955 and early 1956 remained the ideological guideline, meant that those like Zhou pursuing the new course ran into considerable opposition and even had to exhibit "courage" in the circumstances, while those disinclined to the policies felt they had leeway to fight on. In this critical sense, even the relatively inactive Mao had a crucial influence on the calculations of other actors concerning economic policy.

A similar if more dramatic situation can be seen during the abortive effort to "cool down" from fall 1958. On the surface Mao frequently did not get his way: calls for greater realism did not prevent the continued pursuit of wild goals or "leftist" officials such as the provincial leaders at Wuchang from arguing against the more cautious views expressed by the Chairman in his presence. Mao would, disingenuously, later speak of developments in this period as something he was almost powerless to curb.[10] Yet as in 1956, and with considerably more reason following the sweeping attacks on past policies and top leaders at Nanning and during subsequent conferences, other actors in the system were convinced of Mao's basic "anti-rightist" posture, believing that continued pursuit of his visionary objectives was more in tune with his "line" and an ultimately safer course of action. There was, fundamentally, a clear perception that for all his words about "cooling down," the Chairman was unshakably attached to the Great Leap Forward. Those such as Chen Yun who were more inclined to Mao's various "realistic" sentiments nevertheless moved with the greatest caution, obviously concerned that they were reading too much into Mao's remarks and fearing the gravest consequences if they ventured too far to the "right." Divining the Chairman's "real" intentions was the primary requirement for all players in the Chinese political game throughout this period. Such divining had always been a central aspect of the court politics around Mao, but since the launching of the Great Leap it had become a particularly dangerous game for all concerned. Nowhere, despite growing signs of an unraveling policy consensus, was there any indication of opposition to Mao.[11] Indeed, the theme that no one would *dare* to oppose a

---

[10] See especially his references to the January 1959 Beijing conference. Gu Longsheng, *Mao Zedong jingji nianpu*, p. 606; and above, p. 142.

[11] This, of course, runs against the dominant interpretation of events at the Lushan conference, an interpretation refuted in Epilogue 1. For a well researched and carefully argued study positing a case of "fierce opposition" during the pre-Lushan period to at least Mao's policies, see Michael Schoenhals, "Yang Xianzhen's Critique of the Great Leap Forward," *Modern Asian Studies*, vol. 26, no. 3 (1992). We believe that Schoenhals' data only demonstrate a similar "dialectic" position on the part of Yang (initially another ardent supporter of the leap) to that of Mao in late 1958, while the Central Party School head's much more disillusioned view and indeed disgust with the leap by mid-1959 in no way represented a political challenge to Mao. As Schoenhals notes (p. 607), Yang's (private) strictures (much as Mao's milder complaints), were

firmly committed Mao throughout the mid and late 1950s came up more times than can be remembered in interviews with Party historians.

To elaborate further the findings of this study we will conclude by providing an overview of the roles of the key actors throughout the 1955-59, period[12]: Mao himself, other top Party leaders, key economic coordinating bodies, central spending bureaucracies, and local leaders.

Mao Zedong. While the preceding chapters should, we hope, demonstrate Mao's ultimate and absolute authority throughout 1955-59, including those periods when an "un-Maoist" approach dominated and/or he claimed his wishes were thwarted, his role in the events of the time require further analysis. Enormous power meant immense responsibility, including for one of the greatest tragedies in modern Chinese history. Yet the horrors which grew out of the Great Leap should not blind us to the fact that there were essentially two Maos in these years. The first, in evidence prior to late 1957, while certainly strong-willed and prone to an explosive temper making life difficult for those around him,[13] as suggested above nevertheless did function as a basically rational policy maker who sought the counsel of his top colleagues and specialist officials, and who by and large pursued goals which, if sometimes overambitious as in the "little leap," were nevertheless not obviously unattainable. The results of these policies, moreover, were not only successful from the perspective of a modernizing communist elite, but tolerable or better for substantial segments of the Chinese population.[14] And while the Chairman's tendency to ambiguity, changes of position, and unexpressed reservations were a definite feature of his style, they generally did not have the explosive consequences of the Great Leap period.[15]

As he began to grope toward the Great Leap and then throughout its unfolding during both the utopian and "cooling down" stages, Mao's politically relevant behavior became much more dangerous for his colleagues. This was seen in both the status of his targets, with Politburo Standing Committee members now dressed down in inner-Party fora for the first time,

---

directed at lower-level cadres and steered well clear of the Chairman. It is, however, notable that Yang's 1959 scathing criticisms were marked by a near absence of any reference to Mao's ideological authority. *Yang Xianzhen zhuan* [Biography of Yang Xianzhen] (Beijing: Zhonggong dangshi chubanshe, 1996), pp. 248-50, 252-54.

12 We exclude here Mao's secretaries and household personnel generally as sufficient data exists only for the "cooling down" phase and is summarized above, pp. 167-69.

13 For several first-hand examples, see Li Zhisui, *Private Life*, pp. 97-98, 159-60.

14 For an overview arguing success in terms of regime goals through 1957, see Teiwes, "Establishment." For a stimulating discussion of the *dissatisfactions* of various groups in the mid-1950s, see Domenach, *Origins*, ch. 2.

15 A limited exception concerned Deng Zihui during the cooperativization debates of 1955. Deng's real sin, however, was to continue to argue *after* Mao had made his position clear; see Teiwes and Sun, *The Politics of Agricultural Cooperativization*, pp. 13, 16, 20-21. Cf. also the rather more explosive events surrounding Bo Yibo during 1953; Teiwes, *Politics at Mao's Court*, pp. 62-71.

and in the threatening nature of the criticism ("you are 50 meters from the rightists"). Moreover, danger was implicit in the aforementioned difficulty of divining his "real" intentions. Indeed, perhaps the most remarkable feature of the "great helmsman's" performance in 1958-59 was not his wrongheaded push for unprecedented objectives through fall 1958 which brooked no expression of reservations, but the nature of his responses thereafter as he realized something was going wrong. While his occasional dissembling (e.g., the claim that he was too preoccupied with the August 1958 Taiwan crisis to give too much attention to the unfolding leap at the Beidaihe conference[16]) is unattractive, what is especially notable in Mao's statements is the sheer intellectual incoherence of his views. Whether it was appeals to Stalin's authority for more attention to "objective laws" while at the same criticizing his excessively professional orientation, or criticizing Henan's excesses but later drawing encouragement from that province's false claims, the broader political elite could have no confident idea of what was required and often fell back on the prudent understanding that "left is better than right." When intellectual fuzziness was linked to unpredictability and ill-tempered outbursts the situation was exacerbated: even as shrewd a participant as Chen Yun, after cautiously acting on Mao's more "realistic" signals in late 1958-early 1959, quickly pulled his head in once the Chairman ominously raised the question of "line."

If Mao's elusiveness caused difficult and enduring problems for other actors in the political system,[17] what moved the Chairman himself? While Mao, particularly before the Third Plenum, was not and could not be impervious to objective reality, the answer would seem to lie in his subjective attitudes, or his thought as Party historians would put it. While necessarily speculative, Mao's motivations appear to be largely a combination of two factors — a grand vision for his country, and an inability to accept personal failure which translated into petty impulses toward his colleagues. Although the view of some Party historians that Mao *always* favored rapid economic development is overdrawn as can be seen in his policy stance for most of 1956-57, he nevertheless desperately wanted China to advance to the first rank of nations as quickly as possible. Thus his great displays of positive emotion came at times of rapid advance. In early 1956 he declared himself even more elated with the progress of cooperativization, whose mobilizational approach he had by that time extended to the economy, than he had been over the victory of 1949.[18] At the Third Plenum he reportedly became "very excited"

---

16   See "unpublished Chinese document no. 6," pp. 157-58.

17   The Chairman's elusiveness should be seen in the context of his and the CCP's increasing rejection of the Soviet model. In contrast to the comparatively clear framework of the early and mid-1950s, the lack of models and precedents gave Mao increasing opportunities to put his personal stamp on China's economic development, but it also left enormous room for uncertainty. Cf. Teiwes, "Establishment," pp. 15-18.

18   Pang Xianzhi, "Mao Zedong he Tian Jiaying," p. 24.

when local leaders voiced the *duo, kuai, hao, sheng* slogan. And in June 1958 his mood was described as "extraordinary happiness" when Bo Yibo declared the steel target could be doubled and Britain overtaken in three years. There can be no doubt that Mao was driven by genuine if misguided hopes for a stronger China.

Yet at the same time there was a darker, hubris-driven side to Mao's actions. Personal pride meant that Mao, notwithstanding his emotional assertion of his own responsibility for Great Leap "disasters" at Lushan, could never genuinely accept that his own actions were the cause of what went wrong. In attacking Zhou Enlai, Chen Yun *et al.* for encouraging "anti-Party rightists" and violating Party discipline he neglected not only his own backing of *fanmaojin* but also his much more cavalier treatment of Party resolutions. Mao appeared driven to find scapegoats, whether Zhou, Chen, or by the time of Lushan the exceedingly loyal but hapless Li Fuchun, and he overinterpreted and took personally unanticipated setbacks. Thus the "rightists" of the failed Hundred Flowers experiment seemed to represent a personal affront, a development which not only led to an excessively harsh campaign against those intellectuals but a search for explanations which illogically settled on opposing rash advance, not his own miscalculation in inviting intellectuals to participate in Party rectification, as the cause of the failed experiment. As we have argued, this rationalization contributed mightily to Mao's growing emotional commitment to the leap forward. And once information appeared concerning serious problems with the (as he and other leaders believed) hugely successful leap, at the same time as calling for greater efforts at realism, he lashed out at Chen Yun in January 1959, at a whole range of top leaders at Shanghai, and finally at those who dared to broach sensitive matters at Lushan. What was involved was not simply an unwillingness to change basic policy, but seemingly a deep psychological inability to admit that *his* initiatives had gone seriously wrong.[19] The tragic consequences for China were enormous.

The Top CCP Leadership. As already indicated, life for the CCP's other top leaders, defined loosely as Politburo and particularly Standing Committee members,[20] necessarily followed the different approaches to leadership exercised by Mao over the 1955-59 period. Prior to the Great Leap there was ample room for debate and the initiative of other top leaders, as particularly revealed by Zhou Enlai's boldness in shaping the *fanmaojin* policies. But with the Great Leap Forward, and especially after the Nanning conference when Mao made economic policy a question of political line, the leadership equation was fundamentally altered. Alternative opinions could not be aired,

---

[19]   Cf. our interpretation of Mao's motives in launching the Great Leap; above, pp. 78-79.

[20]   There is obviously an overlap of categories for some Politburo members such as Li Fuchun who is also discussed under coordinating bureaucracies below, while Ke Qingshi and Li Jingquan are treated basically as local leaders despite their elevation to this body in 1958.

as illustrated by Zhou's drastically altered behavior and Chen Yun's marginalization until Mao decided in summer 1958 that his talents were needed to tighten implementation of the leap. And even when Mao began to encourage alternative views from November 1958, as demonstrated by Chen's cautious on-again off-again performance, this was hardly the type of vigorous debate which marked economic policy during opposition to rash advance. The more threatening atmosphere had sharply reduced the scope of expression and action for Mao's leading comrades — men who were, after all, heroes of the Chinese revolution.

Their predicament notwithstanding, a great deal of responsibility rests with these leaders. To a man, they not only offered no resistance to Mao's radical departure in early 1958, they also seemed more than prepared to give him the benefit of any doubts, with even Chen Yun described by a participant as having "some belief" in the leap. Clearly fear and calculation were important elements in following Mao, but the evidence suggests both shared goals with and enormous faith in the Chairman within the top circles as well. Mao was not only regarded as the architect without whom revolutionary victory was impossible, but the leader who, against the virtually unanimous views of his colleagues, insisted on involvement in the Korean war which was perceived to have had a "victorious" outcome.[21] In the context of the time, moreover, the "high tide" of agricultural cooperativization in 1955 was viewed as a great success leading to high optimism among the top leadership, including the pragmatic Zhou Enlai by the end of the year.[22] During the Great Leap the pronounced fear factor complicates any assessment, particularly as problems became apparent, but close Chinese observers believe that a common desire for a more powerful China generated genuine enthusiasm at the outset among such diverse figures as Liu Shaoqi, Deng Xiaoping, Peng Dehuai, and Zhang Wentian. In this sense, during the early stages of the leap decision making remained "democratic" in that the overwhelming majority backed Mao without major reservation.

A feature of the period as it wore on was uncertainty as to who exactly were the top leaders — or more precisely the policy relevant top leaders. There was little doubt during the *fanmaojin* episode that Party position and status largely indicated real power and policy authority. With the Great Leap, however, the positions and influence of top leaders became more fluid. While Liu Shaoqi and Deng Xiaoping suffered no known setbacks in this regard, the positions of Zhou Enlai and Chen Yun were clearly vulnerable to the extent that Chen feared for his Party membership and Zhou offered to resign as Premier. Mao shifted leading responsibilities at will: overall economic responsibility was stripped from Chen Yun in early 1958, passed in a quasi-formal sense to the less competent but more pliable Li Fuchun while Mao

---

21   This is the assessment of an oral source with access to the top leadership in this period.

22   Even the sceptical Deng Zihui, if Bo Yibo's account is accurate, came to believe Mao was correct as the cooperativization movement unfolded. *Huigu*, vol. 1, pp. 354-55.

himself exercised real authority, and then briefly and partially returned to Chen after the 1959 Shanghai conference. And significantly, when apportioning blame for the leap's setbacks at Lushan, the Chairman singled out three comparatively marginal members of the top elite: Tan Zhenlin, a driving force for radicalism in the rural sector who was raised to the Politburo only at the Second Session of the Eighth Congress, Ke Qingshi, normally a consistent radical also promoted to the Politburo in 1958 but only a local leader, and Wang Heshou, only an *alternate* Central Committee member but the minister responsible for one of Mao's great passions — steel production.[23]

More broadly, our analysis has shown that while the top leadership, apart from those directly concerned with economic management such as Zhou Enlai and Chen Yun, was involved in shaping economic policy during 1955-57 (note especially the role of Liu Shaoqi in initiating the discussions leading to the "Ten Great Relationships" and then in shaping the June 20, 1956, editorial on rash advance), with the leap forward their role as a group significantly contracted, specifically with regard to initiating policy. There is little sign of any input by these leaders during the crucial period from the Third Plenum to Nanning when the basic course of policy was altered — at the Nanning conference these top officials sat in virtual silence as Mao sketched out the new course. Thereafter key individuals such as Liu (the successor) and Deng Xiaoping (characterized by Mao as the vice marshal or deputy commander by spring 1959) in particular played major roles in pushing the new program forward, and later from spring 1959 in implementing Mao's new calls for greater realism. But in both periods the driving forces for policy change, apart from Mao himself, were relative "outsiders" — local leaders in the case of launching the leap, and in May-June 1959 Chen Yun — a marginal player at that point despite his high Party status due to his association with *fanmaojin*.

The irony is that the logic of the Great Leap vested great but paradoxically insubstantial power in the hands of central *Party* leaders; despite the extensive decentralization the leap resulted in incessant orders from the top and, as chief of the Party Secretariat, Deng Xiaoping in particular now exercised enormous administrative clout. Beyond personalities, this also reflected on the Party as an institution. It has long been a staple of analysis that during the leap forward the Party reigned supreme among China's official institutions, now appropriating functions previously under the control of the

---

23   See Li Rui, *Lushan shilu*, pp. 175-76. In this passage Mao also assigned "a bit of responsibility" to Li Fuchun, a less marginal Politburo member given his full membership since 1956 and his role as SPC head, but one who was still considerably less significant than Chen Yun in economic policy before the Great Leap. Mao, however, reserved the greatest responsibility for himself; see also *Chinese Law and Government*, Winter 1968/69, pp. 41-42; and *Case of Peng*, p. 25. Others at Lushan had a similar list of culprits with Hu Qiaomu blaming, in order, Ke Qingshi, Wang Heshou, and Li Fuchun for the 1958 steel target (see Li Rui, pp. 47-48), and Peng Dehuai regarding Tan Zhenlin as having primary responsibility for rural disasters (*ibid.*, p. 285).

state apparatus.[24] To the extent the "Party" refers to provincial Party committees, this was certainly true and will be examined when we discuss local leaders. It also is relevant for top leaders such as Deng whose writ now extended unprecedentedly deep into economic matters, and in a sense for Li Fuchun in that his new position on the Secretariat was probably more authoritative than his SPC role. But what did this mean for such leaders or the "Party" as a whole? Deng and Li seemingly had limited policy-formulating roles — they largely applied pressure to lower levels in an effort to satisfy Mao's wishes. And the central Party apparatus, for all its increased clout, was not developing any enhanced *sustainable* organizational power or interests.[25] As with all other organizational actors, it too lived in a pressure cooker and was forced to implement policies that could only result in the restoration of the influence of government specialists once the resultant difficulties were recognized.

A final aspect of the politics of the leadership just below Mao requiring comment is that there appears to have been relatively little conflict among these leaders throughout the entire 1955-59 period. Thus Liu Shaoqi, whose position as number two in the Party and his own basic inclination made him a close follower of Mao, cooperated fully with the *fanmaojin* program. More broadly, there is no evidence of sharp dissent from the prevailing policies by any Politburo member during 1955-57. With the Great Leap, moreover, even though the circumstances of the time were notionally congenial to attacks from within the top elite on those who committed the "error" of *fanmaojin*, in contrast to attacks from lower-ranking figures, such as those against Zhou Enlai in early 1958, harsh criticism of Politburo colleagues does not appear to have happened to any great extent before the Lushan conference[26]; a case in

---

24   E.g., see Michel Oksenberg, "The Political Leader," in Dick Wilson, ed., *Mao Tse-tung in the Scales of History* (Cambridge: Cambridge University Press, 1977), p. 92. Cf. above, pp. 106-107, 117-18.

25   Bachman, *Bureuacracy*, especially ch. 6, argues that the Party had a vested interest in mobilizational policies. While true to a degree, and undoubtedly contributing to the enthusiasm of provincial-level Party leaders, the point here is twofold: first, the *central* leaders of the Party played no major identifiable role in the shift from *fanmaojin* to the Great Leap, and once the leap was launched its fundamentally antibureaucratic nature meant no genuine institutional interests could be sustained on a medium or long-term basis.

26   The most likely exception was in January 1959, when following Mao's raising of the question of "line," "some comrades" (identified as Li Fuchun and Tan Zhenlin by an oral source) criticized Chen Yun for "rightist" tendencies; see above, p. 142. On attacks by local leaders, see above, pp. 73, 74, 97.

      While the fact that all top central leaders had supported *fanmaojin* was clearly a factor in dampening conflict, this would have been no bar to opportunistic attacks as seen in Zhou Enlai's behavior during the Cultural Revolution; see Teiwes and Sun, *The Tragedy of Lin Biao*, pp. 95, 98. Not only is there no clear documentary evidence of intraleadership conflict at the highest level (i.e., below Mao), but an oral source with

point is Deng Xiaoping's apparent defusing of the question of Zhou's resignation in June 1958. A large part of this phenomenon has to do with revolutionary status. The perpetrators of opposing rash advance, above all Zhou, had enormous prestige, and no other top leader seemed willing to launch excessive personal attacks. The much vaunted unity of the Yan'an leadership, so called into question by the Cultural Revolution, nevertheless seemed real even in this stressful period. This unity was not necessarily based on personal affection (although it was to a considerable degree in Zhou's case) but rather, as intimated, on one's contributions to the revolution. Remarkably, as discussed in Epilogue 1, even when Peng Dehuai, a personally unpopular member of the top group, came under Mao's direct attack at Lushan, there were initial efforts by various leaders, including those who strongly disagreed with Peng on policy grounds, to try (unsuccessfully) to ameliorate his plight.[27] On this matter as all else the top leadership caved in to Mao's wishes and participated in harsh attacks on Peng, but the degree of restraint and respect within this "collective" during this uncertain period was still remarkable.

The Economic Coordinating Bodies. These bodies consisting of the two planning committees, Li Fuchun's SPC and Bo Yibo's SEC, and Li Xiannian's Ministry of Finance, were as vulnerable as any other actors to the whims of Chairman Mao. As with top leaders, their roles changed significantly with the coming of the Great Leap Forward. During 1956-57 they, especially the planning agencies whose power in a communist developing state was always greater than that of any financial body, stood at the apex of a Stalinist economy. While subject to the course set by their political masters, these bodies had great input into the drafting of overall economic policy — the plan — and of course operational authority to oversee its implementation. But concerning the origins of the leap forward the role of these organs was either absent or derivative: there is no sign of any policy initiative on their part at the Third Plenum, and as with top Party leaders silence was their basic posture at Nanning. Some role was apparent, however, in (moderately) increasing targets in late 1957-early 1958 under Mao's pressure, and especially in Bo Yibo producing the concept of two sets of accounts at Nanning "in order to avoid being called a conservative."[28] Moreover, following the launching of the leap the established routines built up over the previous eight years were ruptured, and the formally great powers of the SPC in particular could not hide the fact that the planning function had been drastically weakened, eventually leading even Mao to complain about the planners abandoning their duties. Finally, as problems became apparent from late 1958, the Chairman began to listen to the advice of the leaders of

---

personal knowledge of elite interaction in this period asserts the absence of attacks on leading figures within this circle, apart from Mao's own comments.

27   Note also the comfort mission to Li Fuchun at Lushan; above, p. 172n142. On the question of revolutionary status, see Teiwes, *Politics and Purges*, pp. lxiii-lxvii.

28   See above, p. 87.

these organizations who now, Li Fuchun normally apart, began to reflect the seriousness of the situation, and the planning agencies, as seen in the SEC assuming control of industrial policy in March 1959, regained some of their traditional functions.

Even during the "bureaucratic" phase of 1956-57, the distinction must be made between these institutions and their leaders who sat on the Politburo — the two Lis and Bo Yibo. It was not only Mao who could dominate the central bureaucracies; to a lesser degree other top leaders of the revolutionary generation also had a very strong position *vis-à-vis* these organs. Moreover, in the relations among the leading economic policy makers, power and influence came less from the organizational "power bases" of these individuals than from their Party status. This was clear in the preeminent role of Chen Yun in economic policy before the leap. Chen held the comparatively minor bureaucratic post of Minister of Commerce in this period, but he had enormous status as a CCP Vice Chairman and a Politburo member since the early 1930s, and great prestige from his past leading role in the key area of Party organization work as well as from his successes in guiding China's post-1949 economic recovery and launching the FFYP. Among those concerned with the economy Chen's position was authoritative. As noted previously, Chen (subject to Mao's and Zhou's consent) formulated policy while Li Fuchun, Li Xiannian, and Bo Yibo took charge of concrete implementation, and even if the others were unhappy with Chen's positions it was difficult for them to express their discontent given Chen's superior status. Chen clearly operated at a higher generalist level within the economic sphere, involving himself heavily in the affairs of both the planners and the financial types. He certainly was not coopted by any particular organization. That his views by fall 1956 had a congruence with some of the organizational missions of the "financial coalition" is best understood as a byproduct of his own reading of the current situation and not as the result of institutional influence.

This leads to a broader observation. While certainly a degree of cooptation took place, perhaps especially in the case of Li Fuchun who had headed heavy industry and the planning bureaucracies since 1950,[29] this arguably occurred to a lesser degree than what normally happens in more institutionalized political systems. The individuals who took charge of China's economic bureaucracies were on the whole self-confident revolutionaries who saw themselves on a transformative mission and who believed in a higher loyalty to the CCP as a whole. To paraphrase a Party historian who has written on the period, although the phenomenon of differences resulting from departmental interests existed, the overall Party unity of the period clearly overrode any partial interest. While the heads of departments would have to respond to organizational objectives, they themselves acted somewhat

---

[29]   In comparison, Li Xiannian only took up his duties as Minister of Finance in 1954, while Bo Yibo had earlier held that post from 1949 to 1953 before assuming positions in the "planning coalition" in 1954.

independently and took into account the overall Party interest. The institutional influence, this scholar concluded, was relatively smaller. Moreover, the strictures of Party discipline meant that there were severe limitations on information below the very top central bureaucrats, a situation clearly inhibiting the ability of those organizations *qua* organizations to exercise power. Thus, according to a ministerial official of the period, when criticism of *fanmaojin* at the Third Plenum emerged, ministers kept the identity of Zhou Enlai and his associates as the perpetrators of the "mistake" secret from their subordinates out of respect and a sense of discipline since this information was restricted to very high-level cadres. That such information about the broad policy orientations of top leaders *could* be kept secret says volumes about the limits of organizational power in a system dominated by a revolutionary generation.

As noted, during the *fanmaojin* period the coordinating bureaucracies were clearly the dominant actors in economic policy under the direction of Zhou Enlai and Chen Yun and, of course, subject ultimately to Mao. All of the relevant organs carried out the program of opposing rash advance, and all of their Politburo-level leaders supported those policies. There was no split between "planners" and "budgeteers": while acknowledging some influence of organizational missions,[30] Party historians reject the notion of competing "coalitions" and see the interaction of the two groups as fundamentally cooperative in support of *fanmaojin* in 1956-57, and as essentially irrelevant afterwards when the Great Leap thoroughly disrupted organizational routine. The differences which did appear were between Li Fuchun and the other leaders, including fellow planner Bo Yibo, and were largely reflected in his less active involvement in the process. Although various considerations arguably contributed to this development,[31] the strongest factor most likely had to do with Li's personality and political style — particularly his lack of assertiveness and initiative — rather than institutional considerations. While organizational factors may have also been present, for example the fact that the SPC's revised SFYP came under Zhou Enlai's criticism in May 1956, this did not stop SPC personnel from working closely with Zhou on the *fanmaojin* effort, or, in other circumstances in 1959, from contributing to the "cool heads" on the steel question, while Li personally — apparently hesitant to risk departing from Mao's basic "line" — adhered to a much "hotter" advocacy.

Thus the real bureaucratic conflict in Beijing took place between these coordinating agencies and the spending ministries.[32] Clearly there was a clash of missions here, with the ministries wanting more resources for their

---

[30]   An example of minor differences was the more prominent role of the Ministry of Finance in the initial anti-rash advance efforts of January-February 1956; above, pp. 24f.

[31]   See the summary above, pp. 49-51.

[32]   This, of course, is not to say there was no bureaucratic tension among these agencies, including between the SPC and the SEC, whose responsibilities especially for annual plans shifted over the whole period.

particular tasks and the SPC, SEC, and Ministry of Finance (during 1956-57) seeking to achieve overall balance and restrain excessive demands.[33] While constant quarreling over resources was a general phenomenon according to a participant in the process, it clearly became especially intense during the *fanmaojin* period as the planning agencies repeatedly tried to wind back the demands of the ministries. That this effort was eventually successful owes a great deal to the organizational power of the SPC and SEC before the leap forward, but more to Zhou Enlai's persistence and Mao's acceptance of Zhou's program.

During the Great Leap the situation changed in several senses. First, leading planners such as Bo Yibo had to invent new schemes in order "[not to appear] conservative" and also to compete with the spending bureaucracies in proposing vast increases in targets, while at the same time an inversion in the previous organizational relationship took place. Whereas the coordinating agencies were the undisputed masters before 1958 even if much bureaucratic argument was involved, with the leap these bodies were placed in a relatively passive position in that they had to meet the demands for more resources from their "subordinate" spending ministries (as well as from the localities). The situation was most dramatic in the case of steel: given Mao's fixation with increasing steel production any projection by Minister of Metallurgy Wang Heshou — one of those singled out by the Chairman at Lushan as responsible for the leap's shortcomings — had to be accepted by the planners. Not only was the planning function degraded, but ministries which had previously been under the thumb of the planners now had the upper hand.

A final aspect of the situation is that while Mao seemingly held the coordinating agencies in high regard during 1956-57, from early 1958 his attitude was negative, and often harshly so. As the leap forward took shape he sharply criticized their methods and performance, basically calling for a whole new set of work methods to replace the Soviet-style approach of the FFYP. Even when the planners, as with Bo Yibo's dual accounts, provided him with new methods suited to rapid development, there is little to indicate any special regard on his part toward these agencies *qua* organizations. Soon their inability to provide meaningful coordination precisely because of his demands led to further disillusionment on his part, including sharp comments especially at Shanghai and Lushan. It was not only a case of the economic coordinating agencies having no choice but to follow Mao, it was also a situation where they earned his displeasure no matter what they did in attempting to achieve his objectives.

The Central Spending Ministries. The basic bureaucratic position of the spending ministries is apparent from the preceding discussion, as is the fact that these organizations and their leaders were also at the mercy of the

---

33   An official who was involved in the process emphasizes that the main conflict of the ministries was with the planning agencies which controlled spending, not with the Ministry of Finance whose central task was to collect funds.

Chairman's fluctuating attitudes. As suggested, in a fundamental sense their position was similar to that of the localities. Both wanted more money to spend, thus making them competitors for scarce resources, but also making them allies against the coordinating agencies (and Zhou Enlai, Chen Yun *et al.*) in the repeated bureaucratic battles of the *fanmaojin* period. Yet in certain senses the respective roles of the spending ministries and the localities differed significantly, particularly following the Third Plenum, when the Great Leap began to take shape and through the Nanning conference.

In 1955-57, as the centralized Soviet model dictated, the spending ministries had a greater input into economic policy making than the localities. This is perhaps most clearly indicated by Mao's opening statement in the "Ten Great Relationships" where he noted that his speech was a summarization of the discussions with the 34 ministries over the previous two months.[34] In contrast, the Chairman's similar encounters with provincial representatives during the same period and subsequently seemingly did not have the same impact. Both groups forcefully articulated their organizational interests in the relatively permissive atmosphere of the time,[35] but the model meant that the representations of the ministries whose tasks focused on the modern sector were the most significant for overall economic policy. But as the Great Leap took shape initially, despite their basic interest in rapid growth and the increased resources it implied, the spending ministries seemingly played an even smaller role than the economic coordinating agencies. Not only is there no sign of their initiative at the Third Plenum or at Nanning, but these central organs lagged behind the localities in raising targets. A key problem, of course, was that Mao lumped these bureaucracies together with the planning agencies as "those people in Beijing" who had succumbed to the erroneous Soviet methods of economic management. Particularly at Nanning, this was not a situation conducive to bold contributions to the policy process.

This, of course, did not prevent the influence of particular ministries and ministers as the leap developed — provided they appealed to Mao's enthusiasms. This was most clearly the case with Wang Heshou given the Chairman's passion for steel, but it is useful to remember that Wang too was apparently silent at Nanning. Ministerial influence can also be seen in other cases where Mao's approval was obtained as a result of the rhetoric and declared ambition of these bodies: this occurred with regard to the optimistic reports of 12 ministries to the Wuchang conference where, he noted, "The report by [Vice Minister of Railroads] Lü Zhengcao is very daring, I greatly enjoyed it."[36] The actual benefit of the Chairman's enjoyment was less clear, however. While it may have produced additional resources for the ministry,

---

[34]   *SW*, V, 284.

[35]   In addition to the articulation of local interests at the Eighth Party Congress described by MacFarquhar, *Origins 1*, pp. 130-33, see the discussion of various presentations of ministerial officials on that occasion in Bachman, *Bureaucracy*, pp. 108-11.

[36]   *SS*, p. 506. Cf. above, pp. 93-94, 100.

Mao's accompanying question "whether we can achieve [the ministry's targets], whether there is a basis" underlined the dilemma of the spending ministries. Although expressions of bold optimism possibly earned greater resources, they also tied those organizations to tasks that could not be fulfilled, something it appears various ministerial officials became aware of comparatively early in the leap forward.[37] This dilemma suggests that, while institutional interests were relevant, the fundamental factors affecting the behavior of the spending ministries during the leap forward were the broadly shared desire for a strong China and the political pressure brought to bear from above.

The spending ministries were caught up in bureaucratic tensions throughout the entire period, and not just with the coordinating agencies. Not only was tension with the localities inherent in the competition for scarce resources, but the decentralization debate produced a significant clash of interests as reflected at the January 1957 conference of provincial secretaries and also in more muted form in 1958 under the impact of a more radical devolution of power. While the Great Leap was not a time when open opposition to administrative devolution was possible, some central officials feared that the localities lacked the expertise to run modern sector enterprises effectively.[38] Moreover, the spending ministries competed with one another for resources during both the *fanmaojin* and Great Leap phases.[39] Yet such "natural" conflicts sometimes became embroiled in larger policy political questions, particularly during the leap forward. The clearest case concerns two ministries at the center of the modern sector, the Ministry of Metallurgy which was responsible for steel production, and the First Ministry of Machine Building, a user of high quality steel output, particularly for military products. At the Eighth Party Congress in 1956, the two ministries openly debated over whether steel or machine building should be the most important component of the heavy industry sector, a debate which machine building apparently lost as

---

[37]   See above, p. 115. Note also Li Rui's warnings from mid-1958. In this respect Li's "other" position as a leading official in the electric power sector was undoubtedly crucial, even if his status as Mao's secretary presented the opportunity to express his concerns to the Chairman. See above, pp. 114n81, 151.

[38]   According to our central bureaucrat (see above, p. 17), he did not regard this as primarily a struggle for institutional control, noting that he himself was quite in favor of decentralizing his sector and concluding that the concern over requisite expertise was quite genuine. On the January 1957 clash, see above, p. 60.

[39]   Bachman, *Bureaucracy*, pp. 111-12, argues that particularistic interests were generally subsumed by the larger interests of the "coalition." Concerning our perspective of conflict with the coordinating bodies, a participant in the process reports that the ability of the spending ministries to push their case against the planners during the *fanmaojin* phase was inhibited by the fact that interaction among ministries was to a large degree limited to forums controlled by the planning agencies. On the tendency of bureaucratic units to stick to themselves in another context, see Teiwes and Sun, *The Politics of Agricultural Cooperativization*, p. 18.

its funding declined while metallurgy's increased.[40]

With the Great Leap — and Mao's fixation on steel — the preeminence of metallurgy was even greater, meaning that it obtained the largest share of investment, thus squeezing other sectors seemingly including machine building. Another source of tension concerned the quality of steel output: metallurgy's pursuit of maximum gross output conflicted with machine building's need for quality products.[41] All this underlay the contrasting advocacy of the two ministries' leaders once Mao called for greater realism in late 1958, but arguably it was existing political postures that were telling. Wang Heshou seemed unwilling to depart from the relatively "hot" position he had occupied since the start of the leap, apparently remaining silent when Bo Yibo and Zhao Erlu suggested a significantly reduced steel target at Wuchang and holding out for a higher target against the Chen Yun review in May 1959. Zhao, representing machine building,[42] seemingly was unburdened with such prominent advocacy of wild claims, and could more comfortably adopt a position of relative moderation.

Ironically, while the spending ministries had a genuine interest in the increased investments brought about by the leap, they neither played a significant role in the emergence of that policy nor, like other actors, were they able to use those investments to produce sustainable growth in the sectors under their responsibility. Ultimately, while clearly involved in a competition for resources, they were engaged in a more fundamental competition to display loyalty to Mao. Their plight was familiar, being forced to follow Mao in carrying out policies disruptive to the national economy as well as to their own more parochial interests, but in contrast to provincial leaders they received no particular sympathy from the Chairman.

Provincial Leaders. Two things stand out in any general assessment of the role of provincial-level Party leaders over the 1955-59 period. First, of all the players in elite politics, this group most consistently pursued a course that in some rational sense was congruent with its own interests. Second, in the post-Third Plenum period these leaders, particularly activist elements among them such as Ke Qingshi in the initial formative and utopian phases, played the most influential role of any of the actors around Mao and thus on the course of the Great Leap Forward by stimulating and encouraging the

---

40   See Bachman, *Bureaucracy*, pp. 108-10, 118.

41   Li Rui, *Lushan shilu*, pp. 40, 53-54; and oral source. The imbalance in sectoral allocations was also noted in Chen Yun's May 1959 oral report to Deng Xiaoping where he noted that "more care should be given to the petroleum and chemical industries, to construction materials, as well as to various light industries"; Sun Yeli and Xiong Lianghua, *Gongheguo jingji fengyun zhong de Chen Yun*, pp. 181-82.

42   Zhao became Minister of the First Ministry of Machine Building following the February 1958 death of Huang Jing, the official who was also in charge of the State Technological Commission.

Chairman to develop his initiative to even more unsustainable heights.[43] In addition, local leaders continued to hold a favored place in Mao's affections even after the period of his initial enthusiasm. Yet ultimately, for all their influence on and support of Mao, they too were completely dependent on the Chairman's fluctuating views.

Mao's favorable attitude toward the localities was apparent even before the Great Leap. In this earlier period local leaders did receive sympathetic audiences with Mao during his various inspection tours of the provinces, and clearly there was some influence, as in his late 1955-early 1956 tour concerning not only the development of the 40-article agricultural draft which so captured his fancy, but also in his calling for attention to their requests for decentralization. Subsequently, it may have been the input of provincial officials which led the Chairman to float the idea of an increase in capital construction expenditure at the April 1956 Politburo meeting, and following the meeting he again received provincial leaders on another of his inspection trips. This work method of visiting the provinces to find out what was really going on, together with an antibureaucratic bias against central officials remote from the "masses," seemingly brought Mao close to local leaders physically and psychologically. Yet in the end it was not sufficient to expand their role in economic policy before the Third Plenum: the constraints of the Soviet model meant the action was elsewhere, while Mao's contemporary confidence in Zhou Enlai, Chen Yun *et al.* meant that the budget cutters had their way in denying the localities the resources they sought. Interestingly, if necessarily speculatively, it appears that local leaders were somewhat bolder than central ministerial officials in grumbling about this result,[44] perhaps reflecting both a greater physical distance from Zhou and the other architects of *fanmaojin* in Beijing and the sensitivity of nonspecialist Party officials to the overall ideological "line."

The remarkable, indeed astonishing, influence of provincial leaders from the time of the Third Plenum undoubtedly reflects Mao's continuing attentiveness to those "close to the masses," but it more profoundly relates to the mutual reinforcement of the Chairman's new departure and the enthusiasm of the provinces for that course. Thus Mao reportedly was "very excited" when local leaders revived the *duo, kuai, hao, sheng* slogan at the Third Plenum, later asked Zhou Enlai if he could write an article as good as Ke Qingshi's, and ordered the *People's Daily* to learn from the localities.[45] For their part, provincial leaders not only vigorously articulated the rhetoric of the

---

[43]   A similar if more restrained role had been played by this group and Ke personally during the 1955 cooperativization debate; see Teiwes and Sun, *The Politics of Agricultural Cooperativization*, p. 20.

[44]   While one should be wary of making too much of a single incident, the report of Ke Qingshi expressing "dissatisfied feelings" over the June 20, 1956, editorial is intriguing; see above, p. 32.

[45]   See *SS*, p. 394; and above, pp. 69, 74.

emerging leap, they launched a mass mobilization water conservancy campaign, proposed significantly increased production targets substantially before the central ministries, and strongly took up the criticism aimed at top leaders such as Zhou Enlai who were tarred with the brush of opposing rash advance. Moreover, in terms of influencing policy, apart from Mao's own initiatives, one of the most critical factors — arguably even more significant than Bo Yibo's dual accounts or Wang Heshou's role in doubling the 1958 steel target in June, both of which came under Mao's direct personal pressure — was Ke Qingshi's East China coordinating region's promise of a huge increase of that region's steel output for the following year in late May 1958, an action which both led other regions to offer similar unrealizable targets and came *before* Bo, Wang, and others at the Center drastically raised their projections in the Chairman's presence.

Clearly a number factors fueled this enthusiasm. Undoubtedly most basic was the vision of a strong China, but a vision which fit perfectly with their sense of local interests. Throughout the entire 1955-59 period provincial leaders wanted rapid economic growth to build up their areas. This was not linked to any particular economic strategy — the localities pressed for more resources for their regions under the centralized Soviet system, even when actual control would remain with Beijing. But various features of the Great Leap struck a deep chord with these leaders who, in the perhaps overstated but still suggestive view of a former central official, found Mao expressing what they thought but hitherto had not dared to say. These features included an even more radical version of decentralization than what they had advocated, a version which gave them much greater control of local industrial development, greatly enhanced financial and material resources, and a mass mobilization approach that was familiar to the Party cadres who now ventured forth to oversee the modern sector.

In addition to furthering local interests, at least some provincial leaders were affected by genuine ideological enthusiasm and/or opportunism. Arguably, both can be seen in the case of Shanghai's Ke Qingshi. Throughout his career Ke frequently stood on the "left" of Party opinion on key issues and developments. While we should not forget his role as the first major public advocate of "the whole nation as a chessboard" in February 1959, "leftism" certainly was the distinctive feature of his Great Leap performance, as in the unrestrained utopianism of his Chengdu proposal that everyone become university students by 1967. Indeed, according to an authoritative oral source, Ke was always a "leftist," and his activism (along with that of other local leaders) following the Third Plenum came when change was in the air but its parameters were still quite uncertain. Nevertheless, the view of Ke put forward by Bo Yibo as someone who "figured out very well Chairman Mao's thinking and what he liked"[46] is also suggestive and certainly points to a phenomenon

---

[46] Bo's remark occurred in the context of his analysis of the 1955 agricultural cooperativization debate; see Teiwes and Sun, *The Politics of Agricultural*

not unknown in elite politics in China or elsewhere. Finally, the enthusiasm of the localities has been linked to the comparatively low level of education and sophistication of their leaders, an observation which may have some relevance concerning lack of formal training in the specialized modern sector, but which fails to explain why some of the most radical provincial leaders were among the best educated. Ke Qingshi was well educated, lecturing at Fudan University among his other duties, while Tao Zhu and Wang Renzhong — radicals in 1958 before veering toward moderation in 1959 — were regarded as *caizi*, i.e., talented men of letters whose accomplishments exceeded those of *xiucai*.[47] Indeed, one is tempted to suggest on the basis of their performance, as well as that of the *xiucai*, that high levels of *literary* education were conducive to radicalism.

Of course, provincial leaders were never a unified group, as graphically illustrated by the fact that some, although a definite minority in number and clout,[48] were purged during the early days of the Great Leap. Earlier, at the Eighth Congress, varying demands were articulated by different provinces according to their respective natural endowments.[49] And even during the intense utopian phase of the leap some provinces lagged despite the intense pressure from above.[50] But the significant divisions among provincial leaders emerged as the leap ran into problems. Initially the most important of these provincial figures, notwithstanding some recognition of problems and a role in bringing them to Mao's attention particularly in the context of his inspection tours, remained on the "left" of the spectrum — even to the point of directly contesting his more "realistic" opinions. But as time wore on the results of "practice" produced sharp differences of views, as strikingly visible in the clash of radicals Ke Qingshi and Li Jingquan *versus* "moderates" Wang

---

Cooperativization, pp. 11-12, 15, 20. Ke remains a controversial figure in the eyes of CCP scholars. The research of David Chambers, making substantial use of interviews with Shanghai Party historians, has revealed that completion of a detailed chronology of the post-1949 Shanghai CCP has foundered in part because of the difficulty of reaching a consensus on Ke. While some view him in the decidedly negative light so common in Western analyses, others conclude that he did the best he could under difficult circumstances, playing a constructive role in the development of Shanghai's industrial base and protecting several leading city figures from leftist attack in the early stages of the 1957 anti-rightist campaign. Work began on the chronology in 1986; it was still incomplete in late 1997.

[47] See *Xuexi ziliao*, vol. 3, p. 219; and Quan Yanchi, *Zhongguo zuida baohuangpai — Tao Zhu fuchenlu* [China's Number One Royalist — The Rise and Fall of Tao Zhu] (Hong Kong: Tiandi tushu chubanshe, 1991), p. 13. Cf. the discussion above, p. 175. On the *xiucai*, see above, p. 131.

[48] See Teiwes, *Politics and Purges*, pp. 275, 285-86.

[49] See MacFarquhar, *Origins 1*, pp. 130-33.

[50] See the discussion of Liaoning, the only province whose leadership was purged in 1958 *after* the Second Session of the Eighth Congress, in Chan, "Agricultural Development in the Great Leap," especially pp. 63-64, 68n.

Renzhong and Tao Lujia at Shanghai. But what is perhaps most remarkable is that both sides in this debate of the localities received a sympathetic hearing from Mao. While the Chairman certainly handed out doses of criticism to various provincial figures,[51] on the whole he seemed to maintain a sympathetic attitude, giving some encouragement to Wang Renzhong and Tao Lujia, while drawing solace from the "leftist" Wu Zhipu. Thus those local leaders pushing moderation had an impact, even if the overall incoherence of Mao's position prevented more than a fitful "cooling down" effort. Again, the Chairman looked benignly on the localities: his enigmatic visage toward the debating provincial leaders at Shanghai stood in significant contrast to both his dressing down of Bo Yibo and Li Fuchun for their planning failures and his harsh speech criticizing a large section of the top leadership for alleged historical sins on the same occasion.

Thus by the end of the period under study both "hot" and "cool" heads among the provincial leaders retained a remarkable degree of influence and favor with Mao. This was not because of any needed support to secure his policies, it was rather due to a predisposition toward them as a group, not simply because of their enthusiasm in the period when he formulated *his* Great Leap, but more generally because they had been relatively removed from the "failed" policies and methods of the initial eight years of the PRC and were notionally closer to the grass roots and China's "masses" than any other elite grouping.

The "Missing" Actor: The Military. A final brief comment is required concerning the one major institution which has hardly featured in our story — the PLA. This may appear odd given not only the dismissal of Peng Dehuai and army Chief of Staff Huang Kecheng at Lushan, not to mention Mao's fulminations about an alleged "military club," but also because of the presumptive link noted in Western studies between the peasant-based army and the interests of China's rural population.[52] Certainly army leaders appear in the events examined, with Huang Kecheng serving on the small group responsible for the economy until its reorganization in June 1958, military representatives participating in major meetings and less formal discussions initiated by Mao,[53] while Peng in his role as a Politburo member shifted from

---

51   E.g., Mao criticized Guangdong's Tao Zhu in early 1959 but also praised him somewhat later. See MacFarquhar, *Origins 2*, pp. 155-56; and above, p. 143.

52   See Michel Oksenberg, "Occupational Groups in Chinese Society and the Cultural Revolution," in Oksenberg, Carl Riskin, Robert A. Scalapino, and Ezra F. Vogel, *The Cultural Revolution: 1967 in Review* (Ann Arbor: Michigan Papers in Chinese Studies no. 2, 1968), p. 5. Another factor commonly argued as placing military interests, and Peng Dehuai personally, in conflict with the Great Leap was the desire for good relations with the Soviet Union in order to further military modernization; see Lieberthal, "Great Leap Forward," pp. 307-308.

53   For example, the January 1959 occasion when Peng Dehuai was summoned along with Chen Yun, Li Fuchun, Bo Yibo, and Li Xiannian to discuss economic and industrial questions; see above, p. 141. The generally low profile of military leaders is reflected in

early enthusiast to sceptic as a result of his rural investigations during the "cooling off" phase. Ironically, the clearest army-Great Leap link before Lushan came during the utopian phase. This was in the context of the attack on "dogmatism" — an attack *led by* Peng Dehuai — at the May-July 1958 Military Affairs Committee conference, where the similarity between criticism of Soviet military and economic methods was obvious and explicitly emphasized by Mao who directed a stream of economic reports to the meeting. But thereafter the PLA was fully absorbed in military tasks — the Taiwan Straits crisis of summer 1958 and the Tibetan rebellion of 1959. Indeed, it is worth noting that Huang did not initially go to Lushan, while Peng attempted to beg off on grounds of military work. In fact, the army's greatest input into economic matters seemingly came during the *fanmaojin* phase when Huang occupied a seat on the small group and organizational representation was the order of the day, while during the entire pre-Lushan Great Leap phase the military role was marginal at best, if not nonexistent.[54]

The key features of CCP economic policy making over the 1955-59 period are now clear in considerably greater depth and nuance: an absolutely dominant Mao, albeit one who chose to exercise that dominance in the economic sphere only with the Great Leap Forward, and a drastic change in the roles and clout of other political players during the leap which reduced or made sporadic the role of the Chairman's top Party colleagues, inverted the relationship of the economic coordinating agencies and spending ministries, and gave provincial leaders an unusual influence in launching, pushing to extremes, and attempting to modify the leap forward. The ultimate responsibility for the radical break from a system which — for all its faults and totalitarian nature — nevertheless functioned in a relatively systematic fashion and, in its own terms, reasonably well, to a regime which set impossible goals, destroyed tested organizational routines, and made policy advocacy (at least of a "moderate" type) an exceedingly risky business, of course lies with Mao. But what is perhaps most striking is the complicity of all other actors in what turned out to be such a great tragedy. On one level, this is understandable. All sections of the elite, the beneficiaries of the unexpected and indeed amazing victory of the communist revolution, had enormous faith in Mao whom they firmly believed was the key ingredient in that victory, and suspended credulity and followed their "ever correct leader" — even to the extent that relatively clear-sighted leaders still clung to belief in the general line as conditions deteriorated in 1959.[55] And interlaced with such faith was

---

their limited participation in the major meetings of 1958-59, particularly when the presence of PLA figures with Politburo status is factored out; see Appendix 1.

54   See *Mao wengao*, vol. 7, pp. 273-76, 278-80, 289-91, 326-27, 416-17, 437-38, 454-56, vol. 8, pp. 245-46, 310; Teiwes, "Peng and Mao," pp. 87-89; idem, *Politics and Purges*, pp. 293-96; MacFarquhar, *Origins 2*, pp. 195-200; and Schram, *Mao Unrehearsed*, pp. 126-30. Cf. below, p. 229n38.

55   Cf. the belief of early Soviet leaders that Lenin should be obeyed even against the convictions of one's own understanding because he had been repeatedly proven correct

fear[56] based on the universal understanding that opposing Mao, not that anyone had any wish to do so, would be futile as it was simply impossible and not the way to achieve desired policy change. As Zhang Wentian commented in the context of Lushan, accusations of seeking to overthrow Mao were absurd as only the Chairman could rectify the excesses of the Great Leap. Thus political prudence and — as especially seen in the case of Chen Yun — any possibility of shifting policy for the better both required subservience to Mao.[57]

Yet as understandable and indeed inevitable as these considerations may be, in the end the elite politics of the Great Leap Forward must strike an observer as depressing — perhaps not as grotesque as that of the Cultural Revolution,[58] but depressing nevertheless. For what we have, in intellectual terms, is a set of political actors accepting untested methods and developmental projections that no one should have believed, actors including in Chen Yun a man of shrewdness and sophistication who reportedly had "some belief," and men of honor such as Peng Dehuai and Zhang Wentian[59]

---

by revolutionary practice. Arguably the phenomenon was even stronger in the PRC given the importance of obedience in Chinese culture. See Teiwes, *Leadership*, p. 47.

56   Fear and faith can also be seen in the broader perspective of the leadership's inability to separate Mao the individual from the Party and regime as a whole. Thus faith in the Chairman involved not simply following his Great Leap policies in the belief that he had discovered a new way to rapid growth, it was also reflected in expectations that he would "do the right thing" and make the necessary changes to save the country as was his moral obligation. At the same time, there was at least a subconscious fear that the regime could not withstand a break with Mao, that the entire system might collapse into disorder given not only his Lushan threat to "go to the countryside to lead the peasants and overthrow the government" (*Case of Peng*, p. 21), but more fundamentally due to the very fact that so much ideological legitimacy and political power was vested in his person. We are indebted to Peter Kuhfus for emphasizing these points. See also Teiwes, *Politics and Purges*, p. 331.

57   On Zhang Wentian's comment, see below, p. 208. In addition to the necessity of currying Mao's favor in order influence policy positively, the provincial leader we interviewed at some length made a point of emphasizing the concrete work of leaders such as Zhou Enlai, Chen Yun, and Li Xiannian to ameliorate conditions. He further argued the need to take into account such beneficial developments as increased inputs of fertilizer into agricultural production in order to achieve a "balanced" view of the leap. For memoir accounts of the role of Zhou Enlai and others in coping with the serious grain situation, see *Wenxian he yanjiu*, [Documents and Research], no.3 (1984), pp. 19-25; Yang Shaoqiao and Zhao Fasheng, "Liangshi diaodu de zong zhihui" [The General Director of Grain Transfers], in Guo Simei and Tian Yu, eds, *Wo yan zhong de Zhou Enlai* [Zhou Enlai as I Saw Him] (Shijiazhuang: Hebei renmin chubanshe, 1993), pp. 225-29; and below, p. 216n10.

58   For an analysis of the grotesque politics of this period, see Teiwes and Sun, *The Tragedy of Lin Biao*.

59   For light on the characters of Peng and Zhang, see Teiwes, "Peng and Mao"; idem, *Politics and Purges*, pp. xxxiv-xxxv, liii-liv; and idem with Sun, *Formation of the*

who exhibited positive enthusiasm in the early stages of the leap. And in terms of political courage, despite the honored role of Hai Rui in the larger political culture we have at most individual actors willing to exploit (cautiously) small windows of opportunity opened by Mao, only to retreat at any sign of the Chairman's disapproval, as in the case of Chen Yun's early 1959 self-criticism. As China drifted toward disaster no one stood up to say "enough is enough" — not even at Lushan.[60] Loyalty, fear, and the sheer incapacity to imagine any situation where Mao's word was not law were the underlying factors leading the PRC to its first great tragedy.

Maoist Leadership, pp. 4, 12, 14-15, 48.

[60]   Zhang Wentian arguably came closer to standing up to Mao at Lushan than Peng Dehuai, but even Zhang's criticisms were aimed at the desperate situation rather than confronting the Chairman. See below, p. 208.

Epilogue 1

THE LUSHAN CONFERENCE, JULY-AUGUST 1959[1]

How do the events at the summer 1959 Lushan conference which culminated in the dismissal of Minister of Defense Peng Dehuai square with the preceding analysis? The broad outline of developments at Lushan has long been well known: after an early initial stage of the meeting when Mao seemed prepared to make significant modifications to Great Leap policies, Peng authored a far-reaching critique of the leap in his "letter of opinion" which drastically altered the Chairman's attitude, and led him to demand the dismissal of Peng and others who had demonstrated scepticism concerning those policies, most notably alternate Politburo member Zhang Wentian.[2] The activities of Peng and the others have long been regarded in Western literature as a challenge to or even "an all-out attack on [Mao's] policies"[3] and indeed on the Chairman himself, with Mao then prevailing in the subsequent struggle. While official CCP accounts deny such a political struggle, they cause difficulty for our analysis by picturing a brave and upright Peng Dehuai who dared to stand up for the suffering masses. While there is a substantial element of truth in this, although arguably even greater credit should go to Zhang Wentian than Peng, the overall story of Lushan like so much else is more depressing. For once Mao chose to interpret events as an attack on him, the problems of the leap were overwhelmed by the political drama, and the fates of Peng *et al.* were sealed without serious resistance.

---

[1]   This epilogue is based on the 1993 account in Teiwes, *Politics and Purges*, pp. xxxi-xxxvi, liii-lvi, as supplemented by more recent sources. For further detail on the conference, see *ibid.*, ch. 9; and MacFarquhar, *Origins 2*, ch. 10.

[2]   The key leaders named as principal members of Peng's "anti-Party clique" at the conference were Zhang, PLA Chief of Staff Huang Kecheng, and Hunan First Secretary Zhou Xiaozhou. Also affected at a lower level was Mao's secretary Li Rui who three decades later authored the most authoritative account of the meeting in *Lushan shilu*. For a listing of those known to have suffered after Lushan during the campaign against "right opportunism" that was designed to target people of like thinking, see Teiwes, *Politics and Purges*, pp. 336-37.

[3]   Jürgen Domes, *Peng Te-huai: The Man and the Image* (London: C. Hurst and Co., 1985), p. 91. See MacFarquhar, *Origins 2*, pp. 216, 403, for a more nuanced version of this position.

The unanimous view of the Party historians consulted during our interviews is that although Peng Dehuai, Zhang Wentian, and others in the alleged "anti-Party clique" represented a broad strand of opinion within the leadership, their aim was not to confront Mao but to deepen the trend of correcting the excesses of the leap which the Chairman himself had set in motion. While there were concerns with Mao's "undemocratic" tendencies which had been so pronounced since the Nanning conference, the main story was the familiar one of divining the Chairman's intentions and making use of the opportunities they presented to advance one's policy preferences. That Mao's desire to correct the "left" was, notwithstanding all the ambiguity and ambivalence of previous months, widely perceived during the "first stage" of the Lushan conference is amply demonstrated by the range of officials who adopted this perspective. They included not only government administrators like Zhou Enlai who now had scope to express their presumably moderate inclinations, but even such Great Leap radicals as Shanghai leader Ke Qingshi who brought materials critical of leftist phenomena to Lushan, and Mao's long-time secretary and trouble-shooter, Chen Boda, who both openly aired concern in group meetings and joined in private criticisms of the leap with the Chairman's other secretaries Hu Qiaomu, Tian Jiaying, and Li Rui, as well as *People's Daily* head Wu Lengxi. That these leaders of different ideological tendencies, work responsibilities, and Party rank — but who all had a significant degree of personal access to Mao — were on the same track indicates that an anti-left posture was seen as important for retaining or regaining the Chairman's favor.[4]

But while the main direction was relatively clear as Party leaders gathered at Lushan, there was considerable ambiguity as to the precise policy implications of this direction and particularly concerning how far Mao was prepared to go in correcting left errors. This was inherent in the Chairman's attitude since late 1958 that the Great Leap concept was correct and errors were limited to concrete work problems (not to mention his more blatant self-contradictions), a view reflected in his assessment on the eve of Lushan that was intended to set the tone for the conference discussions: although problems

---

4   *Women de Zhou Zongli,* pp. 303-304; Li Rui, *Huainian nianpian* [Twenty Articles in Remembrance] (Beijing: Sanlian chubanshe, 1987), pp. 258-59; idem, *Lushan shilu,* pp. 184-85; and oral sources.

Chen Boda's attitude was a case of someone who had been out of Mao's favor for his excessively leftist stance earlier. As indicated previously, Mao sharply criticized Chen at the November 1958 Zhengzhou conference for his advocacy of abolishing commodities and money and he was now excluded from the key committee set up to draft an outline for the Lushan meeting. Thus he may have felt it necessary to join in the anti-left trend to repair this damage, and/or his new position may have reflected a genuine change of view. Also, the fact that Chen lived together with Hu, Tian, and Wu under the Lushan arrangements facilitated his participation in their discussion sessions, which were also joined by two former/concurrent Mao secretaries, Zhou Xiaozhou and Li Rui. Li Rui, *Huainian nianpian,* pp. 35, 62; oral source; and above, pp. 127-28.

were "quite a few," "our achievements are great ... and the future is bright." As demonstrated in Chapter 4, in this general context many officials had earlier chosen to ignore Chen Yun's moderating suggestions, and Chen, assertedly mistakenly, even felt it necessary to make a self-criticism in early 1959 following a sharp comment from Mao, while others stifled their critical opinions given the uncertainty of the situation notwithstanding Mao's more cautious bent. Thus when the Lushan meetings began, even allowing for the critical comments being made, considerable restraint was evident. As Peng Dehuai observed, people were not airing opinions freely, a situation undoubtedly due to fear of offending the Chairman. Moreover, Hunan First Secretary Zhou Xiaozhou, a secretary of Mao's in the 1930s who would, arguably more because of coincidence than common advocacy, soon be labeled a leading member of Peng Dehuai's "clique," even raised his concern that people were not speaking out, that many didn't dare to talk about shortcomings in a private conversation with Mao, and he received a sympathetic hearing.[5]

Given this situation Peng could later reasonably interpret his actions at Lushan as designed to overcome such hesitancy and foster the process of correcting the left trend by gaining Mao's backing, for problems "could be easily resolved" if the Chairman endorsed correct policies. Such a calculation, of course, was based on the principle that Mao was unchallengeable — a principle that informed his actions and those of others in his "clique" throughout the Lushan meetings. This was not unrelated to a concern about Mao's arbitrary tendencies; Zhang Wentian was most acute on this point. Speaking to his secretary, Zhang complained that the Party had become arrogant and had lost its perspective, things were becoming like Stalin's later period, collective leadership was no longer tenable, and although he was a Politburo member he didn't know what was going on. In another more celebrated conversation with Peng Dehuai, Zhang again raised the Stalin analogy but, ironically, Peng sought to defend Mao by arguing he was different from Stalin and far superior in his recognition of nonantagonistic contradictions, although Peng went on to complain that the Chairman only

---

5   Cong Jin, *Quzhe fazhan*, p. 188; Zheng Longpu, trans., *Memoirs of a Chinese Marshal — The Autobiographical Notes of Peng Dehuai (1898-1974)* (Beijing: Foreign Languages Press, 1984), p. 502; Li Rui, *Lushan shilu*, pp. 78-79; Teiwes, *Politics and Purges*, pp. 310, 311-12; and oral sources. Hunan Party Secretary Zhou Hui was also involved in expressing concerns in the conversation with Mao, but despite being criticized later in the conference he held his position before being demoted in the second half of 1960. See Quan Yanchi and Huang Linuo, *Tiandao — Zhou Hui yu Lushan huiyi* [Heaven's Way — Zhou Hui and the Lushan Conference] (Guangzhou: Guangdong lüyou chubanshe, 1997), p. 336; and Liu Jintian and Shen Xueming, eds, *Lijie Zhonggong zhongyang weiyuan renmin cidian* [*Biographic Dictionary of Previous Central Committee Members*] (Beijing: Zhonggong dangshi chubanshe, 1992), p. 251. On the reasons for Zhou Xiaozhou's fate, see below, p. 211.

criticized others and would never admit his own mistakes.[6] But these discontents notwithstanding, such grumbling was private and those seeking a change in policy hoped to achieve it *through* Mao rather than against him.

Rather than having a plan to confront Mao, Peng did not even want to go to Lushan, preferring instead to remain in Beijing overseeing military affairs, and only went when, among others, the Chairman himself rang up and urged him to attend. Similarly, Peng's greatest ally at Lushan, Zhang Wentian (a Vice Minister of Foreign Affairs as well as an alternate Politburo member) was also somewhat reluctant to go, but was persuaded to attend by Foreign Minister Chen Yi who argued that it would not produce problems since Mao had raised no objections to the critical remarks concerning the leap expressed by both Chen and Zhang at a June foreign affairs conference. Thus both Peng Dehuai and Zhang Wentian — their deep concern over the economic situation and subsequent actions notwithstanding — manifested caution about even attending the conference.[7]

Once present, other signs of concern were in evidence. Peng later claimed he felt uneasy about raising difficult questions at group discussions as it could produce "confusion," while in several talks with Zhou Xiaozhou, the two men sought not simply to reinforce each other's critical opinion of the leap, but also apparently to urge one another to raise their concerns with the Chairman directly. In the event, it was only after Zhou Xiaozhou did see Mao and reported back that the Chairman was sincere that Peng decided to approach Mao himself. Yet Peng's uneasiness did not stifle his legendary bluntness, particularly in small group meetings during the early stage of the conference. He not only made various provocative comments, he also reportedly hoped his caustic criticisms would reach Mao and angrily reacted when discovering that the summary reports of the group sessions which were sent on to Mao omitted his harshest criticisms. In any case, although Peng was wary that his impetuous nature might result in giving offence to the Chairman, by his subsequent account he had already concluded that at worst Mao would sack him as Minister of Defense, with the effect of promoting his close colleague, Chief of Staff Huang Kecheng, to the post.[8]

---

6   *Memoirs of a Chinese Marshal*, p. 503; *Huiyi Zhang Wentian* [Remember Zhang Wentian] (Changsha: Hunan renmin chubanshe, 1985), p. 313; and Li Rui, *Lushan shilu*, pp. 130-31.

7   *Memoirs of a Chinese Marshal*, p. 489; MacFarquhuar, *Origins 2*, p. 200; and *Liaowang* [Outlook], no. 32 (1985), p. 20. Those besides Mao urging Peng to attend were Zhang Wentian and Huang Kecheng. See Zhang Peisen, ed., *Zhang Wentian yanjiu wenji*, p. 356; and Li Rui, *Lushan shilu*, p. 127.

8   *Memoirs of a Chinese Marshal*, pp. 490-91, 503; Li Rui, *Lushan shilu*, pp. 128-30; *CB*, no. 851, pp. 24-25, 29; *Peng Dehuai zhuan*, pp.588-89; and Xie Chuntao, *Lushan fengyun: 1959 nian Lushan huiyi jianshi* [Storm at Lushan: A Simplified History of the 1959 Lushan Conference] (Beijing: Zhongguo qingnian chubanshe, 1996), pp.63-66.

Apart from his comments at group meetings, post-Mao sources also point to one

Moved by these factors, Peng went to the Chairman's quarters only to find Mao asleep. This led to Peng's fateful decision to write his "letter of opinion," a private letter that could not be regarded as an open attack on Mao. Although at the time Peng claimed that he wrote the letter himself in a fit of frustration, it was actually carefully prepared and revised with the assistance of one his secretaries. Once written, the letter was circulated on Mao's instruction by the Central Committee's General Office — not by Peng as sometimes thought. Thus Peng's private communication was turned into an inner-Party document. Peng seemed concerned that the very fact of making the letter public could mean trouble and asked the General Office to take it back, thereby indicating that he saw even the possible perception that he was criticizing Mao as politically dangerous. But once Mao did launch his attack on Peng, the old marshal, like many other participants at Lushan, was astonished by the ferocity of the Chairman's reaction. Peng could not see how a letter meant only for Mao's eyes could be interpreted by the Chairman as a political attack, and he bitterly asked himself why after thirty years of close collaboration Mao could not have privately talked with him if he had made such a grave mistake. Peng's anger, as well as the circumstances of his letter, strongly suggest that he did not conceive of it as an attack on the Chairman.[9]

Yet we are left with the curious nature of the letter itself: part a polite memorial to the throne which, as the editors of the "self-statement" subsequently prepared by Peng under duress assert, "seems diplomatic and mild,"[10] yet which clearly contained some barbed commentary on the contemporary situation.[11] The answer to this paradox lies in Peng's provocative nature which had already been on display in his comments at small group meetings that had failed to reach Mao. Peng had a history of not

apparently testy exchange between Peng and Mao over the amount of waste caused by the steel campaign at an early to mid-July Politburo Standing Committee meeting. Arguably the sharpness of Peng's tongue reflected his anger at developments three months earlier at the Shanghai conference where he had also raised Mao's ire for reasons that are unclear but which led the Chairman to claim that "Peng Dehuai hates me." Li Rui, *Lushan shilu*, pp. 92, 125, 128; and above, p. 153. These events point to a larger pattern which perhaps goes a long way toward explaining the eventual fury of Mao's explosion at Lushan — three decades of repeated instances of personal friction and ill temper albeit within a larger framework of political cooperation. For an overview of this pattern, see Teiwes, "Peng and Mao," pp. 83-87. After Peng's letter, Mao distorted the extent of these tensions with the conclusion that his relations with Peng had consisted of 30 percent cooperation and 70 percent conflict; Cong Jin, *Quzhe fazhan*, p. 218.

9   *Memoirs of a Chinese Marshal*, pp. 494, 503-506; and *Peng Dehuai zhuan*, p. 595.

10   *Memoirs of a Chinese Marshal*, p. 1. Peng's letter is appended to his "self-statement" (*zishu*), i.e., the autobiographical notes written in response to interrogations during the Cultural Revolution and later published and translated as his *Memoirs*.

11   For the view of Peng's letter as a "memorial to the emperor," see Teiwes, *Politics and Purges*, pp. 322-23. For a persuasive case emphasizing the biting criticism included in the letter, see MacFarquhar, *Origins 2*, pp. 213-16.

simply speaking his mind, but also of provoking people to get them to do what he wanted. He had spoken crudely to the Comintern's military representative, Otto Braun, during the fifth encirclement campaign in 1934 in an effort to secure a change in tactics,[12] and now he attempted to use a more measured variation of the same approach on Mao. After writing his letter Peng told Zhang Wentian that he believed Mao's pre-Lushan measures to modify the Great Leap had not gone far enough, and he deliberately included a few stings (*ci*) in the letter to induce Mao to go further.[13] Thus the letter was not quite a polite memorial, nor does it appear to have been an effort to shift the blame to Liu Shaoqi as has been suggested.[14] Rather, the aim was to provoke Mao through a private communication, not to challenge him politically, but in hopes of producing the desired policy change. It was disastrous psychology, and produced fateful results for China in retarding the process of redressing the excesses of the Great Leap as well as for Peng personally. Indeed, Mao subsequently pointed to Peng's indiscretion as the key factor in derailing the rectification of leap excesses and thus propeling China further along the road to disaster.[15]

That Peng's letter was not meant as a political attack, as well as the importance of anticipating Mao's attitude, is also suggested by the reactions of other leaders following the circulation of the letter. These reactions varied: indeed, it appears Mao's intent was to draw out opinions by adding the neutral comment "issue to each comrade" when the letter was distributed. At first many participants at the conference not only agreed with the letter's policy advocacy, but significantly saw no major political problem with it. For example, Zhou Enlai, a sensitive observer of the Chairman who had rededicated himself to understanding Mao's meaning following his humiliation in early 1958, commented that there was nothing to worry about, while a leading provincial secretary "could not see anything wrong, although we were uncomfortable with [phrases like] "petty bourgeois fanaticism."

---

12   *Memoirs of a Chinese Marshal*, pp. 354-57; and oral source.

13   Li Rui, *Lushan shilu*, p. 281; and oral sources. In Li Rui's account, in an early August speech Lin Biao claimed that Peng had told someone that his letter contained stings. An authoritative oral source identified this person as Zhang Wentian, but another well-informed source said Jia Tuofu was the leader in question. There are, in any case, several other versions not necessarily in contradiction with the above on the question of stings in Peng's letter. One is that Peng's friend, Huang Kecheng, said with some alarm after reading the letter that it contained stings; Cong Jin, *Quzhe fazhan*, p. 206. Another is that people unsympathetic to Peng like Ke Qingshi pointed to the stings as evidence that the letter was an attack on Mao; Peng Cheng and Wang Fang, *Lushan 1959* [Lushan 1959] (Beijing: Jiefangjun chubanshe, 1988), pp. 93, 187.

14   This was speculatively suggested in Teiwes, *Politics and Purges*, pp. 323-24.

15   In a mid-1961 conversation with Anhui's Zeng Xisheng Mao complained that Peng had "messed up" his plan to tackle leftist mistakes at Lushan; Wang Lixin, *Anhui "dabaogan" shimo — 1961, 1978* [Anhui's "Big Responsibility (System)" from Beginning to End — 1961, 1978] (Beijing: Kunlun chubanshe, 1989), p. 43.

Others close to Mao, however, sensed that a delicate situation had arisen. Thus secretary Li Rui felt that Peng had shown a lot of daring that was virtually unique in writing the letter, even though he too did not anticipate any serious consequences. Hu Qiaomu was even more wary, observing privately that the letter might cause trouble. Still others of demonstrated leftist inclination, such as Ke Qingshi and Sichuan's Li Jingquan, began to criticize the letter whether because they felt its policy implications went further than they could accept, that in their view it genuinely did slight the Chairman, or in anticipation of Mao's displeasure with Peng. In any case, these initial reactions suggest that the letter was far from universally perceived as an attack on Mao, but that some at Lushan had an inkling that the Chairman might respond badly.[16]

One of the most revealing responses was that of Zhang Wentian who shared Peng's dim view of the consequences of the leap and who had exchanged views privately with him before and during the conference. Zhang's response was revealing both in that it demonstrated the outer limit that any leader was prepared to go, and the understanding that everything rested in Mao's hands. In the new, more uncertain situation created by Peng's letter, Zhang was determined to support Peng's views by giving a speech that would argue the case more rigorously than Peng had. As he prepared his speech he was warned by Hu Qiaomu that it was not a wise thing to do, but at a time when Peng was seeking to have his letter withdrawn from circulation, Zhang decided to go ahead even though he recognized that it could potentially cause severe repercussions. He subsequently argued to his wife who questioned his involvement in a situation where, as a foreign affairs official, he had no direct responsibility, that in view of the dire plight of the masses he had an obligation to speak up regardless of the consequences. In the event, his speech on July 21 was an ordeal for Zhang given frequent hostile interjections. Yet even at this stage he could not have known the full implications of what he had done, implications which began to become clear when Mao addressed the conference on July 23. Once Mao had spoken and Zhang faced demands that he confess to seeking to overthrow Mao, Zhang commented on the absurdity of the accusation to his secretary by observing, in a manner similar to Peng Dehuai's rationale for acting in the first place, that such an aim was simply impossible and only the Chairman could solve the problems caused by the Great Leap.[17]

The emotional, intemperate nature of Mao's outburst on the 23rd has long been apparent, but post-Mao sources give a much clearer picture of its impact. The immediate impact was to astonish the audience: it was not only Peng who was taken aback by Mao's ferocity. Perhaps most revealing was the fact that four of the Chairman's secretaries, including Chen Boda who would soon

---

[16]   Cong Jin, *Quzhe fazhan*, p. 206; Li Rui, *Lushan shilu*, pp. 94, 135-53, 164; and oral sources.

[17]   Li Rui, *Lushan shilu*, pp. 156-57; Zhang Peisen, *Zhang Wentian yanjiu wenji*, p. 357; *Huiyi Zhang Wentian*, pp. 19-20, 314-16, 319; and oral source.

change his colors to adopt a posture sharply critical of Peng, returned from the meeting to sit in stunned silence with no one speaking for half a day. Yet given Mao's track record of harsh attacks that were not followed by severe punishment — as had been demonstrated the previous year concerning Zhou Enlai and Chen Yun — many leaders apparently still believed the situation could be repaired and sought to play down the transgressions of Peng and Zhang over the following days. Thus Bo Yibo and An Ziwen, two officials who had clashed with Peng in the past and were specially summoned to Lushan following Peng's letter, limited their criticisms of Peng to historical questions, while other leaders as varied as revolutionary military commander in chief, Zhu De, and the leftist agricultural boss, Tan Zhenlin, sought to lighten Peng's sins. The case of Tan is particularly interesting given his policy stance. On July 26 Tan declared he would engage in principled struggle against Peng's letter to the end, but at the same time he lauded Peng as a good comrade who was loyal to the Party and country with many contributions to the revolution, and he even praised the writing of the letter as a brave act, as a very good thing. Yet despite his attitude, which was reportedly representative of the feelings of many others, Tan was forced to withdraw his remarks two days later as the pressure grew following new remarks by Mao, also on the 26th, that people and not just the issues had to be dealt with, and it quickly became clear that the Chairman was demanding Peng's head regardless of the widespread desire to cool matters down. As so often before, and as would be the case again in the future, now that Mao's attitude was completely unambiguous the resistance of his colleagues collapsed and attention focused on intensified criticism of Peng, Zhang, and others now implicated in their "clique."[18]

Thus once Mao had placed his authority on the line the leadership closed ranks behind him. This did not mean that individuals did not object to what had happened, but their objections were limited to private expressions of sorrow rather than resulting in any attempt to curb the Chairman. The sympathy that existed was now channeled into persuading Peng, whose options had been reduced to stubbornly holding his ground in the face of massive attack, engaging in self-criticism, or, apparently, suicide, to make the

---

[18]   Li Rui, *Huainian nianpian*, p. 35; idem, *Lushan shilu*, pp. 87, 181-83, 196; *Renmin ribao*, June 30, 1988, p. 5, October 23, 1988, p. 4; Cong Jin, *Quzhe fazhan*, pp. 218, 306-307; and oral source. The ineffectualness of the efforts to stand up for Peng are further illustrated by the actions of Zhu De and Bo Yibo. Zhu, undoubtedly the most sympathetic of all on a personal basis, could only try to assist Peng by making his criticism as mild as possible under the circumstances, an effort which resulted in Zhu also coming under harsh criticism at both Lushan and the Military Affairs Committee meeting convened soon after. As for Bo, when Foreign Minister Chen Yi, who had not been present at Lushan, questioned him on what happened and expressed disappointment with the undemocratic way of handling Peng's views, Bo agreed but quickly added that they could only exchange these opinions in private.

necessary demeaning self-examination.[19] Peng finally accepted pleas to "consider the interests of the whole situation" and undertook the required self-criticism in deference to Party unity and Mao's prestige, but he remained bitter over the fact that "For the first time in my life, I have spoken out against my very heart!"[20] Despite significant elite reservations over Mao's actions as well as his policies, the most his leadership colleagues were willing to do was to try and find a way to ease Peng's dilemma while protecting the Chairman's prestige and giving him the outcome he wanted.

In terms of the various actors we have been examining throughout this study, the Lushan meeting saw a wide range of individuals including Politburo colleagues, central economic officials, provincial Party leaders, and Mao's own secretaries who either shared Peng's views on the need for a further retreat and/or sympathized with his efforts and sought to ameliorate his situation. This inclination was shared by various army leaders at the conference — notably PLA Chief of Staff Huang Kecheng who had been summoned to Lushan during the conference and subsequently found himself declared a principal member of the "anti-Party clique." As with the other "clique" members there is no evidence of anti-Mao intent; when the issue of Peng's letter exploded with Mao's July 23rd speech, Huang, like others, initially felt "The matter will be cleared up, the Chairman will not err." The PLA as an institution or interest group, moreover, remained essentially peripheral to the drama, notwithstanding Mao's fanciful claim that a "military club" (*junshi julebu*) had formed around Peng and Western analyses pointing to military interests. In fact, the reaction of army leaders both at Lushan and at the subsequent September Military Affairs Committee conference had far less to do with opinions concerning the Great Leap than with attitudes toward Peng (including for many a sense of injustice over his situation), and of course with loyalty to Mao.[21]

---

19   The suicide option is implied by Peng's promise to Mao at Lushan that he would not take his own life; *Memoirs of a Chinese Marshal*, p. 522. The efforts of leaders including Nie Rongzhen, Ye Jianying, Zhu De, Liu Shaoqi, and Zhou Enlai to persuade Peng to give in are reported in *ibid.*, p. 507; Domes, *Peng*, p. 98; and by oral sources. The suicide option seems more a worry of other leaders, who were perhaps affected by the memory of Gao Gang taking his own life when facing political disgrace in 1954, than any serious intention on Peng's part. In any case, measures were taken to guard against any possibility of his suicide; see *Zhonggong dangshi ziliao*, no. 28 (1988), p. 96.

20   According to a 1978 letter by Huang Kecheng cited in Domes, *Peng*, p. 98.

21   On Huang Kecheng, see *Memoirs of a Chinese Marshal*, pp. 494, 505-506. For Mao's views concerning the "military club" which by his definition consisted of five members, three of whom (Zhang Wentian, Zhou Xiaozhou, and Li Rui) assertedly joined the core group of Peng and Huang although they were not army officers, see Li Rui, *Lushan shilu*, pp. 267, 326; and *Xuexi ziliao (1957-1961)*, pp. 387-88. For an analysis arguing the dissatisfaction of Peng and his PLA colleagues at Lushan with the Great Leap based on a combination of military *v.* political priorities, foreign policy differences, and sensitivity to the peasantry which provided the army's soldiers and food, see Chang,

The evidence further suggests that for Mao, while criticism of *his* Great Leap was crucial, it was less policy views *per se* or the organizations people represented than a number of other, often coincidental factors which ultimately determined his reaction to individuals. Going beyond Peng Dehuai's provocations and Zhang Wentian's insistence on ignoring Hu Qiaomu's warnings to offer a systematic critique of the Great Leap as late as July 21, why were Huang Kecheng and Zhou Xiaozhou designated leading members of the "clique"? In Huang's case his close personal and work ties to Peng was undoubtedly a key factor. Zhou Xiaozhou, who had spoken out in support of Peng's views about the same time as Zhang Wentian, may have been affected by the coincidence that many of Peng Dehuai's opinions were based on investigations conducted in Hunan and the two Hunanese exchanged views at Lushan. Arguably particularly important for both Huang and Zhou was Mao's observation of their reluctance to join in the criticism of Peng, to "draw a line" quickly with Peng Dehuai. That policy as such was not decisive can be seen in the case of Hu Qiaomu who, in his role as the key drafter of the conference outline emphasized leap shortcomings and came under strong attacks for views as controversial as those of Peng. Nevertheless, Hu's "case" was not fatal once Mao remarked that the *xiucai* are "our men." Yet another *xiucai*, Li Rui who was now denied such status by Mao, did suffer, and here the role of coincidence or sheer bad luck seemingly was crucial. For on the night of Mao's July 23rd outburst Hunan native Li who had worked in the province in the early 1950s joined long-standing Hunan officials Zhou Xiaozhou and Zhou Hui at fellow provincial Huang Kecheng's residence, and were present when Peng dropped by to discuss a military matter concerning Tibet with Huang. As another provincial leader who had been equally critical of leap excesses commented, he (who was not a Hunanese) was lucky not to attend this gathering which was subsequently denounced as sinister by Minister of Public Security Luo Ruiqing.[22]

Once Mao forced the issue virtually all actors, however reluctantly for some, joined in the required denunciations of Peng and the others. Among the most prominent critics were those with demonstrated radical inclinations,

---

Power and Policy, pp. 110-14. Cf. above, p. 198. Teiwes, *Politics and Purges*, pp. 332-35, details the post-Lushan military personnel changes which seemingly, as in the case of Huang Kecheng, had more to do with guilt by association than common advocacy, and argues against the significance of military issues for developments at the conference. Subsequent analysis using post-Mao Party history sources demonstrates that Peng, rather than being the military modernizer *par excellence* as usually portrayed, had in fact strongly backed Mao's political emphasis during the spring 1958 military affairs conference; see above, pp. 198-99.

[22] *Memoirs of a Chinese Marshal*, pp. 494, 505; Li Rui, *Lushan shilu*, pp. 78, 298, 326; and interview with participant at Lushan, Beijing, 1997. All of those including Peng at this gathering except Zhou Hui who, despite being a Jiangsu native was considered a Hunanese by Mao, were Hunan natives, and all except Peng had worked in Hunan during the early 1950s.

notably provincial-level leaders Ke Qingshi and Li Jingquan and alternate Politburo member Kang Sheng. But also making some of the most severe attacks were PLA leaders; in the memory of conference participants these included Marshal He Long, General Political Department Deputy Director Xiao Hua, and Nanjing Military Region Commander Xu Shiyu as well as Luo Ruiqing who would soon succeed Huang Kecheng as PLA Chief of Staff. Not to be outdone, top leaders also joined the harsh criticisms with the contribution of Liu Shaoqi particularly sticking in the mind of the above participant and, according to a senior Party historian, Zhou Enlai being even worse than radicals Ke Qingshi and Li Jingquan. In the face of Mao's fury, ideological proclivities, timidity and opportunism, and loyalty to the Chairman determined behavior, while the policy preferences and institutional interests that were influential at the start of the conference took a decidedly back seat.[23]

"Party unity" had been restored, but completely on Mao's terms and with scant concern for the plight of China's masses. Indeed, as has been long understood, while targets were reduced at the Central Committee plenum that completed the conference, the political atmosphere created by the dismissal of Peng *et al.* and the subsequent campaign against "right opportunism" overrode any policy caution as once again unrealistic claims by officials fearing the "rightist" label created a push for a renewed and intensified leap forward in 1960. By the time the leadership finally faced up to the dire nature of the situation in the second half of 1960, a disaster of truly unprecedented dimensions had engulfed the nation.

---

23   Li Rui, *Lushan shilu*, pp. 178-79, 183-84, 294-96, 2nd revised edition (Zhengzhou: Henan renmin chubanshe, 1994), pp. 235, 240-44, 250-51, 283, 303; Xiong Huayuan and Liao Xinwen. *Zhou Enlai Zongli shengya*, p. 241; and oral sources. The participant who particularly remembered Liu's harsh language did not, however, have a clear recollection of Zhou's offering. The account of He Long's role conflicts with that of Cultural Revolution sources which claim his reluctance to criticize Peng, arguably in order to blacken He's name; see MacFarquhar, *Origins 2*, p. 240

Epilogue 2

THE RETREAT FROM THE GREAT LEAP, 1960-62[1]

As in 1956-57, the retreat from the Great Leap Forward from mid-1960 through to the summer 1962 Beidaihe meeting and subsequent Tenth Plenum is clearly an "un-Maoist" period. Mao's beloved Great Leap was effectively dismantled, other leaders were prominent in cleaning up the mess, and the ideological themes of 1958-59 largely disappeared, to be replaced by the pragmatism of "investigation and research." Inevitably, this has also been widely regarded in Western analyses as a period of political eclipse for Mao, something he had to endure out of weakness until he again somehow turned the tables on his opponents, raising the slogan of "never forget class struggle" as a key national guideline at the Tenth Plenum.[2] Once again, such interpretations are wide of the mark. In a manner both similar to yet profoundly different from the *fanmaojin* experience, Mao retained unchallenged authority, endorsed what happened, yet was ambivalent about the measures which repaired the situation. Like 1956-57 Mao was somewhat distant from the process, but now his role was much more critical. The Chairman was central to correcting the terrible disaster he more than anyone had created, while those around him were much more attuned to the problems inherent in his ambiguous positions than they had been half a decade earlier. The eventual outcome in 1962, however, was all too familiar.

---

[1] While this epilogue is not based on the same degree of comprehensive and in-depth research as all other parts of this study, we have examined a considerable range of post-Mao Party history sources to support the interpretation which follows. A debt is owed to the fine analysis in Dali Yang, *Calamity and Reform*, ch. 3, which provides one basis for much of our account. Another useful secondary source, albeit one flawed by both a power struggle interpretation of the period and grossly inadequate footnoting, is Becker, *Hungry Ghosts*. Becker's book is reviewed by Frederick C. Teiwes in *CQ*, no. 149 (1997). Finally, MacFarquhar's *Origins 3*, which came to hand at the very last moment, provides a rich history of the period which is by and large compatible with our analysis; see, however, below, pp. 225-26n30, 228n34.

[2] See, e.g., Chang, *Power and Policy*, ch. 5, especially pp. 130-31; Byung-joon Ahn, "Adjustments in the Great Leap Forward and Their Ideological Legacy, 1959-62," in Chalmers Johnson, ed., *Ideology and Politics in Contemporary China* (Seattle: University of Washington Press, 1973), especially pp. 294-300; and Lieberthal, "Great Leap Forward," pp. 319ff.

Mao's policy stance after the dismissal of Peng Dehuai still retained the elusive ambivalence of the period from fall 1958 to the Lushan conference. He not only endorsed the cutback in targets approved by the August plenum, in November 1959 he echoed his February comments at Zhengzhou by again enjoining basic-level cadres to "pay absolutely no attention to the directives from a higher level," and advising them that claims of high yields "really can't be done, so what is the use of such boasts?"[3] As before, some leading officials used the Chairman's more realistic impulses to restrain radicalism, as in February 1960 when Guangdong leaders Tao Zhu and Zhao Ziyang strictly limited the number of communes that could experiment with commune-level accounting — a modest initiative in substance but a notable one given the general climate. The dominant trend, clearly fueled by the post-Lushan campaign against "right opportunism," was for even greater radicalism as seen in the Center's March 1960 directive that 80 percent of the peasants should eat in communal mess halls, and a February report from Guizhou of the province's determination to at least double the size of mess halls and turn over private plots to them — a report that earned Mao's enthusiastic praise and demand for nationwide emulation. Overall, the emphasis was on upgrading collective organization while largely ignoring the increasingly desperate situation.[4]

The failure to respond meaningfully had several causes. Mao subsequently claimed that with the Sino-Soviet dispute escalating in 1960, "the central leadership comrades devoted their main energy to international questions."[5] But undoubtedly more significant was the political paralysis created as a result of Lushan and the onslaught against "right opportunism." There is no indication of any top-level leader taking a major initiative to deal with the unfolding disaster, while provincial reports reaching the Center downplayed problems as isolated occurrences within a generally favorable situation and Mao seemingly regarded deviations as easily correctable. A case in point took place in March 1960 when reports of starvation in local areas in Anhui came to the attention of Mao and his colleagues. As we have seen, Anhui First Secretary Zeng Xisheng was a leading provincial radical during the leap forward whose excesses had produced serious difficulties in Anhui from 1959 or indeed earlier. But now news of the depth of the crisis reached

---

3   *CB*, no. 891, pp. 34-35, cited in Stuart R. Schram, "Introduction: The Cultural Revolution in Historical Perspective," in idem, ed., *Authority, Participation and Cultural Change* (London: Cambridge University Press, 1973), p. 63.

4   See Yang, *Calamity and Reform*, pp. 58, 71-72, 74-75. Yang draws heavily on the important collection of central and local documents prepared by the Guojia Nongye Weiyuanhui Bangongting [State Agricultural Commission General Office], *Nongye jitihua zhongyao wenjian huibian* [Compendium of Important Documents on Agricultural Collectivization], vol. 2: 1958-1981 (Beijing: Zhongyang dangxiao chubanshe, 1981).

5   *Miscellany of Mao Tse-tung Thought (1949-1968)*, part II, *Joint Publications Research Service*, no. 61269-2, February 20, 1974, p. 238.

the Center through an appeal by a member of the provincial Political Consultative Conference. In the event, Zhou Enlai wrote to Zeng asking him to investigate the claims and duly noting that in comments concerning the Shandong situation Mao had "stressed that we should take this [type of phenomena] seriously." Zhou, however, characteristically added that "Perhaps this has been exaggerated," and "this sort of *individual case* happened in every province ... last year."[6] Clearly, there was little will at the top to address the fundamental issues.

Things began to change by summer 1960, however. While Mao's later claim that starvation "was not reported to the Center until the summer of 1960" is not strictly accurate, it does appear that only at this time did substantial numbers of reports suggesting the true scale of the famine begin to be received in Beijing — a situation also brought home by diminishing grain reserves in China's big cities.[7] While, as we shall see, the substantive response remained ambivalent, clearly a new stage of awareness had been attained, and by no one more so than Mao. The most dramatic evidence was the Chairman's altered mood. According to Mao's librarian, he had rarely been so depressed and said little during summer 1960, while an authoritative Party history account claims that in subsequent months Mao had difficulty eating and sleeping and gave up meat, in order to share the difficulties of the people.[8]

Policy did change significantly, although with important limitations initially and political hesitations throughout. The annual summer leadership gathering in Beidaihe saw some notable retreats: Mao declared that rather than a transition to a commune-based rural economy the position of the production brigade was guaranteed for five years, peasants should be allowed private

---

6   *Zhou Enlai nianpu*, vol. 2, p. 299 (emphasis added). See also Jiang Kunchi, "Zeng Xisheng 'zuo' hou jiu 'zuo'" [Zeng Xisheng from "Leftism" to Correcting "Leftism"], *Renwu*, no. 5 (1997), pp. 9, 12, 14; and above, pp. 122, 130, 151.

7   Mao's March 1961 claim concerning reports of starvation is from Pang Xianzhi, "Mao Zedong he Tian Jiaying," p. 50. See also Yang, *Calamity and Reform*, pp. 72, 75-76, 278n23, 279n41; and below, n. 10. Evidence of earlier reports of starvation can be traced to fall 1958, although that Anhui case was treated as isolated and having been quickly put right; see above, p. 122. However, other claims of earlier reporting, e.g., that Peng Dehuai warned of the danger of starvation in a telegram to Beijing in fall 1958 (Becker, *Hungry Ghosts*, p. 87), and that top secret messages reporting famine deaths reached the Center in the immediate post-Lushan period (see Yang, *Calamity and Reform*, p. 278n23) are undocumented and, we believe, unlikely given both the broader evidence available and the prevailing political circumstances.

8   Pang Xianzhi, "Mao Zedong he Tian Jiaying," p. 56; and Liu Yishun, "Mao Zedong zai Anhui tuiguang zerentian de qianqian houhou" [Mao Zedong before and after Anhui's Promotion of Responsibility Fields], *Zhonggong dangshi ziliao* [Materials on CCP History], no. 54 (1995), p. 102. A shorter version of the latter authoritative Party history article is idem, "60 niandaichu Anhui nongcun zerentian shimo" [The Early 1960s Anhui Village Responsibility Fields from Beginning to End], *Dangshi yanjiu ziliao* [Research Materials on Party History], no. 8 (1994).

plots, and the Center's approval of the February Guizhou report on expanded mess halls he had so enthusiastically endorsed should be altered. In addition, the meeting addressed the desperate agricultural situation by giving priority to grain production while labor was to be shifted from other activities to farming. And by the end of August a new slogan proposed by Li Fuchun and Zhou Enlai of "adjustment, consolidation, filling out, and improvement" foreshadowed a new overall economic policy of reduced targets, attention to quality, and emphasis on coordination. Yet at the same time the Beidaihe meeting affirmed the "unlimited vitality" of the Great Leap and communes, declared the economic situation "good," called on the peasants to do a good job of running the mess halls, and decided on a mass campaign to produce steel. As Dali Yang has acutely observed, it was — and not for the first time — a mixed message, one that left considerable leeway to provincial leaders to devise appropriate responses.[9]

Subsequent measures in the second half of 1960 and early 1961 manifested further retreat, continuing ambivalence, and the crucial role of Mao. The Chairman directed Zhou Enlai to oversee drafting of the November 1960 emergency letter on communes (the 12 articles) which extended some production rights down to the lowest collective unit, the production team, and stipulated that 5 percent of cultivated land could be private plots, while Mao himself drafted a directive calling for rectifying the "five winds" (*wufeng*) of communism, exaggeration, commandism, cadre privileges, and blindly leading production. But official policy still stipulated continuing the supply system and communal mess halls, and there were also warnings against "rightist mistakes." Further steps came at the December-January Beijing conference followed by the Ninth Plenum: the limit for private plots was increased to 7 percent of cultivated land, compensation was ordered for property seized during the leap, agricultural procurement prices were increased, and — while it did not prevent tragedies caused by the internal movement of grain[10] — the decision was taken to import food. But the most

---

9   See Yang, *Calamity and Reform*, pp. 73-74, 277n8.

10   When Beijing, Shanghai, Tianjin, and especially the nuclear industry test areas (*he gongye jidi*) suffered from severe grain shortages beginning in late spring 1960, Zhou Enlai called on Zeng Xisheng to transfer grain from the deeply affected Anhui to these areas. This process reportedly left Zhou in tears and Zeng engaging in ideological struggle with himself, but in the end 500 million catties of grain were transferred to the benefit of the "overall situation" but to the decided detriment of an Anhui increasingly racked by starvation. See Jiang Kunchi, "Zeng Xisheng," p. 10. A similar situation occurred in Sichuan (whose leader Li Jingquan boasted at the 1959 Shanghai conference that the province would supply grain to other areas) which apparently continued to send grain elsewhere until 1961 while suffering the nation's highest death toll. See Becker, *Hungry Ghosts*, pp. 94, 162-64; S. G. Wheatcroft, "Comparing the Great Chinese and Soviet Famines of the Twentieth Century," paper presented to the 23rd General Population Conference of the International Union of Population Studies, Beijing, October 1997, pp. 16-18; and above, p. 150.

important outcome was Mao's call for 1961 to become a year for seeking truth from facts and his emphasis on investigation and research, thus opening the way to more vigorous questioning of existing policies. He followed this up by organizing three investigation groups, each headed by one of his secretaries,[11] and himself departed for investigations in the south. As a result Mao became aware that the measures introduced by the 12 articles were insufficient, and he set in motion the process that produced under his direct leadership the 60 articles on communes which further liberalized rural policy at the March 1961 Guangzhou conference.[12]

While the retreat from the Great Leap over the summer 1960 to mid-1962 period had many aspects and leaders other than Mao played the innovative roles on most of these matters,[13] the Chairman's advocacy of investigation and research not only cleared the political path for these developments but in the critical agricultural area it was his policy initiatives (the 12 and 60 articles) that were crucial. We can better understand the overall process, including the roles of various actors, by focusing on one area of rural policy, the trend toward household-based farming. The central figures in this drama were the erstwhile provincial radical, Anhui's Zeng Xisheng, and Mao himself. An authoritative Party history account regards the rise as well as the fall of the Anhui responsibility fields system (zerentian) which led the trend as "inseparable from Mao Zedong's attitude," and attributes the spread of the Anhui system to "Zeng Xisheng's ... courage, [but] even more to Mao Zedong's ... attitude."[14] While it is possible that the tendency of official Party history to give Mao the benefit of the doubt is operative here, we believe these statements are accurate and go to the core of a political process that ultimately remained little changed by disaster conditions.

Zeng Xisheng had indeed demonstrated courage in making an early turn from his previous position in August 1960. Several weeks after the mixed message of Beidaihe Zeng proposed to an Anhui cadres conference the method of assigning production tasks to small groups within the team as a good way of assuring responsibility, and in October he proposed further measures to strengthen the smallest collective units. Zeng's activities in strengthening basic-level responsibility intensified in the wake of the encouragement provided by November's 12 articles, and further encouragement, a "big enlightenment" according to Party history sources,

---

[11] Chen Boda headed a group to Guangdong, Hu Qiaomu another one to Hunan, and Tian Jiaying a third group to Zhejiang.

[12] Liu Yishun, "Mao Zedong," pp. 102-104; and Yang, *Calamity and Reform*, pp. 76-78.

[13] For an overview of the retreat, see Teiwes, *Politics and Purges*, pp. 346-50, 369-76. For a detailed official account recording the roles of various leaders, see *Guanyu jianguo yilai dang de ruogan lishi wenti de jueyi zhuyiben (xiuding)* [Revised Notes on the Resolution on Certain Questions in the History of Our Party since the Founding of the State] (Beijing: Renmin chubanshe, 1985), pp. 271-317.

[14] Liu Yishun, "Mao Zedong," pp. 102, 109.

resulted from Zeng hearing Mao declare at a winter conference of regional secretaries that it was permissable to restore the field management system of the higher cooperatives period which involved contracting labor to peasant households (*baogong daohu*). Mao's remarks led Zeng to review issues arising from the entire cooperative experience, conduct research on responsibility systems, conclude that such systems were crucial to good work, and by the turn of the year carry out experiments in contracting production to individual households (*baochan daohu*). Nevertheless, Zeng's activities should be recognized as representing *prudent* courage as seen in his end-of-year advocacy of trials of *baochan daohu* in an isolated mountainous area.[15]

But even with Mao's green, or more accurately amber, light, the issue was extremely sensitive. Similar to 1956, even though a moderate policy trend was evident, the fact that the political line had not been altered engendered both resistance to change and caution on the part of those seeking to push the trend further. Thus Zeng Xisheng prudently sought Mao's blessing for his new course, asking the Chairman both to approve the disbanding of mess halls and to allow him to return to Anhui from his temporary concurrent posting as Party leader in Shandong so that he could correct his own previous mistakes, requests which were apparently granted. But when Zeng, even more aware of the deteriorating famine situation following early February investigations, put his household responsibility policies to an Anhui secretaries conference in the middle of the month as necessary to secure the smooth development of the socialist system and the support of the masses, although his proposals were approved locally, various places throughout the country criticized the practice of *baochan daohu*. Moreover, when Anhui reported to Ke Qingshi in his role as first secretary of the East China Bureau in late February, Ke's response was that the method should not be popularized, only experimented with. All of this produced a sense of danger which undoubtedly was behind renaming the practice with the less politically problematic term "responsibility fields," as well as influencing Zeng's study of editorials and essays published since the Lushan conference criticizing *baochan daohu* in order to obtain guidance for the implementation of the system.[16]

The sensitivity of the issue was further underlined at the March 1961 Guangzhou conference, the very meeting which adopted Mao's 60 articles stipulating further retreats on rural policy even though production teams were still urged to run mess halls as long as possible. Interestingly, Mao's proposal to make the production team the unit of accounting within the communes was not taken up by the meeting — probably due to a diffident attitude on his part. In any case, the proposal for responsibility fields which Zeng Xisheng raised in the East China group at the conference was an even greater retreat — one

---

15   *Ibid.*, pp. 105-106; and Jiang Kunchi, "Zeng Xisheng," p. 14.

16   Liu Yishun, "Mao Zedong," pp. 106-107; Wang Lixin, *Anhui "dabaogan" shimo*, p. 41; Jiang Kunchi, "Zeng Xisheng," pp. 16-17; *Dangdai Zhongguoshi yanjiu*, no. 1 (1994), p. 57; and Yang, *Calamity and Reform*, p. 82.

which could be interpreted as being a retreat from socialism itself. And in fact it was so interpreted, with group meeting participants accusing him of encouraging "going it alone," making the state into a rentier *vis-à-vis* the peasants, and returning China to the time of land reform. Zeng, facing such opposition, went to Mao to argue his case directly, and the Chairman responded with "Try it out! If it stuffs up, then just make a self-criticism. If it goes well we can increase grain output by 1 billion catties, and that would be a great thing." This response elated Zeng who immediately phoned the Anhui provincial Party committee with instructions to start popularizing the system, saying "it's been approved by the top, we can do it!"[17]

Others were worried, however, whether out of uncertainty given Mao's mercurial track record or genuine concern over the implications for socialism — in fact, most likely a combination of both. In the circumstances, Tian Jiaying, Mao's secretary who had become critical of Great Leap excesses in 1959 but now worried about the threat to the collective sector, played a key role in altering the drift of policy. At the conference, along with many others including Tao Zhu, Tian sharply criticized the household responsibility field system. His views, although frowned upon by Chen Yun, brought great pressure to bear on Zeng Xisheng. Of particular importance, Tian wrote to Mao after receiving materials on the Anhui system from a responsible East China official and argued that the province's proposal reflected panic in the face of difficulties and did not consider the wider consequences. This seemingly had an impact on Mao who now directed Zeng via Ke Qingshi only to experiment with the system on a small scale. Zeng subsequently sought to explain his proposal in great detail in a letter to Mao and other top leaders which emphasized that he was proposing a trial to determine the advantages and disadvantages of the system, that it was different from *baochan daohu*, and that he would not adopt it immediately or unchanged. This, however, bore no fruit as Mao never responded to the letter.[18]

As a result, despite having "received the Emperor's blessing" (*tongtian*) for a larger experiment only a short time earlier, Zeng addressed the Anhui provincial standing committee in late March and, echoing Mao's more restrictive view, said "we will trial it this year, if it's proven good we'll continue it, if it's proven bad we'll just drop it." Crucially, he ordered the Anhui authorities to stop popularization of responsibility fields, but they had already spread widely to reach nearly 40 percent of all production teams by the time Zeng spoke, and given the desperate nature of the situation "everyone" felt the fields had to be accepted, with the result that Zeng's order

---

17   Liu Yishun, "Mao Zedong," pp. 109-10; Jiang Kunchi, "Zeng Xisheng," p. 19; Wang Lixin, *Anhui "dabaogan" shimo*, p. 42; and Yang, *Calamity and Reform*, pp. 78, 82.

18   Sun Yeli and Xiong Lianghua, *Gongheguo jingji fengyun zhong de Chen Yun*, pp. 256-57; Liu Yishun, "Mao Zedong," p. 110; Pang Xianzhi, "Mao Zedong he Tian Jiaying," pp. 65-66; Jiang Kunchi, "Zeng Xisheng," p. 19; Wang Lixin, *Anhui "dabaogan" shimo*, p. 42; and above, p. 168.

was not carried out. But while the "majority of the masses" reportedly supported the system, within and outside the province different views among cadres resulted in many letters to higher authorities with the issue of whether the responsibility fields were suitable for socialism prominent. In this context, the provincial committee sent many reports to Mao, the Party Center, and the East China Bureau seeking support, with the key argument that responsibility fields did not mean individual farming. Meanwhile, the post-Guangzhou investigations of top leaders including Liu Shaoqi and Zhou Enlai uncovered further problems, leading them — now with Mao's backing — to disband mess halls, a development followed up by major changes to the provisions of the 60 articles concerning mess halls and the supply system at the May-June Beijing conference. The element of caution was still very much in evidence, however, as seen in Liu's restrictive pre-conference suggestion that "some piecemeal (*lingxing*) production can be contracted down to the household." The conference also saw a noted self-criticism by Mao where he acknowledged the gravity of the situation and declared that achieving socialism would take at least 50 years — albeit a self-criticism that Liu Shaoqi prudently declined to transmit to lower levels.[19]

In this context of policy retreat but continuing ideological debate, Zeng again sought out Mao during one of the Chairman's inspection tours in mid-July in a new effort to obtain his support. Zeng carefully explained the advantages for production of the responsibility fields compared to other work point systems then being tried in the provinces, while cautiously noting that there were some problems. Zeng also made a point of admitting Anhui's errors including two matters of direction (*fangxiang wenti*): "one is making a decline in production into an increase; the second is opposing what was originally 'left' deviationism in the countryside as 'right' deviationism." After advising Zeng to correct his earlier "subjective bureaucratism" and to engage in self-criticism, Mao responded by giving the go-ahead for further development of the responsibility field system: "If you don't think there are any problems you can popularize [this method] on a widespread basis.... If responsibility fields really have good points, they can be developed a bit more." The Chairman also adopted a benign view on the related issue of private plots, arguing that 5 percent of cultivated land as private plots "is not enough, [we should give] even more land to avoid more deaths by starvation!" When Zeng mentioned increasing the amount to 7 or 8 percent (7 percent having been set in January by the Ninth Plenum), Mao rejoined with "What about 10 percent?" With Mao's endorsement Anhui quickly extended the responsibility fields, and nearly 75 percent of all brigades were implementing the system by mid-August, although not without attracting inner-Party criticism. While Party history accounts rightly point to Mao's backing as a key factor in this speedy

---

19   Liu Yishun, "Mao Zedong," pp. 110-11; Jiang Kunchi, "Zeng Xisheng," pp. 19-20; *Dang de wenxian*, no. 4 (1992), p. 12; Yang, *Calamity and Reform*, pp. 78-79; Teiwes, *Politics and Purges*, pp. xxxvii, 377; and oral source.

development of the responsibility fields, equally significant was the familiar equivocal nature of his support. As leading Party historian Cong Jin has observed, the Chairman's relatively tolerant attitude toward Zeng and other local leaders seeking to deal with the situation was predicated on a recognition that new ways to curb "egalitarianism" had to be found, but he wanted the effort restricted to policy trials rather than full-scale approval.[20]

While official policy developed further in a moderate direction as seen in Mao's September letter to the Politburo Standing Committee noting that "serious egalitarianism" still existed and the team rather than the brigade should be the accounting unit, the responsibility system remained a matter of contention. As one Party history source put it, disputes over direction and line continued without interruption. While the peasants supported the system for its obvious benefits and over 90 percent of Anhui production teams adopted it by the end of the year, officials worried that it was not suited to the "big and public" nature of the people's communes. Contrary to his image from the post-Mao period, one of the main critics of the Anhui scheme was Hu Yaobang, then first secretary of the Young Communist League. In a report to the Center in the second half of 1961 following investigations in Anhui, Hu characterized the responsibility fields as a "dangerous method" which, although having the support of the masses, gave rise to contradictions and disputes that were difficult to resolve and could give rise to exploitation, damage collective viewpoints and organization, and, if their development was unchecked, could reduce the productive level of society. According to an authoritative Party history analysis, with Hu and others contributing to the stormy debate it "could not but influence Mao Zedong's attitude."[21]

Whether Mao needed contributions from leaders such as Hu Yaobang is a moot point, but in November 1961 the Center called for socialist education in the countryside in a directive which stated that contracting output to households was not in accord "with the principles of the socialist collective economy." The following month Mao sought out Zeng for a report, and in the ensuing conversation addressed the issue of whether the responsibility field system should be continued in view of the decision to make the production

---

[20]   Liu Yishun, "Mao Zedong," p. 112; Wang Lixin, Anhui "dabaogan" shimo, pp. 43-46; Jiang Kunchi, "Zeng Xisheng," pp. 20-21; Cong Jin, Quzhe fazhan, p. 486; and Yang, Calamity and Reform, pp. 83-84.

[21]   Liu Yishun, "Mao Zedong," pp. 115-16; Jiang Kunchi, "Zeng Xisheng," pp. 17, 21; and Yang, Calamity and Reform, p. 80.

Hu Yaobang's opposition to the Anhui system is also discussed in Becker, Hungry Ghosts, pp. 243, 328-29, although unfortunately with little documentation. According to Becker, following his inspection of Anhui, Hu attacked Zeng for abandoning communism. In addition, Hu reportedly confessed in 1980 to lying to Mao about his findings on an inspection in Hunan due to fear of being purged had he told the truth (p. 237). Another unsubstantiated claim of Becker's calling into question stereotyped views of Party leaders is that in summer 1961 Peng Dehuai criticized Zeng's method in his letter begging for rehabilitation (p. 243).

team the basic accounting unit. In a reportedly consultative manner Mao noted that production had begun to revive and he asked whether the system could be changed. Zeng responded by requesting that the fields be allowed to continue for a short period as the peasants had only begun to taste their benefits, but Mao did not express an unequivocal position. Zeng seemingly put a favorable interpretation on Mao's failure to reveal disagreement with the responsibility fields and continued to promote the system, but as with other leaders earlier he misread the Chairman who had decided that the retreat to the production team level was as far as he was willing to go. This became apparent at the famous 7,000 cadres conference in January-February 1962.[22]

While the 7,000 cadres conference endorsed a wide range of measures systematizing the retreat from the Great Leap, including making the production team the rural accounting unit, the responsibility fields came under sharp attack. Zeng Xisheng and the other Anhui delegates to the conference were required to stay behind for serious criticism of "mistakes in direction," Zeng was transferred out of Anhui, and the provincial committee was reorganized under Li Baohua who was dispatched from a central government posting. The new provincial committee then engaged in a review of the responsibility field system and dutifully concluded that while the system was the result of good intentions at a time of disaster, the Anhui method was the road of retrogression and with the new policy of team accounting the production activism of the masses could be sustained through the collective approach. Moreover, at the same time back in Beijing Liu Shaoqi strongly endorsed the restrictive line, also arguing that the responsibility fields were clearly a retrogressive path.[23]

But if Mao and other top Party leaders left the 7,000 cadres conference feeling they had set a course to see them through the difficulties created by the Great Leap, they were soon disabused of such optimism. When first front leaders met in Mao's absence in Beijing for the Xilou conference later in February, new information produced a considerably bleaker assessment. The overall economic situation was particularly dire, with new figures on the budget deficit leading Liu Shaoqi and others to conclude that previous measures were inadequate and the economy was "on the verge of collapse." Liu then proposed, and gained Mao's assent, that Chen Yun be assigned a key economic role akin to his 1950s position as the country's economic czar. With Chen apparently playing a leading role, policies of further retreat, including new sharp cutbacks in construction and investment, were adopted. In these circumstances rural policy became a major focus of concern. At the grass roots individual farming and household contracting continued to spread throughout

---

22   Liu Yishun, "Mao Zedong," p. 116; *Dangdai Zhongguoshi yanjiu*, no. 1 (1994), p. 61; and Yang, *Calamity and Reform*, pp. 84-85.

23   Liu Yishun, "Mao Zedong," pp. 116-17. For more detail on the policy and political ramifications of the 7,000 cadres conference, see Teiwes, *Politics and Purges*, pp. xxxix-xli, 369-71.

the spring and summer, while various leaders began to rethink the issue of household contracting. As for Mao, he organized further investigations of the rural situation, apparently gave guarded approval to some measures of the resumed retreat, and remained noncommittal on others. This was not a new situation, but given the extreme nature of the situation facing the country various figures demonstrated an unusual degree of boldness.[24]

What is perhaps most remarkable is the range of actors who by mid-1962 endorsed, or virtually endorsed, household contracting. Yet it is important to emphasize that for these actors the process of coming to support this policy was a gradual one, often arrived at only after considerable hesitation. Perhaps the most interesting case was Deng Zihui, theoretically the official responsible for agriculture as head of the Party Center's Rural Work Department, but whose influence had been sharply curtailed as a result of arguing with Mao for greater caution during the cooperativization drive in 1955, with Tan Zhenlin taking over as the dominant leader on the agricultural front during the leap forward. As Deng commented in summer 1962, his thinking had evolved: "I originally disapproved of household contracting." Deng had returned to an active role after more than a year of sick leave in September 1960 and proceeded to undertake rural investigations at the invitation of the leadership. These efforts were effusively praised by Mao at the March 1961 Guangzhou conference where Deng reportedly voiced support for Anhui's responsibility fields, but in a late October conversation with Mao, the period when the Chairman began to distance himself from the responsibility fields, Deng declared his backing of production team accounting as the long-term solution. With the new grim view of the situation, in spring 1962 Deng renewed his interest in household contracting but with a degree of circumspection. In an early May speech he advocated contracting "anywhere hit by disaster, or where the collective economy has not been done well," endorsed Henan's approach of lending the land with a view to "taking it back" rather than Anhui's more radical departure, and set a limit of 20 percent to the amount of land that could be contracted. Later in the month a still cautious Deng reported to Mao and the Center to warn of the lack of peasant trust in Party policies and that without effective action individual farming would undermine the commune system.[25]

In the coming weeks Deng's position moved toward less hesitant backing of household contracting. Apparently moved by a report from a district Party

---

[24] See Teiwes, *Politics and Purges*, pp. 371-72, 374-75; and Yang, *Calamity and Reform*, pp. 85-86. In addition to the high level individuals discussed below, lower-level officials within Anhui wrote to Mao, the Center, and the provincial committee opposing changing the responsibility fields, as did several higher-ranking regional and central cadres; see Liu Yishun, "Mao Zedong," pp. 117-18.

[25] *Deng Zihui zhuan* [Biography of Deng Zihui] (Beijing: Renmin chubanshe, 1996), pp. 534, 537, 547, 614; Liu Yishun, "Mao Zedong," p. 119; *Dang de wenxian*, no. 4 (1992), pp. 12-13; *Deng Zihui wenji* [Collected Works of Deng Zihui] (Beijing: Renmin chubanshe, 1996), pp. 587, 595; Yang, *Calamity and Reform*, p. 86; and oral source.

secretary arguing the case for the responsibility fields, Deng sent work teams to Anhui in May and June to determine whether the fields qualified as a form of collective management which could be developed in other provinces, in the second instance with the intent of strengthening his case in persuading an unconvinced Mao of the need for greater change. Deng also spoke positively of responsibility systems in a number of talks in June-July, sent a further inspection team to Anhui in July, subsequently arguing that the responsibility fields could not be knocked down at one stroke, and finally prepared a report supporting the system for the annual Beidaihe meeting which began in early August. Meanwhile, on July 17, Deng, who correctly believed that "the crux of whether household contracting [and] responsibility fields can be carried out lies with Mao Zedong," met with Mao to argue once again the virtues of the responsibility system, with the Chairman responding by asking to see Deng's and local reports. Despite warnings from colleagues, Deng persisted in attempting to bring Mao around, although by then (see below) it was too late. It was, as one account observed, a performance (like 1955) where Deng "did not calculate individual gains and losses."[26]

If Deng Zihui was ultimately true to form but developed his views throughout, changing views also marked the behavior of "a comrade working closely with Mao," the Chairman's secretary Tian Jiaying. One of the radical *xiucai* for much of the 1950s, Tian had become critical of the excesses of the Great Leap in the period leading up to the 1959 Lushan conference, but at Guangzhou in 1961 he sharply attacked the responsibility field system and was crucial in undercutting Zeng Xisheng's efforts. Following the 7,000 cadres conference Mao asked Tian to lead an inspection team to Hunan in late March. To the surprise of the investigators, the local peasants demanded household contracting with the result that Tian then changed his mind. Tian soon made his views known to top leaders. At a small work conference in May attended by Liu Shaoqi, Zhou Enlai, Chen Yun, and Deng Xiaoping, Tian reportedly emphasized the need to criticize leftist tendencies, and apparently most participants were favorably disposed to household contracting.[27]

Seemingly shortly afterwards Tian reported on his findings to Mao in Shanghai, a meeting also attended by Chen Yun. Chen responded positively to

[26]   *Deng Zihui zhuan*, pp. 564-65; Wang Lixin, *Anhui "dabaogan" shimo*, pp. 48-49; Liu Yishun, "Mao Zedong," p. 119; and Yang, *Calamity and Reform*, pp. 87-89.

    On Deng Zihui in 1955, see Teiwes and Sun, *The Politics of Agricultural Cooperativization*, especially pp. 13-14, 15, 43, 44. On that occasion Deng continued to argue with Mao after the Chairman had made up his mind on faster development of cooperatives, and in the process brushed aside pleas from colleagues who implored him not to "risk disaster."

[27]   Pang Xianzhi, "Mao Zedong he Tian Jiaying," pp. 63-65; Yang, *Calamity and Reform*, pp. 88-89; and above, pp. 131n41, 168, 219. We are somewhat sceptical of the claims concerning the "small work conference in May" cited by Yang which are based on the often unreliable book by the exiled Ruan Ming, *Deng Xiaoping: Chronicle of an Empire* (Boulder: Westview Press, 1994), p. 5.

Tian's report, praising it for its "distinctive viewpoint." Mao, however, in the observation of Tian's assistant, was very indifferent, not even reading the outline but only listening to the oral report. The Chairman described household contracting as a type of retreat that reflected the backward views of the masses, and commented that "We should follow the mass line, but sometimes we cannot completely follow the masses, for example in contracting output to the household." While, in the view of Tian's assistant, this was a case of Mao making his attitude clear on household contracting, when Tian subsequently returned to Beijing at the end of June and reported separately to Liu Shaoqi and Deng Xiaoping,[28] the two leaders were persuaded of the need for household contracting. It was in this context, at and following a late June Secretariat meeting where the East China Bureau's rural work office harshly criticized Anhui and opinion was divided (with Liu urging against premature determinations on the Anhui system pending the outcome of the Beidaihe meeting), that Deng made his famous remark (in fact quoting Liu Bocheng) that it didn't matter if a cat was black or white as long as it caught the mouse. Deng, however, hedged his bets, with his July 7 endorsement of the responsibility system limited to a trial until the Party — i.e., Mao — determined the best way to go. [29]

With top leaders, the redoubtable Deng Zihui, and Mao's own secretary persuaded of the virtues of household contracting, SPC head Li Fuchun, the embodiment of the "leftist faction" of planners in Mao's early 1958 assessment, also voiced support for Anhui's responsibility fields in a June letter to the Center. This leaves something of a puzzle: if Mao had clearly indicated his dissatisfaction with household contracting at Shanghai, why were so many leaders persisting, to varying degrees, in supporting the policy? The possibility that, Chen Yun aside, other leaders were not aware of his Shanghai comments, seems unconvincing. More likely is a combination of the seriousness of the situation emboldening such leaders to test the limits of Mao's tolerance — perhaps wistfully hoping, as Chen Yun stated in early 1962, that as in the pre-Great Leap period "differences of opinion are entirely normal" — and the fact that Mao's Shanghai message, particularly in view of his ongoing activities, was not all that clear.[30]

---

28 According to *Deng Zihui zhuan*, p. 564, Tian also reported to Chen Yun and Li Fuchun in addition to Liu and Deng at this juncture, securing the "complete agreement" of all concerned.

29 Pang Xianzhi, "Mao Zedong he Tian Jiaying," pp. 66-68; Bo Yibo, *Huigu*, vol. 2, p. 1084; *Deng Zihui zhuan*, p. 564; *Dang de wenxian*, no. 4 (1992), pp. 13-14; Ruan Ming, *Zhonggong renwu lun* [Essays on CCP Personalities] (New Jersey: Global Publishing Co., 1993), pp. 64-65; Yang, *Calamity and Reform*, pp. 88-89; and MacFarquhar, *Origins 3*, pp. 233, 268.

30 Liu Yishun, "Mao Zedong," p. 119; Bo Yibo, *Huigu*, vol. 2, p. 1081; *Chen Yun wenxuan (1956-1985 nian)*, p. 182; and above, p. 50.

   Another explanation of such phenomena in the first half of 1962 is offered by

This explanation is suggested by Mao's reaction to further support for responsibility systems from regional and provincial leaders, most notably Central-South Bureau First Secretary Tao Zhu and Hubei Party leader Wang Renzhong, two particular favorites of the Chairman when it came to rural policy in this period. Tao and Wang carried out rural investigations in Guangxi in early June and became convinced of the need for a responsibility system. Wang reported to Mao near Changsha on his way back to Hubei, indicating that he and Tao favored giving peasant households responsibility for managing land and output while the collective organized plowing and seeding. In seeming contradiction to his Shanghai remarks, Mao responded positively: "Yes, it's contracting output to the household, not dividing up land for individual farming." Thus encouraged, Tao and Wang drafted a report for the Center which packaged advocacy of individual responsibility within the collectives and tolerance of some individual farming together with claims of improved conditions, mass support for socialism, and the superiority of collective production — as long as it embraced a responsibility system. Mao's seeming receptiveness to the Tao-Wang plan may have encouraged other leaders to persist with household contracting, notwithstanding his Shanghai remarks, and shortly before the Beidaihe meeting he ordered that the record of Tao and Wang's discussions in Guangxi be distributed to conference participants, commenting that the opinions put forward were Marxist.[31]

Whatever Mao's precise views on household contracting or the calculations of his colleagues, once the Chairman returned to Beijing by early July the pressure for adopting such a system had counterproductive results. Two private meetings appear to have done considerable damage. First, Tian Jiaying saw Mao, aware of both the critical need for household contracting and the support of many top leaders, but also — as his assistant put it — that the strategic point was obtaining Mao's agreement. Tian thus gave a

---

MacFarquhar in *Origins 3*, ch. 12: after the 7,000 cadres conference Mao "abdicated" in favor of Liu Shaoqi (p. 262) with the result that various actors operated on the assumption that power had indeed been transferred. While we agree that in this period Mao retreated more deeply onto the "second front" than in any other period, we do not believe either that he intended to cede ultimate power or that other leaders would have believed in anything other than the Chairman's final authority whenever he chose to exercise it. This is the lesson of the present analysis, and indeed is supported by MacFarquhar's own observation that "Whatever leadership arrangements were in place at the time, Tian [Jiaying] was well aware that *baochan daohu* needed to get the Chairman's approval" (p. 266).

31   Cong Jin, *Quzhe fazhan*, pp. 489-90; Zheng Xiaofeng and Shu Ling, *Tao Zhu zhuan*, pp. 8-9, 282-85; *Mao wengao*, vol. 10 (January 1962-December 1963) (Beijing: Zhongyang wenxian chubanshe, 1996), pp. 114-16; and Yang, *Calamity and Reform*, pp. 89-91. Mao's special regard for Tao and Wang can be seen in their assignments as head and deputy head of the drafting committee for the 60 articles on communes. It is unclear to what degree Tao and Wang's clever packaging in contrast to the bluntness of others (see Yang, pp. 90-91) accounts for Mao's approval, or to what extent actual differences in the methods proposed were decisive for the Chairman.

systematic report arguing that 30 percent of the peasantry was already using household contracting and more were sure to follow, and that it would be better to give official sanction so as to exercise leadership over these developments. While this might lead to 40 percent of peasant households engaging in such activities, it was a necessary tactical concession until agricultural production recovered when the collective economy could again be emphasized. While Mao did not directly comment on the correctness or otherwise of the proposal, he did leave Tian speechless by asking provocatively, "Are you in favor of a predominantly collective or predominantly private economy."[32]

The second meeting with Chen Yun about the same time[33] seemingly was even more fateful. Ironically, given his normal pattern of extreme caution, Chen might have been better advised to back quietly the Tao Zhu-Wang Renzhong proposal, although we cannot be sure he was aware of it. Chen told Mao that it appeared the individual economy would exist for a considerable period, and advocated "dividing the fields to the households" (*fentian daohu*). But as at Lushan, if less spectacularly, the Chairman reacted badly. While apparently saying little at the encounter itself, the next day Mao's anger at what he interpreted as advocacy of dividing land for individual farming (*fentian dan'gan*) exploded. He denounced this as Chinese revisionism that would destroy the communes, and quickly embarked on a number of actions which dramatically altered the direction of official policy and the tone of leadership politics. Mao dressed down Liu Shaoqi for paying too much attention to Chen Yun and criticized Tian Jiaying for advocating household contracting rather than revising the 60 articles, now assigning Chen Boda the task of drafting a directive on agriculture and consolidating the collective economy. Despite the Chairman's favorable comment on the Tao Zhu-Wang Renzhong approach on the eve of the Beidaihe gathering, key top leaders were already starting to scramble to adjust to the Chairman's new drift. Significantly, Liu Shaoqi suddenly and drastically reversed course and adopted Mao's view, Chen Yun begged off going to Beidaihe on health grounds and indicated his support of Chen Boda's draft, while Deng Xiaoping had Hu Yaobang revise a draft of his (Deng's) July 7 speech to the Youth

---

32   Pang Xianzhi, "Mao Zedong he Tian Jiaying," pp. 68-69; and Yang, *Calamity and Reform*, pp. 91, 92.

33   There are conflicting reports concerning the date. Sun Yeli and Xiong Lianghua, *Gongheguo jingji fengyun zhong de Chen Yun*, p. 261, place the meeting on the evening of the 9th, which was given as the day of Mao's return to Beijing. The more authoritative *Zhou Enlai nianpu*, vol. 2, p. 488, however, has Mao, clearly after his meeting with Chen, calling in Zhou, Liu Shaoqi, Deng Xiaoping, and Chen Boda on the 8th to express his condemnation of household contracting. Thus the most likely date for the Mao-Chen meeting is July 7. It was apparently immediately after the meeting with Mao on the 8th that Deng Xiaoping (see below) asked Hu Yaobang to delete the reference to "cat theory" from the record of his speech on the 7th; see Ruan Ming, *Zhonggong renwu lun*, pp. 64-65.

League, eliminate references to the color of cats, and add support for consolidating the collective economy.[34]

Once the Beidaihe meeting began on July 25,[35] there were other reminders of Lushan. Notwithstanding Mao's reaction to Tian and Chen, there apparently still were expectations of a relatively moderate outcome, expectations undoubtedly encouraged by Mao's request to Tao Zhu, Wang Renzhong, and Hunan leader Zhang Pinghua that they draft a Central Committee directive approving household contracting as a method within the collective economy and his eve of the meeting self-categorization as a "middle of the roader." Yet with discussion at Beidaihe focusing on weaknesses, and a regional first secretary — perhaps Ke Qingshi or Li Jingquan[36] — claiming household contracting *was* individual farming, to the surprise of the gathered leaders Mao now decisively turned against the approach as a "wind of individual farming" (*dan'gan feng*). At Beidaihe and the subsequent Tenth Plenum Mao further voiced a sweeping range of discontent with both the policies of retreat and those advocating or implementing them on the first front: the 1962 economic plans were "capitulation to the bourgeoisie," the reversal of verdicts against right opportunists had become another "wind" (*fan'an feng*), Zeng Xisheng and other local leaders who had advocated household contracting were categorized as representatives of rich peasants and bad elements, Chen Yun was declared "always a rightist," Deng Zihui was not only dismissed but his rural work department was disbanded, and Liu Shaoqi was belabored for establishing an "independent kingdom." In the face of this onslaught, *à la* Lushan the leadership once again caved in, with even Deng Zihui, after an effort to defend his stance at Beidaihe, undertaking self-criticism by the end of the meeting and continuing his self-examination at the Tenth Plenum.[37]

---

34   *Chen Yun yu jingji jianshe*, pp. 168-69; Sun Yeli and Xiong Lianghua, *Gongheguo jingji fengyun zhong de Chen Yun*, pp. 260-62; Bo Yibo, *Huigu*, vol. 2, p. 1086; Zheng Qian and Han Gang, *Mao Zedong zhi lu: wannian suiyue* [Mao Zedong's Road: The Last Years] (Beijing: Zhongguo qingnian chubanshe, 1993), pp. 177-78; Bo Yibo, *Huigu*, vol. 2, pp. 1085-86; *Dang de wenxian*, no. 4 (1992), p. 20; Huang Zheng, *Liu Shaoqi yisheng* [Life of Liu Shaoqi] (Beijing: Zhongyang wenxian chubanshe, 1995), pp. 391-92; Ruan Ming, *Deng Xiaoping*, p. 5; idem, above, n. 33; and Yang, *Calamity and Reform*, pp. 91-92, 283n119. Cf. MacFarquhar, *Origins 3*, p. 268, for a somewhat different view of Liu's reaction.

35   While the Beidaihe meeting is usually given as starting on August 6 (see Yang, *Calamity and Reform*, p. 93), in fact it began on July 25 and lasted until August 24. It was quickly followed by preparatory sessions from August 26 to September 23 in Beijing for the Tenth Plenum, and the plenum itself was held on September 24-27. Bo Yibo, *Huigu*, vol. 2, p. 1071.

36   Li led the attack on Deng Zihui at Beidaihe; *Deng Zihui zhuan*, p. 567.

37   Zheng Xiaofeng and Shu Ling, *Tao Zhu zhuan*, p. 285; Zheng Qian and Han Gang, *Mao Zedong zhi lu*, pp. 196-97; *Xuexi ziliao*, vol. 3, p. 40; Liu Yishun, "Mao Zedong," p. 119;

The story of the "un-Maoist" retreat from the Great Leap Forward in 1960-62, then, served only to underline dramatically Mao's unchallengeable authority. At a time of the gravest threat to the regime, it took the Chairman's cognizance of the severity of the problem, albeit in conjunction with the grass-roots pressure generated by the unfolding disaster, to set in motion a serious policy response. This response, however, was at all times inhibited by both ideological concerns over the dangers to socialism and the shifting and limited nature of Mao's own attitudes. Even in the first half of 1962 when a deeper understanding of the disaster led Mao's top colleagues, the head of the SPC, key provincial leaders, and his own trusted secretary to advocate household contracting, this popular method was swept away in the face of the Chairman's anger. Certainly there were elements of the leadership sharing Mao's view,[38] but accounts of Beidaihe convey personal dominance rather than a process of gathering support; at most, other actors influenced Mao by articulating views in accord with his own biases.[39] The Party history observation that "the rise, fall, and fate of the Anhui responsibility fields cannot be separated from the attitude of Mao Zedong"[40] is indisputably verified by the starts and stops in the unfolding of the policy. As throughout the 1955-59 period, and especially from late 1957, Mao's word — clearly expressed — carried the day. When, as so often, Mao's position was unclear or ambivalent, various actors attempted to shape the debate according to their preferences and to persuade the Chairman of their views. But when Mao turned decisively against their counsel, even in these dire circumstances they saw no option except to obey.

Deng Zihui zhuan, pp. 566-69; Yang, *Calamity and Reform*, pp. 92-94; and Teiwes, *Politics and Purges*, pp. 375-76.

[38]   Lieberthal, "Great Leap Forward," p. 330, in speaking of the entire first half of 1962, claims that Mao was supported by "at least some provincial officials, by Lin Biao in the military and by people in the heavy industry sector." Our own detailed examination of Lin Biao's career (see Teiwes and Sun, *The Tragedy of Lin Biao*, especially pp. 187-98), finds no evidence of such support by Lin and again indicates little military involvement in domestic debates, except perhaps a proposal by Luo Ronghuan and Xiao Hua in November 1960 for a greater PLA role in local affairs, a proposal *rejected* by Lin as anti-Party (see pp. 191, 193-94). Of course, Lin's speech at the 7,000 cadres conference praising Mao was a significant political statement, although the speech as a whole dealt with military affairs (see p. 196). There is also some questionable evidence suggesting that Lin actually supported household contracting (p. 197).

[39]   In addition to the regional first secretary who claimed household contracting was individual farming, Mao was seemingly influenced by a Beidaihe participant who complained that people were only allowed to discuss mistakes and problems; see Yang, *Calamity and Reform*, p. 93.

[40]   Liu Yishun, "Mao Zedong," p. 102.

APPENDICES

Appendix 1

PARTICIPANTS IN PARTY CONFERENCES, JANUARY 1958-APRIL 1959

A series of high-level Party meetings beginning with the January 1958 Hangzhou conference set the course of CCP policy during the initial upsurge of the Great Leap Forward and then during the effort to "cool down." The participants in these meetings varied significantly; this can be seen in the lists below of known participants in the most significant gatherings through to the March-April 1959 Shanghai conference and Central Committee plenum. The main positions of each participant at the time of the particular meeting are also given. Only Politburo members are listed for plenums, while the listings for conferences are either complete or incomplete due to limited information as indicated. Participants are given in the order listed in the most authoritative source available; where only scattered references are available, those present are recorded according to their Party rank in the Politburo or Central Committee, or according to lesser position. Sources for each listing are provided.

1. The Hangzhou conference, January 2-4, 1958 (seemingly complete list)

Mao Zedong	CCP Chairman, PRC Chairman
Zhou Enlai	CCP Vice Chairman, Premier
Bo Yibo	Alternate Politburo, Chairman SEC
Ke Qingshi	1st Secretary Shanghai
Shu Tong	1st Secretary Shandong
Zeng Xisheng	1st Secretary Anhui
Liu Shunyuan	Party Secretary Jiangsu
Jiang Weiqing	1st Secretary Jiangsu
Ye Fei	1st Secretary Fujian
Jiang Hua	1st Secretary Zhejiang
Hu Qiaomu	secretary to Mao Zedong
Chen Pixian	Party Secretary Shanghai
Lin Tie	1st Secretary Hebei
Shi Ximin	Director Propaganda Shanghai

Zhang Chunqiao	Deputy Director Propaganda Shanghai

Source: Jin Chongji, *Zhou Enlai zhuan*, vol. 3, pp.1364-65.

2. The Nanning conference, January 11-22, 1958 (complete list)

Mao Zedong	CCP Chairman, PRC Chairman
Liu Shaoqi	CCP Vice Chairman
Zhou Enlai	CCP Vice Chairman, Premier
Peng Zhen	Politburo, Central Secretariat, 1st Secretary Beijing
Li Fuchun	Politburo, Chairman SPC
Li Xiannian	Politburo, Minister of Finance
Bo Yibo	Alternate Politburo, Chairman SEC
Ke Qingshi	1st Secretary Shanghai
Li Jingquan	1st Secretary Sichuan
Ouyang Qin	1st Secretary Heilongjiang
Liu Ren	2nd Secretary Beijing
Shi Xiangsheng	Party Secretary Henan
Tao Zhu	1st Secretary Guangdong
Wang Renzhong	1st Secretary Hubei
Yang Shangkui	1st Secretary Jiangxi
Zhou Xiaozhou	1st Secretary Hunan
Liu Jianxun	1st Secretary Guangxi
Wei Guoqing	Party Secretary and Governor Guangxi
Wang Heshou	Minister of Metallurgy
Zhao Erlu	Minister of 2nd Machine Building
Huang Jing	Chairman State Technological Commission, Minister of 1st Machine Building
Chen Boda	Alternate Politburo, secretary to Mao Zedong
Hu Qiaomu	secretary to Mao Zedong
Wu Lengxi	chief editor *People's Daily*
Tian Jiaying	secretary to Mao Zedong
Li Rui (from January 18)	Assistant Minister Electric Power
Lin Yishan (from January 18)	Director Yangzi Water Conservancy Commission

Sources: Li Rui, *"Dayuejin" qinliji*, p. 30; "unpublished Chinese document no. 2," p. 182; and Jin Chongji, *Zhou Enlai zhuan*, vol. 3, p. 1366. Li Rui lists Zhao Erlu but not Wei Guoqing, while the listing in "unpublished Chinese document no. 2" is the reverse. Although he was not included in Mao's original list of invitees, Zhao's participation is credible in view of Wang Heshou's presence in particular, while Wei's attendance is confirmed by the authoritative *Zhou Enlai zhuan*. Li Rui also lists Zhu De but we doubt this is correct in that *Zhu De nianpu* [Chronicle of Zhu De] (Beijing: Renmin chubanshe, 1986), p. 424, while placing Zhu in Nanning at least at the start of the conference does not list him as a participant which is the normal practice in *nianpu*; nor does *Zhou Enlai zhuan* mention Zhu. In addition, while the first two sources above listed Shaanxi 1st secretary Zhang Desheng, *Zhou Enlai zhuan* records that although invited Zhang did not attend.

3. The Chengdu conference, March 8-26, 1958 (complete list)

Mao Zedong	CCP Chairman, PRC Chairman
Liu Shaoqi	CCP Vice Chairman
Zhou Enlai	CCP Vice Chairman, Premier
Chen Yun	CCP Vice Chairman, Minister of Commerce
Deng Xiaoping	General Secretary, Politburo Standing Committee
Luo Ronghuan	Politburo, Vice Chairman Military Affairs Committee
Li Fuchun	Politburo, Chairman SPC
Peng Dehuai	Politburo, Minister of Defense
Li Xiannian	Politburo, Minister of Finance
Ulanfu	Alternate Politburo, 1st Secretary Inner Mongolia
Chen Boda	Alternate Politburo, secretary to Mao Zedong
Bo Yibo	Alternate Politburo, Chairman SEC
Tan Zhenlin	Central Secretariat
Hu Qiaomu	secretary to Mao Zedong
Wu Lengxi	chief editor *People's Daily*
Tian Jiaying	secretary to Mao Zedong
Li Rui	Assistant Minister Water Conservancy and Electric Power, corresponding secretary to Mao
Wang Heshou	Minister of Metallurgy
Liao Luyan	Minister of Agriculture
Teng Daiyuan	Minister of Railways
Peng Tao	Minister of Chemical Industry
Lin Tie	1st Secretary Hebei
Liu Ren	2nd Secretary Beijing

Tao Lujia	1st Secretary Shanxi
Huang Huoqing	1st Secretary Tianjin
Ouyang Qin	1st Secretary Heilongjiang
Huang Oudong	1st Secretary Liaoning
Wu De	1st Secretary Jilin
Ke Qingshi	1st Secretary Shanghai
Tao Zhu	1st Secretary Guangdong
Wang Renzhong	1st Secretary Hubei
Li Jingquan	1st Secretary Sichuan
Xie Fuzhi	1st Secretary Yunnan
Zhou Lin	1st Secretary Guizhou
Zhang Desheng	1st Secretary Shaanxi
Zhang Zhongliang	1st Secretary Gansu
Gao Feng	1st Secretary Qinghai
Wang Enmao	1st Secretary Xinjiang
Li Dazhang	Party Secretary Sichuan

Sources: Li Rui, *"Dayuejin" qinliji*, p. 160; and "unpublished Chinese document no. 3," pp. 274-75.

4. The Second Session of the Eighth Party Congress, May 5-23, 1958 (Congress Presidium Standing Committee and delegation leaders only)

Mao Zedong	CCP Chairman, PRC Chairman
Liu Shaoqi	CCP Vice Chairman
Zhou Enlai	CCP Vice Chairman, Premier
Zhu De	CCP Vice Chairman
Chen Yun	CCP Vice Chairman, Minister of Commerce
Deng Xiaoping	General Secretary, Politburo Standing Committee
Peng Zhen	Politburo, Central Secretariat, 1st Secretary Beijing
Ulanfu	Alternate Politburo, 1st Secretary Inner Mongolia
Ke Qingshi	elected to Politburo at Congress, 1st Secretary Shanghai
Li Jingquan	elected to Politburo at Congress, 1st Secretary Sichuan
Lin Tie (North China)	1st Secretary Hebei
Tao Lujia (North China)	1st Secretary Shanxi
Ouyang Qin (Northeast)	1st Secretary Heilongjiang
Wu De (Northeast)	1st Secretary Jilin
Zeng Xisheng (East China)	1st Secretary Anhui

Tao Zhu (Central-South)   1st Secretary Guangdong
Wang Renzhong (Central-Sth)   1st Secretary Hubei
Xie Fuzhi (Southwest)   1st Secretary Yunnan
Zhang Desheng (Northwest)   1st Secretary Shaanxi
Zhang Zhongliang (Northwest)   1st Secretary Gansu
Nie Rongzhen (PLA)   Vice Premier, Vice Chairman
                                   Military Affairs Committee
Xiao Hua (PLA)   Deputy Director PLA General
                                   Political Department
Yang Shangkun (central organs) Director CC General Office

Source: "Unpublished Chinese document no. 3," p. 54.

5. The Beidaihe conference, August 17-31, 1958 (incomplete list)[1]

Mao Zedong   CCP Chairman, PRC Chairman
Liu Shaoqi   CCP Vice Chairman
Zhou Enlai   CCP Vice Chairman, Premier
Zhu De   CCP Vice Chairman
Chen Yun   CCP Vice Chairman,
                            Minister of Commerce
Deng Xiaoping   General Secretary,
                            Politburo Standing Committee
Li Fuchun   Politburo, Central Secretariat,
                            Chairman SPC
Peng Dehuai   Politburo, Minister of Defense
He Long   Politburo, Vice Premier,
                            Vice Chairman Military Affairs
                            Committee
Bo Yibo   Alternate Politburo,
                            Chairman SEC
Hu Qiaomu   secretary to Mao Zedong
Ye Fei   1st Secretary Fujian
Jiang Weiqing   1st Secretary Jiangsu
Wang Shangrong   Director PLA War Strategy Department
Wu Lengxi (from August 23) chief editor *People's Daily*

Sources: Bo Yibo, *Huigu*, vol. 2, pp. 705-707; Wu Lengxi, *Yi Mao Zhuxi*, pp. 73-78; Jiang Weiqing, *Qishinian zhengcheng*, p. 425; *Zhu De nianpu*, p. 436; and *He Long*

---

[1] In his speeches to the conference Mao mentioned Li Xiannian, Chen Boda, Wang Heshou, Zhao Erlu, Vice Minister of Water Conservancy and Electic Power Li Baohua, and Deputy Director of the Central Rural Work Department Chen Zhengren in a manner suggesting they were present, but this is not definite. See *SS*, pp. 397-441.

nianpu [Chronicle of He Long] (Beijing: Zhonggong zhongyang dangxiao chubanshe, 1988), p. 389.

6. The First Zhengzhou conference, November 2-10, 1958 (incomplete list)[2]

Mao Zedong	CCP Chairman, PRC Chairman
Liu Shaoqi (from November 7)	CCP Vice Chairman
Deng Xiaoping	General Secretary, Politburo Standing Committee
Li Fuchun	Politburo, Central Secretariat Chairman SPC
Ke Qingshi	Politburo, 1st Secretary Shanghai
Chen Boda	Alternate Politburo, chief editor *Red Flag*, secretary to Mao
Shu Tong	1st Secretary Shandong
Lin Tie	1st Secretary Hebei
Wu Zhipu	1st Secretary Henan
Zeng Xisheng	1st Secretary Anhui
Zhang Desheng	1st Secretary Shaanxi
Jiang Weiqing	1st Secretary Jiangsu
Wang Renzhong	1st Secretary Hubei
Zhang Zhongliang	1st Secretary Gansu
Tao Lujia	1st Secretary Shanxi
Zhou Xiaozhou	1st Secretary Hunan
Wu Lengxi	chief editor *People's Daily*
Tian Jiaying	secretary to Mao Zedong

Sources: Bo Yibo, *Huigu*, vol. 2, pp. 808-10; Wu Lengxi, *Yi Mao Zhuxi*, pp. 100-104; *Liu Shaoqi nianpu 1898-1969* [Chronicle of Liu Shaoqi, 1898-1969] (Beijing: Zhongyang wenxian chubanshe, 1996), vol. 2, p. 443; Tao Lujia, *Yige shengwei shuji*, pp. 70-74; *SS*, pp. 443-79; Jiang Weiqing, *Qishinian zhengcheng*, p. 433; and Tan Qilong, "Jianchi shishi qiushi," p. 239.

---

2   Zhou Enlai did not attend; *Zhou Enlai nianpu*, vol. 2, pp. 186-89. Shandong Second Secretary Tan Qilong's memoirs refer to himself, Shanghai's Deputy Director of Propaganda Zhang Chunqiao, and *Red Flag* editor in charge of daily work Li Youjiu in the context of the meeting, but in an ambiguous manner concerning their actual presence. Tan Qilong, "Jianchi shishi qiushi," p. 239.

7. The Wuchang conference, November 21-27, 1958 (incomplete list)[3]

Mao Zedong	CCP Chairman, PRC Chairman
Liu Shaoqi	CCP Vice Chairman
Chen Yun	CCP Vice Chairman,
	Chairman State Capital
	Construction Commission
Deng Xiaoping	General Secretary,
	Politburo Standing Committee
Peng Zhen	Politburo, Central Secretariat,
	1st Secretary Beijing
Li Fuchun	Politburo, Central Secretariat,
	Chairman SPC
Li Xiannian	Politburo, Central Secretariat,
	Minister of Finance
Ke Qingshi	Politburo, 1st Secretary Shanghai
Li Jingquan	Politburo, 1st Secretary Sichuan
Tan Zhenlin	Politburo, Central Secretariat
Zhang Wentian	Alternate Politburo,
(from November 25)	Vice Minister Foreign Affairs
Bo Yibo	Alternate Politburo,
	Chairman SEC
Wang Jiaxiang	Vice Minister Foreign Affairs
Li Baohua	Vice Minister Water Conservancy
	and Electric Power
Lin Tie	1st Secretary Hebei
Zhao Erlu	Minister of 1st Machine Building
Ouyang Qin	1st Secretary Heilongjiang
Lü Zhengcao	Vice Minister of Railways
Tao Zhu	1st Secretary Guangdong
Zeng Xisheng	1st Secretary Anhui
Zhang Desheng	1st Secretary Shaanxi
Zhang Linzhi	Minister of Coal Industry
Jiang Weiqing	1st Secretary Jiangsu
Wang Heshou	Minister of Metallurgy
Wang Renzhong	1st Secretary Hubei
Zhou Xiaozhou	1st Secretary Hunan

---

[3]   In addition, Shanxi's Tao Lujia and Central Committee General Office Director Yang Shangkun are known to have met with Mao in Wuchang on the eve of the conference; Bo Yibo, *Huigu*, vol. 2, p. 812. According to Jiang Weiqing, *Qishinian zhengcheng*, p. 433, each province reported on its situation, but few specific provincial leaders were mentioned. Jin Chongji, *Zhou Enlai zhuan*, vol. 3, pp. 1444-45, clearly states that the visit of Kim Il Sung and other duties kept Zhou away from the Wuchang conference as well as from the preceding Zhengzhou meeting.

Wu Lengxi (to November 23)	chief editor *People's Daily*
Tian Jiaying	secretary to Mao Zedong
Li Rui	Assistant Minister Water Conservancy and Electric Power, corresponding secretary to Mao

Sources: Bo Yibo, *Huigu*, vol. 2, pp. 812-16; Tao Lujia, *Yige shengwei shuji*, p. 74; *SS*, p. 493; *Bainianchao*, no. 4 (1997), p. 8; Wu Lengxi, *Yi Mao Zhuxi*, pp. 106-13; *Liu Shaoqi nianpu*, vol. 2, pp. 443-44; *Zhu De nianpu*, p. 442; *Huiyi Zhang Wentian*, p. 307; Jiang Weiqing, *Qishinian zhengcheng*, pp. 433-34; and Kenneth G. Lieberthal and Bruce J. Dickson, *A Research Guide to Central Party and Government Meetings in China 1949-1986*, revised and expanded edition (Armonk: M.E. Sharpe, 1989), p. 77.

8. **The Sixth (Wuhan) Plenum of the Eighth Central Committee, November 28-December 12, 1958 (complete list of full Politburo members attending among 84 full and 82 alternate Central Committee members, plus additional central personnel and provincial first secretaries)**

Mao Zedong	CCP Chairman, PRC Chairman
Liu Shaoqi	CCP Vice Chairman
Zhou Enlai (from November 30)	CCP Vice Chairman, Premier
Zhu De	CCP Vice Chairman
Chen Yun	CCP Vice Chairman, Chairman State Capital Construction Commission
Lin Biao	CCP Vice Chairman
Deng Xiaoping	General Secretary, Politburo Standing Committee
Lin Boqu	Politburo
Dong Biwu	Politburo
Peng Zhen	Politburo, Central Secretariat, 1st Secretary Beijing
Luo Ronghuan	Politburo, Vice Chairman Military Affairs Committee
Chen Yi	Politburo, Minister of Foreign Affairs
Li Fuchun	Politburo, Central Secretariat, Chairman SPC
Peng Dehuai	Politburo, Minister of Defense
Liu Bocheng	Politburo, Vice Chairman Military Affairs Committee

He Long	Politburo, Vice Premier, Vice Chairman Military Affairs Committee
Li Xiannian	Politburo, Central Secretariat, Minister of Finance
Ke Qingshi	Politburo, 1st Secretary Shanghai
Li Jingquan	Politburo, 1st Secretary Sichuan
Tan Zhenlin	Politburo, Central Secretariat

Sources: *PDA*, p. 484; and *Zhou Enlai nianpu*, vol. 2, p. 192.

9. The Beijing conference of provincial and municipal secretaries, January 26-February 2, 1959 (incomplete list)[4]

Mao Zedong	CCP Chairman, PRC Chairman
Liu Shaoqi	CCP Vice Chairman
Chen Yun	CCP Vice Chairman, Chairman State Capital Construction Commission
Deng Xiaoping	General Secretary, Politburo Standing Committee

Sources: Bo Yibo, *Huigu*, vol. 2, p. 819; *Liu Shaoqi nianpu*, vol. 2, p. 447; and *Mao wengao*, vol. 8, p. 31.

10. The Second Zhengzhou conference, February 27-March 5, 1959 (known participants of 29 provincial-level Party secretaries with primary responsibility for the rural areas, plus 18 leaders from the Center)

Mao Zedong	CCP Chairman, PRC Chairman
Liu Shaoqi	CCP Vice Chairman
Zhou Enlai (from March 2)	CCP Vice Chairman, Premier
Chen Yun (from March 2)	CCP Vice Chairman, Chairman State Capital Construction Commission

---

4   Given the nature of the meeting various provincial leaders clearly attended; unfortunately no names are given in the available sources. Zhou Enlai did not attend; *Zhou Enlai nianpu*, vol. 2, pp. 204-205.

Deng Xiaoping	General Secretary, Politburo Standing Committee
Peng Zhen	Politburo, Central Secretariat, 1st Secretary Beijing
Chen Yi (from March 2)	Politburo, Minister of Foreign Affairs
Li Fuchun (from March 2)	Politburo, Central Secretariat, Chairman SPC
Peng Dehuai (from March 2)	Politburo, Minister of Defense
Li Xiannian	Politburo, Central Secretariat, Minister of Finance
Ke Qingshi	Politburo, 1st Secretary Shanghai
Li Jingquan	Politburo, 1st Secretary Sichuan
Tan Zhenlin	Politburo, Central Secretariat
Lu Dingyi (from March 2)	Alternate Politburo, Director CC Propaganda
Kang Sheng (from March 2)	Alternate Politburo
Bo Yibo (from March 2)	Alternate Politburo, Chairman SEC
Huang Kecheng	Vice Minister of Defense, PLA Chief of Staff
Tan Zheng	Vice Minister of Defense, Director PLA General Political Department
Hu Qiaomu	secretary to Mao Zedong
Xiao Hua (from March 2)	Deputy Director PLA General Political Department
Wu Zhipu	1st Secretary Henan
Zhang Desheng	1st Secretary Shaanxi
Zhang Zhongliang	1st Secretary Gansu
Tao Lujia	1st Secretary Shanxi
Shi Xiangsheng	Party Secretary Henan

Sources: *Mao wengao*, vol. 8, pp. 87, 91; Tao Lujia, *Yige shengwei shuji*, pp. 74-76; idem, *Mao Zhuxi jiao women dang shengwei shuji*, p.96; and *Dang de wenxian*, no. 6 (1992), pp. 91-92.

11. The Shanghai conference, March 25-April 1, 1959 (incomplete list)

Mao Zedong	CCP Chairman, PRC Chairman
Liu Shaoqi	CCP Vice Chairman
Zhou Enlai	CCP Vice Chairman, Premier

Chen Yun[5]	CCP Vice Chairman, Chairman State Capital Construction Commission
Deng Xiaoping	General Secretary, Politburo Standing Committee
Peng Zhen	Politburo, Central Secretariat, 1st Secretary Beijing
Li Fuchun	Politburo, Central Secretariat, Chairman SPC
Li Xiannian	Politburo, Central Secretariat, Minister of Finance
Peng Dehuai	Politburo, Minister of Defense
He Long	Politburo, Vice Premier, Vice Chairman Military Affairs Committee
Ke Qingshi	Politburo, 1st Secretary Shanghai
Li Jingquan	Politburo, 1st Secretary Sichuan
Tan Zhenlin	Politburo, Central Secretariat
Zhang Wentian (from March 27)	Alternate Politburo, Vice Minister Foreign Affairs
Bo Yibo	Alternate Politburo, Chairman SEC
Hu Qiaomu	secretary to Mao Zedong
Zeng Xisheng	1st Secretary Anhui
Wang Renzhong	1st Secretary Hubei
Tao Lujia	1st Secretary Shanxi
Li Rui	Assistant Minister Water Conservancy and Electric Power, corresponding secretary to Mao

Sources: Bo Yibo, *Huigu*, vol. 2, pp. 829ff; Tao Lujia, *Yige shengwei shuji*, pp. 76-77, 81ff; *Zhou Enlai nianpu*, vol. 2, p. 214; *Bainianchao*, no. 4 (1997), p. 9; *Peng Dehuai zhuan*, p. 589; *Huiyi Zhang Wentian*, p. 309; Gu Longsheng, *Mao Zedong jingji nianpu*, p.460; and Lieberthal and Dickson, *Research Guide*, p. 86.

---

5   Although Deng Liqun, *Xiang Chen Yun Tongzhi xuexi zuo jingji gongzuo* [Learn Economic Work from Comrade Chen Yun] (Beijing: Zhonggong zhongyang dangxiao chubanshe, 1981), p. 13, states that "Comrade Chen Yun did not attend that meeting," *Peng Dehuai zhuan*, p. 589, makes clear that Chen was present.

12. **The Seventh (Shanghai) Plenum of the Eighth Central Committee, April 2-5, 1959 (incomplete list of Politburo members attending among 81 full and 80 alternate Central Committee members, plus additional central personnel and provincial first secretaries)**[6]

Mao Zedong	CCP Chairman, PRC Chairman
Liu Shaoqi	CCP Vice Chairman
Zhou Enlai	CCP Vice Chairman, Premier
Zhu De	CCP Vice Chairman
Chen Yun	CCP Vice Chairman, Chairman State Capital Construction Commission
Deng Xiaoping	General Secretary, Politburo Standing Committee
Li Fuchun	Politburo, Central Secretariat, Chairman SPC
He Long	Politburo, Vice Premier, Vice Chairman Military Affairs Committee
Ke Qingshi	Politburo, 1st Secretary Shanghai
Zhang Wentian	Alternate Politburo, Vice Minister Foreign Affairs

Sources: Ma Qibin, *Zhizheng sishinian*, p. 165; Bo Yibo, *Huigu*, vol. 2, pp. 831-32; Tao Lujia, *Yige shengwei shuji*, pp. 81ff; *Liu Shaoqi nianpu*, vol. 2, p. 453; *Zhu De nianpu*, p. 447; *Zhou Enlai nianpu*, vol. 2, p. 215; *He Long nianpu*, p. 394; Jiang Weiqing, *Qishinian zhengcheng*, p. 451; and Lieberthal and Dickson, *Research Guide*, p. 87.

---

6   It can be assumed that most Politburo members who attended the Shanghai conference stayed on for the plenum, most likely joined by other Politburo members who did not participate in the preceding meeting.

Appendix 2

SELF-CRITICISMS BY THE ARCHITECTS OF
OPPOSING RASH ADVANCE, JANUARY-MAY 1958

The impetus for the Great Leap Forward was created when Mao Zedong raised the issue of *fanmaojin* to the level of a question of political line at the January 1958 Nanning conference. This not only produced a situation where "no one could say anything different," but one where some of the highest leaders of the Party and state concerned with economic policy were forced to engage in a series of self-criticisms for their role in opposing rash advance. The most important of these self-criticisms by Zhou Enlai, Chen Yun, Li Xiannian, and Bo Yibo came at Nanning, the March Chengdu conference, and the Second Session of the Eighth Party Congress in May. In addition, we include a self-examination at Chengdu by Liu Shaoqi, who although not an architect of *fanmaojin* nevertheless had provided important political backing in 1956. The available excerpts from these self-criticisms translated below shed considerable light not only on the specific issue, but more importantly on the dynamics of CCP leadership politics during this crucial period when the Great Leap took shape.

1. The Nanning conference, January 11-22, 1958

At this watershed meeting Zhou Enlai, Li Xiannian, and Bo Yibo offered self-examinations for their *fanmaojin* "errors," but a brief excerpt of Zhou's statement is all that is available. As Chen Yun was not at Nanning, he was not involved in the process at this stage.

Zhou Enlai, January 19, 1958

"For a period (summer to winter 1956) this problem of opposing rash advance produced wavering and errors in guiding policy.... Opposing rash advance resulted from not understanding or not fully understanding that, following the transformation of the relations of production, the forces of production will undergo a leap forward in development. Consequently, I recoiled from fully arousing the masses for socialist revolution and construction, and often focused on things rather than people, especially in exaggerating numerous isolated phenomena into general or the main phenomena. This was right-deviationist conservative thinking.... Opposing rash advance has damaged three things: the committee to promote progress, the 40 articles on agriculture, and the [policy of] more, faster, better, and more economical. This had some effect on industrial and agricultural production in 1957, and some capital construction projects were also cut, but most importantly the zeal of the masses and cadres did not receive support. On the contrary, it was hampered, bringing some harm to our guiding policy, of [conducting socialist] construction through the masses.... This was a retrogressive guiding policy, counter to the Chairman's guiding policy of advance. Carrying out this policy, no matter what your subjective intention, was bound to deviate from the Chairman's guiding policy. The less one was aware of this deviation, the graver and more dangerous it became.... I must shoulder the main responsibility for the error of opposing rash advance."

Sources: *Bainianchao*, no. 6 (1997), p. 18; and Jin Chongji, *Zhou Enlai zhuan*, vol. 3, pp. 1368-69.

2. The Chengdu conference, March 8-26, 1958

Following self-criticisms by several leaders after the Nanning conference, the Chengdu conference became the occasion for extensive self-examinations by various high-ranking figures, including several without direct economic responsibilities such as Liu Shaoqi and Deng Xiaoping. We provide a brief excerpt from Liu, while according to a participant at Chengdu Deng seemingly gave only a very general self-criticism that did not touch upon *fanmaojin*. Of the architects of opposing rash advance, an excerpt from Zhou Enlai's self-criticism and a more lengthy one from Chen Yun are available. Presumably Li Xiannian and Bo Yibo also offered self-examinations on this occasion.

Liu Shaoqi during the conference

"Chairman Mao has criticized some comrades as not ready for socialist construction. Although I'm not unready — I thought about it during the democratic revolution, over the years I have felt Chairman Mao's superiority. I am unable to keep up with his thought. Chairman Mao has a remarkable knowledge, especially of Chinese history which no one else in the Party can reach. [He] has practical experience, especially in combining Marxist theory and Chinese reality. Chairman Mao's superiority in these aspects is something we should admire and try to learn from [like] the student of Confucius who described Confucius as someone so superior that students can never catch up but should [try to] move in that direction....

"[I made mistakes concerning] cooperatives in 1951, initially thinking they should be delayed for 15 years, that we should make use of the great incentives for peasants resulting from land reform. Although cooperatives were the [correct] direction, at the time I thought they might damage peasant incentives."

Source: Interview with a participant at Chengdu, Beijing, 1997. The interviewee read from a record of Liu's statement.

Chen Yun, March 21, 1958

"Opposing rash advance at the Second Plenum of the Eighth Congress was to a certain extent my idea, and I ought to take primary responsibility. At the time, I had in mind many financial and trade problems. I had no doubts about the cooperatives or irrigation works, believing that whatever couldn't be done by individual peasants, could now be done. I'd heard some debate about well-digging, but didn't have any objections. However, I did have many doubts about other aspects of agriculture, such problems as seeding, the rate of spreading the double-cropping system for rice, the relatively high targets set by the plan's production quotas, the promotion and spread of the two-wheeled double-furrow plough and so on.

"The influence of the erroneous opposition to rash advance mainly affected areas [I previously regarded as] excessive, [namely,] basic construction and financial investment. This was due to my failure to realize that during a production high tide certain shortcomings are always unavoidable, [hence acceptable]. [My] right-deviationist conservative thinking is therefore related to the following two aspects:

"The first is making no distinction between [different types of] financial deficits, one being wartime, the other peacetime. I was panicked by the financial deficit which appeared in 1955. The characteristic of wartime deficits is that they are compelled, since war is the order of the day, so there are frequently deficits, and these affect long-term price fluctuations. The War to Resist America and Aid Korea was fought abroad, the domestic order remained normal, but managing barely to avoid a deficit was still a constant worry. Since March 1944, I've been in financial and economics work for 14 years (it was out of my hands for only one year, while [I was] in the Northeast). And in this war situation my mind was preoccupied with price fluctuations and financial deficits, and they left a deep impression. During peacetime construction, deficits may also occur. The two deficits of 1953 and 1956 were rather accidental and not inevitable, they resulted from negligence. At the time I didn't feel it was a deficit budget, but believed the budget could be balanced. Peacetime deficits can also have a corresponding effect on prices, the situation is like that of wartime. But it can also be rapidly eliminated, and the ways of doing this are many, such as economizing, increasing production, and digging into reserves, and it can be solved by the next year. This kind of contingent deficit is no more frightening than a wartime one. [Nevertheless,] at the time I didn't make such a distinction, and ended up with undue alarm. In the future this situation may occur again, and having sized it up, it can be turned around.

"During the Soviet Union's FFYP, the people's living conditions were extremely fraught, and that had an influence on us. In 1935 they had a severe shortage of goods and presumably a sizeable deficit. This was made up for by issuing currency, and consequently purchasing power and the supply of goods were out of balance. It is difficult to judge whether the Soviet Union could have avoided this situation. This kind of deficit during the Soviet Union's program of construction left an impression on us, and we wanted to do our utmost to avoid it. Thus, [we] often repeated: [it is] better to have a slower rate of construction and maintain price stability. In terms of more and less, faster and slower, positive and negative [balance], this was different from the Chairman's guiding policy of more, faster, better, and more economical.

"Second, [we had] not relayed the situation to the Chairman and the Politburo frequently enough. Rather than a steady drizzle [of information], it was always dropped in one mighty downpour. [Chairman Mao] has criticized [us] many times, [but we] have failed to rectify [this] resolutely. In essence this was blocking the passage of information. In winter 1955 the Premier convened a meeting of the Standing Committee of the State Council which discussed the work of all the financial and economics ministries. It was felt that it was difficult for one or two people to report on the situation, and the comprehensive situation should be reported to the Chairman and the [Politburo] Standing Committee, but again we fell back into working on documents. There was no timely reporting. In the future there will be these stipulations:

—The leaders of each financial and economics ministry, such as Wang Heshou and Peng Tao, will report separately to and obtain instructions from the Chairman, and only in this way can problems be clearly addressed.

—Documents related to finance and economics must be vetted [and discussed] by the Secretariat. [After all,] Fuchun and Xiannian are already participating in the work of the Secretariat.

—Resolve to write brief reports in concise language. But oral reports will be more important than written ones.

—Issue a *Bulletin* (*lingxun*) edited by Xue Muqiao. It will print some controversial things, and they can be debated internally. There shouldn't be any fear of it 'finding its way outside,' without [such things] it would be a bore. It can print things that are just a little bit more expansive.

—The Politburo can have informal discussions, a bit more relaxed, with each department in turn giving written and oral reports. Everyone can raise questions, and attendance can be freer. If there are two people in attendance we can begin.

—Comrades of the central financial and economics small group can regularly attend meetings of the [economic] coordination regions, and they can convene meetings of provincial and municipal planning committee (or financial committee) directors in places where the coordination region heads are stationed. Now Beijing convenes meetings of over a hundred people, so it's difficult to discuss issues. With fewer people, we can talk in greater depth. Two or three times a year, various places can take turns in hosting [such meetings]. Financial and economics work is the main issue for the coordination regions. Comrades doing financial and economics work should pay attention to politics, their thinking should not be too narrow."

Source: Li Rui, "*Dayuejin" qinliji*, pp. 222-24.

Zhou Enlai, March 25, 1958

"At the time, I didn't take in the views of many sides and had no contact with the masses and reality. Rather, I was tied up in conference halls and the office, so I saw even less clearly that a mass movement demanding major [economic] development was rising after the transformation of ownership had liberated the forces of production. On the contrary, we only saw lifeless things and not people full of life, [and] attended to concrete tasks but not principles (*wushi er bu wuxu*). The report proposing 'opposition to rash advance' for which I was chiefly responsible poured cold water on the mainstream of the high tide of mass production. Thus it was not an advance but a retrogression, not more, faster, better, more economical, but less, slower, worse, and more wasteful, and the 40 articles [on agriculture] were placed in limbo. This is the essence of the problem. I also believe that the essence of the problem is not one of wartime and peacetime deficits. Although the two types of deficits have different circumstances, for us communists there is one guiding principle to solving these two types, which is that we can only rely on the energy of the people....

"At the time, I really didn't understand this. Only after the rightists had taught me a lesson, and the Chairman had reminded me, and mass practice had further enlightened me, did I finally slowly begin to realize that this was an error concerning the guiding principles of socialist construction. Put more profoundly, I didn't see, and naturally as a result didn't grapple with, the essence of the socialist revolution's liberation of the forces of production, the mainstream of socialist construction in arousing the masses, and the development of production."

"I did not follow a dialectical materialist approach and failed to see the key issue, its fundamental essence, and the lesson of opposing rash advance that we should listen more to opinions from all sides and not just stay in our offices and deal with statistics. We must visit the countryside and grass roots. I failed to realize properly how following the three [socialist] transformations [in 1955-56] incentives were encouraged and productivity was liberated, I failed to see the human factor. I gave too much attention to things and not enough attention to theory, too much to practical things. Regarding opposing rash advance I began to realize something was wrong at the Third Plenum but at that time didn't think it was so serious. It was only after the Hangzhou and Nanning conferences that I realized it was a mistake in line."

Sources: Jin Chongji, *Zhou Enlai zhuan*, vol. 3, p. 1383 (paragraphs 1 and 2); and interview with a participant at Chengdu, Beijing, 1997 (paragraph 3). The interviewee read from a record of Zhou's statement.

3. The Second Session of the Eighth Party Congress, May 5-23, 1958

None of the self-examinations offered by the proponents of opposing rash advance at Nanning and Chengdu or elsewhere satisfied Mao. The Second Session of the Eighth Party Congress became a formal occasion when these leaders were required to make written self-criticisms whereas previously only oral remarks had been proffered. While there was considerable dissatisfaction with these leaders from the assembled lower-ranking delegates to the Congress, in the end Mao declared that the process had been completed to his satisfaction. Excerpts are available from self-criticisms by all the main architects of *fanmaojin*, except for the less deeply involved Li Fuchun who seemingly was spared from making a contribution.

Li Xiannian, May 15, 1958

"In recent years, under the leadership of Party committees at the Center and at every level, financial work has enjoyed success; it has basically implemented the Party's general line and general guiding policy. However, shortcomings in work have certainly arisen, to the degree that for a period of time and over certain issues there were errors in guiding policy. [Of course,] our financial work must concentrate capital and ensure key point construction and the needs of developing construction enterprises; it must also attend to the balance between income and expenditure and ensure the stability of market prices. All of these are necessary. However, in our work we invariably gave more consideration to balance and stability, and less consideration to the speed of construction. As always, we first feared that the budget would go into deficit, and then [we] feared market fluctuations.... This was because our thinking was lopsided, sometimes overstressing the approach of negative methods and constraints so that all we could do was to get bogged down in budgetary income and expenditure figures, never arriving at a way out. As a result, we were left muddled and downcast, and not vigorous, taking all before us. Certain instances of imbalance in supply and demand can occur during the advance of construction, yet we behaved with exceptional sensitivity, blindly howling about strains. When certain isolated shortcomings emerged in the 1956 construction leap, we only grasped the partial phenomena of things and didn't grasp the essence of things, exaggerating shortcomings and underrating achievements, calling the 1956 leap forward a 'rash advance.' The error of opposing 'rash advance' caused considerable damage to [our] work, and I must assume responsibility here. Fortunately, the [Party] Center made timely corrections, otherwise I don't know how great the damage might have been."

Sources: Li Rui, *"Dayuejin" qinliji*, pp. 335-36; and Cong Jin, *Quzhe fazhan*, p. 131.

Chen Yun, May 16, 1958

"In the period from the second half of 1956 to the first half of 1957, I underestimated the development trend of social productive forces following the three transformations of agriculture, handicrafts, and capitalist industry and commerce. I underestimated the great achievements of the 1956 production high tide. And I overestimated the scattered problems which had emerged during the great leap forward of [1956], problems that were chiefly a consequence of employing excessive numbers of new workers and of inappropriate wage rises in certain sectors which created strains in the supply of goods and in finance. When I was thinking over and raising these problems, I always viewed them from the standpoint of the condition of the financial and trade system, and I did not give enough attention either to the conditions of most central departments in industry and transportation or to the various tasks of the localities across the country. Having proceeded from partial circumstances to solve these problems, I could not correctly understand the question of nine fingers versus one finger, and then unavoidably committed errors. The method of obtaining market stability and fiscal balance which I stated at the provincial and municipal secretaries conference in January 1957 was premised on these partial concerns. Therefore, I did not take the positive approach [of] devising every possible way to arouse the masses and increase production to surmount these difficulties, but [instead] adopted negative methods which gave in to the difficulties. I paid too much attention to things and underestimated the revolutionary enthusiasm of the masses; I paid too much attention to allocative relations, but did not give enough emphasis to expanding production. I paid too much attention to so-called 'stability' (*wen*), and did not enthusiastically strive for all that was possible. These errors damaged the enthusiasm of the masses and slowed the pace of economic growth in 1957. The error of 'opposing rash advance' then was to overlook and underrate the great achievements of the high tide of mass production, and to overestimate financial and market strains. At the Second Plenum of November 1956, although I myself only reported on problems of grain, pig raising, vegetable oils, and foodstuffs, and did not even touch on the problems of overall finances, [in fact] the incorrect opinions concerning financial and market strains were first and foremost my opinions. Therefore, I must take primary responsibility for the error in guiding policy of 'opposing rash advance,' and above all, in terms of its influence on [my colleagues'] thinking, I take primary responsibility.... If [we] had not received Chairman Mao's timely correction, and let this mistake develop further, it would have caused our endeavors to suffer very serious damage."

Sources: Li Rui, *"Dayuejin" qinliji*, pp. 334-35; and Cong Jin, *Quzhe fazhan*, pp. 128-29.

Bo Yibo, May 16, 1958

"The Great Leap Forward of the national economy is the main feature of our country's current trend. This trend has certainly not arisen fortuitously. This is a victory for Chairman Mao's general guiding policy and the general line of socialist construction. Since the Third Plenum, especially since Chairman Mao affirmed the achievements of the first leap forward in 1956 at the Nanning conference, thoroughly condemning the error of opposing 'rash advance,' and further expounding the general guiding policy and line for building socialism of going all out, aiming high, and more, faster, better, and more economical [results], ... the present new trend has quickly emerged. This new developing trend offers us the possibility to develop our country's national economy at an even faster pace than the FFYP. In the second set of accounts for the 1958 national plan approved by the [Party] Center, the rate of industrial development is 34 percent; the rate of agricultural development is 21 percent.... It's now clear that the opposition to 'rash advance' of 1956 was completely wrong, that this was a mistake in guiding policy. I also bear responsibility for this error. The [achievement] of the 1956 leap forward was tremendously significant in enabling us to finish the FFYP early and increase our country's pace of socialist construction. Though some temporary and partial difficulties inevitably emerged, it was never anything to be scared of. However, I didn't make a very good analysis of these trends, didn't grasp the general direction of these developing trends. I didn't take positive steps when difficulties emerged over strains in materials [supply], mobilizing and relying on the masses and doing everything possible to surmount [these difficulties]; rather, in playing up these difficulties, I believed that, as primary materials production couldn't keep up, the pace of basic construction could not be too fast. Regarding the relationship between accumulation and consumption, I

[only] saw our country's large population and heavy consumption, emphasizing the difficulties in raising the proportion of accumulation, and I did not first emphasize that, with more people, production can be greater and accumulation also greater. Consequently, I bear a share of responsibility for the error of opposing 'rash advance.' The 1957 plan which was drafted under the influence of the opposing 'rash advance' error was a conservative one. And the first set of accounts for the 1958 plan, which was drafted in circumstances where our thinking was not fully liberated, underestimated as well the trend of the present Great Leap Forward. Viewed from today, the gravity of the problem did not lie in whether production and construction targets were higher or lower, but in the great damage which opposing 'rash advance' did to the enthusiasm of the masses and the great number of cadres, pouring cold water on the high tide of mass production and construction which had just begun. This must be taken as a lesson for us....

"In our present era, the question of our socialist construction is not just an economic question, but above all a political one; not only does it have tremendous significance for our country, but also for the world.... If we don't strive to develop rapidly our national economy, it would mean that we prolong the suffering of the people, and that we draw out the time needed to vanquish capitalism from the world arena. The problem before us is simply as serious as this, yet previously some of us comrades engaged in economics and planning work did not truly comprehend this problem....

"Recently, in reviewing Chairman Mao's writings and speeches of recent years, I profoundly realized that Chairman Mao's general guiding policy and line of socialist construction were put forward long ago, and [the situation] has been continuously improving.... With a helmsman like Chairman Mao, with such brilliant leadership, so long as we behave ourselves, learn from him and follow his instructions, we can [certainly] avoid committing an error such as opposing 'rash advance,' and we can achieve even greater successes in economic construction."

Sources: Cong Jin, *Quzhe fazhan*, pp. 129-31; and Li Rui, *"Dayuejin" qinliji*, pp. 336-37.

Zhou Enlai, May 17, 1958

"This meeting is a conference for the liberation of thought, and a conference brimming with communist mettle. The speeches have been rich and varied, and have vividly reflected the construction miracles and revolutionary vigor of the people during the Great Leap Forward in production and liberation of thought. Truly, one day is equal to twenty years, and half a year surpasses several thousand years. In this great epoch, so long as one is a genuine revolutionary, one cannot but be stirred by the exalted feelings and aspirations of this type of communism, and cannot but wholeheartedly acknowledge the correctness of the line for construction of the Party Center and Chairman Mao. At the same time, one understands even more the seriousness of the 'opposing rash advance' error. I was the one mainly responsible for the error of 'opposing rash advance,' and [I] ought to draw even more lessons from this error. I will now talk about my own knowledge [of this matter].

"The building of socialism encompasses problems of objectives and of methods. Whether or not to build socialism is a problem of objectives; to build socialism this way or that way is a question of methods. The former belongs to contradictions between the enemy and ourselves; the latter belongs to internal contradictions within the people and the Party. Chairman Mao has repeatedly instructed us that there can be two methods in undertaking the building of socialism: one faster and better; one slower and worse. The former is the more, faster, better, more economical method, and it carries out the Party's mass line, relying on the leadership of Party committees at every level, going all out to mobilize the masses, and bringing every positive factor into play to build socialism. The latter is the fewer, slower, worse, more wasteful method, and it violates the Party's mass line, paying no attention to safeguarding the enthusiasm of the cadres and masses. It does not go all out to mobilize the masses, and mainly relies on administrative orders to build socialism. These two different methods are also different guiding policies. Those who have made the 'opposing rash advance' error were building socialism according to the latter method. Clearly this runs directly counter to the guiding policy of building socialism more, faster, better, and more economically put forward by Chairman Mao. Moreover, for a short time in the past, it slowed our country's speed of construction, and hurt the enthusiasm of the cadres and masses for production and construction. Therefore, it was not an error over isolated questions, rather for a time it was an error of guiding policy over the questions of the scale and pace of socialist construction. For a considerable time, I remained unaware of this, and therein lay the seriousness of [my] problem."

[*In this self-criticism there is a section on "learning from Chairman Mao" through which one can understand the pressure which Zhou Enlai was then under — comment by Li Rui*]: "China's historical experience of decades of revolution and construction demonstrates that Chairman Mao is the representative of the truth. When we have deviated from or disobeyed his leadership and instructions, we have frequently lost our direction and errors have occurred, damaging the interests of the Party and the people. The repeated errors which I have committed are evidence enough of this. On the other hand, when I've acted correctly and whatever I've done right are inseparable from Chairman Mao's correct leadership and leading thought....

"The error of 'opposing rash advance' was reflected in a concentrated manner in my report to the Second Plenum of the Eighth Central Committee in November 1956. At the time I misjudged certain shortcomings and difficulties that had emerged in the construction achievements and leap forward of 1956. I exaggerated shortcomings which in fact amounted to less than one finger out of ten, I confirmed that the plan for 1956 had 'blown out' (*'mao' le*), and proposed to reduce appropriately the scale of construction. At this conference, Chairman Mao spoke last, steadfastly maintaining that the construction achievements of 1956 remained primary and that progress and development were the general trend. He pointed out that the enthusiasm of the broad cadres and masses must be safeguarded, cold water should not be poured on them, and there should be no 'committee for retrogression' (*cutuihui*). Soon after the Party Center again adopted a positive guiding policy based on Chairman Mao's speech to small group leaders [at the plenum], launching a national movement to increase production and economize. Only in this way was the trend turned around, enabling the production and construction plan for 1957 to be completed relatively smoothly. Yet, despite this, comparing rates of production and construction for the previous three years, it can be seen clearly that the error of 'opposing rash advance' dampened the enthusiasm of the broad cadres and masses, and had no small effect on our country's construction efforts in 1957. This was also raised by many comrades in their speeches.... This fact shows how the two different types of methods create two different types of results. The Great Leap Forward gives us positive education. The 'opposing rash advance' error has taught us by negative example, and just as Comrade Shaoqi has said, 'It is as a result of this reversal that the correctness of the Party's line for building socialism can be seen ever more clearly.'"

[*Zhou Enlai was left with no choice but to connect painfully the error of "opposing rash advance" with the "furious attack" of the [bourgeois] rightists [in 1957] — comment by Li Rui*]: "The error of the 'opposing rash advance' was grave, but thanks to the correct leadership and timely redress of the Party Center and Chairman Mao, and resistance to these errors from cadres and masses inside and outside the Party, as well as the negative lesson given by the bourgeois rightists, this error did not continue developing into an even more serious one. When the bourgeois rightists were furiously attacking the Party in the spring of 1957, they exploited the error of 'opposing rash advance' to negate totally the construction achievements of 1956. They exaggerated certain shortcomings during the 1956 leap forward into an 'all out rash advance,' and further they negated the construction achievements of the FFYP. Confronted by this grave class struggle, I began to wake up. Consequently, in the government work report of June 1957, I completely abandoned my incorrect assessment of a 'rash advance' in construction during 1956 and resolutely affirmed that construction in 1956 had been a leap forward in development. This was a turning point in my thinking. This was a lesson gained from the enemy, but still more important was the lesson of Chairman Mao's declaration about reviving the more, faster, better, more economical policy, the 40 articles on agriculture, and the 'committee to promote progress' at the Third Plenum, and then the rectification at the Hangzhou, Nanning, and Chengdu conferences. At the same time, I also had contact with some mass activities of the Great Leap Forward in production. Only from rectification and from practice did I truly understand the incomparable brilliance and limitless energy of the Party's line on socialist construction....

"The error of 'opposing rash advance' was not accidental. The ideological sources of the error lay in subjectivism and [hollow] metaphysics. For most issues, this was manifested as [bourgeois] empiricism; for certain issues, it was manifested as dogmatism; in others these two were intermingled. These errors in mode of thinking eventually resulted in the error of right-deviationist conservatism in construction work. This then violated the general line of socialist construction consistently advocated by Chairman Mao....

"Here I should explain how in guiding national economics work my administration incorrectly adopted an approach of mechanical static balancing. For example, during the leap forward in socialist construction of 1956, some isolated shortcomings appeared, bringing certain difficulties to our country's economic life. There was never any need for alarm about these momentary difficulties, and provided we followed Chairman Mao's thinking and relied on the Party and masses, trusted the localities, gave full play to the masses, and continued to develop production unwaveringly, these temporary difficulties absolutely could have been surmounted, and production could have developed even more. This point is amply demonstrated by the facts of our country's economic Great Leap Forward in the past half year. At the time, however, I, and certain comrades engaged in government work, wrongly believed that the excessive scale and pace of basic construction had created strains in market supply and demand and had led to many instances of imbalance. To stabilize the market and maintain balance, we then adopted a mechanical static balancing method, and strove to reduce the scale of construction and to compress consumption, striving for balance only from the side of allocation. This was a way of striving for balance by 'chopping one's feet to fit the shoes'; not only was it unable to promote production, it actually obstructed the development of production.... Chairman Mao taught us at the Second Plenum of the Eighth Central Committee when he said, balance is relative [and] temporary, but imbalance is absolute and constant.... Our opinions at that time about imbalance and the methods we adopted for achieving balance were precisely the opposite to what Chairman Mao taught us, only looking to lifeless goods and numbers, and not seeing the decisive factor in productive forces — living people...."

[*He also offered the following self-criticism, echoing Mao Zedong's harsh language in his repeated accusations against "opposing rash advance" — comment by Li Rui*]: "Apart from these errors in understanding and method, it should also be observed that the error of 'opposing rash advance' is inseparable from the tendency of government work to become divorced from the Party's leadership and from the masses. For a period, government work, especially in financial and economics construction work, has stressed professional tasks to the neglect of politics, attending to 'concrete matters' but neglecting ideological precepts (*wu 'shi' bu wuxu*), grasping small things but not big ones, and not distinguishing between the major and minor [aspects].

Requests for instructions or reports concerning some major work problems were not promptly sent to the [Party] Center, even less was the situation regularly and systematically relayed to the [Party] Center. Even if [we] requested instructions or made reports, we presented these in one 'mighty downpour' rather than as a 'steady flow,' in a big pile of figures which made it too late for the [Party] Center to consider closely the decisions it had to make about these issues. [We] were guilty of lacking serious consideration and discussion of the instructions given by the [Party] Center and Chairman Mao, our understanding was neither deep nor thorough, and hence we did not carry them through further in government work."

Sources: Li Rui, *"Dayuejin" qinliji*, pp. 330-34; and Cong Jin, *Quzhe fazhan*, pp. 123-26.

ANNOTATED BIBLIOGRAPHY OF MAJOR SOURCES

1. *Jianguo yilai Mao Zedong wengao* [Mao Zedong's Manuscripts since the Founding of the State]. 13 vols (September 1949 — July 1976). Beijing: Zhongyang wenxian chubanshe, 1987-98.

This fascinating *neibu* compilation of Mao's post-1949 manuscripts ranks with the "imperial notes" of any earlier "emperor" in terms of the richness of information, the intensity of activities, and, more importantly, the ideas that dictated the course of historical events. Volumes 4 to 10 covering January 1953 to December 1963 relate to this study in terms of the events covered themselves, background developments such as the 1955 agricultural cooperativization campaign, and the subsequent retreat from the Great Leap Forward covered in Epilogue 2. Despite indications that the collection would not be extended to the problematic Cultural Revolution period of the "later Mao," two final volumes covering this period, up to two months before the Chairman's death, have recently appeared. (See Teiwes, "Mao Texts," for a detailed review of the collection through the first eight volumes.)

The manuscripts selected for this collection take various forms ranging from literary drafts, instructions, comments, speech outlines, marginal remarks, letters, poems, insertions on Party documents, speeches, records of conversations, and writings published under Mao's name. Of the last three genres only items approved or revised by Mao personally are included in the present compilation. Conceivably, Chen Boda, Mao's ranking secretary during the period of the study, played a significant role in drafting, editing, or stylistically polishing contemporary items.

Given Mao's pivotal role in CCP decision making, these materials are of extraordinary value in demonstrating the nature of his impact on key events. The relevant volumes which include the period through the Eighth Party Congress in 1956, generally described as Mao's most "democratic," demonstrate how the great majority of major decisions can be traced back to Mao. The chronologically arranged materials not only testify to the obvious truth of Mao being at *the center* of power, but also reveal that he was often *the origin* of history-making events.

The bulk of the selections consists of either Mao's manuscripts that are published for the first time or those that were circulated previously as internal materials on a highly restricted basis. The compilation contains many condensed notes not initially meant for public consumption. For example, see Mao's speech outlines for the three major meetings in the first half of 1958 (namely the Nanning and Chengdu conferences and the Second Session of the Eighth Congress: vol. 7, pp. 16-18, 108-25, 194-211). These items as a rule are more telling than the complete speeches precisely because they are crude, less rhetorical, and hence to the point.

There is no evidence that these documents have been doctored by the compilers, although one can be certain that a great many of Mao's manuscripts have been deliberately excluded. The editors' attitude is conscientious, and their footnotes are extremely useful. In short, compelling reading shedding new light on the wonder that was Mao.

2. *Zhonggong dangshi jiaoxue cankao ziliao* [CCP History Teaching Reference Materials]. Vols. 20-24 (January 1953-May 1966). N.p.: Zhongguo Jiefangjun Guofang Daxue dangshi dangjian zhenggong jiaoyanshi, April-July 1986.

These five volumes covering the mid to late 1950s and the early 1960s are drawn from the National Defense University's 27 volume set of what is undoubtedly the best comprehensive compilation of Party history materials yet produced. (See Warren Sun, "The National Defense University's *Teaching Reference Materials*," in Cheek and Saich, *New Perspectives on State Socialism in China*, for a discussion of the entire collection which spans the period from the founding of the CCP to the end of the "Cultural Revolution decade.") The relevant years leading up to the Great Leap in these volumes are among the most thoroughly documented in the entire compilation, with over 300 pages of contemporary materials from 1955 (vols. 20-21), roughly 450 pages from 1956 (vol. 21), and a bit less than 400 pages from 1957 (vol. 22), but as the leap and post-leap crisis emerged the coverage tapers off to about 230 pages each for 1958 (vol. 22) and 1959 (vol. 23), and further to 200 pages or less for 1960, 1961 (vol. 23), and 1962 (vol. 24). The editorial board in charge of the project consisted of a dozen leading NDU scholars, including Lin Yunhui and Cong Jin who clearly have made excellent use of these extraordinarily valuable materials (see items 6 and 7, below).

The types of documents included are quite varied in terms of both nature and previous availability. They include open contemporary sources such as important *People's Daily* editorials and major Party and state decrees, internal materials which had previously been published in other *neibu* collections (see the discussion of materials on agricultural cooperativization, below), and documents such as various reports and speeches related to the Gao Gang affair (see Deng Xiaoping's March 1955 report in vol. 21, pp. 512-25) which are not known to be available in any other source. As a comprehensive collection the coverage spans virtually all fields with key political issues, economic affairs, foreign policy, and security matters all included.

Even such an extensive collection inevitably leaves things out. One type of exclusion seems based on common sense. With Mao's *Selected Works* universally available in Party history circles, there is no need to reproduce them here; thus such key items as his July 1955 speech on cooperatives or his February 1957 contradictions speech are missing. A second type of exclusion is undoubtedly a function of comprehensive coverage which demands careful selection in each specialized field. Thus with regard to the agricultural cooperativization debate in 1955 the collection clearly draws on the "secret documents" compiled by the State Agricultural Commission, *Nongye jitihua zhongyao wenjian huibian* [A Collection of Important Documents on Agricultural Collectivization], vol. 1: 1949-1957 (Beijing: Zhonggong zhongyang dangxiao chubanshe, 1981). Nearly all the NDU documents appeared in the earlier collection which also contained a significant number of additional materials, mostly of a more technical nature.

A final type of exclusion, however, appears more political in nature. Thus there are no materials on the key January 1958 Nanning meeting where Mao openly and harshly attacked Zhou Enlai and other leaders for their alleged deviations with regard to "opposing rash advance," nor are the revealing self-criticisms of Zhou and others to the May 1958 Second Session of the Eighth Party Congress included despite their availability to the editors (see item 7). One can only assume that some pressure to protect Mao's reputation, and perhaps that of Zhou Enlai as well, was at work here.

This invaluable collection is unfortunately not widely available either inside China or abroad, but volumes 12-24 are held by the Universities Service Centre, Hong Kong, and at Harvard's Fairbank Center.

3.   *Dang de wenxian* [The Party's Documents], sponsored by Zhonggong zhongyang wenxian yanjiushi [CCP Central Documents Research Office] and Zhongyang dang'anguan [Central Archives]. Beijing: Zhongyang wenxian chubanshe, 1988-19...

Undoubtedly the most authoritative Party history journal since its founding in 1988, *The Party's Documents* is the successor to earlier journals separately put out by its two sponsors. These were the CCP Central Documents Research Office's *Wenxian he yanjiu* [Documents and Research], a journal similar to its successor which was published from 1982 to 1987, and the Central Archives' *Dang'anguan congkan* [Archives Journal] which dealt more with technical issues concerning archives during its existence in 1986-87. The collaborative sponsorship makes sense given the close functional and bureaucratic relationship of the two organs which are of independent equal rank under the Central Committee's General Office, with the Research Office having priority use of Archives material and the right to decide what to publish.

This bimonthly journal covers the full span of CCP history and combines original documents on a particular theme, whether those published for the first time or others that have been published elsewhere previously, and analytic pieces. There are inevitably one or more analytic articles attached to the documents presented, as well as a large range of research papers on other subjects in any given issue. Apart from examinations of specific events and issues, these papers include discussions of editing work on particular major projects and reviews of scholarly work on specific areas including that done abroad. Also published from time to time are the reflections of "retired" leaders on various past events, as well as announcements of new publications.

The scope of what is covered can be conveyed more concretely by considering the contents of issue no. 1 of 1989. The lead article is an account of the first nine months of the liberation war in the Northeast by one of the leading personalities involved at the time, Peng Zhen. The major documentary collection of the issue brings together materials on agricultural cooperativization beginning with Liu Shaoqi's July 1951 comment on Shanxi cooperatives and ending with Mao's May 1955 call for a faster pace of cooperativization (see Teiwes and Sun, *The Politics of Agricultural Cooperativization*, for translations of most of the 1955 items). These documents were previously included in the NDU collection (item 2), but presumably reached a wider audience within China through the journal. Attached to the documents are three analytic articles, including one by Du Runsheng, a major actor in the 1955 events.

Other subjects covered in the above issue include Mao's 1925 analysis of classes in Chinese society (both the original document and an analysis), scholarly pieces on the "collapse" of the Gang of Four, Stalin's advice opposing the crossing of the Yangzi, the Xi'an incident, the *Since the Sixth Congress* collection that was studied during the Yan'an rectification, Mao's comments on Hai Rui before and after the 1959 Shanghai meetings, and errors in Mao's views on class struggle during the early period of socialist construction. In addition, discussions of research on Zhou Enlai conducted in 1978-88, the editorial process concerning the *Selected Works of Ren Bishi*, and the publication of two volumes of Mao writings were included.

As with scholarly journals anywhere, the quality of offerings varies, but it is usually of good standard and highly informative. Unfortunately, *The Party's Documents* is not readily found outside China despite the fact that it is no longer classified as a *neibu* publication and has been advertised as available for foreign purchase. In practice, regular purchase or exchange remains difficult, but it is well worth making special efforts to obtain copies. Researchers will discover ongoing attention to difficult questions in CCP history; a case in point relevant here is several articles concerning *fanmaojin* (no. 4, 1992, pp. 88-89; and no. 5, 1992, pp. 43-46) which form part of continuing studies of and documents concerning economic policy in the 1950s.

4.   *Zhongguo Gongchandang zhizheng sishinian (1949-1989)* [The CCP's Forty Years in Power, 1949-1989], edited by Ma Qibin, Chen Wenbin, Lin Yunhui, Cong Jin, Wang Nianyi, Zhang Tianrong, and Bu Weihua. 1st edition, Beijing: Zhonggong dangshi ziliao chubanshe, 1989. 2nd expanded edition, Beijing: Zhonggong dangshi chubanshe, 1991.

This is undoubtedly the best general chronology of post-1949 PRC developments. In 586 double-columned large pages (in the 2nd edition) a wealth of detailed information is provided on Party and state meetings, important directives, and political developments more generally. In addition there is considerable attention to economic targets and performance, with the entries for each year concluding with a statistical summary of the main results.

The superiority of this volume can be illustrated by comparison to two other prominent general chronologies, *Zhonggong dangshi dashi nianbiao* [Chronology of Events in CCP History] (Beijing: Renmin chubanshe, 1987), and *Zhongguo Gongchandang lishi dashiji (1919.5-1990.12)* [Chronology of Events in CCP History, May 1919-December 1990] (Beijing: Renmin chubanshe, 1991), both compiled by the CCP Central Party History Research Office. *Forty Years* focuses on the post-1949 period in contrast to the entire CCP history coverage of the others, with the result that much more information is conveyed; for example, it devotes 18 pages to 1957, while the other two chronologies respectively contain 8 and 6 far smaller pages on this year.

As a result *Forty Years* covers some of the less prominent meetings of specific bureaucratic organs, such as the SPC (see, e.g., 2nd ed., pp. 121, 129) not included in the other general chronologies. Its superiority, however, is apparent in ways other than simple number of entries. Concerning entries on the same event, such as the critical Nanning conference in January 1958 (2nd ed., p. 138), it provides not only more information than that in the other two books, but also a better feel for what took place. Thus this account notes the *severe* criticism of *fanmaojin*, and that Mao raised the matter to a political question, although it too refrained from naming Zhou Enlai *et al.* as the targets of Mao's strictures. Also, the individual mood of Mao is conveyed on occasion in contrast to flat accounts normal to chronologies, as in the Chairman's "extraordinary happiness" upon being told in June 1958 that the steel target could be doubled (2nd ed., p. 146).

In addition to the chronology, the book contains useful appendices on Party, state, military, and mass organization personnel, including leading figures at the provincial level. These name-lists are particularly valuable for providing a record of dates of service, but they are limited to the most prominent positions.

The rich detail of this volume, particularly when taken in conjunction with the extensive NDU documentary collection (item 2), provides an incomparably rich overview of the ebb and flow of events in the PRC. The expanded edition simply extends the chronology of the 1st edition which ended in November 1987 despite the book's title through to the start of October 1989, and updates the appendices accordingly.

5.   Bo Yibo. *Ruogan zhongda juece yu shijian de huigu* [Reflections on Certain Major Decisions and Events]. Vol. 1, Beijing: Zhonggong zhongyang dangxiao chubanshe, 1991; vol. 2, 1993.

In these two volumes on the period from 1949 to the start of the Cultural Revolution, Bo Yibo — one of the most important two dozen CCP leaders and one of the top economic officials of the period — offers his reflections on some of the most significant events and policy decisions of the 1950s. These include land reform, the general line for the transition period, the Gao-Rao affair, the speed-up of agricultural cooperativization in 1955 (see Teiwes and Sun, *The Politics of Agricultural Cooperativization*, for a translation of the relevant sections), the "Ten Great Relationships," the *fanmaojin* program of 1956-57, and the course of the Great Leap and its aftermath in 1958-62.

Bo's reflections are different from the usual CCP memoirs in that they do not necessarily focus on the activities of the author. They deal with events where Bo played a key role, but also with those where he had no direct involvement. In some instances they provide a vivid picture of Bo's state of mind, as in his anxiety when he found himself receiving Mao's criticism at the Nanning conference (vol. 2, pp. 638, 682), while in others like the 1955 cooperativization debate Bo's involvement was minimal and his account is that of a very well-supported researcher. Thus, while there are various elements of the memoir in this book — not least Bo's reflections on the rightness or otherwise of various decisions, it is also a substantial research work which was assisted by established scholars such as Cong Jin (see item 7).

Given his very high status in the Party and role as a member of the Party history leadership small group (*dangshi lingdao xiaozu*), Bo presumably had virtually unsurpassed access to inner-Party records. Such access, together with his personal understanding of the individuals involved, allows a more detailed and more finely nuanced account of leadership interaction than Party historians can normally achieve, even in cases like cooperativization where he was not an important figure. This is perhaps most clearly seen in his analysis of the "change in May [1955]" concerning cooperativization where he chides "some historical works in recent years" (clearly a reference to item 6) for "not exploring or explaining clearly the causes of the change" (vol. 1, p. 369). Yet it is his presence on the scene which produces Bo's most illuminating material as, for example, his report of Mao's observation at the November 1956 Central Committee plenum where *fanmaojin* had allegedly reached its peak that the type of rightism having to do with the speed of economic construction was perfectly all right (vol. 1, p. 556).

In terms of "bias," Bo's assessment mirrors the official 70 percent good 30 percent mistaken summary of Mao, with attention to both his faults and where his views were correct. Thus on cooperativization, Bo not only notes Deng Zihui's "correct" views, but also indicates where Deng made policy errors and Mao's views were superior (vol. 1, p. 338). On the political issue, however, Bo adheres to the post-Mao consensus — the Chairman erred seriously in raising a policy dispute to the level of political principle. In terms of his own role, Party historians and contemporary participants consider Bo's version generally fair, although some suspect a slight skewing of the record to make himself look a bit better than the actual reality.

6. **Lin Yunhui, Fan Shouxin, and Zhang Gong.** *1949-1989 nian de Zhongguo: kaige xingjin de shiqi* **[China 1949-1989: The Period of Triumph and Advance]. Zhengzhou: Henan renmin chubanshe, 1989.**

This book, undoubtedly the best comprehensive history of the period from the founding of the PRC to the eve of the 1956 Eighth Party Congress, makes excellent companion reading to Bo Yibo's *Reflections* (item 5). The first of the acclaimed 4 volume series on post-1949 Party history, the study, like volumes 2 (see item 7) and 3 (Wang Nianyi's survey of the "Cultural Revolution decade" — see *CCP Research Newsletter*, no. 3, 1989, p. 57), has strong links to the NDU documentary collection (item 2) through the first listed author serving on the editorial board for the collection. It is perhaps work on compiling this collection that facilitated the "many new materials" which Liao Gailong noted in his foreword as distinguishing the book.

While volumes 2 and 3 are solely produced by NDU scholars and the less useful volume 4 on the reform era is the work of a team of researchers from the CCP Central Party History Research Office, this book is a collaborative effort of senior scholars from three peak Party history institutions. Initially the work was to be the prime responsibility of Zhang Gong from the Party History Research Office, but major problems with his eyes led Zhang to call in Lin Yunhui from the NDU and Fan Shouxin from the CCP Central Party School to undertake the bulk of the work.

In comparison to Bo Yibo's first volume, this volume has a broader coverage of events; it seeks to be inclusive whereas Bo tended to focus on economic questions and major political issues, often those involving Cultural Revolution charges against his main patron, Liu Shaoqi. In producing a more comprehensive picture Lin *et al.* often give briefer accounts of the events Bo covers, and for all the richness of their new materials they often fail to match Bo in the details and flavor of elite interaction. Thus with regard to the background to *fanmaojin*, their account of the emergence of the "more, faster, better, more economical" slogan (pp. 615-617) fails to mention the roles of Zhou Enlai, Bo, and Li Fuchun in formulating the slogan, nor does it capture the extent of elite enthusiasm for the first leap forward at the end of 1955. The book, however, often gives greater attention to background conditions, as in its discussion of the 1955 cooperativization debate (as with Bo's account translated in Teiwes and Sun, *The Politics of Agricultural Cooperativization*) where it examines the actual problems in the villages and the responses of local officials, particularly after Mao's July 1955 speech.

Although Liao Gailong also refers to the book's "new viewpoints," its treatment of events is compatible with the 1981 *Historical Resolution* but without the obvious impulse to defend Mao that is apparent in Bo's volume. Thus with regard to Mao's clash with Deng Zihui over cooperativization, this matter-of-fact account implicitly assumes Mao was wrong in both policy and politics in contrast to Bo's attempt to strike a more subtle balance. On this issue and others, a reading of the two books in conjunction with one another will greatly enhance understanding of the formative years of the PRC.

7.   **Cong Jin.** *1949-1989 nian de Zhongguo: Quzhe fazhan de suiye* **[China 1949-1989: The Years of Circuitous Development]. Zhengzhou: Henan renmin chubanshe, 1989.**

Arguably ranking as the best of the *China 1949-1989* volumes along with Wang Nianyi's account of the "Cultural Revolution decade," this book (cf. *CCP Research Newsletter*, nos. 6 & 7, 1990, p. 62) takes up the story where item 6 leaves off with the Eighth Party Congress in September 1956 and continues through to the eve of the Cultural Revolution in May 1966. As volume 1, it is a comprehensive study covering all the key developments of the period, and clearly benefits from the author's role as a member of the editorial board of the NDU collection (item 2).

One of major features of the book is its use of previously unavailable sources. Of particular interest in terms of this chapter is the valuable documentation of the crucial period from the Nanning conference to the Second Session of the Eighth Party Congress in January-May 1958 which had previously been underexamined in Party history literature, documentation which gives a vivid sense of the political pressure unleashed by Mao against the architects of *fanmaojin*. Most valuable are the extracts from the self-criticisms to the Congress of Zhou Enlai, Chen Yun, Li Xiannian, and Bo Yibo, especially that of the Premier (pp. 123-31 and reproduced in Appendix 2.3). Of note is the fact that these documents and others from the period are not included in the NDU collection. Given that Cong Jin was involved in both projects, one can only assume that an easing of restrictions took place in the roughly three years between the issuing of the collection and the page-proof stage of the book.

What makes the documentation so exciting is the light it sheds on the texture of the Mao-centered political process in a period of, to adopt the words of the title, circuitous development. Thus we see the Party shaken by Mao's imperious attack on Zhou *et al.* at Nanning (pp. 111-12), Zhou dealing with the situation via excessive self-criticism and extreme praise of Mao much as he had in Yan'an, Mao's extreme pleasure in June 1958 when Bo Yibo pandered to his enthusiasm for the Great Leap by declaring Britain could be overtaken in two or three years (p. 138), and Mao starting to modify his position in late 1958 but in such an ambivalent fashion as to inhibit his colleagues from forcefully pursuing new directions (p. 256). In these and later instances in the pre-Cultural Revolution years Cong provides a combination of new materials and subtle analysis to deepen understanding of what it was like to operate in a political system where so much depended on keeping up with an unpredictable, volatile Chairman.

The excellence of Cong Jin's book tangentially draws our attention to a couple of key problems in the Party history field. If he could go further on the events of the first half of 1958 than was possible for the NDU documents three years earlier, in the more restrictive if uneven atmosphere since the Beijing spring of 1989 some studies making even more detailed use of materials from the period have reportedly been suppressed (see item 10). Perhaps even more serious is that the lure of the market has apparently drawn Cong, after a brief period assisting Bo Yibo, away from Party history and into business activities. The loss of such an excellent scholar, and undoubtedly others, surely diminishes Party history studies in the PRC.

8.   **Li Rui. *Lushan huiyi shilu* [True Record of the Lushan Conference]. Beijing: Chunqiu chubanshe, 1989. 2nd revised edition, Zhengzhou: Henan renmin chubanshe, 1994.**

This outstanding account of the July-August 1959 Lushan conference offers a unique insight into one of the major turning points in both CCP history and Mao's leadership style. While the broad outlines and many details of events at Lushan have been well known through a variety of other sources, this book not only provides an unprecedented inside story of the meeting but also illuminates many developments in the elite politics of the entire Great Leap Forward period after the January 1958 Nanning conference. The resultant picture of the Mao-centered political process which sheds new light on both the Chairman's nervous Politburo colleagues and reactive Party and state institutions is unsurpassed.

No one was in a better position to give a credible account of the Lushan conference than Li Rui, Mao's secretary since shortly after the Nanning meeting and the only survivor among the members of the alleged anti-Party clique at Lushan. Li Rui was not only an active participant throughout the critical events of the conference, he is the only remaining witness to the July 31-August 1 Politburo Standing Committee meeting where Peng Dehuai's fate was sealed. The true story of this highest-level meeting, previously not accessible to even other top officials, is revealed for the first time by this book. Li's account is based on his detailed notes taken during the conference which miraculously escaped subsequent destruction, and thus is both highly credible and rare since comprehensive notetaking was generally not allowed in meetings of the Party Center from about the late 1950s.

When the book was first published in 1989 it quickly became a classic, hotly sought after by Party historians as well as overseas experts despite criticism from conservative veteran leaders. Encouraged by its success, the author has incorporated several new sections in the revised edition. Most revealing is the discussion of small group meetings in which various leaders such as Kang Sheng and Xiao Hua launched ruthless attacks on members of the so-called "military club" of people associated with Peng Dehuai. While, as the first edition demonstrated, there were attempts by senior leaders to soften the blow to Peng and the others at Lushan, this addition demonstrates how vestiges of humanity withered at the Chairman's court once Mao unleashed his full fury.

In short, this book ranks as one of the very best ever to come out of the PRC: an original, compelling, and thought-provoking account of a crucial turning point in CCP history based on the detailed records of a key participant.

9.   Li Rui. *"Dayuejin" qinliji* [A Personal Historical Record of the "Great Leap Forward"]. Shanghai: Shanghai yuandong chubanshe, 1996.

Following the success of *Lushan shilu*, Li Rui has become one of the foremost chroniclers of the Great Leap Forward. His efforts include articles — notably "'Dayuejin' de xumu — Nanning huiyi" [The Prelude to the Great Leap Forward — the Nanning Conference], *Zhonggong dangshi ziliao*, no. 57 (1996), "Zhonggong zhongyang Wuchang huiyi he bajie liuzhong quanhui" [The CCP Central Committee's Wuchang Conference and the Sixth Plenum of the Eighth Central Committee], *ibid.*, no. 61 (1997), and "'Dayuejin' qijian wo gei Mao Zedong de sanzi shangshu" [The Three Letters I Gave Mao Zedong during the "Great Leap Forward"], *Bainianchao*, no. 4 (1997) — but most significantly this book covering the crucial formative period from the Nanning conference in January 1958 to the Second Session of the Eighth Party Congress in May. Li reportedly is engaged in a subsequent volume that will take up the story following the Second Session.

The book reflects Li Rui's dual role as Mao's secretary — or corresponding secretary (*tongxin mishu*) to be precise — and a bureaucrat in the power industry as Assistant Minister of Electric Power and later of Water Conservancy and Electric Power. The first chapter describes how this dual role came about with Li summoned to the Nanning conference to debate the issue of the Three Gorges dam with another comparatively low-ranked official, impressing the Chairman with his argument, and then being invited to become one of Mao's secretaries. Li, however, chose to remain in his post, but accepted the status of secretary which allowed him both a degree of access to Mao and the opportunity to participate in most of the high-level meetings of 1958-59.

In subsequent chapters Li devotes, somewhat self-indulgently, considerable attention to developments in his own functional area, an account which gives a sense of the pressures bureaucrats were under as the Great Leap heated up. But from the point of view of Party history, it is the detailed discussion of the three major meetings that are most valuable. Ironically, it was only partially that Li's "personal historical record" illuminates these meetings. While he certainly provides first-hand witness to the Chengdu conference which he attended throughout, he only arrived at Nanning late in the day and much of his knowledge of that crucial meeting came via the accounts of other participants after his arrival, and he did not attend the Second Session since he had not been elected a delegate. Thus much of his account relies on written sources, such as the "unpublished documents" (item 10) and even more detailed records.

In any case, the detail provided by Li is considerably richer than in any other available sources. We not only have another version of the Second Session self-criticisms of Zhou Enlai *et al.* (see item 7 and Appendix 2.3), but lengthy extracts from Mao's many speeches to these gatherings and from key speeches by such critical leaders at the time as Ke Qingshi, Chen Boda, and Tan Zhenlin, as well as summaries of the representations of various provinces and ministries. The exceptional detail is indicated by the fact that Li's account of the Chengdu conference runs to 105 pages, compared to 25 pages in "unpublished document no. 3" (see item 10).

While Li interjects his own views and personal exchanges with others at the time, often he simply provides texts of what was said at the meetings concerned without comment. The net result is a curiously uneven book which never reaches the heights of *Lushan shilu*, but nevertheless one which is extremely valuable for an understanding of the Great Leap Forward.

10.   "Unpublished Chinese documents on opposing rash advance and the Great Leap Forward nos. 1-6." N.p.: c. 1992.

These six studies by Party historians covering the period from late 1955 to the early stage of the 1959 Lushan conference were suppressed by the Party history establishment. Having come into our possession via a senior source outside Party history circles, they provide an extraordinarily detailed account of the *fanmaojin* program and the various major conferences of 1958-59 that affected the course of the Great Leap. Together they shed invaluable light on the dynamics of the period.

Document no. 1 provides a detailed history of "opposing rash advance," covering events up to fall 1957. Documents nos. 2, 3, and 4, dealing respectively with the Nanning conference, the Chengdu conference, and the Second Session of the Eighth Party Congress in the January-May 1958 period, are of particular interest in revealing the political dynamics of the launching of the Great Leap Forward. Document no. 5 examines the August 1958 Beidaihe conference which drove the leap to even more extreme heights, while document no. 6 covers the two Zhengzhou conferences, the Wuchang and Shanghai conferences, and the Sixth and Seventh Plenums as well as the start of the Lushan meeting from November 1958 to July 1959 which saw the abortive effort to "cool down" the movement and correct "leftist" excesses.

Documents nos. 2-4 not only provide full lists of participants of the crucial meetings of spring 1958 (in the case of the larger-scale Second Session it is impossible and unnecessary to list the 1,364 delegates, but all the standing members of the Congress Presidium, big region leaders and deputies, military representatives, and keynote speakers are clearly identified), they also recount Mao's Great Leap agenda by detailing his "whipping the horses," so to speak, and the actual proceedings (on what day who said what). They further reveal the close interaction between Mao and local leaders, and convey a general sense of the mood and atmosphere of these meetings.

These studies also contain many lengthy extracts from Mao's speeches which are rarely available in official party histories, let alone in Volume V of Mao's *Selected Works* published nearly two decades ago which stopped at the end of 1957. These extracts clearly reaffirm the authenticity of Red Guard collections of Mao's speeches and writings which appeared during the 1966-69 Cultural Revolution period, the only period when access to such classified materials became possible due to the anarchical situation and factional fighting. This reinforces our view that Red Guard materials should be reexamined when sifting official Party histories.

Through these unpublished documents careful readers can also capture a strong sense of Mao's centrality in kick-starting the leap forward program and the hugely significant role and input of the localities which enabled the campaign to gain and maintain its great momentum, as well as the awkward situation of the central bureaucracies, financial and planning alike, that were caught by surprise by pressure, from both above and below, to toe the new line. In short, these extremely valuable materials should be viewed as indispensable for any scholar of the Great Leap Forward, especially on questions concerning its origins.

The fact that these materials were suppressed indicates the extreme, indeed rather irrational attitude of the Party history authorities. They are simply factual, providing more detail than any other previous source, but basically consistent with the highly official if internal *Mao wengao* documents (see item 1, above). To the extent they offer an opinion of the events concerned it is entirely consistent with the official orthodoxy. Fortunately at least three of the documents have been published in condensed form in recent years. Nevertheless, that mere detail could have been seen to be threatening is sad commentary indeed.

Deposit copies of these documents are available at the Menzies Library, the Australian National University, and the Fairbank Center Library at Harvard University.

BIBLIOGRAPHY

Chinese-Language Sources

(a) Books

Bo Yibo. *Ruogan zhongda juece yu shijian de huigu* [Reflections on Certain Major Decisions and Events]. Vol. 1, Beijing: Zhonggong zhongyang dangxiao chubanshe, 1991. Vol. 2, 1993.

Chen Xuewei. *Mao Zedong yu dangdai Zhongguo jingji* [Mao Zedong and China's Contemporary Economy]. Henan: Zhongyuan nongmin chubanshe, 1993.

Chen Yun yu Xin Zhongguo jingji jianshe [Chen Yun and New China's Economic Construction]. Beijing: Zhongyang wenxian chubanshe, 1991.

Cheng Hua. *Zhou Enlai he tade mishumen* [Zhou Enlai and his Secretaries]. Beijing: Zhongguo guangbo dianshi chubanshe, 1992.

Cheng Zhongyuan. *Zhang Wentian zhuan* [Biography of Zhang Wentian]. Beijing: Dangdai Zhongguo chubanshe, 1993.

Cong Jin. *1949-1989 nian de Zhongguo: Quzhe fazhan de suiye* [China 1949-1989: The Years of Circuitous Development]. Zhengzhou: Henan renmin chubanshe, 1989.

Dang de wenxian bianjibu [*The Party's Documents* editorial department], ed. *Gongheguo zouguode lu* [The Road Traveled by the People's Republic]. Beijing: Zhongyang wenxian chubanshe, 1991.

Deng Liqun. *Xiang Chen Yun Tongzhi xuexi zuo jingji gongzuo* [Learn Economic Work from Comrade Chen Yun]. Beijing: Zhonggong zhongyang dangxiao chubanshe, 1981.

Deng Zihui zhuan [Biography of Deng Zihui]. Beijing: Renmin chubanshe, 1996.

Dong Baochun. *Tan Zhenlin waizhuan* [Unofficial Biography of Tan Zhenlin]. Beijing: Zuojia chubanshe, 1992.

Dong Bian, Tan Deshan, and Zeng Zi, eds. *Mao Zedong he tade mishu Tian Jiaying* [Mao Zedong and His Secretary Tian Jiaying]. Beijing: Zhongyang wenxian chubanshe, 1990. Expanded edition, 1996.

Gai Jun. *Zhongguo Gongchandang bolan zhuangkuo de qishinian* [The CCP's Seventy Years of Large-Scale Surging Forward]. Beijing: Zhongguo qingnian chubanshe, 1991.

Guo Simin, ed. *Wo yan zhongde Chen Yun* [Chen Yun as I Saw Him]. Beijing: Zhonggong dangshi chubanshe, 1995.

_____ and Tian Yu, eds. *Wo yan zhongde Zhou Enlai* [Zhou Enlai as I Saw Him]. Shijiazhuang: Hebei renmin chubanshe, 1993.

Hu Sheng, ed. *Zhongguo Gongchandang qishinian* [The CCP's Seventy Years]. Beijing: Zhonggong dangshi chubanshe, 1991.

Huainian Zhou Enlai [In Memory of Zhou Enlai]. Beijing: Renmin chubanshe, 1986.

Huang Zheng. *Liu Shaoqi yisheng* [Life of Liu Shaoqi]. Beijing: Zhongyang wenxian chubanshe, 1995.

Huiyi Zhang Wentian [Remember Zhang Wentian]. Changsha: Hunan renmin chubanshe, 1985.

Jiang Weiqing. *Qishinian zhengcheng: Jiang Weiqing huiyilu* [Seventy Years' Journey: The Memoirs of Jiang Weiqing]. Nanjing: Jiangsu renmin chubanshe, 1996.

_____. *Tan Zhenlin zhuan* [Biography of Tan Zhenlin]. Hangzhou: Zhejiang renmin chubanshe, 1992.

Jin Chongji, ed. *Zhou Enlai zhuan* [Biography of Zhou Enlai]. 4 vols. Beijing: Zhongyang wenxian chubanshe, 1998.

Jin Ye, ed. *Huiyi Tan Zhenlin* [Remember Tan Zhenlin]. Hangzhou: Zhejiang renmin chubanshe, 1992.

Li Guang'an, Wang Guizhen, and Qin Ming, eds. *Jinian Li Fuchun* [Remember Li Fuchun]. Beijing: Zhongguo jihua chubanshe, 1990.

Li Ping. *Kaiguo Zongli Zhou Enlai* [Founding Premier Zhou Enlai]. Beijing: Zhonggong zhongyang dangxiao chubanshe, 1994.

Li Rui. *"Dayuejin" qinliji* [A Personal Historical Record of the "Great Leap Forward"]. Shanghai: Shanghai yuandong chubanshe, 1996.

_____. *Huainian nianpian* [Twenty Articles in Remembrance]. Beijing: Sanlian chubanshe, 1987.

_____. *Lushan huiyi shilu* [True Record of the Lushan Conference]. Beijing: Chunqiu chubanshe, 1989. 2nd revised edition, Zhengzhou: Henan renmin chubanshe, 1994.

Lin Yunhui, Fan Shouxin, and Zhang Gong. *1949-1989 nian de Zhongguo: Kaige xingjin de shiqi* [China 1949-1989: The Period of Triumph and Advance]. Zhengzhou: Henan renmin chubanshe, 1989.

Lin Zhijian, ed. *Xin Zhongguo yaoshi shuping* [Commentary on New China's Important Affairs]. Beijing: Zhonggong dangshi chubanshe, 1994.

Ling Chuanji, ed. *Tian Jiaying Jiashan diaocha yu renmin gongshe "liushi tiao" de zhiding* [Tian Jiaying's Jiashan Investigation and the Drafting of the 60 Articles on the People's Communes]. Beijing: Dongfang chubanshe, 1997.

Liu Zhende. *Wo wei Liu Shaoqi dang mishu* [I Was Liu Shaoqi's Secretary]. Beijing: Zhongyang wenxian chubanshe, 1994.

Mianhuai Mao Zedong [Cherish the Memory of Mao Zedong]. Vol. 1, Beijing: Zhongyang wenxian chubanshe, 1993.

Peng Cheng and Wang Fang. *Lushan 1959* [Lushan 1959]. Beijing: Jiefangjun chubanshe, 1988.

Peng Dehuai zhuan [Biography of Peng Dehuai]. Beijing: Dangdai Zhongguo chubanshe, 1993.

Quan Yanchi. *Zhongguo zuida baohuangpai — Tao Zhu fuchenlu* [China's Number One Royalist — The Rise and Fall of Tao Zhu]. Hong Kong: Tiandi tushu chubanshe, 1991. Hong Kong edition of book by PRC writer.

_____. *Zouxia shentande Zhou Enlai* [Zhou Enlai Down to Earth]. Taibei: Xinrui chubanshe, 1994. Taiwan edition of book by PRC writer.

_____ and Huang Linuo. *Tiandao — Zhou Hui yu Lushan huiyi* [Heaven's Way — Zhou Hui and the Lushan Conference]. Guangzhou: Guangdong lüyou chubanshe, 1997.

Ruan Ming. *Zhonggong renwu lun* [Essays on CCP Personalities]. New Jersey: Global Publishing Co., 1993. Book by exiled PRC official.

Shi Zhongquan. *Mao Zedong de jianxin kaituo* [Mao Zedong's Arduous Pioneering]. Beijing: Zhonggong dangshi ziliao chubanshe, 1990.

_____. *Zhou Enlai de zhuoyue fengxian* [Zhou Enlai's Brilliant Commitment]. Beijing: Zhonggong zhongyang dangxiao chubanshe, 1993.

Sun Yeli and Xiong Lianghua. *Gongheguo jingji fengyun zhongde Chen Yun* [Chen Yun in the Storms of the Republic's Economy]. Beijing: Zhongyang wenxian chubanshe, 1996.

Tao Lujia. *Mao Zhuxi jiao women dang shengwei shuji* [Chairman Mao Teaches Us Provincial Secretaries]. Beijing: Zhongyang wenxian chubanshe, 1996.

_____. *Yige shengwei shuji huiyi Mao Zhuxi* [A Provincial Party Secretary Remembers Chairman Mao]. Taiyuan: Shanxi renmin chubanshe, 1993.

Tong Xiaopeng. *Fengyu sishinian (dierbu)* [Forty Years of Trials and Hardships (second part)]. Beijing: Zhongyang wenxian chubanshe, 1996.

Wang Lixin. *Anhui "dabaogan" shimo — 1961, 1978* [Anhui's "Big Responsibility (System)" from Beginning to End — 1961, 1978]. Beijing: Kunlun chubanshe, 1989.

Weida de renmin gongpu — huainian Li Xiannian Tongzhi [A Great Public Servant of the People — In Memory of Comrade Li Xiannian]. Beijing: Zhongyang wenxian chubanshe, 1993.

Women de Zhou Zongli [Our Premier Zhou]. Beijing: Zhongyang wenxian chubanshe, 1990.

Wu Lengxi. *Yi Mao Zhuxi — Wo jinsheng jingli ruogan zhongda lishi shijian pianduan* [Remembering Chairman Mao — Fragments of My Personal Experience with Certain Major Historical Events]. Beijing: Xinhua chubanshe, 1995.

Xie Chuntao. *Dayuejin kuanglan* [Raging Waves of the Great Leap Forward]. Henan: Henan renmin chubanshe, 1990.

_____. *Lushan fengyun: 1959 nian Lushan huiyi jianshi* [Storm at Lushan: A Simplified History of the 1959 Lushan Conference]. Beijing: Zhongguo qingnian chubanshe, 1996.

Xiong Huayuan and Liao Xinwen. *Zhou Enlai Zongli shengya* [Premier Zhou Enlai's Career]. Beijing: Renmin chubanshe, 1997.

Xu Zehao. *Wang Jiaxiang zhuan* [Biography of Wang Jiaxiang]. Beijing: Dangdai Zhongguo chubanshe, 1996.

Xue Muqiao. *Xue Muqiao huiyilu* [Memoirs of Xue Muqiao]. Tianjin: Tianjin renmin chubanshe, 1996.

Yang Shangkun *et al. Wo suo zhidao de Hu Qiaomu* [The Hu Qiaomu I Knew]. Beijing: Dangdai Zhongguo chubanshe, 1997.

Yang Xianzhen zhuan [Biography of Yang Xianzhen]. Beijing: Zhonggong dangshi chubanshe, 1996.

Ye Yonglie. *Chen Yun quanzhuan* [Complete Biography of Chen Yun]. Taibei: Zhouzhi wenhua chubanshe, 1995. Taiwan edition of book by PRC writer.

Zhang Peisen, ed. *Zhang Wentian yanjiu wenji* [Collected Research on Zhang Wentian]. Beijing: Zhonggong dangshi ziliao chubanshe, 1990.

Zheng Qian and Han Gang. *Mao Zedong zhi lu: wannian suiyue* [Mao Zedong's Road: The Last Years]. Beijing: Zhongguo qingnian chubanshe, 1993.

Zheng Xiaofeng and Shu Ling. *Tao Zhu zhuan* [Biography of Tao Zhu]. Beijing: Zhongguo qingnian chubanshe, 1992.

Zhou Enlai yanjiu xueshu taolunhui lunwenji [Collected Conference Papers on the Study of Zhou Enlai]. Beijing: Zhongyang wenxian chubanshe, 1988.

Zhou Weiren. *Jia Tuofu zhuan* [Biography of Jia Tuofu]. Beijing: Zhonggong dangshi chubanshe, 1993.

Zhou Xiaozhou zhuan [Biography of Zhou Xiaozhou]. Changsha: Hunan renmin chubanshe, 1985.

(b) Major Party History Journals

Bainianchao [The Hundred Years' Tide]. Beijing: Zhonggong zhongyang dangshi yanjiushi, 1997- .

Dang de wenxian [The Party's Documents]. Beijing: Zhongyang wenxian chubanshe, 1988- .

Dangdai Zhongguoshi yanjiu [Research on Contemporary Chinese History]. Beijing: Dangdai Zhongguo chubanshe, 1994- .

Dangshi tongxun [Party History Bulletin]. Beijing: Zhongyang dangshi yanjiushi, 1983-87.

Dangshi wenhui [Collected Articles on Party History]. Taiyuan: Zhonggong Shanxi shengwei dangshi yanjiushi, 1985- .

Dangshi yanjiu [Research on Party History]. Beijing: Zhonggong zhongyang dangxiao chubanshe, 1980-87.

Dangshi yanjiu ziliao [Research Materials on Party History]. Beijing: Zhongguo geming bowuguan, 1980- .

Renwu [Personalities]. Beijing: Renmin chubanshe, 1980- .

Wenxian he yanjiu [Documents and Research]. Beijing: Renmin chubanshe, 1982-87.

Zhonggong dangshi tongxun [CCP History Bulletin]. Beijing: Zhonggong dangshi chubanshe, 1989-95.

Zhonggong dangshi yanjiu [Research on CCP History]. Beijing: Zhonggong dangshi chubanshe, 1988- .

Zhonggong dangshi ziliao [Materials on CCP History]. Beijing: Zhonggong dangshi ziliao chubanshe, 1981- .

(c) Articles

Bo Yibo. "Chongjing he huainian" [Respect and Rememberance]. *Hongqi* [Red Flag], no. 13 (1981).

Chen Guodong. "Chen Guodong tan Zhou Enlai yu liangshi gongzuo" [Chen Guodong Discusses Zhou Enlai and Grain Work]. *Wenxian he yanjiu* [Documents and Research], no. 3 (1984).

Chen Pixian. "Gungun pujiangshui, nansu sinianqing" [Even the Endless Torrent of the Huangpu River Cannot Convey My Feelings (toward Premier Zhou)]. In *Women de Zhou Zongli* [Our Premier Zhou]. Beijing: Zhongyang wenxian chubanshe, 1990.

Chen Pu. "Mao Zedong wushi niandai houqi de tansuo silu he ta du jibenshu de qingxing" [Exploring Mao Zedong's Thinking in the Later Period of the 1950s and the Circumstances of His Reading of Several Books]. Part 1, *Dang de wenxian* [The Party's Documents], no. 4 (1993). Part 2, *Dang de wenxian* [The Party's Documents], no. 5 (1993).

Chen Xuewei. "50 niandai guanyu jingji jianshe fangzhen de lunzheng — shuping 1956 nian jingji jianshe zhongde maojin yu fanmaojin, he dui 1956 nian fanmaojin de pipan" [The Debate in the 1950s about the Guiding Principles of Economic Construction — An Account of the Rash Advance and Anti-Rash Advance in Economic Construction in 1956, and of the Criticism of the Anti-Rash Advance of 1956]. *Dangshi wenhui* [Collected Articles on Party History], no. 2 (1989).

Chen Zhiling. "Li Fuchun" [Li Fuchun]. In *Zhonggong dangshi renwu zhuan* [Biographies of Personalities in CCP History], edited by Hu Hua. Vol. 44, Xi'an: Shaanxi renmin chubanshe, 1990.

Dong Zhikai. "Mao Zedong zai 'bada' qian-hou gaige jingji guanli tizhi de shexiang" [Mao Zedong's Conceptions of the Reform of Economic Management Structure Before and After the Eighth Party Congress]. *Dangdai Zhongguoshi yanjiu* [Research on Contemporary Chinese History], no. 1 (1994).

Fan Ruoyu. "Zai Zhou Enlai shenbian de rizili" [Days by the Side of Zhou Enlai]. *Renwu* [Personalities], no. 1 (1986).

Fang Liubi. "Zhou Enlai zai guomin jingji tiaozheng shiqi wei liangshi gongzuo xinqin caolao" [Zhou Enlai's Toil for Grain Work During the Period of National Economic Adjustment]. *Wenxian he yanjiu*

[Documents and Research], no.3 (1984).

Gao Lu. "Chen Yun yu dang de bada qian-hou de jingji tizhi gaige juece" [Chen Yun and Economic Structure Reform Policy Making Before and After the Party's Eighth Congress]. *Dang de wenxian* [The Party's Documents], no. 6 (1989).

Gu Zhuoxin, An Zhiwen, Li Renjun, Gu Ming, and Fang Weizhong. "Li Fuchun Tongzhi dui jingji jihua gongzuo de zhongda gongxian" [Comrade Li Fuchun's Great Contributions in Economic Planning Work]. In *Jinian Li Fuchun* [Remember Li Fuchun], edited by Li Guang'an, Wang Guizhen, and Qin Ming. Beijing: Zhongguo jihua chubanshe, 1990.

Han Gang. "1958 nian Beidaihe huiyi" [The 1958 Beidaihe Conference]. *Zhonggong dangshi ziliao* [Materials on CCP History], no. 47 (1993).

Jiang Kunchi. "60 niandaichu Zeng Xisheng zai Anhui tuixing zerentian shimo" [Zeng Xisheng's Implementation of Responsibility Fields in Anhui during the Early 1960s from Beginning to End]. *Dangdai Zhongguoshi yanjiu* [Research on Contemporary Chinese History], no. 1 (1994).

———. "Zeng Xisheng 'zuo' hou jiu 'zuo'" [Zeng Xisheng from "Leftism" to Correcting "Leftism"]. *Renwu* [Personalities], no. 5 (1997).

Jiang Yingguang and Zhang Decheng. "Yijiuwuliu nian liuyue *Renmin ribao* 'fanmaojin' de shelun yao chongxin pinglun" [We Must Discuss Anew the 1956 *People's Daily* "Opposing Rash Advance" Editorial]. *Dangshi yanjiu* [Research on Party History], no. 6 (1980).

Jiang Yizhen. "Tan Zhenlin zai nongye zhanxian de gongji" [Tan Zhenlin's Achievements on the Agricultural Front]. In *Huiyi Tan Zhenlin* [Remember Tan Zhenlin], edited by Jin Ye. Hangzhou: Zhejiang renmin chubanshe, 1992.

Li Chengrui. "'Dayuejin' yinqi de renkou biandong" [Population Changes Produced by the "Great Leap Forward"]. *Zhonggong dangshi yanjiu* [Research on CCP History], no. 2 (1997).

Li Gui. "Xiao Hua" [Xiao Hua]. In *Zhonggong dangshi renwu zhuan* [Biographies of Personalities in CCP History], edited by Hu Hua. Vol. 45, Xi'an: Shaanxi renmin chubanshe, 1990.

Li Ping. "Zhou Enlai" [Zhou Enlai]. In *Zhonggong dangshi renwu zhuan* [Biographies of Personalities in CCP History], edited by Hu Hua. Vol. 49, Xi'an: Shaanxi renmin chubanshe, 1991.

Li Rui. "'Dayuejin' qijian wo gei Mao Zedong de sanzi shangshu" [The Three Letters I Gave Mao Zedong during the "Great Leap Forward"]. *Bainianchao* [The Hundred Years' Tide], no. 4 (1997).

———. "Zhonggong zhongyang Wuchang huiyi he bajie liuzhong quanhui" [The CCP Central Committee's Wuchang Conference and the Sixth Plenum of the Eighth Central Committee]. *Zhonggong dangshi ziliao* [Materials on CCP History], no. 61 (1997).

Liao Jili. "Luoshi 1959 nian gangtie zhibiao wenti de huigu" [Recalling the Issue of Implementing the 1959 Steel and Iron Targets]. In *Chen Yun yu Xin Zhongguo jingji jianshe* [Chen Yun and New China's Economic Construction]. Beijing: Zhongyang wenxian chubanshe, 1991.

Liu Wusheng. "Zong diyici Zhengzhou huiyi dao Lushan huiyi qianqi dui Mao Zedong jiu 'zuo' de lishi kaocha" [A Historical Investigation of Mao Zedong's Rectifying the "Left" from the First Zhengzhou Conference to the Early Stage of the Lushan Conference]. *Zhonggong dangshi ziliao* [Materials on CCP History], no. 48 (1993).

Liu Yishun. "60 niandaichu Anhui nongcun zerentian shimo" [The Early 1960s Anhui Village Responsibility Fields from Beginning to End]. *Dangshi yanjiu ziliao* [Research Materials on Party History], no. 8 (1994).

_____. "Mao Zedong zai Anhui tuiguang zerentian de qianqian houhou" [Mao Zedong Before and After Anhui's Promotion of Responsibility Fields]. *Zhonggong dangshi ziliao* [Materials on CCP History], no. 54 (1995).

Liu Zihou. "Huiyi Mao Zhuxi zai Hebei de jige pianduan" [Some Recollections of Chairman Mao in Hebei]. In *Mianhuai Mao Zedong* [Cherish the Memory of Mao Zedong]. Vol. 1, Beijing: Zhongyang wenxian chubanshe, 1993.

Ma Zhisun. "Zhou Enlai de wushi jingshen yu fanmaojin, fan 'zuo' qing" [Zhou Enlai's Spirit of Dealing with Concrete Work and Opposing Rash Advance, Opposing "Left" Tendencies]. *Dang de wenxian* [The Party's Documents], no. 5 (1992).

Pang Xianzhi. "Mao Zedong he tade mishu Tian Jiaying" [Mao Zedong and His Secretary Tian Jiaying]. In Dong Bian, Tan Deshan, and Zeng Zi, eds. *Mao Zedong he tade mishu Tian Jiaying* [Mao Zedong and His Secretary Tian Jiaying]. Beijing: Zhongyang wenxian chubanshe, 1990.

Pei Di. "1958 nian Nanning huiyi shuping" [An Account of the 1958 Nanning Conference]. *Dangshi tongxun* [Party History Bulletin], no. 12 (1987).

Qiang Yuangan and Chen Xuewei. "Chongping yijiuwuliu nian de 'fanmaojin'" [Again Reviewing "Opposing Rash Advance" in 1956]. *Dangshi yanjiu* [Research on Party History], no. 6 (1980).

Rong Zihe. "Zhou Zongli shi zenyang zhua caizheng gongzuo de" [How Premier Zhou Grasped Financial Work]. In *Women de Zhou Zongli* [Our Premier Zhou]. Beijing: Zhongyang wenxian chubanshe, 1990.

Shi Wei. "Maojin, fanmaojin, fan fanmaojin" [Rash Advance, Opposing Rash Advance, and Opposing Opposing Rash Advance]. *Dang de wenxian* [The Party's Documents], no. 2 (1990). Republished in *Gongheguo zouguode lu* [The Road Traveled by the People's Republic], edited by *Dang de wenxian* bianjibu [*The Party's Documents* editorial department]. Beijing: Zhongyang wenxian chubanshe, 1991.

Shi Zhongquan. "Dierci lishixing feiyue de qianzouqu — Zhongguo Gongchandang zai 1956 qian-hou dui shehuizhuyi jianshe daolu tansuo" [Prelude to the Second Historical Leap — The CCP's Explorations concerning the Road of Socialist Construction Before and After 1956]. *Dang de wenxian* [The Party's Documents], no. 6 (1988).

Sun Gang and Wang Mingjian. "Mao Zedong guanyu ba dang de gongzuo zhongdian zhuandao jishu geming he jianshe shanglai de sixiang de kaocha" [Observations on Mao Zedong's Thinking concerning Changing the Focus of Party Work to the Technological Revolution and Socialist Construction]. *Dang de wenxian* [The Party's Documents], no. 6 (1991).

Tan Qilong "Jianchi shishi qiu shi shenru diaocha yanjiu" [Uphold Seeking Truth From Facts, Immerse Oneself in Investigation and Study]. In *Mianhuai Mao Zedong* [Cherish the Memory of Mao Zedong]. Vol. 1, Beijing: Zhongyang wenxian chubanshe, 1993.

Wang Heshou and Lü Dong. "Mao Zedong Tongzhi dui woguo gangtie gongye de zhanlüe zhidao" [Comrade Mao Zedong's Strategic Guidance of Our Country's Iron and Steel Work]. In *Mianhuai Mao Zedong* [Cherish the Memory of Mao Zedong]. Vol. 1, Beijing: Zhongyang wenxian chubanshe, 1993.

Wang Heshou, Lü Dong, and Yuan Baohua. "Huiyi Chen Yun Tongzhi zai 'erwu' shiqi de jige guanjian shike" [Remembering Comrade Chen Yun at Several Critical Moments during the Second Five-Year Plan]. In *Chen Yun yu Xin Zhongguo jingji jianshe* [Chen Yun and New China's Economic Construction]. Beijing: Zhongyang wenxian chubanshe, 1991. Also in *Wo yan zhongde Chen Yun* [Chen Yun as I Saw Him], edited by Guo Simin. Beijing: Zhonggong dangshi chubanshe, 1995.

Wu Lengxi. "Tong Jiaying gongshi de rizi" [My Time Working Alongside Jiaying]. In *Mao Zedong he tade mishu Tian Jiaying (zengdingben)* [Mao Zedong and His Secretary Tian Jiaying (Expanded Edition)], edited by Dong Bian, Tan Deshan, and Zeng Zi. Beijing: Zhongyang wenxian chubanshe, 1996.

Wu Qungan. "Shilun woguo diyige wunian jianshe jihua de jige wenti" [A Preliminary Assessment of Several Issues about Our Country's First Five-Year Construction Plan]. In *Gongheguo zouguode lu* [The Road Traveled by the People's Republic], edited by *Dang de wenxian* bianjibu [*The Party's Documents* editorial department]. Beijing: Zhongyang wenxian chubanshe, 1991.

————. "Zhou Enlai yu Xin Zhongguo jingji jianshe" [Zhou Enlai and New China's Economic Construction]. *Dang de wenxian* [The Party's Documents], no. 4 (1993).

Wu Zhihong. "Zhou Enlai guanyu zhongyang yu difang guanxi sixiang lunxi" [An Analysis of Zhou Enlai's Thinking concerning the Relationship between the Center and the Localities]. *Dang de wenxian* [The Party's Documents], no. 1 (1993).

Xiao Yang. "Yi Lushan huiyi qian-hou de Zhang Wentian Tongzhi"

[Remember Comrade Zhang Wentian Before and After the Lushan Conference]. In *Huiyi Zhang Wentian* [Remember Zhang Wentian]. Changsha: Hunan renmin chubanshe, 1985.

Xiong Huayuan. "Guanyu ji fanbaoshou you fanmaojin de fangzhen tichu de shijian" [Concerning the Timing of the Raising of the Guiding Policy of Both Opposing Conservatism and Opposing Rash Advance]. *Dang de wenxian* [The Party's Documents], no. 4 (1992).

―――――. "Lun Zhou Enlai zai fanmaojin zhongde tansuo" [Explorations concerning Zhou Enlai during Opposing Rash Advance]. *Dang de wenxian* [The Party's Documents], no. 2 (1988).

―――――. "Zai xiandaihua jianshe zhongde fenqi" [Differences of Opinion concerning Modernizing Construction]. In *Xin Zhongguo yaoshi shuping* [Commentary on New China's Important Affairs], edited by Lin Zhijian. Beijing: Zhonggong dangshi chubanshe, 1994.

Xu Qingqing and Wang Diming. "Mao Zedong lingdaole bada wenjian de qicao gongzuo" [Mao Zedong Led the Drafting Work of the Eighth Party Congress Documents]. *Zhonggong dangshi yanjiu* [Research on CCP History], no. 2 (1990).

Xue Muqiao. "Jiechu de jingji gongzuo lingdaozhe — Chen Yun Tongzhi" [An Outstanding Leader of Economic Work — Comrade Chen Yun]. In *Chen Yun yu Xin Zhongguo jingji jianshe* [Chen Yun and New China's Economic Construction]. Beijing: Zhongyang wenxian chubanshe, 1991.

Yang Shaoqiao. "Wei minshi jiejin xinli" [Strenuous Efforts for the People's Food]. In *Weida de renmin gongpu — huainian Li Xiannian Tongzhi* [A Great Public Servant of the People — In Memory of Comrade Li Xiannian]. Beijing: Zhongyang wenxian chubanshe, 1993.

――――― and Zhao Fasheng. "Liangshi diaodu de zong zhihui" [The General Director of Grain Transfers]. In *Wo yan zhongde Zhou Enlai* [Zhou Enlai as I Saw Him], edited by Guo Simin and Tian Yu. Shijiazhuang: Hebei renmin chubanshe, 1993.

Yu Jianting. "Chen Yun yu dierge wunian jihua qijian de jingji tiaozheng" [Chen Yun and the Economic Readjustment During the Second Five-Year Plan]. In *Chen Yun yu Xin Zhongguo jingji jianshe* [Chen Yun and New China's Economic Construction]. Beijing: Zhongyang wenxian chubanshe, 1991.

Yu Zhan. "Liushi niandaichu woguo bufen diqu nongcun shixing baochan daohu shengchan zerenzhi de shijian yu jingyan" [The Practice and Experience of Some Rural Areas of Our Country in the Early 1960s in Implementing Responsibility Systems of Contracting Production to Individual Households]. *Dang de wenxian* [The Party's Documents], no. 4 (1992).

Zhang Peisen. "Zhang Wentian Lushan fayan sixiang de youlai he fazhan" [The Origins and Development of the Thinking in Zhang Wentian's Lushan Speeches]. In *Zhang Wentian yanjiu wenji* [Collected Research on Zhang Wentian], edited by Zhang Peisen. Beijing; Zhonggong dangshi ziliao chubanshe, 1990.

Zhang Qiuyun and Zheng Shulan. "Yipian fanmaojin shelun de youlai" [The Origins of an Editorial Opposing Rash Advance]. *Dang de wenxian* [The Party's Documents], no. 2 (1990).

Zheng Geheng *et al.* "Jia Tuofu" [Jia Tuofu]. In *Zhonggong dangshi renwu zhuan* [Biographies of Personalities in CCP History], edited by Hu Hua. Vol. 46, Xi'an: Shaanxi renmin chubanshe, 1991.

Zheng Xiaofeng and Shu Ling. "Tao Zhu" [Tao Zhu]. In *Zhonggong dangshi renwu zhuan* [Biographies of Personalities in CCP History], edited by Hu Hua. Vol. 43, Xi'an: Shaanxi renmin chubanshe, 1990.

Zhonggong Youxian dangshi bangongshi [Party History Office of the You County Party Committee]. "Yi jiao liu jiaxiang" [A Legacy of Wisdom for the Home Town]. In *Huiyi Tan Zhenlin* [Remember Tan Zhenlin], edited by Jin Ye. Hangzhou: Zhejiang renmin chubanshe, 1992.

Zhou Cheng'en. "Shehuizhuyi jianshe zongluxian shuping" [A Review of the General Line for Socialist Construction]. *Dang de wenxian* [The Party's Documents], no. 2 (1992).

"*Zhou Enlai zhuan* xuanzhai: cong bajie sanzhong quanhui dao bada erci huiyi" [Selections from the *Biography of Zhou Enlai*: From the Third Plenum to the Second Session of the Eighth Congress]. *Bainianchao* [The Hundred Years' Tide], no. 6 (1997).

Zhou Taihe. "Chen Yun Tongzhi sixia nongcun diaocha de qian-hou" [Before and After Comrade Chen Yun's Four Rural Investigations]. In *Chen Yun yu Xin Zhongguo jingji jianshe* [Chen Yun and New China's Economic Construction]. Beijing: Zhongyang wenxian chubanshe, 1991.

(d) Chronologies, Documentary Collections, Personnel Directories, etc. (excluding Red Guard Publications)

Bo Yibo wenxuan (1937-1992 nian) [Selected Works of Bo Yibo, 1937-1992]. Beijing: Renmin chubanshe, 1992.

Chen Yun wenxuan (1956-1985 nian) [Selected Works of Chen Yun, 1956-1985]. Beijing: Renmin chubanshe, 1986.

Deng Xiaoping wenxuan (1938-1965 nian) [Selected Works of Deng Xiaoping, 1938-1965]. Beijing: Renmin chubanshe, 1989.

Deng Zihui wenji [Collected Works of Deng Zihui]. Beijing: Renmin chubanshe, 1996.

"Guanyu fanmaojin de wenxian sipian (1956 nian siyue — qiyue)" [Four Documents concerning Opposing Rash Advance, April-July 1956]. *Dang de wenxian* [The Party's Documents], no. 2 (1990).

Guanyu jianguo yilai dang de ruogan lishi wenti de jueyi zhuyiben (xiuding) [Revised Notes on the Resolution on Certain Questions in the History of Our Party since the Founding of the State], compiled by Zhonggong zhongyang wenxian yanjiushi [CCP Central Documents Research Office]. Beijing: Renmin chubanshe, 1985.

"Guanyu shehuizhuyi jianshe zongluxian de lunshu xuanzai (yijiuwuliu nian yiyue — yijiuliuyi nian yiyue)" [Selections concerning the General Line for Socialist Construction, January 1956-January 1961]. *Dang de wenxian* [The Party's Documents], no. 2 (1992).

He Long nianpu [Chronicle of He Long]. Beijing: Zhonggong zhongyang dangxiao chubanshe, 1988.

Jianguo yilai Mao Zedong wengao [Mao Zedong's Manuscripts since the Founding of the State]. 13 vols. (September 1949-July 1976). Beijing: Zhongyang wenxian chubanshe, 1987-98.

Li Fuchun xuanji [Selected Works of Li Fuchun]. Beijing: Zhongguo jihua chubanshe, 1992.

Li Xiannian lun caizheng jinrong maoyi (1950-1991) [Li Xiannian on Finance, Banking, and Trade, 1950-1991]. Vol. 1, Beijing: Zhongguo caizheng jingji chubanshe, 1992.

Li Xiannian wenxuan (1935-1988 nian) [Selected Works of Li Xiannian, 1935-1988]. Beijing: Renmin chubanshe, 1989.

Lijie Zhonggong zhongyang weiyuan renmin cidian [Biographic Dictionary of Previous Central Committee Members], edited by Liu Jintian and Shen Xueming. Beijing: Zhonggong dangshi chubanshe, 1992.

"Liu Shaoqi, Deng Xiaoping, Deng Zihui deng guanyu nongye shengchan zerenzhi de lunshu xuanzai (yijiuliuyi nian wuyue — yijiuliuer nian qiyue)" [Selections from Liu Shaoqi, Deng Xiaoping, Deng Zihui, etc. concerning Agricultural Responsibility Systems, May 1961-July 1962]. *Dang de wenxian* [The Party's Documents], no. 4 (1992).

Liu Shaoqi nianpu 1898-1969 [Chronicle of Liu Shaoqi, 1898-1969], edited by Zhonggong zhongyang wenxian yanjiushi [CCP Central Documents Research Office]. 2 vols., Beijing: Zhongyang wenxian chubanshe, 1996.

Liu Shaoqi xuanji [Selected Works of Liu Shaoqi]. Vol. 2, Beijing: Renmin chubanshe, 1985.

Mao Zedong dacidian [Dictionary of Mao Zedong], edited by He Ping. Beijing: Zhongguo guoji guangbo chubanshe, 1992.

Mao Zedong jingji nianpu [Chronicle of Mao Zedong on the Economy], edited by Gu Longsheng. Beijing: Zhonggong zhongyang dangxiao chubanshe, 1993.

Mao Zedong xuanji [Selected Works of Mao Zedong]. Vol. V, Beijing: Renmin chubanshe, 1977.

Nongye jitihua zhongyao wenjian huibian [Compendium of Important Documents on Agricultural Collectivization], edited by Guojia Nongye Weiyuanhui Bangongting [State Agricultural Commission General Office]. 2 vols., Beijing: Zhonggong zhongyang dangxiao chubanshe, 1981.

Peng Dehuai zishu [Peng Dehuai's Self-statement]. Beijing: Renmin chubanshe, 1981.

Xin Zhongguo biannianshi [Chronological History of New China], edited by Liao Gailong. Beijing: Renmin chubanshe, 1989.

Yejin gongye de zuji: Wang Heshou wenji [The Tracks of the Metallurgical Industry: The Collected Works of Wang Heshou], edited by Zhongguo yejin zhigong sixiang zhengzhi gongzuo yanjiu hui [The Chinese Metallurgical Workers Ideological and Political Work Research Society]. Beijing: Sanlian shudian, 1990.

"Yijiuwuba nian Mao Zedong guanyu yao ba dang he guojia de gongzuo zhongdian zhuandao jishu geming he shehuizhuyi jianshe shanglai de lunshu xuanzai (yijiuwuba nian yiyue — sanyue)" [Selections from Mao Zedong in 1958 Expounding on the Need to Change the Focus of Party and State Work to the Technological Revolution and Socialist Construction, January-March 1958]. *Dang de wenxian* [The Party's Documents], no. 6 (1991).

"Yijiuwuliu nian qian-hou Mao Zedong deng tongzhi tansuo shehuizhuyi jianshe daolu wenti de wenxian wupian (yijiuwuliu nian siyue ershibari — yijiuwuqi nian siyue liuri" [Five Documents by Mao Zedong and Other Comrades Before and After 1956 Exploring Questions of the Path of Socialist Construction, April 28, 1956-April 6, 1957]. *Dang de wenxian* [The Party's Documents], no. 6 (1988).

Zhang Wentian Lushan huiyi fayan [Zhang Wentian's Lushan Conference Speeches]. Beijing: Beijing chubanshe, 1990.

Zhang Wentian xuanji [Selected Works of Zhang Wentian]. Beijing: Renmin chubanshe, 1985.

Zhonggong dangshi dashi nianbiao [Chronology of Events in CCP History], compiled by Zhonggong zhongyang dangshi yanjiushi [CCP Central Party History Research Office]. Beijing: Renmin chubanshe, 1987.

Zhonggong dangshi jiaoxue cankao ziliao [CCP History Teaching Reference Materials]. Vols. 20-24 (January 1953-May 1966). N.p.: Zhongguo Jiefangjun Guofang Daxue dangshi dangjian zhenggong jiaoyanshi, April-July 1986.

Zhonggong dangshi renwu zhuan [Biographies of Personalities in CCP History], Vols. 1-50, edited by Hu Hua. Xi'an: Shaanxi renmin chubanshe, 1980-91. Vols. 51-60, edited by Wang Qi and Chen Zhiling. Xi'an: Shaanxi renmin chubanshe, 1994-96.

Zhonggong dangshi wenxian xuanbian: shehuizhuyi geming he jianshe shiqi [Selected Documents on CCP History: The Period of Socialist Revolution and Construction], edited by Zhonggong zhongyang dangxiao jiaocai shending weiyuanhui [CCP Central Party School Teaching Materials Approval Committee]. Beijing: Zhonggong zhongyang dangxiao chubanshe, 1992.

Zhongguo Gongchandang huiyi gaiyao [Outline of CCP Meetings], edited by Jiang Huaxuan *et al.* Shenyang: Shenyang chubanshe, 1991.

Zhongguo Gongchandang lici zhongyao huiyiji (xia) [Collected Important Meetings of the CCP (vol. 2)], edited by Zhonggong zhongyang dangxiao jiaoyanshi ziliaozu [CCP Central Party School Teaching and Research Office Materials Group]. Shanghai: Shanghai renmin chubanshe, 1983.

Zhongguo Gongchandang lishi dashiji (1919.5-1987.12) [History of the Chinese Communist Party: A Chronology of Events, May 1919-December 1987], compiled by Zhonggong zhongyang dangshi yanjiushi [CCP Central Party History Research Office]. Beijing: Renmin chubanshe, 1989.

Zhongguo Gongchandang zhizheng sishinian (1949-1989) [The CCP's Forty Years in Power, 1949-1989], edited by Ma Qibin, Chen Wenbin, Lin Yunhui, Cong Jin, Wang Nianyi, Zhang Tianrong, and Bu Weihua. 1st edition, Beijing: Zhonggong dangshi ziliao chubanshe, 1989. 2nd expanded edition, Beijing: Zhonggong dangshi chubanshe, 1991.

Zhongguo Gongchandang zuzhi gongzuo dashiji [Chronology of CCP Organizational Work], edited by Zhao Bo *et al*. Beijing: Zhongguo guoji guangbo chubanshe, 1991.

Zhongguo Gongchandang zuzhishi ziliao huibian [Compilation of Materials on CCP Organizational History], edited by Wang Jianying. Beijing: Hongqi chubanshe, 1983. 2nd revised edition, from the 1st to 14th Party Congresses, Beijing: Zhonggong zhongyang dangxiao chubanshe, 1995.

Zhonghuarenmingongheguo fengyun shilu, edited by Su Donghai. [True Record of the PRC's Storms]. Vol. 1, Hebei: Hebei renmin chubanshe, 1994.

Zhonghuarenmingongheguo guomin jingji he shehui fazhan jihua dashi jiyao 1949-1985 [Outline of Events in PRC National Economic and Social Development 1949-1985], edited by "Dangdai Zhongguo de jihua gongzuo" bangongshi [General Office of "Contemporary China Planning Work"]. Beijing: Hongqi chubanshe, 1987.

Zhonghuaremingongheguo guoshi quanjian (dierjuan) (1954-1959) [An Encyclopedia of the National History of the PRC, vol. 2, 1954-1959]. No publication data.

Zhonghuarenmingongheguo jingji dashiji (1949-1980 nian) [Chronology of Economic Events in the PRC, 1949-1980], edited by Fang Weizhong. Beijing: Zhongguo shehui kexue chubanshe, 1984.

Zhonghuarenmingongheguo jingji guanli dashiji [Chronology of Events in Economic Administration in the PRC], edited by "Dangdai Zhongguo de jingji guanli" bianjibu ["Contemporary China Economic Administration" Editorial Department]. Beijing: Zhongguo jingji chubanshe, 1986.

Zhonghuarenmingongheguo jingji zhuanti dashiji, 1949-1965 [Chronology of PRC Special Economic Topics, 1949-1965], edited by Zhao Desheng. Henan: Henan renmin chubanshe, 1989.

Zhonghuarenmingongheguo lishi changbian [PRC History Compendium], edited by Liu Shao. Vol. 2, Nanning: Guangxi renmin chubanshe, 1994.

Zhonghuarenmingongheguo shilu [True Record of the PRC]. *Jueqi yu fendou — Gongheguo dansheng zhichu, 1953-1956* [The Rising (Nation) and Marching Forward — The Early Years of the Republic]. Vol. 1, part 2, edited by Liu Guoxin. Changchun: Jilin renmin chubanshe, 1994.

_____. *Quzhe yu fazhan — tansuo daolu de jianxin* [Complications and Development — Hardships on the Path of Exploration]. Vol. 2, part 1, edited by Li Chen. Changchun: Jilin renmin chubanshe, 1994.

Zhonghuarenmingongheguo zhiguan zhi [Directory of Officials in the PRC], compiled by He Husheng *et al.* Beijing: Zhongguo shehui chubanshe, 1993.

"Zhou Enlai fanmaojin wenxian wupian" [Five Zhou Enlai Documents on Opposing Rash Advance]. *Dang de wenxian* [The Party's Documents], no. 2 (1988).

Zhou Enlai jingji wenxuan [Selected Works of Zhou Enlai on the Economy], compiled by Zhonggong zhongyang wenxian yanjiushi [CCP Central Documents Research Office]. Beijing: Zhongyang wenxian chubanshe, 1993.

Zhou Enlai nianpu 1949-1976 [Chronicle of Zhou Enlai, 1949-1976], edited by Zhonggong zhongyang wenxian yanjiushi [CCP Central Documents Research Office]. 3 vols., Beijing: Zhongyang wenxian chubanshe, 1997.

Zhou Enlai xuanji [Selected Works of Zhou Enlai]. Vol. 2, Beijing: Renmin chubanshe, 1984.

Zhou Zongli shengping dashiji [Chronicle of Premier Zhou's Life], edited by Huai En. Chengdu: Sichuan renmin chubanshe, 1986.

Zhu De nianpu [Chronicle of Zhu De], edited by Zhonggong zhongyang wenxian yanjiushi. Beijing: Renmin chubanshe, 1986.

(e) Speeches and Reports Not Included in the above Collections

Bo Yibo. "Zai Guowuyuan changwei huiyi shang de fayan" [Speech at the Meeting of the State Council Standing Committee] (June 5, 1956). In *Gongheguo zouguode lu* [The Road Traveled by the People's Republic], edited by *Dang de wenxian* bianjibu [*The Party's Documents* editorial department]. Beijing: Zhongyang wenxian chubanshe, 1991.

"Bo Yibo Fuzongli tan zai jiben jianshe gongzuo zhong ruhe jinxing zhengfeng" [Vice Premier Bo Yibo Talks on How to Conduct Rectification in Capital Construction Work]. *Xinhua banyuekan* [New China Semi-Monthly], no. 11 (1957).

"Bo Yibo xiang Tianjinshi ganbu baogao bianzhi 1958 nian jihua kongzhi shuzi wenti" [Bo Yibo Reports to Tianjin Municipal Cadres on the

Control Figures Drafted for the 1958 Annual Plan]. *Xinhua banyuekan* [New China Semi-Monthly], no. 17 (1957).

"Dierge wunian jihua jueda bufen jianshe xiangmu woguo neng ziji shehua" [Our Country Is Capable of Designing Most of the Projects Set Out in the Second Five-Year Plan]. *Xinhua banyuekan* [New China Semi-Monthly], no. 13 (1957).

"Guowuyuan guanyu Guojia Jihua Weiyuanhui guanyu 1956 niandu jiben jianshe he wuzi pingheng wenti de buchong baogao de pishi" [State Council Comments on the Supplementary Report of the State Planning Commission Concerning the Problem of Basic Construction and Balance of Materials in 1956] (April 14, 1956). In *Gongheguo zouguode lu* [The Road Traveled by the People's Republic], edited by *Dang de wenxian* bianjibu [*The Party's Documents* editorial department]. Beijing: Zhongyang wenxian chubanshe, 1991.

"Li Fuchun, Bo Yibo zai Chongqing tan guanche qinjian jianguo fangzhen zhongde wenti" [Li Fuchun and Bo Yibo Canvass Issues of Implementing the Policy of Building the Nation Through Thrift at Chongqing]. *Xinhua banyuekan* [New China Semi-Monthly], no. 12 (1957).

Li Xiannian. "Zai Guowuyuan changwei huiyi shang de fayan" [Speech at the Meeting of the State Council Standing Committee] (June 5, 1956). In *Gongheguo zouguode lu* [The Road Traveled by the People's Republic], edited by *Dang de wenxian* bianjibu [*The Party's Documents* editorial department]. Beijing: Zhongyang wenxian chubanshe, 1991.

"Quanguo jihua huiyi" [The National Planning Conference]. *Xinhua banyuekan* [New China Semi-Monthly], no. 18 (1957).

"Quanguo sheji huiyi" [The National Design Conference]. *Xinhua banyuekan* [New China Semi-Monthly], no. 13 (1957).

Zhou Enlai. "Jiben jianshe guimo yiding yao shiying keguan jingji tiaojian" [The Scale of Basic Construction Must Accord with Objective Economic Conditions] (June 1, 1956). In *Gongheguo zouguode lu* [The Road Traveled by the People's Republic], edited by *Dang de wenxian* bianjibu [*The Party's Documents* editorial department]. Beijing: Zhongyang wenxian chubanshe, 1991.

_____. "Yusuan shuzi yao jianli zai kekao de jichu shang, ji fandui baoshou you fandui maojin" [The Budget Figures Must be Established on a Reliable Basis, Opposing Conservatism and Opposing Rash Advance] (June 5, 1956). In *Gongheguo zouguode lu* [The Road Traveled by the People's Republic], edited by *Dang de wenxian* bianjibu [*The Party's Documents* editorial department]. Beijing: Zhongyang wenxian chubanshe, 1991.

_____. "Zai Guowuyuan changwei huiyi shang de jianghua" [Talk to the Meeting of the State Council Standing Committee] (July 17, 1956). In *Gongheguo zouguode lu* [The Road Traveled by the People's

Republic], edited by *Dang de wenxian* bianjibu [*The Party's Documents* editorial department]. Beijing: Zhongyang wenxian chubanshe, 1991.

(f) Photocopies of Unpublished PRC Materials

"Unpublished Chinese documents on opposing rash advance and the Great Leap Forward nos. 1-6." N.p.: c. 1992. Deposit copies available at the Menzies Library, the Australian National University, and the Fairbank Center Library, Harvard University.

(g) Red Guard Cultural Revolution Publications

Mao Zedong sixiang wansui [Long Live Mao Zedong Thought]. Red Guard collection of Mao's talks and speeches, 2 vols., [Taibei]: 1967, 1969.

_____. Red Guard collection of Mao's talks and speeches covering 1917-66, Hebei: Hebei Daxue Mao Zedong sixiang "8.18" hongweibing xuanchuanbu [Hebei August 18 Red Guard Propaganda Department], March 1967.

_____. Red Guard collection of Mao's talks and speeches covering 1950-65, n.p.: May 1967. Copy held at the Menzies Library, the Australian National University.

_____. Red Guard collection of Mao's talks and speeches covering October 1949-September 1965, n.p.: June 1967. Copy held at the Menzies Library, the Australian National University.

_____. Red Guard collection of Mao's talks and speeches covering 1951-67, n.p.: July 1967. Copy held at the Menzies Library, the Australian National University.

_____. Red Guard collection of Mao's talks and speeches covering 1950-67, n.p.: September 1967. Copy held at the Menzies Library, the Australian National University.

_____. Red Guard collection of Mao's talks and speeches covering 1958-63, n.p.: September 1967.

_____. Red Guard collection of Mao's talks and speeches covering 1950-57, n.p.: 1967.

_____. Red Guard collection of Mao's talks and speeches covering 1917-August 1949, n.p.: n.d.

_____. Red Guard collection of Mao's talks and speeches, 2 vols., n.p.: n.d. Vol. 1 [1949-57]; vol. 2 [1958-59]. Copy held at the Menzies Library, the Australian National University.

_____. Red Guard collection of Mao's talks and speeches covering 1951-58, n.p.: n.d. Copy held at the Menzies Library, the Australian National University.

_____. Red Guard collection of Mao's talks and speeches covering 1953-65, n.p.: n.d. Copy held at the Menzies Library, the Australian National University.

Xuexi wenxuan [Selected Study Materials]. Red Guard collection of Mao's talks and speeches, 4 vols., [Beijing]: 1967. Vol. 1 [1949-July 1957]; vol. 2 [October 1957-1958]; vol. 3 [1959-63]; vol. 4 [1964-67]. Copy held at the Menzies Library, the Australian National University.

Xuexi ziliao [Study Materials]. Red Guard collection of Mao's talks and speeches, 4 vols., [Beijing: 1967]. Vol. 1 [1949-56]; vol. 2 [1957-61]; vol. 3 [1962-67]; vol. 4 [1949-67], *xuyi* [Supplement 1]. Copy held at the Menzies Library, the Australian National University.

Primary Chinese Sources in English

(a) Books and Monographs

Li Zhisui. *The Private Life of Chairman Mao: The Memoirs of Mao's Personal Physician*. London: Chatto & Windus, 1994.

Memoirs of a Chinese Marshal — The Autobiographical Notes of Peng Dehuai (1898-1974), translated by Zheng Longpu. Beijing: Foreign Languages Press, 1984. English translation of *Peng Dehuai zishu* [Peng Dehuai's Self-statement]. Beijing: Renmin chubanshe, 1981.

Ruan Ming. *Deng Xiaoping: Chronicle of an Empire*. Boulder: Westview Press, 1994.

(b) Articles, Documents, Speeches, etc.

Bo Yibo. "Principles for 1958 Economic Plan Outlined by Po I-po" (August 9, 1957). In *Survey of China Mainland Press*, no. 1602 (September 3, 1957).

_____. "Relationship between Accumulation and Consumption in Socialist Construction" (September 18, 1956). In *Current Background*, no. 416 (October 9, 1956). Also in *Eighth National Congress of the Communist Party of China*. Vol. II (Speeches). Peking: Foreign Languages Press, 1956.

_____. "Working of the National Economic Plan for 1956 and Draft National Economic Plan for 1957" (July 1, 1957). In *Current Background*, no. 465 (July 9, 1957).

Chen Yun. "A Letter to Comrade Mao Zedong concerning Problems in the Steel Target" (May 1959). In *Chen Yun's Strategy for China's Development: A Non-Maoist Alternative*, edited by Nicholas R. Lardy and Kenneth Lieberthal. Armonk: M.E. Sharpe, 1983.

_____. "New Issues Since the Basic Completion of the Socialist Transformation" (September 20, 1956). In *Chen Yun's Strategy for China's Development: A Non-Maoist Alternative*, edited by Nicholas

R. Lardy and Kenneth Lieberthal. Armonk: M.E. Sharpe, 1983. Also in *Eighth National Congress of the Communist Party of China*. Vol. II (Speeches). Peking: Foreign Languages Press, 1956.

_____. "Problems We Must Pay Attention to After the Reform of the System" (September 1957). In *Chen Yun's Strategy for China's Development: A Non-Maoist Alternative*, edited by Nicholas R. Lardy and Kenneth Lieberthal. Armonk: M.E. Sharpe, 1983.

_____. "Regulation on the Improvement of the Industrial Management System" (November 1957). In *Chen Yun's Strategy for China's Development: A Non-Maoist Alternative*, edited by Nicholas R. Lardy and Kenneth Lieberthal. Armonk: M.E. Sharpe, 1983.

_____. "The Problem of Making Practicable the Steel Target" (May 1959). In *Chen Yun's Strategy for China's Development: A Non-Maoist Alternative*, edited by Nicholas R. Lardy and Kenneth Lieberthal. Armonk: M.E. Sharpe, 1983.

_____. "The Scale of Construction Should Be Compatible with National Strength" (January 1957). In *Chen Yun's Strategy for China's Development: A Non-Maoist Alternative*, edited by Nicholas R. Lardy and Kenneth Lieberthal. Armonk: M.E. Sharpe, 1983.

"Communique of the Sixth Plenary Session of the Eighth Central Committee" (December 17, 1958). In *Communist China 1955-1959: Policy Documents with Analysis*, with a foreword by Robert R. Bowie and John K. Fairbank. Cambridge: Harvard University Press, 1965.

[Deng Xiaoping]. "Report on the Rectification Campaign" (September 23, 1957). In *Communist China 1955-1959: Policy Documents with Analysis*, with a foreword by Robert R. Bowie and John K. Fairbank. Cambridge: Harvard University Press, 1965.

"[The] Draft Program for Agricultural Development, 1956-1967" [the 40 articles] (January 23, 1956). In *Communist China 1955-1959: Policy Documents with Analysis*, with a foreword by Robert R. Bowie and John K. Fairbank. Cambridge: Harvard University Press, 1965.

[Jia Tuofu]. "Chia To-fu Summarizes Planning Conference" (August 22, 1957). In *Survey of China Mainland Press*, no. 1607 (September 11, 1957).

[Jiang Hua]. "Adhere to the Correct Line of the Party and Win Victory of the Rectification Campaign on Every Front" (December 9, 1957). In *Communist China 1955-1959: Policy Documents with Analysis*, with a foreword by Robert R. Bowie and John K. Fairbank. Cambridge: Harvard University Press, 1965.

[Li Fuchun]. "Report on the First Five-Year Plan, 1953-1957" (July 5-6, 1955). In *Communist China 1955-1959: Policy Documents with Analysis*, with a foreword by Robert R. Bowie and John K. Fairbank. Cambridge: Harvard University Press, 1965.

_____. "Strengthen State Planning Work for Socialist Construction" (September 24, 1956). In *Current Background*, no. 416 (October 9,

1956). Also in *Eighth National Congress of the Communist Party of China*. Vol. II (Speeches). Peking: Foreign Languages Press, 1956.

[Li Xiannian]. "Final Accounts for 1956 and the 1957 State Budget" (June 29, 1957). In *Current Background*, no. 464 (July 5, 1957).

_____. "Price Policy That Promotes Production" (September 22, 1956). In *Current Background*, no. 416 (October 9, 1956). Also in *Eighth National Congress of the Communist Party of China*. Vol. II (Speeches). Peking: Foreign Languages Press, 1956.

Liao Kai-lung [Liao Gailong]. "Historical Experiences and Our Road of Development." Part II, *Issues & Studies*, November 1981.

Liu Shaoqi. "Political Report of the Central Committee" (September 15, 1956). In *Communist China 1955-1959: Policy Documents with Analysis*, with a foreword by Robert R. Bowie and John K. Fairbank. Cambridge: Harvard University Press, 1965. Also in *Eighth National Congress of the Communist Party of China*. Vol. I (Documents). Peking: Foreign Languages Press, 1956.

_____. "The Present Situation, the Party's General Line for Socialist Construction and Its Future Tasks" (May 5, 1958). In *Communist China 1955-1959: Policy Documents with Analysis*, with a foreword by Robert R. Bowie and John K. Fairbank. Cambridge: Harvard University Press, 1965.

Mao Zedong. "Criticism of *People's Daily*, Which Should Not 'Oppose Adventurism' (Draft Transcript)" (January 1958). In *The Secret Speeches of Chairman Mao: From the Hundred Flowers to the Great Leap Forward*, edited by Roderick MacFarquhar, Timothy Cheek, and Eugene Wu. Cambridge: Harvard Council on East Asian Studies, 1989.

_____. "Intraparty Correspondence" (March-October 1959). In *Miscellany of Mao Tse-tung Thought*. Part 1, *Joint Publications Research Service*, no. 61269-1, February 20, 1974.

_____. "Request for Opinions on the Seventeen-Article Document concerning Agriculture Work" (December 21, 1955). In *Selected Works of Mao Tsetung*. Vol. V, Peking: Foreign Languages Press, 1977. Also in *The Writings of Mao Zedong, 1949-1976. Volume I, September 1949-December 1955*, edited by Michael Y. M. Kau and John K. Leung. Armonk: M.E. Sharpe, 1986.

_____. "Sixteen Articles Concerning Work Methods" (May 1959). In *Miscellany of Mao Tse-tung Thought*. Part 1, *Joint Publications Research Service*, no. 61269-1, February 20, 1974.

_____. "Sixty Points on Working Methods" (February 19, 1958). In *Mao Papers: Anthology and Bibliography*, edited by Jerome Ch'en. London: Oxford University Press, 1970.

_____. "Speech at Conference of Provincial and Municipal Secretaries" (February 2, 1959). In *Miscellany of Mao Tse-tung Thought*. Part 1, *Joint Publications Research Service*, no. 61269-1, February 20, 1974.

_____. "Speech at Moscow Celebration Meeting" (November 6, 1957). In *Communist China 1955-1959: Policy Documents with Analysis*, with a foreword by Robert R. Bowie and John K. Fairbank. Cambridge: Harvard University Press, 1965. Also in *The Writings of Mao Zedong, 1949-1976. Volume II, January 1956-December 1957*, edited by John K. Leung and Michael Y. M. Kau. Armonk: M.E. Sharpe, 1992.

_____. "Speech at the Conclusion of the Third Plenum of the Eighth Central Committee" (October 9, 1957). Official version in *Selected Works of Mao Tsetung*. Vol. V, Peking: Foreign Languages Press, 1977. This version and Red Guard text in *The Writings of Mao Zedong, 1949-1976. Volume II, January 1956-December 1957*, edited by John K. Leung and Michael Y. M. Kau. Armonk: M.E. Sharpe, 1992.

_____. "Speech at the Conference of Heads of Delegations to the Second Session of the 8th Party Congress" (May 18, 1958). In *Miscellany of Mao Tse-tung Thought*. Part 1, *Joint Publications Research Service*, no. 61269-1, February 20, 1974.

_____. "Speech at the Group Leaders' Forum of the Enlarged Meeting of the Military Affairs Committee" (June 28, 1958). In *Mao Tse-tung Unrehearsed, Talks and Letters: 1956-71*, edited by Stuart Schram. Harmondsworth: Penguin Books, 1974.

_____. "Speech at the Lushan Conference" (July 23, 1959). In *Mao Tse-tung Unrehearsed, Talks and Letters: 1956-71*, edited by Stuart Schram. Harmondsworth: Penguin Books, 1974. Another version in *Chinese Law and Government*, Winter 1968/69. Also in *The Case of Peng Teh-huai*. Hong Kong: Union Research Institute, 1968.

_____. "Speech at the Ninth Plenum of the Eighth Central Committee" (January 18, 1961). In *Miscellany of Mao Tse-tung Thought*. Part 2, *Joint Publications Research Service*, no. 61269-2, February 20, 1974.

_____. "Speech at the Second Plenary Session of the Eighth Central Committee of the [CCP]" (November 15, 1956). Official version in *Selected Works of Mao Tsetung*. Vol. V, Peking: Foreign Languages Press, 1977. This version and Red Guard text in *The Writings of Mao Zedong, 1949-1976. Volume II, January 1956-December 1957*, edited by John K. Leung and Michael Y. M. Kau. Armonk: M.E. Sharpe, 1992.

_____. "Speech at the Sixth Plenum of the Eighth Central Committee" (December 19 [sic], 1958). In *Miscellany of Mao Tse-tung Thought*. Part 1, *Joint Publications Research Service*, no. 61269-1, February 20, 1974.

_____. "Speech at the Third Plenum of the Eighth Central Committee" (October 7, 1957). In *The Writings of Mao Zedong, 1949-1976. Volume II, January 1956-December 1957*, edited by John K. Leung and Michael Y. M. Kau. Armonk: M.E. Sharpe, 1992. Also in *Miscellany of Mao Tse-tung Thought*. Part 1, *Joint Publications Research Service*, no. 61269-1, February 20, 1974.

_____. "Speech to Chinese Students and Trainees in Moscow" (November 17, 1957). In *The Writings of Mao Zedong, 1949-1976. Volume II, January 1956-December 1957*, edited by John K. Leung and Michael Y. M. Kau. Armonk: M.E. Sharpe, 1992.

_____. "Speeches at the Second Session of the Eighth Party Congress" (May 8-23, 1958). In *Miscellany of Mao Tse-tung Thought. Part 1, Joint Publications Research Service*, no. 61269-1, February 20, 1974.

_____. "Talk at Seventh Plenum of the Eighth Central Committee" (April 1959). In *Miscellany of Mao Tse-tung Thought. Part 1, Joint Publications Research Service*, no. 61269-1, February 20, 1974.

_____. "Talk at the 8th Plenary Session of the CCP 8th Central Committee" (August 2, 1959). In *The Case of Peng Teh-huai*. Hong Kong: Union Research Institute, 1968.

_____. "Talk on Opposing Right-Deviation and Conservatism" (December 6, 1955). In *The Writings of Mao Zedong, 1949-1976. Volume I, September 1949-December 1955*, edited by Michael Y. M. Kau and John K. Leung. Armonk: M.E. Sharpe, 1986. Also in *Miscellany of Mao Tse-tung Thought. Part 1, Joint Publications Research Service*, no. 61269-1, February 20, 1974.

_____. "Talks at a Conference of Secretaries of Provincial, Municipal and Autonomous Region Party Committees" (January 18 and 27, 1957). Official version in *Selected Works of Mao Tsetung*. Vol. V, Peking: Foreign Languages Press, 1977. This version and Red Guard text in *The Writings of Mao Zedong, 1949-1976. Volume II, January 1956-December 1957*, edited by John K. Leung and Michael Y. M. Kau. Armonk: M.E. Sharpe, 1992.

_____. "Talks at the Beidaihe Conference (Draft Transcript)" (August 17-30, 1958). In *The Secret Speeches of Chairman Mao: From the Hundred Flowers to the Great Leap Forward*, edited by Roderick MacFarquhar, Timothy Cheek, and Eugene Wu. Cambridge: Harvard Council on East Asian Studies, 1989.

_____. "Talks at the Chengtu Conference" (March 1958). In *Mao Tse-tung Unrehearsed, Talks and Letters: 1956-71*, edited by Stuart Schram. Harmondsworth: Penguin Books, 1974.

_____. "Talks at the First Zhengzhou Conference" (November 6-10, 1958). In *The Secret Speeches of Chairman Mao: From the Hundred Flowers to the Great Leap Forward*, edited by Roderick MacFarquhar, Timothy Cheek, and Eugene Wu. Cambridge: Harvard Council on East Asian Studies, 1989.

_____. "Talks at the Hangzhou Conference (Draft Transcript)" (January 3-4, 1958). In *The Secret Speeches of Chairman Mao: From the Hundred Flowers to the Great Leap Forward*, edited by Roderick MacFarquhar, Timothy Cheek, and Eugene Wu. Cambridge: Harvard Council on East Asian Studies, 1989.

_____. "Talks at the Nan-ning Conference" (January 11 and 12, 1958). In *Miscellany of Mao Tse-tung Thought*. Part 1, *Joint Publications Research Service*, no. 61269-1, February 20, 1974.

_____. "Talks at the Wuchang Conference" (November 21-23, 1958). In *The Secret Speeches of Chairman Mao: From the Hundred Flowers to the Great Leap Forward*, edited by Roderick MacFarquhar, Timothy Cheek, and Eugene Wu. Cambridge: Harvard Council on East Asian Studies, 1989.

_____. "The Ten Great Relationships" (April 25, 1956). Official version in *Selected Works of Mao Tsetung*. Vol. V, Peking: Foreign Languages Press, 1977. Red Guard versions: 1. *Mao*, edited by Jerome Ch'en. Englewood Cliffs: Prentice-Hall, 1969. 2. *Mao Tse-tung Unrehearsed, Talks and Letters: 1956-71*, edited by Stuart Schram. Harmondsworth: Penguin Books, 1974. 3. *The Writings of Mao Zedong, 1949-1976. Volume II, January 1956-December 1957*, edited by John K. Leung and Michael Y. M. Kau. Armonk: M.E. Sharpe, 1992.

"Oppose Both Conservatism and Hastiness." *Renmin ribao* editorial, June 20, 1956. In *Survey of China Mainland Press*, no. 1321 (June 27, 1956).

Peng Dehuai. "Excerpts from Peng Teh-huai's Talks at the Meetings of the Northwest Group of the Lushan Meeting" (July, 3-10, 1959). In *The Case of Peng Teh-huai*. Hong Kong: Union Research Institute, 1968.

_____. "Letter of Opinion" (July 14, 1959). In *The Case of Peng Teh-huai*. Hong Kong: Union Research Institute, 1968. Also in *Memoirs of a Chinese Marshal — The Autobiographical Notes of Peng Dehuai (1898-1974)*, translated by Zheng Longpu. Beijing: Foreign Languages Press, 1984.

_____. "Speech at the 8th Plenary Session of the CCP 8th Central Committee (Excerpts)" (August 1959). In *The Case of Peng Teh-huai*. Hong Kong: Union Research Institute, 1968.

"Resolution on Certain Questions in the History of Our Party Since the Founding of the People's Republic of China" (June 27, 1981). In *Beijing Review*, no. 27 (1981).

Zhou Enlai. "Economic Work Should Be Conducted in a Practical Way" (February 8, 1956). In *Selected Works of Zhou Enlai*. Vol. II, Beijing: Foreign Languages Press, 1989.

_____. "On Questions concerning Intellectuals" (January 14, 1956). In *Selected Works of Zhou Enlai*. Vol. II, Beijing: Foreign Languages Press, 1989. Also in *Communist China 1955-1959: Policy Documents with Analysis*, with a foreword by Robert R. Bowie and John K. Fairbank. Cambridge: Harvard University Press, 1965.

_____. "Problems of Policy for Economic Development" [report to the Second Plenum] (November 10, 1956). In *Selected Works of Zhou Enlai*. Vol. II, Beijing: Foreign Languages Press, 1989.

_____. "Report on the Proposals for the Second Five-Year Plan (1958-1962)" (September 16, 1956). In *Communist China 1955-1959: Policy*

Documents with Analysis, with a foreword by Robert R. Bowie and John K. Fairbank. Cambridge: Harvard University Press, 1965. Also in *Eighth National Congress of the Communist Party of China*. Vol. I (Documents). Peking: Foreign Languages Press, 1956. Condensed version in *Selected Works of Zhou Enlai*. Vol. II, Beijing: Foreign Languages Press, 1989.

_____. "Report on the Work of the Government" (June 26, 1957). In *Communist China 1955-1959: Policy Documents with Analysis*, with a foreword by Robert R. Bowie and John K. Fairbank. Cambridge: Harvard University Press, 1965.

(c) Chronologies, Documentary Collections, Personnel Directories, etc.

Chen Yun's Strategy for China's Development: A Non-Maoist Alternative, edited by Nicholas R. Lardy and Kenneth Lieberthal. Armonk: M. E. Sharpe, 1983.

Communist China 1955-1959: Policy Documents with Analysis, with a foreword by Robert R. Bowie and John K. Fairbank. Cambridge: Harvard University Press, 1965.

Eighth National Congress of the Communist Party of China. Vols. I (Documents) and II (Speeches). Peking: Foreign Languages Press, 1956.

History of the Chinese Communist Party: A Chronology of Events (1919-1990), compiled by the Party History Research Centre of the Central Committee of the Chinese Communist Party. Beijing: Foreign Languages Press, 1991.

Mao, edited by Jerome Ch'en. Englewood Cliffs: Prentice-Hall, 1969.

Mao Papers: Anthology and Bibliography, edited by Jerome Ch'en. London: Oxford University Press, 1970.

Mao Tse-tung Unrehearsed, Talks and Letters: 1956-71, edited by Stuart Schram. Harmondsworth: Penguin Books, 1974.

Miscellany of Mao Tse-tung Thought. 2 parts, *Joint Publications Research Service*, nos. 61269-1 and 2, February 20, 1974.

Selected Works of Liu Shaoqi. Vol. II, Beijing: Foreign Languages Press, 1989.

Selected Works of Mao Tsetung. Vol. V, Peking: Foreign Languages Press, 1977.

Selected Works of Zhou Enlai. Vol. II, Beijing: Foreign Languages Press, 1989.

The Case of Peng Teh-huai. Hong Kong: Union Research Institute, 1968.

The Secret Speeches of Chairman Mao: From the Hundred Flowers to the Great Leap Forward, edited by Roderick MacFarquhar, Timothy Cheek, and Eugene Wu. Cambridge: Harvard Council on East Asian Studies, 1989.

The Writings of Mao Zedong, 1949-1976. Volume I, September 1949-December 1955, edited by Michael Y. M. Kau and John K. Leung. Armonk: M.E. Sharpe, 1986.

_____. *Volume II, January 1956-December 1957*, edited by John K. Leung and Michael Y. M. Kau. Armonk: M.E. Sharpe, 1992.

Other Primary Sources

Khrushchov, N. S. *Report of the Central Committee of the Communist Party of the Soviet Union*. Moscow: Foreign Languages Publishing House, 1956.

Stalin, J. V. *Economic Problems of Socialism in the U.S.S.R.* Peking: Foreign Languages Press, 1972.

Secondary Sources

(a) Books

Bachman, David. *Bureaucracy, Economy, and Leadership in China: The Institutional Origins of the Great Leap Forward*. Cambridge: Cambridge University Press, 1991.

Becker, Jasper. *Hungry Ghosts: China's Secret Famine*. London: John Murray, 1996.

Chang, Parris H. *Power and Policy in China*. University Park: The Pennsylvania State University Press, 1975.

Cheek, Timothy, and Tony Saich, eds. *New Perspectives on State Socialism in China*. Armonk: M.E. Sharpe, 1997.

Domenach, Jean-Luc. *The Origins of the Great Leap Forward: The Case of One Chinese Province*. Boulder: Westview Press, 1995.

Domes, Jürgen. *Peng Te-huai: The Man and the Image*. London: C. Hurst and Co., 1985.

Donnelly, Desmond. *The March Wind: Explorations behind the Iron Curtain*. London: Collins, 1959.

Johnson, Chalmers, ed. *Ideology and Politics in Contemporary China*. Seattle: University of Washington Press, 1973.

Lee, Peter N. S. *Industrial Management and Economic Reform in China, 1949-1984*. Hong Kong: Oxford University Press, 1987.

Lieberthal, Kenneth, and Michel Oksenberg. *Policy Making in China: Leaders, Structures, and Processes*. Princeton: Princeton University Press, 1988.

MacFarquhar, Roderick, ed. *China Under Mao: Politics Takes Command*. Cambridge: The M.I.T. Press, 1966.

_____. *The Origins of the Cultural Revolution 1: Contradictions among the People 1956-1957*. New York: Columbia University Press, 1974.

_____. *The Origins of the Cultural Revolution 2: The Great Leap Forward 1958-1960.* New York: Columbia University Press, 1983.

_____. *The Origins of the Cultural Revolution 3: The Coming of the Cataclysm 1961-1966.* New York: Columbia University Press, 1997.

_____, ed. *The Politics of China.* New York: Cambridge University Press, 1993. Expanded 2nd edition, *The Politics of China, Second Edition: The Eras of Mao and Deng.* New York: Cambridge University Press, 1997. Republications of main political articles from vols. 14 and 15 of *The Cambridge History of China,* with additional contributions.

_____ and John K. Fairbank, eds. *The Cambridge History of China:Volume 14, The People's Republic, Part I: The Emergence of Revolutionary China 1949-1965.* New York: Cambridge University Press, 1987.

Oksenberg, Michel, Carl Riskin, Robert A. Scalapino, and Ezra F. Vogel, eds. *The Cultural Revolution: 1967 in Review.* Ann Arbor: Michigan Papers in Chinese Studies no. 2, 1968.

Schoenhals, Michael. *Saltationist Socialism: Mao Zedong and the Great Leap Forward 1958.* Stockholm: Institutionen for Orientaliska Sprak, University of Stockholm, 1987.

Schram, Stuart R., ed. *Authority, Participation and Cultural Change in China.* London: Cambridge University Press, 1973.

Teiwes, Frederick C. *Leadership, Legitimacy, and Conflict in China: From A Charismatic Mao to the Politics of Succession.* Armonk: M.E. Sharpe, 1984.

_____. *Politics and Purges in China: Rectification and the Decline of Party Norms 1950-1965.* 1st edition, White Plains: M.E. Sharpe, 1979. 2nd edition, Armonk: M.E. Sharpe, 1993.

_____. *Politics at Mao's Court: Gao Gang and Party Factionalism in the Early 1950s.* Armonk: M.E. Sharpe, 1990.

_____ and Warren Sun, eds. *The Politics of Agricultural Cooperativization in China: Mao, Deng Zihui, and the "High Tide" of 1955.* Armonk: M.E. Sharpe, 1993.

_____ and Warren Sun. *The Tragedy of Lin Biao: Riding the Tiger during the Cultural Revolution, 1966-1971.* London: C. Hurst and Co., 1996.

_____ with the assistance of Warren Sun. *The Formation of the Maoist Leadership: From the Return of Wang Ming to the Seventh Party Congress.* London: Contemporary China Institute Research Notes and Studies no. 10, 1994.

Westad, Odd Arne, ed. *Brothers in Arms: The Rise and Fall of the Sino-Soviet Alliance, 1945-1963.* Stanford: Stanford University Press, forthcoming.

Yang, Dali L. *Calamity and Reform in China: State, Rural Society, and Institutional Change Since the Great Leap Famine.* Stanford: Stanford University Press, 1996.

Zagoria, Donald S. *The Sino-Soviet Conflict, 1956-61.* Princeton: Princeton University Press, 1962.

(b) Articles

Ahn, Byung-joon. "Adjustments in the Great Leap Forward and Their Ideological Legacy, 1959-62." In *Ideology and Politics in Contemporary China*, edited by Chalmers Johnson. Seattle: University of Washington Press, 1973.

Bachman, David. "Chinese Bureaucratic Politics and the Origins of the Great Leap Forward." *The Journal of Contemporary China*, Summer 1995.

_____. "Response to Teiwes." *Pacific Affairs*, vol. 66, no. 2 (Summer 1993).

Bernstein, Thomas P. "Stalinism, Famine, and Chinese Peasants: Grain Procurements during the Great Leap Forward." *Theory and Society*, May 1984.

Chan, Alfred L. "Leaders, Coalition Politics, and Policy-Formulation in China: The Great Leap Forward Revisited." *The Journal of Contemporary China*, Winter-Spring 1995.

_____. "The Campaign for Agricultural Development in the Great Leap Forward: A Study of Policy-Making and Implementation in Liaoning." *The China Quarterly*, no. 129 (1992).

Cheek, Timothy. "Textually Speaking: An Assessment of Newly Available Mao Texts." In *The Secret Speeches of Chairman Mao: From the Hundred Flowers to the Great Leap Forward*, edited by Roderick MacFarquhar, Timothy Cheek, and Eugene Wu. Cambridge: Harvard Council on East Asian Studies, 1989.

Forster, Keith. "Localism, Central Policy and the Provincial Purges of 1957-58: The Case of Zhejiang." In *New Perspectives on State Socialism in China*, edited by Timothy Cheek and Tony Saich. Armonk: M.E. Sharpe, 1997.

_____. "Mao Zedong on Contradictions under Socialism Revisited." *The Journal of Contemporary China*, Fall 1995.

Klein, Donald W. "The 'Next Generation' of Chinese Communist Leaders." In *China Under Mao: Politics Takes Command*, edited by Roderick MacFarquhar. Cambridge: The M.I.T. Press, 1966.

Lampton, David M. "Health Policy During the Great Leap Forward." *The China Quarterly*, no. 60 (1974).

Lieberthal, Kenneth. "The Great Leap Forward and the Split in the Yenan Leadership." In *The Cambridge History of China:Volume 14, The People's Republic, Part I: The Emergence of Revolutionary China 1949-1965*, edited by Roderick MacFarquhar and John K. Fairbank. New York: Cambridge University Press, 1987. Republished in *The Politics of China*, edited by Roderick MacFarquhar. New York: Cambridge University Press, 1993. Subsequently republished in *The Politics of China, Second Edition: The Eras of Mao and Deng*, edited by Roderick MacFarquhar. New York: Cambridge University Press, 1997.

MacFarquhar, Roderick. "The Secret Speeches of Chairman Mao." In *The Secret Speeches of Chairman Mao: From the Hundred Flowers to the Great Leap Forward*, edited by Roderick MacFarquhar, Timothy Cheek, and Eugene Wu. Cambridge: Harvard Council on East Asian Studies, 1989.

Oksenberg, Michel. "Occupational Groups in Chinese Society and the Cultural Revolution." In *The Cultural Revolution: 1967 in Review*, edited by Michel Oksenberg, Carl Riskin, Robert A. Scalapino, and Ezra F. Vogel. Ann Arbor: Michigan Papers in Chinese Studies no. 2, 1968.

_____. "The Political Leader." In *Mao Tse-tung in the Scales of History*, edited by Dick Wilson. Cambridge: Cambridge University Press, 1977.

Schoenhals, Michael. "Yang Xianzhen's Critique of the Great Leap Forward." *Modern Asian Studies*, vol. 26, no. 3 (1992).

Schram, Stuart R. "Introduction: The Cultural Revolution in Historical Perspective." In *Authority, Participation and Cultural Change in China*, edited by Stuart R. Schram. London: Cambridge University Press, 1973.

_____. "Mao Tse-tung and the Theory of the Permanent Revolution." *The China Quarterly*, No. 46 (1971).

Sun, Warren. "The National Defense University's *Teaching Reference Materials*." In *New Perspectives on State Socialism in China*, edited by Timothy Cheek and Tony Saich. Armonk: M.E. Sharpe, 1997. Originally published in *CCP Research Newsletter*, nos. 10 & 11, 1992.

Teiwes, Frederick C. "A Critique of Western Studies of CCP Elite Politics." *IIAS Newsletter*, Summer 1996.

_____. "Chinese Politics 1949-1965: A Changing Mao." *Current Scene*, January and February 1974. Republished in Frederick C. Teiwes, *Leadership, Legitimacy, and Conflict in China: From A Charismatic Mao to the Politics of Succession*. Armonk: M.E. Sharpe, 1984.

_____. "Establishment and Consolidation of the New Regime." In *The Cambridge History of China:Volume 14, The People's Republic, Part I: The Emergence of Revolutionary China 1949-1965*, edited by Roderick MacFarquhar and John K. Fairbank. New York: Cambridge University Press, 1987. Republished in *The Politics of China*, edited by Roderick MacFarquhar. New York: Cambridge University Press, 1993. Subsequently republished in *The Politics of China, Second Edition: The Eras of Mao and Deng*, edited by Roderick MacFarquhar. New York: Cambridge University Press, 1997.

_____. "Interviews on Party History." In *New Perspectives on State Socialism in China*, edited by Timothy Cheek and Tony Saich. Armonk: M.E. Sharpe, 1997. Originally published in *CCP Research Newsletter*, nos. 10 & 11, 1992.

_____. "Leaders, Institutions, and the Origins of the Great Leap Forward." *Pacific Affairs*, vol. 66, no. 2 (Summer 1993).

_____. "Mao and his Lieutenants." *The Australian Journal of Chinese Affairs*, no. 19-20, 1988.

_____. "Mao Texts and the Mao of the 1950s." *The Australian Journal of Chinese Affairs*, no. 33 (1995).

_____. "Peng Dehuai and Mao Zedong." *The Australian Journal of Chinese Affairs*, no. 16, 1986.

_____. "'Rules of the Game' in Chinese Politics." *Problems of Communism*, September-December 1979.

_____ with Warren Sun. "The Politics of an 'Un-Maoist' Interlude: The Case of Opposing Rash Advance, 1956-1957." In *New Perspectives on State Socialism in China*, edited by Timothy Cheek and Tony Saich. Armonk: M.E. Sharpe, 1997.

Westad, Odd Arne. "Brothers: Visions of an Alliance." In *Brothers in Arms: The Rise and Fall of the Sino-Soviet Alliance, 1945-1963*, edited by Odd Arne Westad. Stanford: Stanford University Press, forthcoming.

Yang, Dali L. "Surviving the Great Leap Famine: The Struggle over Rural Policy, 1958-1962." In *New Perspectives on State Socialism in China*, edited by Timothy Cheek and Tony Saich. Armonk: M.E. Sharpe, 1997.

Yeh, K. C. "Soviet and Chinese Communist Industrialization Strategies." In *Soviet and Chinese Communism: Similarities and Differences*, edited by Donald W. Treadgold. Seattle: University of Washington Press, 1967.

(c) Unpublished Dissertations and Papers

Oksenberg, Michel C. "Policy Formulation in Communist China: The Case of the Mass Irrigation Campaign, 1957-58." Ph.D. dissertation, Columbia University, 1969.

Wheatcroft, S. G. "Comparing the Great Chinese and Soviet Famines of the Twentieth Century." Paper presented to the 23rd General Population Conference of the International Union of Population Studies, Beijing, October 1997.

(d) Research Guides, Biographical and Personnel Collections

A Research Guide to Central Party and Government Meetings in China 1949-1975, by Kenneth Lieberthal. White Plains: International Arts and Sciences Press, 1976.

A Research Guide to Central Party and Government Meetings in China 1949-1986, by Kenneth G. Lieberthal and Bruce J. Dickson. Revised and expanded edition, Armonk: M.E. Sharpe, 1989.

Biographic Dictionary of Chinese Communism 1921-1965, by Donald W. Klein and Anne B. Clark. 2 vols., Cambridge: Harvard University Press, 1971.

Directory of Officials and Organizations in China: A Quarter-Century Guide, by Malcolm Lamb. Armonk: M.E. Sharpe, 1994.

Gendai Chugoku Jimmei Jiten [Modern China Biographic Dictionary]. Tokyo: Gaimusho, 1982.

Who's Who in Communist China. Hong Kong: Union Research Institute, 1966.

INDEX

"adjustment, consolidation, filling out, and improvement" policy, xxv, 216; *see also* economic policy: 8-character principle
"adventurism," 25, 48, 135, 145, 146
agricultural cooperativization, *see* rural policy
agriculture, *see* rural policy
Agriculture, Ministry of, 43, 88; *see also* Liao Luyan
Anhui, xiii, xxv, xxvi, 58, 73, 91n26, 119n2, 122n16, 130, 133, 151, 159n111, 168n135, 174, 175, 207n13, 214, 215n7, 216n10, 217-25, 229; *see also* Chinese Communist Party, Conferences, Zeng Xisheng
annual plans, 11, 190n32, 253; 1955: 21; 1956: 21, 25, 26, 32, 34, 254; 1957: 26, 33-35, 45, 51, 253, 255; 1958: 74, 86, 87, 252, 253; 1959: 109; *see also* Bo Yibo, State Economic Commission
Anshan, 48
anti-right opportunist campaign (1959-60), xxiv, xxvi, 202n2, 212, 214
Anti-Rightist Campaign (1957), 12n21, 44, 53-55, 61n24, 78, 81n88, 89, 197n46
August Harvest Uprising (1927), 162
austerity campaign (1956-57), 41, 44, 64, 65n37, 66

Bachman, David, xi, xii, 6n3, 7, 10-15, 18, 35, 41n60, 42, 45n76, 53, 54n4, 56, 57n10, 59n18, 60n20, 62, 64, 64-65n37, 80-81n86, 87n10, 93n32, 187n25, 193n39
Baotou, 159n111
Becker, Jasper, 5n1, 213n1, 215n7, 221n21

Beidaihe conference (August 1958), *see* Chinese Communist Party, Conferences
Bernstein, Thomas, 5n1, 174n146
"big planning, small freedoms," 61
"blind rash advance," *see* *fanmaojin* program
"blooming and contending," 79
Bo Yibo, xvi, xvii, xix, xx, xxi, 3, 11, 17, 20, 23, 24, 26, 27, 29, 32-35, 41-42, 44, 45n76, 46n81, 47-51, 56, 57, 59, 60, 61, 63, 64, 71, 73, 74, 77, 84, 86, 87, 92, 95, 97, 101, 105-106, 109, 110-11, 113, 120-21, 122-23, 124, 126, 128n31, 133-34n46, 134, 135, 136-37, 141, 142, 143-44, 146, 149, 151, 152, 154, 157, 158, 160, 166n131, 171, 176, 182, 184, 188-91, 194, 196, 198, 209, 263; attendance at conferences, 233-35, 237, 239, 242, 243; resignation as Minister of Finance, 47n84; self-criticism by, xx, 74, 77, 97, 245, 246, 252-53; tour of provinces (spring 1957), 44 Relations with: Chen Yun, 24, 49; Li Fuchun, 62; Li Xiannian, 74; Mao Zedong, xix, 42, 49, 50, 73, 87-88, 105, 106, 124, 135, 137, 141, 166n131, 198, 263; Zhou Enlai, 24, 29, 74 *see also* State Economic Commission, taxation policy
Bo Yibo, *Reflections on Certain Major Decisions and Events*, 262- 63
"bourgeois intellectuals," 77-79
"bourgeois rightists," xv, xviii, 55, 79, 111, 119n2, 120, 127, 131, 255; *see also* Anti-Rightist Campaign
bu kanle, 31
bureaucratic politics model, 7, 11,

About the Authors

Frederick C. Teiwes received his B.A. from Amherst College and his Ph.D. in political science from Columbia University. He subsequently taught and conducted research at Cornell University, the Australian National University, and, since 1976, at the University of Sydney where he currently holds a Personal Chair in Chinese Politics. He is the author of a number of books on Chinese elite politics, including *Politics and Purges in China* (1979, 1993), *Leadership, Legitimacy, and Conflict in China* (1984), and *Politics at Mao's Court* (1990).

Warren Sun received his B.A. from Taiwan National University and his Ph.D. in modern Chinese intellectual history from the Australian National University. He has published on the life and works of Chang Ping-lin, and over the past decade has been engaged in the study of Chinese Communist Party history. He is currently Lecturer in Asian Languages and Studies at Monash University.

Professor Teiwes and Dr. Sun have collaborated on various publications in recent years including *The Politics of Agricultural Cooperativization: Mao, Deng Zihui, and the "High Tide" of 1955* (1993), and most recently *The Tragedy of Lin Biao: Riding the Tiger during the Cultural Revolution, 1966-1971* (1996).